written text, while construction goes beyond and may call in the
aid of extrinsic considerations. "Interpretation," says Dr. Lieber,
"differs from construction in that the former is the art of finding
out the true sense of any form of words, that is, the sense which
their author intended to convey, and of enabling others to derive
from them the same idea which the author intended to convey.
Construction, on the other hand, is the drawing of conclusions, respecting subjects that lie beyond the direct expressions of the text,
from elements known from and given in the text; conclusions which
are in the spirit, though not within the letter, of the text. Interpretation only takes place if the text conveys some meaning or
other. But construction is resorted to when, in comparing two
different writings of the same individual, or two different enactments by the same legislative body, there is found contradiction
where there was evidently no intention of such contradiction one of
another, or where it happens that part of a writing or declaration
contradicts the rest. When this is the case, and the nature of the
document or declaration, or whatever else it may be, is not such
as to allow us to consider the whole as being invalidated by a partial or other contradiction, then resort must be had to construction.
So, too, if required to act in cases which have not been foreseen by
the framers of those rules by which we are nevertheless obliged, for
some binding reason, faithfully to regulate as well as we can our action respecting the unforeseen case."[3] As an illustration of construction, we may suppose the following case: A statute provides a
penalty for any person who offers resistance to "magistrates, sheriffs, constables, bailiffs, marshals, or other officers," in the discharge
of their official duty. The defendant offered resistance to a county
surveyor in the discharge of the latter's official duty. Is the case
within the law? If we observe the rule that general terms following an enumeration by specific terms are to be taken as applying
only to others of the same class with those enumerated; if we notice that the officers enumerated in the statute are all of the class of
officers having to do with the administration of justice or the execution of the laws; if the title of the act shows us that it was intended to be restricted to such officers; if we find from an examination of the condition of affairs which induced the passage of the

---

[3] Lieber, Hermeneutics, 11, 43, 44.

statute, and the evil which it was designed to remedy, that only judicial officers were intended to be thus protected; if we discover that the language of the act was copied from that of a similar statute existing in another state, and the law, in that state, had already received a judicial construction whereby its operation was limited to that class of officers; and if from these several premises (all of which are indicia of the meaning of the legislator) we deduce the conclusion that a county surveyor is not within the terms of the statute, then the process which has led to this result is properly called "construction." On the other hand, it has been settled, by the decisions of the courts, that the term "ex post facto laws," as used in the constitutions, applies only to penal and criminal proceedings and not to civil actions. This explication of the meaning of this term was the result of "interpretation." Again, "the constitution of the United States says that congress shall have the power of regulating commerce, but it does not say how far this regulatory power shall extend. This sentence, then, must be interpreted, if we are desirous to ascertain what precise meaning the framers of our constitution attached to it, and construed, if we are desirous of knowing how they would have understood it respecting new relations, which they could not have known, at the time, and which nevertheless fall decidedly within the province of this provision." [4]

In practice, however, both courts and text-writers are in the habit of using the two terms "interpretation" and "construction" as synonymous or interchangeable. This is because either or both of these methods may be resorted to freely, whenever the necessity of elucidating the meaning of a statute becomes apparent; and niceties of language are not much observed when they do not correspond with an imperative necessity of maintaining a distinction between the things themselves. The technical distinction between the two terms will not be scrupulously observed in the following pages.

It should also be observed that the two terms in question may be applied either to the art, the process, or the result of the elucidation. It is in the latter sense that we employ them when we say that a court has put a "narrow interpretation" upon a statute, or that a case has been brought within the terms of a statute "by construction."

---

[4] Lieber, Hermeneutics, 169.

Different Methods of Interpretation.

The methods of interpretation have been variously classified by different writers. According to one of the most eminent, interpretation is said to be either "legal," which rests on the same authority as the law itself, or "doctrinal," which rests upon its intrinsic reasonableness. Legal interpretation may be either "authentic," when it is expressly provided by the legislator,[5] or "usual," when it is derived from unwritten practice. Doctrinal interpretation may turn on the meaning of words and sentences, when it is called "grammatical," or on the intention of the legislator, when it is described as "logical." When logical interpretation stretches the words of a statute to cover its obvious meaning, it is called "extensive;" [6] when, on the other hand, it avoids giving full meaning to the words, in order not to go beyond the intention of the legislator, it is called "restrictive." [7]

Lieber, in his work on Hermeneutics, gives the following classification of the different kinds of interpretation:

"Close" interpretation is adopted if just reasons connected with the character and formation of the text induce us to take the words in their narrowest meaning. This species of interpretation is also generally called "literal."

"Extensive" interpretation, called also "liberal" interpretation, adopts a more comprehensive signification of the words.

---

[5] The term "authentic" interpretation may also be applied to the interpretation put upon the laws of a given state by its own government, including the judicial department thereof, when the same are required to be interpreted and applied by the tribunals of another state. The courts of one of the states of the American Union will follow the construction put upon the statutes of another state by the courts of the latter state. So the courts of the United States are the "authentic" interpreters of the constitution and laws of the United States, and the courts of the states are bound to follow and adopt their interpretation of those laws. And conversely, the federal courts adopt the construction put upon state statutes by the courts of the state which enacted them. Shelby v. Guy, 11 Wheat. 361; Black, Const. Law, 140.

[6] "The so-called 'extensive' interpretation of statute law ex ratione legis, is the extension of the provisions of the law to a case which they do not comprise because the case falls within the scope of the law, although the provisions of the law do not include it. There is truly an extension of the law." Austin, Jurisprudence, § 913.

[7] Holland, Jurisprudence, 344; Lieber, Hermeneutics, 62, 63.

"Extravagant" interpretation is that which substitutes a meaning evidently beyond the true one. It is therefore not genuine interpretation.

"Free," or unrestricted, interpretation proceeds simply on the general principles of interpretation in good faith, not bound by any specific or superior principle.

"Limited," or restricted, interpretation is when we are influenced by other principles than the strictly hermeneutic ones.

"Predestined" interpretation takes place if the interpreter, laboring under a strong bias of mind, makes the text subservient to his preconceived views or desires. This includes "artful" interpretation, by which the interpreter seeks to give a meaning to the text other than the one he knows to have been intended.[8]

According to the same author, construction is either close, comprehensive, transcendent, or extravagant, the varieties corresponding to the similar species of interpretation.

"Close" construction is that which inclines to the directest possible application of the text, or the principles it involves, to new or unprovided cases, or to contradictory parts.

"Comprehensive" construction is that which inclines to an extensive application of the text, or the principles it involves, to new, unprovided, or not sufficiently specified cases or contradictions.

"Transcendent" construction is that which is derived from or founded upon a principle superior to the text, and nevertheless aims at deciding on subjects belonging to the province of that text.

"Extravagant" construction is that which carries the effect of the text beyond its true limits, and therefore is no longer genuine construction, as the last named species becomes of a more and more doubtful character the more it approaches to this.[9]

There are some other distinguishing terms applied to the interpretation or construction of laws which require a brief mention. Thus, "strict" construction is the construction of a statute according to its letter, which recognizes nothing that is not expressed, takes the language used in its exact and technical meaning, and admits no equitable considerations or implications. It is the same as the "close" or "restrictive" construction of the writers quoted above. Its antithesis is "liberal" construction. Again, interpre-

---

[8] Lieber, Hermeneutics, 54–60.   [9] Id. 65–69.

tation or construction is said to be either prospective or retrospective, according as it makes the provisions of the text apply only to future cases or transactions, or makes them include also cases or transactions which occurred before the passage of the law. Finally, when the words of a law are wrested from their plain and obvious meaning, and made to bear an entirely different meaning (for the sake of avoiding an absurd or unjust consequence), this is called "artificial," "forced," or "strained" construction. It corresponds to the "extravagant" construction or interpretation of Dr. Lieber.

RULES OF CONSTRUCTION NOT MANDATORY.

3. The rules of construction are not rules of positive law, unless expressly provided by statute. They rest on the authority of the courts, which have gradually evolved them, and they are not imperatively binding in the same sense as are the enactments of the legislature.

"Rules of interpretation are not imperative like the mandatory provisions of law; they are rather in the nature of suggestions leading up to the probable meaning where it has been carelessly or inartificially expressed; and where the words are susceptible of more than one interpretation, they (the rules) may possibly guide us to the one intended."[10]   At the same time, it should be noted that these rules of interpretation have now grown into a very complete and detailed system, and that the courts do not feel themselves at liberty to disregard the rules which may be applicable to the given case, unless for very special reasons. And indeed, it has been suggested, and with much plausibility, that the legal rules for the interpretation of statutes form a part of the "jus" or ordinary law the country, which every person is bound to be conversant with at his peril, in accordance with the maxim, ignorantia juris neminem excusat.[11]

[10] Cooley, Taxation, 265   [11] Hardcastle, Stat. Law, 3.

OBJECT OF INTERPRETATION.

4. The true object of all interpretation is to ascertain the meaning and will of the law-making body, to the end that it may be enforced. It is not permissible, under the pretence of interpretation, to make a law, different from that which the law-making body intended to enact.

"Statute law is the will of the legislature; and the object of all judicial interpretation of it is to determine what intention is conveyed, either expressly or by implication, by the language used, so far as it is necessary for determining whether the particular case or state of facts presented to the interpreter falls within it." [12] The wisdom, policy, or expediency of legislation is a matter with which the courts have nothing whatever to do. Whether or not a given law is the best that could have been enacted on the subject; whether or not it is calculated to accomplish its avowed object; whether or not it accords with what is understood to be the general policy of legislation in the particular jurisdiction,—these are questions which do not fall within the province of the courts. And hence a court exceeds its proper office and authority if it attempts, under the guise of construction, to mould the expression of the legislative will into the shape which the court thinks it ought to bear. The sole function of the judiciary is to expound and apply the law. To enact the law is the prerogative of the legislative department of government. Nor can the courts correct what they may deem excesses or omissions in legislation, or relieve against the occasionally harsh operation of statutory provisions, without danger of doing more mischief than good. [13]

[12] Maxwell, Interp. 1.

[13] Sutherland, Stat. Constr. § 235, citing Waller v. Harris, 20 Wend. 562; State v. Heman, 70 Mo. 441.

INTERPRETATION THE OFFICE OF THE JUDICIARY.

5. As between the three departments of government, the office of construing and interpreting the written laws belongs to the judiciary ultimately, although the executive and legislative departments may be required, by necessity, to put their own construction upon the laws in advance of their exposition by the courts.

6. As between the court and the jury, on the trial of a cause, the construction and interpretation of all written instruments, including statutes and constitutions, is for the court.

When there arises a necessity for construing or interpreting the written laws, in order to discover their applicability to a given case or state of facts, the question of the meaning and intention of the legislature in this regard is a question of law, and as such it must be solved by the court; it is not for the determination of the jury.[14] When the question depends upon the meaning of particular words or phrases, it may sometimes be necessary to call in the aid of the jury, but only to ascertain the correct signification of the language used, not to construe or interpret it in its application to the pending case. If the words in question are not technical terms, either as having a special sense by commercial usage, or as having a scientific meaning different from their popular meaning, but are words of common speech, then their interpretation is a matter within the judicial knowledge, and belongs to the court as a question of law.[15]

[14] Dodsworth v. Anderson, T. Jones, 141; Byrne v. Byrne, 3 Tex. 336; Belt v. Marriott, 9 Gill, 331; Large v. Orvis, 20 Wis. 696; Fairbanks v. Woodhouse, 6 Cal. 433; Inge v. Murphy, 10 Ala. 885; Barnes v. Mayor of Mobile, 19 Ala. 707; Thorp v. Craig, 10 Iowa, 461; City of Peoria v. Calhoun, 29 Ill. 317.

[15] Marvel v. Merritt, 116 U. S. 11, 6 Sup. Ct. 207; Nix v. Hedden, 39 Fed. 109; State v. Baldwin, 36 Kans. 1, 22, 12 Pac. 318; Moran v. Prather, 23 Wall. 492. The question whether a statute requiring railroad trains to "slow down to a speed of not more than four miles an hour before running on, or crossing, any drawbridge over a stream which is regularly navigated by vessels," applies to the trestles and approaches leading up to a drawbridge

But when technical terms (other than legal terms) or scientific terms, or the words and phrases of trade and commerce, or mercantile signs or abbreviations, or similarly obscure or specialized expressions, are found in a statute, and their explanation becomes relevant to the case on trial, the testimony of experts is admissible as to their meaning. And thereupon two questions arise, between which it is very necessary to preserve a clear distinction. The first question is, what is the specific meaning of the term as used in the law? This is a question of fact. It is to be determined by the jury, in view of the evidence adduced with regard to it. But the second question is this: What effect has the term, used with this meaning, upon the construction of the statute? And this is a question of law, and is to be determined by the court.[16] "The construction of all written instruments belongs to the court alone, whose duty it is to construe all such instruments, as soon as the true meaning of the words in which they are couched, and the surrounding circumstances, if any, have been ascertained as facts by the jury; and it is the duty of the jury to take the construction from the court, either absolutely, if there be no words to be construed as words of art or phrases used in commerce, and no surrounding circumstances to be ascertained, or conditionally, when those words or circumstances are necessarily referred to them."[17] For example, in a case in Texas, the construction of the word "family," as used in a statute, became necessary to the decision of the case. The court refused to instruct the jury as to what constitutes a "family," but declared that question to be a matter of proof, and authorized the jury to interpret the meaning of the term for themselves. This was held to be error. For the term, when ap-

proper, is a question for the court and not for the jury. Savannah, F. & W. Ry. Co. v. Daniels, 90 Ga. 608, 17 S. E. 647.

[16] See Eaton v. Smith, 20 Pick. 150; Hutchison v. Bowker, 5 Mees. & W. 535; McNichol v. Pacific Exp. Co., 12 Mo. App. 401; Brown v. Brown, 8 Metc. (Mass.) 573; Pitney v. Glen's Falls Ins. Co., 65 N. Y. 6.

[17] Neilson v. Harford, 8 Mees. & W. 806. In Moran v. Prather, 23 Wall. 492, it was said: "Terms of art, in the absence of parol testimony, must be understood in their primary sense, unless the context evidently shows that they were used in the particular case in some other and peculiar sense, in which case the testimony of persons skilled in the art or science may be admitted to aid the court in ascertaining the true intent and meaning of that part of the instrument."

plied to a particular state of facts, presents a mixed question of law and fact; and it is the province of the court to declare the law, so far as the fact is governed by the law; and so far as the fact is a question of proof, it is to be deduced by the jury from the evidence, and not from their personal knowledge.[18]

Similar questions arise as to the construction of foreign laws. It is well settled that foreign laws must be proved as facts, that is, they cannot be judicially noticed. As between the several states of the American Union, the statutes now generally provide that the official publications of the acts of the legislatures or the codes shall be competent original evidence of the existence and terms of those laws. But the rule remains, as always, that foreign laws are to be proved as facts. But, this being established, it is evident that two questions may be presented to the court trying a case in which such foreign laws become relevant. One question is this: What interpretation or construction is put upon the law in question by the courts of the state which enacted it? The other is, what construction should be put upon the statute by the court which is called upon to apply it to a given state of facts? In other words, the tribunal may be called upon either to ascertain, and then apply, the construction which the foreign law bears at home, or else to put its own construction upon it. Now the former of these questions is a question of fact; the latter is a question of law. The construction given to a statute of another state, whether by usage or by judicial decisions, is a part of the unwritten law of that state, and as such it may be proved by parol testimony, and must be found by the jury.[19] But when the existence and terms of the foreign law have been proved as facts, and there is no evidence as to the construction put upon it at home, or when for any reason that con-

---

[18] Goode v. State, 16 Tex. App. 411. Whether or not a given act is a work of necessity, within the meaning of an exception to a statute prohibiting labor on Sunday, is a question of fact to be found by the jury. Smith v. Boston & M. R. Co., 120 Mass. 490; Ungericht v. State, 119 Ind. 379, 21 N. E. 1082; State v. Knight, 29 W. Va. 340, 1 S. E. 569.

[19] Dyer v. Smith, 12 Conn. 384; Kline v. Baker, 99 Mass. 253. But some of the cases appear to hold that if the evidence of the home interpretation of a foreign law consists of judicial decisions, such evidence is properly addressed to the court and not the jury. See Geoghegan v. Atlas Steam-Ship Co. (Com. Pl.) 10 N. Y. Supp. 121; Kline v. Baker, 99 Mass. 253.

struction is not to be followed, but the trial court must construe the law, then there is presented a question with which the jury are not concerned, but it belongs exclusively to the court.[20]

[20] State v. Jackson, 2 Dev. (N. Car.) 563; Cobb v. Griffith & A. S. G. & T. Co., 87 Mo. 90. And see Kline v. Baker, 99 Mass. 253; Bremer v. Freeman, 10 Moore, P. C. 306; Di Sora v. Phillips, 10 H. L. Cas. 624; Molson's Bank v. Boardman, 47 Hun, 135; Ames v. McCamber, 124 Mass. 85; Shoe & Leather Nat. Bank v. Wood, 142 Mass. 563, 8 N. E. 753. Compare Holman v. King, 7 Met. (Mass.) 384.

CHAPTER II.

CONSTRUCTION OF CONSTITUTIONS.

METHOD OF INTERPRETATION.

7. A constitution is not to be interpreted on narrow or technical principles, but liberally and on broad general lines, in order that it may accomplish the objects of its establishment and carry out the great principles of government.

"Narrow and technical reasoning," says Judge Cooley, "is misplaced when it is brought to bear upon an instrument framed by the people themselves, for themselves, and designed as a chart upon which every man, learned or unlearned, may be able to trace the leading principles of government." [1] The constitution "was intended for the benefit of the people, and must receive a liberal construction. A constitution is not to receive a technical construction, like a common-law instrument or a statute. It is to be interpreted so as to carry out the great principles of government, not to defeat

---

[1] Cooley, Const. Lim. 59.

them."[2] Constitutions, it is said in another case, "declare the organic law of a state; they deal with larger topics and are couched in broader phrase than legislative acts or private muniments. They do not undertake to define with minute precision in the manner of the latter, and hence their just interpretation is not always to be reached by the application of similar methods."[3] "A constitution of government does not, and cannot, from its nature, depend in any great degree upon mere verbal criticism, or upon the import of single words. Such criticism may not be wholly without use; it may sometimes illustrate or unfold the appropriate sense; but unless it stands well with the context and the subject-matter, it must yield to the latter. While, then, we may well resort to the meaning of single words to assist our inquiries, we should never forget that it is an instrument of government we are to construe, and that must be the truest exposition which best harmonizes with its design, its objects, and its general structure."[4] It has sometimes been contended that the construction of a constitution should be strict, because it is a grant of powers, and is, to that extent, in derogation of the inherent and natural powers of the people. But on this point it has been very justly observed: "All governments are founded upon a surrender of some natural rights, and they impose some restrictions. Therefore, in construing a constitution of government framed by the people for their own benefit and protection, for the preservation of their rights and property and liberty, where the delegated powers are not and cannot be used for the benefit of their rulers, who are but their temporary servants and agents, but are intended solely for the benefit of the people, no presumption arises of an intention to use the words of the constitution in the most restricted sense. The strict or the most extended sense, being equally within the letter, may be fairly held to be within their intention, as either shall best promote the very objects of the people in the grant, and as either shall best promote or secure their rights, property, or liberty. The words are not, indeed, to be stretched beyond their fair sense; but within that range, the

---

[2] Morrison v. Bachert, 112 Pa. St. 322, 5 Atl. 739; Comm. v. Clark, 7 Watts & S. 127.

[3] Houseman v. Comm., 100 Pa. St. 222. See, also, Greencastle Tp. v. Black, 5 Ind. 557.

[4] 1 Story, Const. § 455.

rule of interpretation must be taken which best follows out the apparent intention. This is the mode, it is believed, universally adopted in construing the state constitutions. It has its origin in common sense. And it can never be an object of just jealousy, because the rulers can have no permanent interest in a free government distinct from that of the people, of whom they are a part, and to whom they are responsible." [5]

But it is here necessary to remark that a distinction must be taken, as regards the strictness or liberality of construction, between the constitution of a state and the constitution of the United States, when either is considered as a grant of governmental powers. Under that aspect, it is only the former which is entitled to be liberally construed, in the fullest sense of the term. The federal constitution, in respect to its clauses which delegate powers to the general government, is to receive a reasonable and fair construction, but is not to be stretched beyond the plain meaning of its terms and the necessary implications arising therefrom. It should also be observed that it is not within the lawful powers of the courts, in any event, "to amend the constitution, under the color of construction, by interpolating provisions not suggested by any part of it. We cannot supply all omissions which we may believe have arisen from inadvertence on the part of the constitutional convention." [6]

INTENT TO BE SOUGHT.

8. It is a cardinal rule in the interpretation of constitutions that the instrument must be so construed as to give effect to the intention of the people, who adopted it. This intention is to be sought in the constitution itself, and the apparent meaning of the words employed is to be taken as expressing it, except in cases where that assumption would lead to absurdity, ambiguity, or contradiction.

Where the meaning shown on the face of the words is definite and intelligible, the courts are not at liberty to look for another meaning, even though it should seem more probable or natural, but

[5] 1 Story, Const. § 413.

[6] Walker v. City of Cincinnati, 21 Ohio St. 14, 53.

they must assume that the constitution means just what it says. "Whether we are considering an agreement between parties, a statute, or a constitution, with a view to its interpretation, the thing we are to seek is the thought which it expresses. To ascertain this, the first resort in all cases is to the natural signification of the words employed, in the order and grammatical arrangement in which the framers of the instrument have placed them. If, thus regarded, the words embody a definite meaning, which involves no absurdity and no contradiction between different parts of the same writing, then that meaning apparent upon the face of the instrument is the one which alone we are at liberty to say was intended to be conveyed. In such a case, there is no room for construction. That which the words declare is the meaning of the instrument, and neither courts nor legislatures have the right to add to, or take away from, that meaning." [7] But if the words of the constitution, thus taken, are devoid of meaning, or lead to an absurd conclusion, or are contradictory of other parts of the constitution, then it cannot be presumed that their prima facie import expresses the real intention. And in that case, the courts are to employ the process of construction to arrive at the real intention, by taking the words in such a sense as will give them a definite and sensible meaning, or reconcile them with the rest of the instrument. And this sense is to be determined by comparing the particular clause with other parts of the constitution, by considering the various meanings, vernacular or technical, which the words are capable of bearing, and by studying the facts of contemporary history and the purpose sought to be accomplished, and the benefit to be secured, or the evil to be remedied, by the provision in question. [8]

[7] Newell v. People, 7 N. Y. 9, 97; City of Beardstown v. City of Virginia, 76 Ill. 34, 40; City of Springfield v. Edwards, 84 Ill. 626; People v. May, 9 Colo. 80, 10 Pac. 641; 1 Story, Const. § 401; Hills v. City of Chicago, 60 Ill. 86.
[8] People v. Potter, 47 N. Y. 375; Taylor v. Taylor, 10 Minn. 107 (Gil. 81).

UNIFORMITY IN CONSTRUCTION.

9. The construction of a constitutional provision is to be uniform.

The constitution cannot be made to mean different things at different times. Its interpretation should not fluctuate according to the changes in public sentiment or the supposed desirability of adjusting the fundamental rules to varying conditions or exigencies. The meaning of the constitution is fixed when it is adopted, and afterwards, when the courts are called upon to interpret it, they cannot assume that it bears any different meaning.[9] "The policy of one age may ill suit the wishes or the policy of another. The constitution is not to be subject to such fluctuations. It is to have a fixed, uniform, permanent construction. It should be, so far at least as human infirmity will allow, not dependent upon the passions or parties of particular times, but the same yesterday, to-day, and forever." [10]

EFFECT TO BE GIVEN TO THE WHOLE.

10. In case of ambiguity, the whole constitution is to be examined in order to determine the meaning of any part; and the construction is to be such as to give effect to the entire instrument, and not to raise any conflict between its parts which can be avoided.

An examination of other parts of the constitution will often enable the court to ascertain the sense in which the words in particular clauses were used. And this method of investigation must be resorted to before aid can be sought from extraneous sources. Moreover, a construction which raises a conflict between different parts of the constitution is not permissible when, by any reasonable construction, the parts may be made to harmonize.[11] But when the constitution speaks in plain language in reference to a

[9] People v. Blodgett, 13 Mich. 127.
[10] 1 Story, Const. § 427.
[11] Cooley, Const. Lim. 58; Manly v. State, 7 Md. 135.

particular matter, the courts have no right to place a different meaning on the words employed because the literal interpretation may happen to be inconsistent with other parts of the instrument in relation to other subjects.[12] And "it is by no means a correct rule of interpretation to construe the same word in the same sense wherever it occurs in the same instrument. It does not follow, either logically or grammatically, that because a word is found in one connection in the constitution with a definite sense, therefore the same sense is to be adopted in every other connection in which it occurs. This would be to suppose that the framers weighed only the force of single words, as philologists or critics, and not whole clauses and objects, as statesmen and practical reasoners."[13] And it must be remembered that a state constitution does not stand alone in regulating the frame of government, or defining the limitations of governmental powers. Just as a statute must be construed with reference to constitutional and statutory provisions on the same subject-matter, so the provisions of a state constitution must be construed with reference to the corresponding or related provisions of the federal constitution, treaties formed by the national authorities, and the acts of congress, and must, if possible, be so interpreted as not to conflict with the same.[14] Where the constitution makes provision for contingencies apprehended, or for occasional or temporary needs, such provisions should not be so interpreted as to clash with the general design, but should be in harmonious subservience thereto, and if their terms conflict with those provisions which are made part of the essential framework of the general plan, and are of usual continuous and necessary operation, the former must yield and adapt themselves to the latter.[15] The bill of rights, commonly incorporated in state constitutions, is not to be interpreted by itself alone, according to its literal meaning. The bill of rights and the constitution together compose the form of government, and they must be interpreted as one instrument. The former announces principles on which the government about to be established will be based. If they differ, the constitution must be taken as a limitation or qualification of the general principles

[12] Cantwell v. Owens, 14 Md. 215.

[13] 1 Story, Const. § 454.

[14] Endlich, Interp. § 523.

[15] People v. Potter, 47 N. Y. 375.

previously declared, according to the subject and the language employed.[16]

COMMON LAW AND PREVIOUS LEGISLATION.

11. A constitution should be construed with reference to, but not overruled by, the doctrines of the common law and the legislation previously existing in the state.

Except in so far as it is superseded by the constitutions, the common law is generally in force in the United States. Hence the importance of comparing constitutional provisions, in order to arrive at the true meaning and effect, with the great body of the common law, both for the purpose of understanding the language employed and of measuring the changes and innovations designed to be introduced. But the constitution is superior to the common law, and is not to be understood as in any way controlled or limited by it. It is a familiar rule that a statute in contravention or derogation of the common law ought not to be extended by construction. And there is always a presumption against an unnecessary change of laws. Accordingly it has been held that when a new constitution makes a change in the pre-existing law, whether common law or statutory, the change is not to be extended by construction beyond the very terms of the constitution.[17] But this is a rule which must be applied with great care. It should never be allowed to detract, in the slightest degree, from the actual meaning and intention of the constitution.

[16] Mayor, etc., of Baltimore v. State, 15 Md. 376, 459. Compare In re Dorsey, 7 Port. (Ala.) 293.

[17] Costigan v. Bond, 65 Md. 122, 3 Atl. 285. See, also, Mayor, etc., of Baltimore v. State, 15 Md. 376; Brown v. Fifield, 4 Mich. 322; Cooley, Const. Lim. 61.

RETROSPECTIVE OPERATION AVOIDED.

12. A constitutional provision should not be construed with a retrospective operation, unless that is the unmistakable intention of the words used or the obvious design of the authors.

It is the invariable rule that a statute will be so construed as to operate prospectively only, unless the words used, or the plain design of the framers of the law, being too clear to admit of any doubt, require that it should have a retrospective effect. This rule, with the very substantial reasons upon which it rests, will be considered in a later chapter. The same reasons apply equally to the interpretation of constitutional provisions. Hence, if the language employed admits of a substantial doubt on this point, the courts should not construe the provision retrospectively. But if such an effect is manifestly intended, they are not at liberty to nar- row the meaning of the constitution from any considerations of justice or expediency. The former part of this rule has not, in- deed, been always accepted. In one of the cases it was said (though the remark was only obiter) that the rule against a retro- spective interpretation has but little application, if any, to the in- terpretation of a constitution. "We are not," said the learned judge, "to interpret the constitution precisely as we would an act of the legislature. The convention was not obliged, like the legis- lative bodies, to look carefully to the preservation of vested rights. It was competent to deal, subject to ratification by the people, and to the constitution of the federal government, with all private and social rights, and with all the existing laws and institutions of the state. If the convention had so willed, and the people had con- curred, all the former charters and grants might have been anni- hilated. When, therefore, we are seeking for the true construction of a constitutional provision, we are constantly to bear in mind that its authors were not executing a delegated authority, limited by other constitutional restraints, but are to look upon them as the founders of a state, intent only upon establishing such principles as seemed best calculated to produce good government and promote the public happiness, at the expense of any and all existing institutions which might stand in their way." [18]

MANDATORY AND DIRECTORY PROVISIONS.

13. **The provisions of a constitution are almost invariably mandatory; it is only in extremely plain cases, or under the pressure of necessity, that they can be construed as merely directory.**

It is not lightly to be presumed that any provision deemed essential to be incorporated in an instrument so solemn and enduring as a constitution, was designed to be merely in the nature of a direction, without imperative force. "It would, in a general sense, be a dangerous doctrine to announce that any of the provisions of the constitution may be obeyed or disregarded at the mere will or pleasure of the legislature, unless it is clear beyond all question that such was the intention of the framers of that instrument. It would seem to be a lowering of the proper dignity of the fundamental law to say that it descends to prescribing rules of order in unessential matters which may be followed or disregarded at pleasure." [19]   As a rule, therefore, whenever the language used in a constitution is prohibitory, it is to be understood as intended to be a positive and unequivocal negation; and whenever the language contains a grant of power, it is intended as a mandate, not a mere direction. [20]   Nevertheless, there may be cases in which a constitutional provision should be held to be merely directory. Thus, where the contrary construction would lead to absurd, impossible, or mischievous consequences, it should not be followed. In Ohio, for example, where a clause of the constitution required that every bill, on its passage through the legislature, should "be fully and distinctly read on three different days," the court held that this provision might be taken as merely directory, and that its observance by the legislature was to be taken as secured by their sense of duty and official oaths, and not by any

[18] In re Oliver Lee & Co.'s Bank, 21 N. Y. 9.

[19] Sutherland, Stat. Constr. § 79; Cooley, Const. Lim. 78.

[20] Varney v. Justice, 86 Ky. 596, 6 S. W. 457; Hunt v. State, 22 Tex. App. 396, 3 S. W. 233; People v. Lawrence, 36 Barb. 177.

supervisory power of the courts. "Any other construction, we incline to think, would lead to very absurd and alarming consequences. If it is in the power of every court (and if one has the power, every one has it) to inquire whether a bill that passed the assembly was 'fully' and 'distinctly' read three times in each house, and to hold it invalid if, upon any reading, a word was accidentally omitted, or the reading was indistinct, it would obviously be impossible to know what is the statute law of the state." [21] And again, it must be remembered that a constitution is to receive a reasonable construction, and such as to carry out the great principles of government, and not to defeat them. Consequently, the principle of strict construction should not be allowed to nullify or frustrate the main objects of the constitution, especially in a newly constructed frame of government. For instance, "it was provided by the first article and third section of the federal constitution that the senate should be composed of two members from each state, chosen for six years, and that 'immediately' after they should be assembled, they should be divided into three classes, in order that one-third of the body might be chosen every second year. Yet, on the principle of strict construction, a postponement of the division for a month or a day would have presented an insuperable obstacle to the organization of the government. Necessarily, the paramount rule of interpretation demands that such provisions be deemed only directory." [22]

IMPLICATIONS.

14. Whatever is necessary to render effective any provision of a constitution, whether the same be a prohibition, or a restriction, or the grant of a power, must be deemed implied and intended in the provision itself. [23]

The principal application of this rule is in respect to the grants of powers contained in the constitutions, which will be considered

---

[21] Miller v. State, 3 Ohio St. 475; Pim v. Nicholson, 6 Ohio St. 176. And see Hill v. Boyland, 40 Miss. 618; McPherson v. Leonard, 29 Md. 377.

[22] Comm. v. Clark, 7 Watts & S. 127.

[23] Endlich, Interp. § 535; 1 Story, Const. § 430; Cooley, Const. Lim. 77.

in the succeeding section. But it is also a rule of construction that "when the constitution defines the circumstances under which a right may be exercised or a penalty imposed, the specification is an implied prohibition against legislative interference to add to the condition or to extend the penalty to other cases. On this ground it has been held that where the constitution defines the qualifications of an officer, it is not in the power of the legislature to change or superadd to them, unless the power to do so is expressly or by necessary implication conferred by the constitution itself." [24] Moreover, the language of a constitution, which cannot enter into minute and detailed specifications to meet possible cases, is subject often to implied exceptions and qualifications, which depend upon the principles of reason, justice, or public policy. Thus, for instance, a constitutional provision giving to county auditors the exclusive right to fix the compensation for all services rendered to the county, should not be held to invest them with the power to fix the compensation for their own services. [25]

GRANTS OF POWERS.

15. Where the constitution grants a power in general terms, the grant includes all such particular and auxiliary powers as may be necessary to make it effectual. Where the means for the exercise of a granted power are specified, all other means are understood to be excluded. Where the means are not specified, any means may be resorted to which are fairly and properly adapted to accomplish the object of the grant of power, if they do not unnecessarily interfere with existing interests or vested rights.

"A constitution cannot, from its very nature, enter into a minute specification of all the minor powers naturally and obviously included in it and flowing from the great and important ones which are expressly granted. It is therefore established as a general

---

[24] Cooley, Const. Lim. 64, citing Thomas v. Owens, 4 Md. 189.

[25] People v. Gies, 25 Mich. 83.

rule that when a constitution gives a general power, or enjoins a duty, it also gives, by implication, every particular power necessary for the exercise of the one or the performance of the other. The implication under this rule, however, must be a necessary, not a conjectural or argumentative one."[26] And when a power is granted in general terms, the power is to be construed as coextensive with the terms, unless some clear restriction upon it is deducible, expressly or by implication, from the context.[27] A power, given in general terms, is not to be restricted to particular cases merely because it may be susceptible of abuse, and, if abused, may lead to mischievous consequences.[28] And on the other hand, a rule of equal importance is not to enlarge the construction of a given power beyond the fair scope of its terms merely because the restriction is inconvenient, impolitic, or even mischievous. Arguments drawn from impolicy or inconvenience ought to have no weight in this connection.[29] But "no construction of a given power is to be allowed which plainly defeats or impairs its avowed objects. If, therefore, the words are fairly susceptible of two interpretations, according to their common sense and use, the one of which would defeat one or all of the objects for which it was obviously given, and the other of which would preserve and promote all, the former interpretation ought to be rejected, and the latter be held the true interpretation. This rule results from the dictates of mere common sense; for every instrument ought to be so construed 'ut magis valeat quam pereat.' "[30]

Where, in a constitution, a power is granted, and the means for its exercise are also specifically granted, no other or different means or powers can be implied on the ground of greater convenience or efficiency.[31] If the means for the execution of the granted power are not specified, it should not fail for the want of such

---

[26] Field v. People, 3 Ill. 79, 83. But where the constitution confers upon a given court certain powers which it specially enumerates, they are all that the court will possess; and it will not be competent for the legislature either to add to or subtract from those powers. State v. Mace, 5 Md. 337.

[27] Cooley, Const. Lim. 64; 1 Story, Const. § 424.

[28] 1 Story, Const. § 425.

[29] Id. § 426.

[30] Id. § 428.

[31] Field v. People, 3 Ill. 79.

enumeration; but in that case it is evident that the depositary of the power will be invested with a discretion as to the choice of the means to be employed, the only restriction being that the means selected shall be fairly and properly adapted and appropriate to the exercise of the power, and shall involve no injustice or hardship which can reasonably be avoided. "When the means for carrying into effect any particular constitutional power are not specified, those means which interfere with established relations, and violate existing rights and obligations, as fixed by law, will not be presumed to be intended, unless they are strictly necessary." [32]

It should also be observed, in this connection, that while the foregoing rules are equally applicable to the constitution of the United States and to those of the states, yet, considered as a grant of powers, the former is to be strictly construed, while the latter are to receive a liberal construction. For instance, the congress of the United States can pass no laws but those which the constitution authorizes, either expressly or by clear implication, while the legislature of a state has jurisdiction of all subjects on which its legislation is not prohibited. [33]

POPULAR AND TECHNICAL SENSE OF WORDS.

16. The words employed in a constitution are to be taken in their natural and popular sense, unless they are technical legal terms, in which case they are to be taken in their technical signification.

It is a general rule that the words of a constitution are to be understood in the sense in which they are popularly employed, unless the context or the very nature of the subject indicates otherwise. [34] "Every word employed in the constitution is to be ex-

[32] Comm. v. Downes, 24 Pick. 227.

[33] Comm. v. Hartman, 17 Pa. St. 118; Weister v. Hade, 52 Pa. St. 474; Black, Const. Law, 260. On the subject of the construction of the constitution of the United States with reference to its grants of legislative power, see Black, Const. Law, 154, 213, 217.

[34] Greencastle Tp. v. Black, 5 Ind. 557; State v. Mace, 5 Md. 337; Manly v. State, 7 Md. 135; People v. Fancher, 50 N. Y. 288.

pounded in its plain, obvious, and common sense, unless the context furnishes some ground to control, qualify, or enlarge it. Constitutions are not designed for metaphysical or logical subtilties, for niceties of expression, for critical propriety, for elaborate shades of meaning, or for the exercise of philosophical acuteness or judicial research. They are instruments of a practical nature, founded on the common business of human life, adapted to common wants, designed for common use, and fitted for common understandings. The people make them, the people adopt them, the people must be supposed to read them, with the help of common sense, and cannot be presumed to admit in them any recondite meaning or any extraordinary gloss." [35] Where a word having a technical (non-legal) meaning, as well as a popular meaning, is used in a constitution, the courts will accord to it its popular signification, unless it is apparent, from the nature of the subject or the connection in which it appears, that it was intended to be used in its technical sense. [36] But there are many technical legal terms employed in the constitutions. And if the technical signification of these words differs from the vernacular, the former is to be preferred in construction. This is because a constitution is a law, and is to be interpreted as such. "No one would doubt," says Story, "when the constitution has declared that 'the privilege of the writ of habeas corpus shall not be suspended,' unless under peculiar circumstances, that it referred, not to every sort of writ which has acquired that name, but to that which has been emphatically so called, on account of its remedial power to free a party from arbitrary imprisonment. So again, when it declares that in suits at 'common law' the right of trial by jury shall be preserved, though the phrase 'common law' admits of different meanings, no one can doubt that it is used in a technical sense." [37] And this rule is particularly true of the terms derived from Magna Charta and the other great English charters, which are to be interpreted in the light of history, and have acquired a fixed and exact technical meaning from the expositions of the courts and the understanding of the people. But where the constitution uses technical terms of law and jurisprudence, which are common to our law and the law of Eng-

[35] 1 Story, Const. § 451.   [36] Weill v. Kenfield, 54 Cal. 111.
[37] 1 Story, Const. § 453.

land, if there is a difference of signification in the two countries, the meaning which they bear in this country is to be preferred.[38]

PREAMBLE AND TITLES.

17. **The preamble to a constitution and the titles of its several articles or sections may furnish some evidence of its meaning and intention; but arguments drawn therefrom are entitled to very little weight.**

"It is evident that only in the most general way can the preamble of a constitution influence the construction of its provisions. As affecting the general character of the instrument, it has, indeed, been resorted to. The weight attached to the phrase 'We, the people,' in the preamble of the federal constitution, and the arguments based upon it, are a familiar instance of this species of construction."[39] And "scarcely any significance can be attached to the wording of the captions or titles of the several articles of the constitution. At most, they do not profess to indicate more than the general character of the article to which they are prefixed. That they are intended as critical and precise definitions of the subject-matter of the articles, or as exercising restraining limitations upon the clear expressions therein contained, cannot be pretended."[40]

INJUSTICE AND INCONVENIENCE.

18. **It is not permissible to disobey, or to construe into nothingness, a provision of the constitution merely because it may appear to work injustice, or to lead to harsh or obnoxious consequences or invidious and unmerited discriminations, and still less weight should be attached to the argument from mere inconvenience.**

In the construction or interpretation of a constitution, the courts have nothing to do with the argument from inconvenience. It is

[38] The Huntress, Daveis, 82, Fed. Cas. No. 6,914.
[39] Endlich, Interp. § 511.
[40] Houseman v. Comm., 100 Pa. St. 222.

their duty to declare what the constitution has said. And while it will not be presumed that the framers of the constitution intended to produce unjust, oppressive, or invidious results, yet if the meaning of the instrument is clear and unambiguous, or is plainly indicated by internal evidence, the courts are not at liberty to disregard this obvious meaning or to depart from it, on any consideration of the consequences which may follow.[41] "The hardships and inconveniences resulting from this construction are urged upon our attention," said the court in Colorado in a recent case. But "to such appeals the language of the courts is uniform. The province of the judiciary is not to make the law, but to construe it. The meaning of a constitutional provision being plain, it must stand, be recognized, and obeyed, as the supreme law of the land."[42] At the same time, "we do not say that if a clause should be found in a constitution which should appear at first blush to demand a construction leading to monstrous and absurd consequences, it might not be the duty of the court to question and cross-question such clause closely, with a view to discover in it, if possible, some other meaning more consistent with the general purposes and aims of these instruments."[43]

EXTRANEOUS AIDS IN CONSTRUCTION.

19. If an ambiguity exists which cannot be cleared up by a consideration of the constitution itself, then, in order to determine its meaning and purpose, resort may be had to extraneous facts, such as the prior state of the law, the evil to be remedied, the circumstances of contemporary history, or the discussions of the constitutional convention.

When the text of a constitutional provision is not ambiguous, the courts, in construing it, are not at liberty to search for its meaning beyond the instrument itself. If the text is ambiguous, the

---

[41] Greencastle Tp. v. Black, 5 Ind. 557; Weill v. Kenfield, 54 Cal. 111; County of Wayne v. City of Detroit, 17 Mich. 390; Oakley v. Aspinwall, 3 N. Y. 547, 568.

[42] People v. May, 9 Colo. 80, 10 Pac. 641.

[43] Cooley, Const. Lim. 73.

endeavor must first be made to arrive at its meaning from other parts of the same instrument.   It is not until the means of solution afforded by the whole constitution have been exhausted without success that the courts are justified in calling outside facts or considerations to their aid.   But when this becomes necessary, it is permissible to inquire into the prior state of the law, the previous and contemporary history of the people, the circumstances attending the foundation of the constitution, the evil intended to be remedied or the benefit sought to be secured by the provision in question, as well as broad considerations of expediency.   The object herein is to ascertain the reason which induced the framers of the constitution to enact the particular provision and the purpose sought to be accomplished thereby, in order so to construe the whole as to make the words consonant to that reason and calculated to effect that purpose.[44]   "It is regarded as appropriate for the courts, and as a matter entitled to their most careful consideration, in giving a construction to the constitution [of the United States] to look back at the situation of the country at the time and antecedent to the time of its adoption, to look at its then existing institutions, at the existence and operation of the then state governments, at the powers and workings of the old confederation, and at all other circumstances which had a tendency to produce or obstruct its formation and ratification; and it is also held that contemporary history and contemporary interpretation may be called in to aid in arriving at just conclusions."[45]   Yet it is very necessary to remember that the plain and obvious meaning of the constitution is not to be overridden by considerations such as these; nor should the purpose and significance of constitutional provisions be sought alone in the facts of antecedent history.   "It will not do to say that an actual, existing, antecedent mischief is essential to support a constitutional limitation or an intent to limit; or that the absence of such an actual mischief excludes an intention to limit. On the other hand, it is safe to say that wherever there is a power liable to be abused, there is to be found a legislative motive for restraint.   The multitudinous restraints of all constitutions proceed

---

[44] Mayor, etc., of Baltimore v. State, 15 Md. 376; Cronise v. Cronise, 54 Pa. St. 255.

[45] Potter's Dwarris on Statutes, 657, citing Stuart v. Laird, 2 Cranch, 309.

largely against possible mischiefs. To leave powers unlimited where there is great temptation to abuse is to invite abuse." [46]

In order to arrive at the reason and purpose of the constitution, it is also permissible to consult the debates and proceedings of the constitutional convention which framed the constitution. But it must be remembered that these are never of binding force, or of anything more than persuasive value. They may throw a useful light upon the purpose sought to be accomplished or upon the meaning attached to the words employed, or they may not. The courts are at liberty to avail themselves of any light derivable from such sources, but are not bound to adopt it as the sole ground of their decision. [47]

[46] People v. May, 9 Colo. 80, 10 Pac. 641.

[47] See City of Springfield v. Edwards, 84 Ill. 626, 643; Coutant v. People, 11 Wend. 511; People v. May, 9 Colo. 80, 10 Pac. 641; People v. Gies, 25 Mich. 83; Taylor v. Taylor, 10 Minn. 107 (Gil. 81). As to the rule which permits recourse to the debates of the constitutional convention, Endlich (Interp. § 510) speaks of it as a great stretch of principle, but says that "it seems upon the whole to be sanctioned by judicial authority; the theory being that, members of the convention having declared that a certain provision was designed to have a certain effect, and no member expressing a different view, the people voted for the constitution in the light of this construction and therefore adopted it; and the limit of the applicability of the rule being that the debates are not to be resorted to when there is no room for construction, but where the meaning from any cause is in doubt, the debates may be considered; and that even the ascertained understanding of the convention is not to be permitted to override the more natural and obvious meaning of the words, in which the people adopting the constitution must be supposed to have understood them." In the case of Comm. v. Balph, 111 Pa. St. 365, 3 Atl. 220, the court said that the debates in the constitutional convention "are of value as showing the views of the individual members, and as indicating the reasons for their votes, but they give us no light as to the views of the large majority who did not talk, much less of the mass of our fellow citizens whose votes at the polls gave that instrument the force of fundamental law. We think it safer to construe the constitution from what appears upon its face." On the other hand, in People v. May, 9 Colo. 80, 10 Pac. 641, the court took judicial notice of an address to the people which had been issued by the constitutional convention upon its adjournment, wherein that body called public attention to the changes made by the new constitution, and explained the reasons for them, and their meaning. And this address was allowed to have some weight in inclining the court to a certain construction of one of the clauses of the constitution therein referred to.

CONTEMPORARY AND PRACTICAL CONSTRUCTION.

20. The contemporary construction of the constitution, especially if universally adopted, and also its practical construction, especially if acquiesced in for a long period of time, are valuable aids in determining its meaning and intention in cases of doubt; but these aids must be resorted to with caution and reserve, and they can never be allowed to abrogate, contradict, enlarge, or restrict the plain and obvious meaning of the text.

By contemporary construction is meant the construction put upon the language or meaning of a constitution, at the time of its adoption, or shortly thereafter, by members of the convention which framed it or by other learned men who expressed their opinions in that regard publicly, though not judicially. It is properly resorted to to illustrate and confirm the text, to explain a doubtful phrase, or to expound an obscure clause. And the credit to which it is entitled is in proportion to the uniformity and universality of that construction, and the known ability and talents of those by whom it was given. But it is to be resorted to with much qualification and reserve. "It can never abrogate the text; it can never fritter away its obvious meaning; it can never narrow down its true limitations; it can never enlarge its natural boundaries." "Nothing but the text itself was adopted by the people. And it would certainly be a most extravagant doctrine to give to any commentary then made, and, a fortiori, to any commentary since made, under a very different posture of opinion and feeling, an authority which should operate as an absolute limit upon the text, or should supersede its natural and just interpretation." [48]

By the practical construction of the constitution is meant the construction put upon it by the legislative body, which is charged with the making of laws in accordance with the constitution, or by the officers of the executive department, whose function is to put into execution the constitution and the laws. "Where there has been a practical construction, which has been acquiesced in for a considera-

---

[48] 1 Story, Const. §§ 406, 407; People v. May, 9 Colo. 80, 10 Pac. 641.

ble period, considerations in favor of adhering to this construction sometimes present themselves to the courts with a plausibility and force which it is not easy to resist.   Indeed, where a particular construction has been generally accepted as correct, and especially when this has occurred contemporaneously with the adoption of the constitution, and by those who had opportunity to understand the intention of the instrument, it is not to be denied that a strong presumption exists that the construction rightly interprets the intention.   And where this has been given by officers in the discharge of their official duty, and rights have accrued in reliance upon it, which would be divested by a decision that the construction was erroneous, the argument ab inconvenienti is sometimes allowed to have very great weight." [49]   And similar respect will be paid to a long, constant, and uniform practical construction of the constitution by the legislature, more especially in relation to those provisions of it which deal with the legislative rights, powers, and duties. [50]

PROVISIONS FROM OTHER CONSTITUTIONS.

21. Where a clause or provision in a constitution, which has received a settled judicial construction, is adopted in the same words by the framers of another constitution, it will be presumed that the construction thereof was likewise adopted.

This rule applies to the case where the constitution of one state copies a clause or provision from the constitution of another state, and also to the case where a new or revised constitution retains a clause or provision from the superseded constitution.   In either such case, the courts will presume that the clause or provision was adopted with a knowledge of its settled judicial construction and with the intention that it should be understood in accordance with that construction.   And the same principle applies, where it can

---

[49] Cooley, Const. Lim. 67, citing Stuart v. Laird, 1 Cranch, 299; Martin v. Hunter's Lessee, 1 Wheat. 304; Cohens v. Virginia, 6 Wheat. 264; U. S. v. Halstead, 10 Wheat. 51; Ogden v. Saunders, 12 Wheat. 290; Minor v. Happersett, 21 Wall. 162. And see McPherson v. Blacker, 146 U. S. 1, 13 Sup. Ct. 3.

[50] Mayor, etc., of Baltimore v. State, 15 Md. 376, 458.

naturally be applied, to the case of a single term or phrase thus transcribed from one constitution to another.[51] Moreover, "clauses that have been eliminated from a constitution by amendment may be referred to in aid of the interpretation of others originally associated with them and remaining in force. And with equal propriety, the differences between the provisions of a new constitution and those of a previous one, and the construction placed upon the latter when in force, may be regarded by the courts in ascertaining the purpose and real meaning of the new provisions. Conversely, identity of language in the old and new constitutions may determine the construction of the latter in accordance with the construction placed upon the former." [52]

SCHEDULE.

22. The office of a schedule to a constitution is temporary only, and its provisions will be understood as merely transitory, wherever that construction is logically possible. The schedule should not be allowed to abrogate or contradict the provisions of the permanent part of the constitution.

A schedule is a statement annexed to a constitution newly adopted by a state, in which are described at length the particulars in which it differs from the former constitution, and which contains provisions for the adjustment of matters affected by the change from the old to the new constitution. "The schedule of a constitution is a temporary provision for the preparatory machinery necessary to put the principles of the same in motion without disorder or collision. It forms, indeed, a part of the constitution, so far as its temporary purposes go, and to that extent is of equal authority with the provisions in the body of the instrument upon the various departments of the state. But its uses are temporary and auxiliary, and its purpose is not to control the principles enunciated in the constitution itself, but to carry the whole into effect without break

[51] Ex parte Roundtree, 51 Ala. 42; Jenkins v. Ewin, 8 Heisk. 456; Commissioners of Leavenworth Co. v. Miller, 7 Kans. 479; Daily v. Swope, 47 Miss. 367.

[52] Endlich, Interp. § 517.

or interval." [53]   If the schedule contains a provision on a certain subject, while the body of the constitution makes no reference thereto, it cannot be understood that the clause in the schedule was designed to supply permanently the omission in the constitution. Rather it will be presumed that the omission in the constitution was intentional and not a mere oversight, and that the provision in the schedule was meant to apply only to the state of affairs existing under the old constitution, and only until the same should be adjusted to the working of the new constitution.[54]

PRINCIPLE OF STARE DECISIS.

23. The principle of stare decisis applies with special force to the construction of constitutions, and an interpretation once deliberately put upon the provisions of such an instrument should not be departed from without grave reasons.

The stability of many of the most important institutions of society depends upon the permanence, as well as the certainty, of the construction placed by the judiciary upon the fundamental law. Hence, when the meaning of the constitution upon a doubtful question has been once carefully considered and judicially decided, every reason is in favor of a steady adherence to the authoritative interpretation, and especially is this so when the question is not simply as to the constitutionality of a law, but involves the validity of contracts, the protection of vested interests, the rights of innocent parties, or the permanence of a rule of property.[55]

---

[53] Endlich, Interp. § 513; Comm. v. Clark, 7 Watts & S. 127.

[54] State v. Taylor, 15 Ohio St. 137.

[55] Maddox v. Graham, 2 Metc. (Ky.) 56.

CHAPTER III.

GENERAL PRINCIPLES OF STATUTORY CONSTRUCTION.

INTENTION OF LEGISLATURE—LITERAL INTERPRETATION.

24. The object of all interpretation and construction of statutes is to ascertain the meaning and intention of the legislature, to the end that the same may be enforced.[1]

25. This meaning and intention must be sought first of all in the language of the statute itself. For it must be presumed that the means employed by the legislature to express its will are adequate to the purpose and do express that will correctly.[2]

26. If the language of the statute is plain and free from ambiguity, and expresses a single, definite, and

---

[1] U. S. v. Hartwell, 6 Wall. 385; Ogden v. Strong, 2 Paine, 584, Fed. Cas. No. 10,460; Smith v. People, 47 N. Y. 330; Koch v. Bridges, 45 Miss. 247; Catlin v. Hull, 21 Vt. 152; Ezekiel v. Dixon, 3 Ga. 146; Noble v. State, 1 Greene (Iowa), 325; State v. Scarborough, 110 N. Car. 232, 14 S. E. 737; State v. Stephenson, 2 Bail. (S. Car.) 334.

[2] Rosenplaenter v. Roessle, 54 N. Y. 262; People v. Schoonmaker, 63 Barb. 44; Barstow v. Smith, Walk. (Mich.) 394; Ezekiel v. Dixon, 3 Ga. 146; Noble v. State, 1 Greene (Iowa), 325; Denn v. Reid, 10 Pet. 524.

sensible meaning, that meaning is conclusively presumed to be the meaning which the legislature intended to convey. In other words, the statute must be interpreted literally. Even though the court should be convinced that some other meaning was really intended by the law-making power, and even though the literal interpretation should defeat the very purposes of the enactment, still the explicit declaration of the legislature is the law, and the courts must not depart from it.[3]

27. If the language of the statute is ambiguous, or lacks precision, or is fairly susceptible of two or more interpretations, the intended meaning of it must be sought by the aid of all pertinent and admissible considerations. But here, as before, the object of the search is the meaning and intention of the legislature, and the court is not at liberty, merely because it has a choice between two constructions, to substitute for the will of legislature its own ideas as to the justice, expediency, or policy of the law.[4]

"It is beyond question the duty of courts, in construing statutes, to give effect to the intent of the law-making power, and to seek for that intent in every legitimate way. But in the construction, both of statutes and contracts, the intent of the framers and parties is to be sought, first of all, in the words employed, and if the words are free from ambiguity and doubt, and express plainly, clearly, and distinctly the sense of the framers of the instrument, there is no oc-

---

[3] Green v. Wood, 7 Ad. & El. (N. S.) 178; Queen v. Armitage, 51 L. J. M. C. 15; Notley v. Buck, 8 Barn. & C. 160; Coe v. Lawrance, 1 El. & Bl. 516; U. S. v. Fisher, 2 Cranch, 358; Doe v. Considine, 6 Wall. 458; Woodbury v. Berry, 18 Ohio St. 456; Newell Universal Mill Co. v. Muxlow, 115 N. Y. 170, 21 N. E. 1048; Bradbury v. Wagenhorst, 54 Pa. St. 180; Cearfoss v. State, 42 Md. 403; Allen v. Mutual Fire Ins. Co., 2 Md. 111; Ezekiel v. Dixon, 3 Ga. 146.

[4] People v. Schoonmaker, 63 Barb. 44; Noble v. State, 1 Greene (Iowa), 325; Ogden v. Strong, 2 Paine, 584, Fed. Cas. No. 10,460.

casion to resort to other means of interpretation. It is not allowable to interpret what has no need of interpretation, and, when the words have a definite and precise meaning, to go elsewhere in search of conjecture in order to restrict or extend the meaning. Statutes and contracts should be read and understood according to the natural and most obvious import of the language, without resorting to subtle and forced construction for the purpose of either limiting or extending their operation. Courts cannot correct supposed errors, omissions, or defects in legislation, or vary, by construction, the contracts of parties. The object of interpretation is to bring sense out of the words used, and not to bring a sense into them." [5] When an act is expressed in clear and concise terms, and the sense is manifest and leads to nothing absurd, there can be no reason not to adopt the sense which it naturally presents. To go elsewhere in search of conjectures, in order to find a different meaning, is not so much to interpret the statute as to elude it. [6] "When the words of an act are doubtful and uncertain, it was proper to inquire what was the intent of the legislature; but it is very dangerous for judges to launch out too far in searching into the intent of the legislature when they have expressed themselves in clear and plain words." [7] So, in Edrich's Case, [8] "the judges said that they ought not to make any construction against the express letter of the statute; for nothing can so express the meaning of the makers of the act as their own direct words, for 'index animi sermo.' And it would be dangerous to give scope to make a construction in any case against the express words, when the meaning of the makers doth not appear to the contrary, and when no inconvenience will thereupon follow; and therefore in such cases 'a verbis legis non est recedendum.'" "Although the spirit of an instrument, especially of the constitution," says the supreme court of the United States, "is to be respected not less than its letter, yet the spirit is to be collected chiefly from its words. It would be dangerous in the extreme to infer from extrinsic circumstances that a case for which the words of the instrument expressly provided shall be exempted from its op-

---

[5] McCluskey v. Cromwell, 11 N. Y. 593, 601.

[6] Vattel, Law of Nat., Bk. 2, c. 17, § 263; Jackson v. Lewis, 17 Johns. 475; People v. New York Cent. R. Co., 13 N. Y. 78.

[7] Colehan v. Cooke, Willes, 393.

[8] 5 Coke, 118a.

eration. Where words conflict with each other, where the different clauses of the instrument bear upon each other, and would be inconsistent unless the natural and common import of words be varied, construction becomes necessary, and a departure from the obvious meaning of words is justifiable. But if, in any case, the plain meaning of a provision, not contradicted by any other provision in the same instrument, is to be disregarded, because we believe the framers of the instrument could not intend what they say, it must be one in which the absurdity and injustice of applying the provision to the case would be so monstrous that all mankind would, without hesitation, unite in rejecting the application." [9]

In the case supposed, where the language of the statute is free from ambiguity and conveys a definite and sensible meaning, the courts should not hesitate to give it a literal interpretation merely because they have doubts as to the wisdom or expediency of the enactment. In such a case, these are not pertinent inquiries for the judicial tribunals. If there be any unwisdom in the law, it is for the legislature to remedy it. For the courts the only rule is "ita lex scripta est." [10] Neither have the judges any authority, in such a case, to put upon the statute a construction different from its natural and obvious meaning in consideration of the consequences which may result from it. Any evil consequences to the public which may flow from the statute may be considered when its meaning is doubtful, in order to give it a more beneficial construction, but when the legislative intent is clearly expressed, such consequences

---

[9] Sturges v. Crowninshield, 4 Wheat. 122, 202. To the same general effect, and as further illustrating the group of rules at the head of this section, the reader may profitably consult the following cases: King v. Inhabitants of Stoke Damerel, 7 Barn. & C. 563; Gardner v. Collins, 2 Pet. 58; U. S. v. Warner, 4 McLean, 463, Fed. Cas. No. 16,643; U. S. v. Ragsdale, 1 Hempst. 497, Fed. Cas. No. 16,113; Bartlett v. Morris, 9 Port. (Ala.) 266; Farrel Foundry v. Dart, 26 Conn. 376; Pearce v. Atwood, 13 Mass. 324; Doane v. Phillipps, 12 Pick. 223; Hyatt v. Taylor, 42 N. Y. 258; Benton v. Wickwire, 54 N. Y. 226; Johnson v. Hudson River R. Co., 49 N. Y. 455; Supervisors of Niagara v. People, 7 Hill (N. Y.) 504; Douglass v. Chosen Freeholders of Essex Co., 38 N. J. Law, 214; State v. Brewster, 42 N. J. Law, 125; Tynan v. Walker, 35 Cal. 634.

[10] State v. Liedtke, 9 Neb. 468, 4 N. W. 68; Horton v. Mobile School Comm'rs, 43 Ala. 598. Compare Opinion of the Justices, 7 Mass. 523.

cannot be at all considered.[11]   And it has been said: "If the precise words used are plain and unambiguous, we are bound to construe them in their ordinary sense, even though it does lead to an absurdity or manifest injustice.   Words may be modified or varied where their import is doubtful or obscure, but we assume the functions of legislators when we depart from the ordinary meaning of the precise words used, merely because we see, or fancy we see, an absurdity or manifest injustice from an adherence to their literal meaning." [12]

Even if the court is fully persuaded that the legislature really meant and intended something entirely different from what it actually enacted, and that the failure to convey the real meaning was due to inadvertence or mistake in the use of language, yet, if the words chosen by the legislature are not obscure or ambiguous, but convey a precise and sensible meaning (excluding the case of obvious clerical errors or elliptical forms of expression), then the court must take the law as it finds it, and give it its literal interpretation, without being influenced by the probable legislative meaning lying back of the words.   In that event, the presumption that the legislature meant what it said, though it be contrary to the evident fact, is conclusive.[13]   A good illustration of this rule is found in the case of Woodbury v. Berry.[14]   It appeared that a section of the code of Ohio provided that when a motion was made to amerce a sheriff or other officer for neglect of duty, he should have two days' written notice thereof.   A subsequent section, which was copied from an earlier statute, provided that "in all cases of a motion to amerce a sheriff or other officer of any county from which the execution issued," he should have a much longer notice.   The court said: "It certainly is difficult, if not impossible, to find any reason why an officer sought to be amerced by motion in the court of his own county should be thus favored in the matter of notice, while, on the other hand, the circumstances of the case to be provided for seem

---

[11] Hines v. Wilmington & W. R. Co., 95 N. Car. 434; Coffin v. Rich, 45 Me. 507; Bosley v. Mattingly, 14 B. Mon. 89.

[12] Abley v. Dale, 11 C. B. 378, 391.

[13] Smith v. State, 66 Md. 125, 7 Atl. 49; Maxwell v. State, 89 Ala. 150, 7 South. 824; St. Louis & I. M. R. Co. v. Clark, 53 Mo. 214; Maxwell v. State, 40 Md. 273.

[14] 18 Ohio St. 456.

to require that the nonresident officer ought to be thus favored. These considerations, and a comparison of the provisions of these sections of the statute, as they stand, with those of the statute which was superseded and repealed by the code of civil procedure, not only suggest the conjecture, but convince us of the fact, that the words 'other than the county,' or some equivalent phrase, must have been, by accident or oversight of the draftsman of the bill to establish a code of civil procedure, or of the clerk who engrossed it, omitted before the words 'from which the execution issued' in section 455. But notwithstanding all this, ita lex scripta est. The language as it stands is clear, explicit, and unequivocal. It leaves no room for interpretation, for nothing in the language employed is doubtful. We are satisfied, by considerations outside the language, that the legislature intended to enact something very different from what it did enact. But it did not carry out its intention, and we cannot take the will for the deed. It is our legitimate function to interpret legislation, but not to supply its omissions."

On the same principle, the literal interpretation cannot be refused, where there is no ambiguity or want of sense, even though the result should be to defeat the very object and purpose of the enactment. Lord Tenterden once said: "Our decision may perhaps, in this particular case, operate to defeat the object of the statute; but it is better to abide by this consequence than to put upon it a construction not warranted by the words of the act, in order to give effect to what we may suppose to have been the intention of the legislature."[15] And though the literal interpretation should permit evasions of the statute, yet, if there is no ambiguity in the law, this consideration cannot be allowed to modify the construction to be put upon it. For example, in an English case,[16] it appeared that a bill of sale had been given by one Price to the plaintiff, but, instead of its being registered before the expiration of the twenty-one days allowed for that purpose by the statute of 17 & 18 Vict. c. 36, another bill of sale was given by Price to the plaintiff in exchange for the first. This was done many successive times, and ultimately the bill of sale last given was registered before the expiration of twenty-one days from the day on which that bill (the last) had been

---

[15] King v. Inhabitants of Barham, 8 Barn. & C. 99. And see Frye v. Chicago, B. & Q. R. Co., 73 Ill. 399.

[16] Smale v. Burr, L. R. 8 C. P. 64.

given. Defendant took Price's goods in execution, and plaintiff brought suit.   In defense, it was charged that the transactions and course of dealing between Price and the plaintiff were fraudulent. This was unquestionably true.   Yet the court was constrained to hold that the plain terms of the law had been literally complied with, and the bill of sale must be held valid.   Although the spirit and purpose of the act had thus been successfully evaded, yet its language being free from ambiguity, it could not be construed to cover the case in hand.

But if the statute is ambiguous, so as to be fairly susceptible of more than one interpretation, then the courts may rightfully exercise the power of controlling its language, so as to give effect to the intention of the legislature, as the same shall be ascertained and determined from pertinent and admissible considerations.[17]   But it is necessary to remember that the intention of the law-making power is to be ascertained by a reasonable construction to be given to the provisions of the act, and not one founded on mere arbitrary conjecture.[18]   And it is always the actual meaning of the legislature which must be sought out and followed, and not the judge's own ideas as to what the law should be.   "It must be borne in mind that it is not competent to a judge to modify the language of an act of parliament in order to bring it into accordance with his own views as to what is right or reasonable."[19]   Finally, although every law must be construed according to the intention of the makers, that intention is never resorted to for any other purpose than to ascertain what they in fact intended to do, and not for the purpose of ascertaining what they have done; that is, the object is to ascertain what the legislature intended to enact, but not to ascertain what is the legal consequence and effect of what they did enact.[20]

[17] Koch v. Bridges, 45 Miss. 247; Bidwell v. Whitaker, 1 Mich. 469; State v. King, 44 Mo. 283; George v. Board of Education, 33 Ga. 344.

[18] Cearfoss v. State, 42 Md. 403.

[19] Hardcastle, Stat. Law, 31.

[20] Leavitt v. Blatchford, 5 Barb. 9.

EQUITABLE CONSTRUCTION.

28. Equitable construction was a principle by which the judges, disregarding the letter of a statute, extended its provisions to cases which, in their judgment, were within the same mischief which the law was designed to remedy, though they were not expressly provided for, or by which, on considerations of justice and right reason, they excepted from the operation of the statute cases which were covered by its terms, but which, in their opinion, were not fairly to be included in it. The power to make such constructions is now disavowed by the courts.

It must not be supposed that "equitable construction" was a method or principle applied by the court of chancery, as distinguished from the courts of law. On the contrary, the idea of it was familiar long before the rise of the extraordinary jurisdiction of the chancellor, and in later times it was in use in the law courts no less than in that of equity. It was based on the historical and fundamental conception of equity. According to this conception, there was a power, existing side by side with the law, yet not in derogation of it, based upon reason, and drawing its inspiration and its guidance from the principles of natural justice, the common sense of fairness, and the dictates of conscience, which power could be appealed to for relief, in particular and individual cases, when it was necessary, in accordance with those principles and precepts, to modify the rigor of the law to suit the case in hand, or to apply its rules to cases which it had not provided for, or to avert the hardship and injustice which the generality of its application would work in the specific instance. This power was called "equity" by the Roman lawyers, and both the name and the idea were adopted in the English jurisprudence. Hence the so-called equitable construction was nothing but the principle of putting such a construction upon the written law as "equity," in this sense, would commend.[21]

[21] See Hammond's note to Lieber, Hermeneutics, 283; 1 Bl. Comm. 61; Maine, Ancient Law, 27.

Equitable construction was principally of two sorts, expansive and contractive. The former is thus described by Lord Coke: "Equity is a construction made by the judges that cases out of the letter of the statute, yet being within the same mischief, or cause of the making of the same, shall be within the same remedy that the statute provideth; and the reason thereof is, for that the lawmakers could not possibly set down all cases in express terms."[22] And conversely, in reference to cases which the judges thought should be excepted out of the statute, though covered by its express terms, because they were not within the mischief which it was intended to remedy, it was said that the law might be construed "contrary to the words," or "contrary to the text." The extent to which this equitable power of the courts was claimed to prevail over the words of the law is shown by the broad statement, made chiefly in reference to the construction of the more ancient statutes, which laid down general rules in the fewest words, that "judges have power over statute laws, to mould them to the truest and best use, according to reason and best convenience," which, of course, would be nothing less than a direct usurpation by the courts of the powers as well as the discretion of the legislature.[23] In the celebrated case of the Postnati of Scotland,[24] Lord Ellesmere laid down the following rule: "Words are to be taken and construed sometimes by extension, sometimes by restriction; sometimes by implication; sometimes a disjunctive for a copulative, or a copulative for a disjunctive; the present tense for the future, or the future for the present; sometimes, by equity, out of the reach of the words; sometimes words taken in a contrary sense; sometimes figuratively, and many other like constructions. And of all these examples be infinite, as well in the civil as common law." Upon this it has been

---

[22] 1 Co. Inst. 24b.

[23] Sheffield v. Ratcliffe, Hob. 346. "The idea that the judges, in administering the written law, can mould it and warp it according to their notions, not of what the legislator said, nor even of what he meant, but of what, in their judgment, he ought to have meant,—in other words, according to their own ideas of policy, wisdom, or expediency,—is so obviously untenable that it is quite apparent that it never could have taken rise except at a time when the division lines between the great powers of government were but feebly drawn, and their importance very imperfectly understood." Sedgwick, Stat. Constr. 265.

[24] Calvin's Case, 2 How. St. Tr. 559, 675.

remarked: "Any one that reads this will easily judge what the scope and consequences of the chancellor's rule may be. And he may as easily discern how far it is capable of being improved, to baffle and elude any law whatsoever, and wrest it from its genuine and native sense to what you please." [25]

The origin and reasons of this extraordinary claim of power have been variously explained. "Equitable construction was said to have been given to ancient statutes in consequence of the conciseness with which they were drawn, though the specific expressions used can hardly be considered more concise than the more abstract terms for which they were, possibly, substituted. It has been explained, also, on the ground that language was used with no great precision in early times, and that acts were framed in harmony with the lax method of interpretation contemporaneously prevalent. It has also been accounted for by the fact that in those times the dividing line between the legislative and judicial functions was feebly drawn, and the importance of the separation imperfectly understood. The ancient practice of having the statutes drawn by the judges from the petitions of the commons and the answers of the king may also contribute to account for the wide latitude of their interpretation. The judges would naturally be disposed to construe the language in which they framed them as their own, and therefore with freedom and indulgence." [26]

The difference between the two kinds of equitable construction, as well as the application of them to specific cases, are learnedly explained by Plowden, in a note to Eyston v. Studd, 2 Plowd. 465. This ancient writer observes: "From this judgment and the cause of it the reader may observe that it is not the words of the law, but the internal sense of it, that makes the law, and our law, like all others, consists of two parts, viz., of body and soul; the letter of the law is the body of the law, and the sense and reason of the law are the soul of the law. * * * And it often happens that when you know the letter you know not the sense; for sometimes the sense is more confined and contracted than the letter, and sometimes it is more large and extensive. And equity enlarges or diminishes the letter according to its discretion, which equity is in two ways. The one Aristotle defines thus: 'Equity is the correction of the law in

[25] Potter's Dwarris on Stat. 237.-   [26] Maxwell, Interp. (2d edn.) 310.

those particulars wherein, by reason of its generality, it is deficient.'
* * * And this correction of the general words is much used in
the law of England.   As when an act of parliament ordains that
whosoever does such an act shall be a felon and shall suffer death,
yet if a man of unsound mind, or an infant of tender age who has
no discretion, does the act, they shall not be felons, nor shall they
be put to death.   And if a statute be made that all persons who
shall receive or give meat or drink or other aid to him that shall do
such an act (knowing the same to be done) shall be accessaries to
the offense and shall be put to death, yet, if a man commits the act,
and comes to his own wife, who, knowing the same, receives him
and gives him meat and drink, she shall not be accessary to his
offense, nor a felon.   For one that is of unsound mind, an infant,
or a wife, were not intended to be included in the general words
of the law.   So that, in those cases, the general words of the
law are corrected and abridged by equity. * * * The other
kind of equity differs much from the former, and is in a manner of
quite a contrary effect, and may well be thus defined: Equity is
giving a more efficacious direction to the words of the law; as if one
thing is specifically provided for by the words of the law, then every
other thing belonging to the same category is to be taken as provided for by the same words.   So that when the words of a statute enact one thing, they enact all other things which are in the like
degree.   As, the statute which ordains that in an action of debt
against executors, he who comes first by distress shall answer, is
extended by equity to administrators, and such of them as come
first by distress shall answer by the equity of the said statute.
* * * And so there are an infinite number of cases in our law
which are in equal degree with others provided for by statutes, and
are taken by equity within the meaning of those statutes.   And
from hence it appears that there is a great diversity between these
two equities, for the one abridges the letter, the other enlarges it;
the one diminishes it, the other amplifies it; the one takes from the
letter, the other adds to it.   So that a man ought not to rest upon
the letter only, for 'qui hæret in litera hæret in cortice;' but he
ought to rely upon the sense, which is tempered and guided by
equity."

The contractive species of equitable construction has been sufficiently explained in the extract given above, but as to the other

variety it is proper to add a few words.   It was a maxim laid down by Lord Coke that "statutum generaliter est intelligendum quando verba statuti sunt specialia, ratio autem generalis."[27]   And "it is not unusual in acts of parliament, especially in the more ancient ones, to comprehend by construction a generality where express mention is made only of a particular; the particular instances being taken only as examples of all that want redress in the kind whereof the mention is made."[28]   In such cases, that which lies outside the letter of the law is said to be within the "equity of the statute." This phrase denotes the construction which admits within the operation of the statute a class of cases which are neither expressly named nor excluded, but which, from their analogy to the cases which are named, are clearly and justly within the spirit and general meaning of the law.   For example, the statute, or writ, called "Circumspecte Agatis," in the 13th year of Edward I., was designed to regulate the boundaries between the ecclesiastical and the temporal jurisdiction.   It directed the judges not to interfere with the Bishop of Norwich or his clergy in suits in the spiritual courts; but it was so construed as to protect all other prelates in the exercise of their proper jurisdiction, for it was held that the Bishop of Norwich was merely put for an example.   So again, uses were not strictly within the statute "De Donis," but they were "taken within the equity," and in Chudleigh's Case,[29] Coke furnishes numerous instances of acts made "against the fraud of uses" having been construed liberally and by equity beyond the letter.   And so, in an American case, where a statute gave to a judgment creditor, who had taken his debtor on a ca. sa., and then released him, the right to proceed against him "by a new execution or such other process as the nature of the case may require," it was held that, "within the equity of the statute," he might pursue him into another state, to which he had departed, and there maintain an action of debt on the judgment.[30]   There were, however, always limitations upon this principle.   Thus, "if the words of a statute do not reach to an inconvenience rarely happening, they shall not be extended to it by an equitable construction; for the objects of statutes are mischiefs 'quæ frequentius accidunt.'   It is good reason in such case, and

---

[27] 10 Coke, 101b.

[28] Platt's Case, Plowd. 36.

[29] 1 Coke, 131.

[30] Simonton v. Barrell, 21 Wend. 362.

therefore sound construction, not to strain the words further than they reach, but the case is to be considered as a casus omissus." [31]

The right to apply an equitable construction to the written laws was often adverted to as one to be exercised with caution, on account of the danger of turning the courts into legislatures, and in modern times it has been disavowed by them, and its principle distinctly repudiated.[32] It is said that the rules for the interpretation of statutes are now the same in courts of equity as in courts of law,[33] and that the dangerous and misleading ancient rule has given way to the more conservative maxim that equity follows the law. And in point of fact, so far as the principle of equitable construction involved the claim of an authority to correct the enacted law, or to mould it to the judge's notions of justice and propriety, or to disregard its positive mandates on any considerations of hardship or inconvenience, it was originally an usurpation and finds no place in modern law. In one of the American cases we find it very clearly stated that the view that the courts may, against the plain language of a statute and in opposition to the intent clearly expressed by the words, mitigate the "violence of the letter" by introducing exceptions where the statute itself makes none, so as to relieve in cases of hardship or particular inconvenience, is not now of force.[34] And

[31] Potter's Dwarris on Stat. 240.

[32] In Brandling v. Barrington, 6 Barn. & C. 467, 475, Lord Tenterden observed: "I think there is always danger in giving effect to what is called the equity of a statute, and that it is much better to rely on and abide by the plain words, although the legislature might possibly have provided for other cases had their attention been directed to them." And in Guthrie v. Fisk, 3 Barn. & C. 178, 183, it was said: "It is a dangerous rule of construction to introduce words not expressed because they may be supposed to be within the mischief contemplated." So, in Monson v. Chester, 22 Pick. 385: "Equitable constructions, though they may be tolerated in remedial and perhaps some other statutes, should always be resorted to with great caution, and never extended to penal statutes or mere arbitrary regulations of matters of public policy. The power of extending the meaning of a statute beyond its words, and deciding by the equity and not the language, approaches so near the power of legislation that a wise judiciary will exercise it with reluctance and only in extraordinary cases." And see Melody v. Reab, 4 Mass. 471.

[33] Talbot's Lessee v. Simpson, Pet. C. C. 188, Fed. Cas. No. 13,730; Ex parte Walton, L. R. 17 Ch. Div. 746.

[34] Encking v. Simmons, 28 Wis. 272. In this case it was said: "When, therefore, the statute says that every mortgage containing a power of sale

in another case, it is declared that a court has no authority to extend a law beyond the fair and reasonable meaning of its terms because of some supposed policy of the law, or because the legislature did not use proper words to express its meaning.[35] But nevertheless, many of the cases which were decided on what was called the "equity of the statute" would now be decided in precisely the same way, though not avowedly on that principle. This is because there was a just and reasonable idea at the base of the principle in question, and this, so far as it is applicable to modern conditions, has survived. This idea was that a given case should not be taken to be within a statute, though apparently covered by its comprehensive terms, unless it is within the spirit and reason of the law. In the next section we shall show the application of this rule in modern practice. Moreover, the courts now claim (and the claim is well recognized) that it is their duty to construe a statute "strictly" when it imposes a burden or penalty or derogates from common right, and "liberally" when it grants a remedy or confers an advantage. This will appear more fully in a later chapter.

SPIRIT AND REASON OF THE LAW.

29. A statute should be construed with reference to its spirit and reason; and the courts have power to declare that a case which falls within the letter of a statute is not governed by the statute, because it is not within the spirit and reason of the law and the plain intention of the legislature.

This rule was very clearly and positively laid down by the supreme court of the United States in an important case which involved a construction of the so-called "Alien Contract Labor Law."

---

may be foreclosed by advertisement, and makes no exception of a mortgage upon lands belonging to an insane person, such mortgage cannot be excluded from the operation of the statute, because that would be repugnant to the intent as clearly expressed by the words. The words cannot be taken to a repugnant intent. In such case, the language of the statute being general, and the particular mortgage not being excepted, the established rule of interpretation is that general words must receive a general construction."

[35] Tompkins v. First Nat. Bank, 18 N. Y. Supp. 234.

This act of congress prohibits the importation into this country of "any" foreigners under contract to perform "labor or service of any kind." The question arose as to its applicability to a clergyman who came to this country under contract to enter the service of a church as its rector. The court conceded that the case came within the letter of the law, but because it was not within the spirit and intent of the law, it was held that the act had no application to the case at bar. "It is a familiar rule," said the court, "that a thing may be within the letter of the statute, and yet not within the statute, because not within its spirit nor within the intention of its makers. This has been often asserted, and the reports are full of cases illustrating its application. This is not the substitution of the will of the judge for that of the legislator; for frequently words of general meaning are used in a statute, words broad enough to include the act in question, and yet a consideration of the whole legislation, or of the circumstances surrounding its enactment, or of the absurd results which follow from giving such broad meaning to the words, makes it unreasonable to believe that the legislator intended to include the particular act." And speaking to the case at bar: "The construction invoked cannot be accepted as correct. It is a case where there was presented a definite evil, in view of which the legislature used general terms with the purpose of reaching all phases of that evil; and thereafter, unexpectedly, it is developed that the general language thus employed is broad enough to reach cases and acts which the whole history and life of the country affirm could not have been intentionally legislated against. It is the duty of the courts, under those circumstances, to say that, however broad the language of the statute may be, the act, although within the letter, is not within the intention of the legislature, and therefore cannot be within the statute." [36]

It would be easy to multiply examples of the application of this rule, both from ancient and modern times. Puffendorf, for example, mentions a law of Bologna which enacted that "whoever drew

[36] Rector, etc., of Holy Trinity Church v. U. S., 143 U. S. 457, 12 Sup. Ct. 511. And see, further, Ex parte Walton, L. R. 17 Ch. Div. 746; U. S. v. Freeman, 3 How. 556; Associates of Jersey Co. v, Davison, 29 N. J. Law, 415; Chase v. Dwinal, 7 Me. 134; People v. Church of Atonement, 48 Barb. 603; Allen v. Mayor, etc., of Savannah, 9 Ga. 286; Castner v. Walrod, 83 Ill. 171; Kennedy v. Kennedy, 2 Ala. 571.

blood in the streets should be punished with the utmost severity." After long debate this was held not to extend to the case of a surgeon who opened the veins of a person who fell down in the street in a fit.[37] So Blackstone says: "The most universal and effectual way of discovering the true meaning of a law, when the words are dubious, is by considering the reason and spirit of it, or the cause which moved the legislator to enact it. An instance of this is given in a case put by Cicero. There was a law that those who, in a storm, forsook the ship, should forfeit all property therein, and that the ship and lading should belong entirely to those who staid in it. In a dangerous tempest, all the mariners forsook the ship, except only one sick passenger, who, by reason of his disease, was unable to get out and escape. By chance the ship came safe to port. The sick man kept possession, and claimed the benefit of the law. Now here all the learned agree that the sick man is not within the reason of the law; for the reason of making it was to give encouragement to such as should venture their lives to save the vessel; but this is a merit which he could never pretend to who neither staid in the ship upon that account nor contributed anything to its preservation."[38] So, in the case of U. S. v. Kirby,[39] the defendants were indicted for the violation of an act of congress providing that "if any person shall knowingly and willfully obstruct or retard the passage of the mail, or of any driver or carrier, or of any horse or carriage carrying the same," he shall suffer a penalty. The charge was that the defendants retarded the passage of one Farris, a carrier of the mail, while he was engaged in the performance of his duty, and also in like manner retarded the steamboat Buell, at that time engaged in carrying the mail. They pleaded that Farris had been indicted for murder by a court of competent jurisdiction, that a bench-warrant had been issued and placed in the hands of the defendant Kirby, the sheriff of the county, commanding him to arrest Farris, and that, in obedience to this warrant, he and the other defendants, as his posse, entered upon the steamboat and arrested Farris, and used only such force as

---

[37] Puffendorf, De Jure Nat., l. 5, c. 12, § 8. It was a maxim of the Roman law that "benignius leges interpretandæ sunt, quo voluntas earum conservetur." Dig. 1, 3, 18.

[38] 1 Bl. Comm. 61.

[39] 7 Wall. 482.

was necessary to accomplish the arrest. It was held by the supreme court that the seizure of Farris was not an obstruction of the mail, or a retarding of the passage of a carrier of the mail, within the meaning of the act. Again, a statute of New York prohibited any sheriff or deputy sheriff, or any one for them, from purchasing any property at any execution sale, and declared void all purchases so made. In an action of ejectment, it appeared that certain premises had been sold by one deputy sheriff, on an execution issued under a judgment owned by another deputy of the same sheriff, and were bid off by the deputy who owned the judgment. It was contended that, under the statute, the sale was void. Plainly the case came within the letter of the law. But it was held that the statute should not apply, because the manifest object of the law was to prevent abuse, and to prohibit sheriffs and their deputies in their official capacity from being purchasers at their own sales, and thus being induced to act corruptly in relation to them, but it could never have been intended to place those persons in a worse situation than others as to the collection of their own demands.[40] Again, it is ruled that the statute of frauds, which requires certain contracts to be in writing, and the consideration expressed therein, applies to executory contracts only, and not to instruments which of themselves pass the estate by words of grant, assignment, surrender, or declaration of trust.[41] And the words "beyond seas," in a state statute of limitations, copied from an English act without due attention to the consequences of incorporating these terms without qualification, have been construed to mean "out of the state." [42] So although a law exempts from execution only such tools of a mechanic as are "necessary to his use and used by him in his trade," a temporary stoppage of his work will not forfeit the exemption; for the object of the law is to prevent those who have become unfortunate from being deprived of the means of making a living, and it must be presumed to contemplate that the loss of all that is not exempt may cause at least a temporary suspension of business.[43] So again, where a statute authorized the conveyance, by a certain county to the state, of certain lands in such distinct lots or parcels "as the said county shall now hold by

---

[40] Jackson v. Collins, 3 Cow. 89.
[41] Cruger v. Cruger, 5 Barb. 225.
[42] Murray v. Baker, 3 Wheat. 541.
[43] Harris v. Haynes, 30 Mich. 140.

virtue of tax deeds issued upon sales for delinquent taxes heretofore made," it was held that the act should be construed not to apply to lands of which the tax deeds held by the county were void
on their face, although there were in fact no lands to which the
act, thus construed, could apply.[44]

In pursuance of the principle of construing a statute according
to its spirit (and also with the help of the presumption that the legislature never intends to make an unnecessary change in the law),
it is held that a penal or criminal statute will not be extended to
cases not plainly within its intention. If the law declares in general and unqualified terms that the doing of a given act shall be a
felony or misdemeanor, or shall be attended with other penal consequences, still it will not be understood as applying to a case where
the act was justifiable or excusable on grounds generally recognized
by law. This is illustrated by the case supposed by some of the
older writers, where a statute should make it a felony to "break
from prison." Yet if the prison should be on fire, and a prisoner
should break out, not to regain his liberty, but to save his life, he
would not be guilty under the statute. As they put it, "he shall
not be hanged because he would not stay to be burned." An important branch of this rule, or corollary from it, may be stated as
follows: As the criminal law generally requires an evil intent, or
guilty mind, to make any act a criminal offense, and as it is not to
be supposed that the legislature intended to abrogate this rule unless by the most explicit language, if an act provides, generally, that
the commission of a given act shall be a crime, or that "any person"
who does the act shall be guilty of a crime, still the courts will understand that it could not have been intended to apply to the case
of a person incapable of a criminal intention, such as a young child,
a madman, or an idiot, and therefore, although such persons may be
within the letter of the statute, an exception will be made in their
favor, in accordance with the reason of the case and the spirit of
the law.[45] So, without reference to the capacity of the person, it

---

[44] Haseltine v. Hewitt, 61 Wis. 121, 20 N. W. 676.

[45] 1 Hale. P. C. 706; Regina v. Moore, 3 Car. & K. 319; Regina v. Tolson,
L. R. 23 Q. B. Div. 168. It should be observed that modern statutes generally
provide against the possibility of this question arising in specific cases, by
declaring that the act denounced shall be a crime when done "wilfully,"
"maliciously," or "knowingly." But it should also be noticed that the words

may be sufficient to take a case out of the statute that the element
of willfulness or malice was wanting. Thus, in Connecticut, where
a statute provided that if "the owner of any ram shall suffer him to
go at large," he should be subject to a penalty, it was said that to
"suffer" a ram to go at large, or out of the owner's enclosure, implied consent or willingness of the mind, and that although the statute intended to enforce strict care on the part of the owner in restraining his ram, it did not require such a degree of care as would
amount to an obligation on him to restrain the animal, at all events,
unless prevented by some uncontrollable cause, nor any greater care
than is usually taken by careful and prudent farmers in like cases.[46]

On a similar principle, it is held that where a statute gives puni-
tive damages, or double or treble damages, against one who cuts
timber growing on the land of another, without the latter's consent,
and converts it to his own use, the law should be confined to cases
where some element of willfulness, wantonness, carelessness, or
evil design enters into the act.   And therefore it does not include
the case of a corporation which enters upon the lands of another
and cuts trees, under a claim of the right of eminent domain, although, in consequence of the failure of the corporation to give
bond or make compensation, as required by law, the taking of the
land was a trespass.[47]   And where a statute imposes liability without qualification (as, where it requires railroad companies to fence
their tracks, and makes them liable for injuries caused by the want
of a fence or its defective condition), it may be construed as intended to impose liability in case of negligence only.[48]   As another
deduction from the same principle, it is said that an act done in

of the act may be so clear and specific as to negative the idea that any exception whatever was intended. And in such cases, the courts have no discretion. They must enforce the law as they find it.

[46] Selleck v. Selleck, 19 Conn. 501. Compare Hall v. Adams, 1 Aik. (Vt.)
166. "No man," says the court in Maryland, "incurs a penalty unless the
act which subjects him to it is clearly both within the spirit and letter of the
statute. Things which do not come within the words are not to be brought
within them by construction; the law does not allow of constructive offenses
or of arbitrary punishment." Cearfoss v. State, 42 Md. 403.

[47] Endlich, Interp. § 129; Cohn v. Neeves, 40 Wis. 393; Kramer v. Good-
lander, 98 Pa. St. 353; Bethlehem South Gas & Water Co. v. Yoder, 112 Pa.
St. 136, 4 Atl. 42.

[48] Murray v. New York Cent. R. Co., 3 Abb. App. Dec. 339.

the honest assertion of a right, which would be good in law if well founded in fact, but which proves unfounded in fact, would not fall within a statute which prohibited it under a penalty, unless, indeed, the penalty was in the nature simply of compensation for a civil injury. So, if a man cut down a tree or demolished a house standing on land of which he was in undisturbed possession and believed himself to be the owner, he would not be punishable under statutes which prohibited such acts in general terms, although it turned out that his title was bad and the property was not his.[49] .

There may also be cases in which ignorance or a mistaken belief in regard to a matter of fact will so far negative the existence of a guilty intent as to take the case out of the comprehensive terms of the statute. In a certain English case, it appeared that a statute "for the better prevention of accidents or injury on railways from the unsafe and improper carriage of certain goods," enacted that every person who should send gunpowder or similarly dangerous articles by the railway should mark or declare their nature, under a penalty. It was held that a guilty knowledge was essential to constitute the crime. And accordingly, an agent, who had sent some cases of dangerous goods by a railway, without mark or declaration, not only in ignorance of their nature, but being misinformed of it by his principal in answer to his inquiries, was not liable to the penalty, on the ground that his ignorance, under such circumstances, proved the absence of a guilty intention. And yet he was under no legal duty to send the goods, and he might have refused to do so without satisfying himself by inspection as to their nature.[50] But it should be carefully remarked that there is a considerable class of statutory crimes in regard to which ignorance of fact, or a mistaken belief as to a fact, is no excuse whatever. This is the case where the criminality of the given act depends upon the existence of some particular independent fact, and it is plainly the intention of the legislature that all persons shall be at their own peril, as to the existence of that fact, if they do the prohibited act. For example, it is generally held (though the authorities are not fully agreed on these points) that if a statute makes it a criminal

---

[49] Maxwell, Interp. (2d edn.) 116; Regina v. Burnaby, 2 Ld. Raym. 900.

[50] Hearne v. Garton, 2 El. & El. 66. See Gordon v. Farquhar, Peck (Tenn.) 155.

offense to sell intoxicating liquor to a minor, any person who makes such a sale will be liable, notwithstanding that he was mistaken as to the buyer's age and honestly believed him to be of full age;[51] that if the law prohibits the sale of adulterated articles of food or drink, it is no defense to a prosecution under it that the seller was ignorant of the fact of adulteration;[52] and that a married person who contracts a second marriage is guilty of bigamy, if the first spouse be still living and undivorced, though the defendant was ignorant of that fact.[53]

The principle of construing a statute according to its spirit and reason has very little connection, if any, with the maxim "cessante ratione legis cessat et ipsa lex." It might be thought that, by virtue of the principle in question, in the case of an obsolete or obsolescent statute, the courts might nullify it by construction. But while the practical desuetude of a law may justify the judicial tribunals in applying to it a greater latitude of construction than would otherwise be permissible, yet the prevailing opinion is that no statute becomes inoperative by mere non-user. It may become obsolete when the object to which it was intended to apply no longer exists; and in that event the maxim quoted has its proper application. But the sole fact that the protection or penalty of the act has not been invoked for a long period of time will not warrant the courts in refusing to enforce it if a state of facts fairly within its purview shall again come before them.[54]

[51] People v. Roby, 52 Mich. 577, 18 N. W. 365; McCutcheon v. People, 69 Ill. 601; State v. Kinkead, 57 Conn. 173, 17 Atl. 855; State v. Hartfiel, 24 Wis. 61. Compare Mulreed v. State, 107 Ind. 62, 7 N. E. 884; Faulks v. People, 39 Mich. 200; Aultfather v. State, 4 Ohio St. 467; Reich v. State, 63 Ga. 616. See Black, Intox. Liq. §§ 417, 418.

[52] Comm. v. Boynton, 2 Allen, 160; People v. Kibler, 103 N. Y. 321, 12 N. E. 795.

[53] Regina v. Gibbons, 12 Cox C. C. 237.

[54] See Comm. v. Hoover, 1 Browne (Pa.) Appendix, xxv.; Austin, Jurisprudence, § 914; Bishop, Written Laws, § 149.

SCOPE AND PURPOSE OF THE ACT.

30. Every statute is to be construed with reference to its intended scope and the purpose of the legislature in enacting it; and where the language used is ambiguous, or admits of more than one meaning, it is to be taken in such a sense as will conform to the scope of the act and carry out the purpose of the statute.[55]

In the construction of statutes, the application of particular provisions is not to be extended beyond the general scope of the statute, unless such extension is manifestly designed. "Legislatures, like courts, must be considered as using expressions concerning the thing they have in hand, and it would not be a fair method of interpretation to apply their words to subjects not within their consideration, and which, if thought of, would have been more particularly and carefully disposed of."[56] If it is the evident and plain purpose of the act to affect only a particular class of persons, the generality of the language employed will not have the effect of including a single individual not belonging to that class, though the mere words might include him.[57] An act extending the bounds of a town over the adjacent navigable waters does not thereby grant the land covered by the waters to the town, but is merely for the purposes of civil and criminal jurisdiction.[58] Again, where a duty is prescribed by statute, and remedies are provided for the breach of it, which remedies cannot be applied to a particular subject, it may be fairly inferred that the subject was not within the view of the legislature when they exacted the duty. This rule was laid down in a case where the question arose under a state pilotage law, requiring vessels to take on pilots when needed, as on leaving a harbor, and subjecting the master to a penalty for refusing to do so, to be recovered in a private action. It was held that this law could not apply to a war vessel of the United States, refusing to take a pilot or taking

---

[55] See Baker v. Terrell, 8 Minn. 195 (Gil. 165); Delafield v. Colden, 1 Paige, 139; Henry v. Thomas, 119 Mass. 583.

[56] Estate of Ticknor, 13 Mich. 44.

[57] U. S. v. Saunders, 22 Wall. 492.

[58] Palmer v. Hicks, 6 Johns. 133.

an unlicensed pilot, because the remedy could not apply, the commanding officer not being liable, and there being no possibility of recovering the penalty against the United States.[59]   On the other hand, it has been held that a statute imposing penalties for "furiously driving any sort of carriage" applies to immoderate speeding on a bicycle.   For although a bicycle is not technically a carriage, yet it is within the scope of the act, and within its purpose, which was to prevent injury from the reckless driving of any sort of vehicle or conveyance.[60]   And so, where a statute provides that persons conspiring and agreeing together to commit any "crimes punishable by imprisonment in the state prison" shall be liable to a prescribed punishment, the phrase quoted means not only such crimes as must be, but such also as may be, so punished.[61]

CASUS OMISSUS.

31. **When a statute makes specific provisions in regard to several enumerated cases or objects, but omits to make any provision for a case or object which is analogous to those enumerated, or which stands upon the same reason, and is therefore within the general scope of the statute, and it appears that such case or object was omitted by inadvertence or because it was overlooked or unforeseen, it is called a "casus omissus." Such omissions or defects cannot be supplied by the courts.**

It was a maxim of the old law that "casus omissus pro omisso habendus est," that is, that a case omitted is to be held as intentionally omitted.[62]   If the statute is sought to be applied to a case or object which is omitted from its terms, but which appears to be within the obvious purpose or plan of the statute, and so to have been omitted merely by inadvertence or accident, still the courts are not at liberty to add to the language of the law; and it must be held that the legislature intended to omit the specific case, how-

---

[59] Ayers v. Knox, 7 Mass. 306.
[60] Taylor v. Goodwin, L. R. 4 Q. B. Div. 228.
[61] State v. Mayberry, 48 Me. 218.
[62] Broom, Max. 46; Trayn. Lat. Max. 67.

ever improbable that may appear in connection with the general policy of the statute.[63] "Where the words of a statute, in their primary meaning, do not expressly embrace the case before the court, and there is nothing in the context to attach a different meaning to them capable of expressly embracing it, the court cannot extend the statute by construction to that case, unless it falls so clearly within the reasons of the enactment as to warrant the assumption that it was not specifically enumerated among those described by the legislature, only because it may have been deemed unnecessary to do so. Where the general intention of the statute embraces the specific case, though it is not enumerated, the statute may nevertheless be applied to it by an equitable construction, in promotion of the evident design of the legislature. But when this is done, it is always presupposed that such a case was within their general contemplation or purview when the statute was enacted; for if the case be omitted in the statute because not foreseen or contemplated, it is a casus omissus, and the court, having no legislative power, cannot supply the defects of the enactment."[64] "Courts of justice can give effect to legislative enactments only to the extent to which they may be made operative by a fair and liberal construction of the language used. It is not their province to supply defective enactments by an attempt to carry out fully the purposes which may be supposed to have occasioned those enactments. This would be but an assumption by the judicial of the duties of the legislative department."[65]

For example, if an act empowers a married woman to sue, but does not authorize her to be sued apart from her husband, no action lies against her.[66] In an English case, it appeared that a statute provided that "if loss of life to any person employed in a coal mine occurs by reason of any accident within such mine, or if any serious personal injury arises from explosion therein, the owner of such mine shall, within twenty-four hours next after such loss of life, send

---

[63] Jones v. Smart, 1 Durn. & E. 44, 52; Jacobs v. U. S., 1 Brock. 520, Fed. Cas. No. 7,157; Peters' Lessee v. Condron, 2 Serg. & R. 80; Moore v. City of Indianapolis, 120 Ind. 483, 22 N. E. 424; Scaggs v. Baltimore & W. R. Co., 10 Md. 268.

[64] Hull v. Hull, 2 Strobh. Eq. 174.

[65] Swift v. Luce, 27 Me. 285.

[66] Hancocks v. Lablache, L. R. 3 C. P. Div. 197.

notice of such accident" to an inspector, or be liable to a penalty.
An accident having occurred which caused serious personal injury
but not loss of life, it was contended that the owner of the mine
ought to have sent notice of the accident, for it was argued that it
was quite clear that there was an accidental omission after the
words "such loss of life," and that the legislature must have intended to insert the words "or such serious personal injury," for otherwise the words "if any serious personal injury arises from explosion therein" would be wholly inoperative.   But the court declined
to imply that these words had been omitted by accident, for "we
cannot," said the court, "take upon ourselves the office of the legislature." [67]   So again, an act which authorizes a municipal corporation to open and widen streets according to the procedure therein
described, and then prescribes no procedure for cases of widening
streets, is to that extent inoperative.[68]   And a statute which directs the comptroller to issue warrants upon the treasury, for costs
chargeable upon the state, in favor of the judge of the county court,
to be paid over to the county trustee, is inoperative and void, if no
provision is made for the payment of this money out of the county
treasury.[69]   The rule which forbids the supplying of a casus omissus by construction has a more peculiarly stringent effect in the
case of enactments creating penal or criminal offenses.[70]

[67] Underhill v. Longridge, 29 Law T. (N. S.) Mag. Cas. 65.

[68] Chaffee's Appeal, 56 Mich. 244, 22 N. W. 871.

[69] Pillow v. Gaines, 3 Lea, 466.

[70] Broadhead v. Holdsworth, L. R. 2 Ex. Div. 321; State v. Peters, 37 La.
Ann. 730.

HARMONIZING THE LAWS.

32. Statutes should be so construed, if possible, as to give effect to all of their clauses and provisions; and each statute should receive such a construction as will make it harmonize with the pre-existing body of law. Antagonism between the act to be interpreted and the previous laws, whether statutory or unwritten, is to be avoided, unless it was clearly the intention of the legislature that such antagonism should arise.[71]

A legislative act is always to be considered with reference to the pre-existing body of law, to which it is added and of which it is thenceforth to form a part. No law can be viewed in a condition of isolation or as the beginning of a legal system. "Every statute," says Dr. Bishop, "operates to modify or confirm something in the law which existed before. No statute is written, so to speak, upon a blank in the institutions of society. No such blank exists or can exist. * * * In every case, the statute is a thread of woof woven into a warp which before existed. It is never to be contemplated as a thing alone, but always as a part of a harmonious whole. * * * A new statutory provision, cast into a body of written and unwritten laws, is not altogether unlike a drop of coloring matter to a pail of water. Not so fully, yet to a considerable extent, it changes the hue of the whole body; and how far and where it works the change can be seen only by him who comprehends the relations of the parts, and discerns how each particle acts upon and governs and is governed by the others."[72]   Now it is always presumed (as will more fully appear in the next chapter) that the legislature does not intend to be inconsistent with itself, that it does not intend to make unnecessary changes in the existing laws, and that statutes are not to be repealed by implication. Hence arises the rule that, in case of any doubt or ambiguity, a statute is to be so construed

---

[71] State v. Babcock, 21 Neb. 599, 33 N. W. 247; U. S. v. Babbit, 1 Black (U. S.) 55; Riggs v. Pfister, 21 Ala. 469; Comm'rs of La Grange Co. v. Cutler, 6 Ind. 354; State v. Bishop, 41 Mo. 16; Smith v. People, 47 N. Y. 330.

[72] Bishop, Written Laws. §§ 4, 5.

as to be consistent with itself throughout its extent, and so as to harmonize with the other laws relating to the same or kindred matters.   It was an ancient maxim of the law that "interpretare et concordare leges legibus est optimus interpretandi modus;" that is, to interpret, and (to do it in such a way as) to harmonize laws with laws, is the best method of interpretation.[73]   It is not permissible, if it can be reasonably avoided, to put such a construction upon a law as will raise a conflict between different parts of it, but effect should be given to each and every clause and provision. But when there is no way of reconciling conflicting clauses of a statute, and nothing to indicate which the legislature regarded as of paramount importance, force should be given to those clauses which would make the statute in harmony with the other legislation on the same subject, and which would tend most completely to secure the rights of all persons affected by such legislation.[74]   And so, where an action is brought under a particular section of a statute, which, considered alone, is in conflict with the constitution, and it appears that such statute, as a whole, is in harmony with the constitution, such construction should be given to the particular section as will harmonize with the statute, when considered in the light of the whole enactment.[75]   Again, where two statutes on the same subject, or on related subjects, are apparently in conflict with each other, they are to be reconciled, by construction, so far as may be, on any fair hypothesis, and validity and effect given to both, if this can be done without destroying the evident intent and meaning of the later act.[76]   Thus, a statutory rule must be construed consistently with the whole system of pleading and practice of which it forms a part.[77]   When the power to hear and determine statutory misdemeanors is given to a municipal corporation, but no words of exclusion or restriction are used, the remedies between the state and the corporation will be construed to be concurrent; but where the manifest intention is that the prosecution shall be limited ex-

[73] Stoughter's Case, 8 Coke, 169a.

[74] Kansas Pac. Ry. Co. v. Wyandotte Co., 16 Kans. 587.

[75] Stump v. Horhback, 94 Mo. 26, 6 S. W. 356.

[76] Beals v. Hale, 4 How. 37; Merrill v. Gorham, 6 Cal. 41; Commercial Bank v. Chambers, 8 Sm. & Mar. 9; Attorney General v. Brown, 1 Wis. 513; Pearce v. Atwood, 13 Mass. 324.

[77] McDougald v. Dougherty, 14 Ga. 674.

elusively to one jurisdiction, that intention must prevail.[78]   Again, of two constructions, either of which is warranted by the words of an amendment to a public act, that is to be preferred which best harmonizes the amendment with the general tenor and spirit of the act amended.[79]   And it has been said that while laws must be construed so as to harmonize, if possible, yet, if two statutes interfere, that should be followed which is recommended by the most beneficial reasons.[80]

IMPLICATIONS IN STATUTES.

33. Every statute is understood to contain, by implication, if not by its express terms, all such provisions as may be necessary to effectuate its object and purpose, or to make effective the rights, powers, privileges, or jurisdiction which it grants, and also all such collateral and subsidiary consequences as may be fairly and logically inferred from its terms.

Doctrine of Implications.

Statutes are seldom framed with such minute particularity as to give directions for every detail which may be involved in their practical application.   Herein they are aided by the doctrine of implications.   This doctrine does not empower the courts to go to the length of supplying things which were intentionally omitted from the act.   But it authorizes them to draw inferences, from the general meaning and purpose of the legislature, and from the necessity of making the act operative and effectual, as to those minor or more specific things which are included in the more broad or general terms of the law, or as to those consequences of the enactment which the legislature must be understood to have foreseen and intended.   This is not the making of law by the judges.   It is educing the will of the legislature by the logical process of inference. "It is a rule of construction that that which is implied in a statute is as much a part of it as what is expressed."[81]   And as a statute

---

[78] State v. Gordon, 60 Mo. 383.

[79] Cæsar Griffin's Case, Chase, Dec. 364, Fed. Cas. No. 5,815.

[80] Kane v. Kansas City, F. S. & M. Ry. Co., 112 Mo. 34, 20 S. W. 532.

[81] Hanchett v. Weber, 17 Ill. App. 114.

must always be construed with reference to the pre-existing law, it will often happen that many details are to be inferred from the general language of the act, which are understood as necessarily involved in it though not enumerated. For example, if a statute creates a new felony, or makes an act a felony which was before innocent, the new crime will necessarily possess all the incidents which appertain to felony by the rules and principles of the common-law. Thus, by necessary implication, all persons who procure or abet the commission of the crime will be principals or accessaries under the same circumstances which would make them such in a felony by the common law.[82]

Remedies Implied from Statute.

As a general principle, whenever a statute creates a new duty or obligation, or prohibits an act which was previously lawful, it also gives, by implication, a corresponding remedy to secure its observance, which remedy may appertain either to the public, when a breach of public duty results from the violation of the act, or to a private person, when he sustains injury by the same violation, and sometimes to both the public and the individual. Thus, it is a general rule of the common law that where a statute prohibits a matter of public grievance, or commands a matter of public convenience, and no special mode of prosecution for a violation of the statute is prescribed, it may be prosecuted by indictment.[83] So, when a remedial statute does not point out the manner in which it shall be enforced, in respect to private rights, an action lies in favor of the party aggrieved, by implication.[84] But when a statute gives a new right or a new power, if it provides a specific, full, and adequate mode of executing the power or enforcing the right given, the fact that a particular mode is prescribed will be regarded as excluding, by implication, the right to resort to any other mode of executing the power or of enforcing the right. Thus, if the charter of a municipal corporation gives it the power to enforce payment of its taxes by a sale of the land on which they are assessed, in accordance with the usual method of tax sales, it will not be permissible for

---

[82] Coalheavers' Case, 1 Leach, C. L. 64.

[83] Colburn v. Swett, 1 Metc. (Mass.) 232; People v. Stevens, 13 Wend. 341.

[84] Com. Dig. "Action upon Statute," A. 1; Van Hook v. Whitlock, 2 Edw. Ch. 304; Bullard v. Bell, 1 Mason, 243, 290, Fed. Cas. No. 2,121.

the municipality to bring suit at law against the owner for the amount of the taxes.[85]   But "where the design is to give additional protection to a subsisting right, and a remedy is provided for its invasion, which is not necessarily exclusive of all others, it is considered as merely cumulative, and the party injured may resort to it, or to the means previously allowed, for redress."[86]   And if the remedy given by the statute is not adequate, there will be no implication that it was intended to be exclusive, and resort may be had, for the execution of the power or the enforcement of the right, to the ordinary process of the law.[87]   Where a statute creates a duty with the object of preventing a mischief of a particular kind, a person who, by reason of another's neglect of the statutory duty, suffers loss or injury of the kind contemplated by the statute, may have redress; but if he suffers a loss of a different kind, though it resulted from a breach of statutory duty, he is not entitled to maintain an action in respect of such loss.[88]   And the fact that a statute gives half a penalty to the complainant does not import authority to bring an action for the penalty in his own name.[89]

Illegality of Contract Implied from Statutory Prohibition.

Where a statute prohibits anything to be done, an act done in contravention of the prohibition must be adjudged void and inoperative; and this is necessary because the statute must be made effectual to accomplish the object intended by its enactment.[90]   Hence it follows that if a law imposes a penalty upon any person who shall do a given act, this implies a prohibition of the act in question; and any contract or agreement which involves the doing of the prohibited act is tainted, in respect to its consideration, by the statutory illegality, and will not be enforced by the courts.[91]

[85] Johnston v. Louisville, 11 Bush. 527.

[86] Smith v. Lockwood, 13 Barb. 209.

[87] Johnston v. Louisville, 11 Bush, 527.

[88] Gorris v. Scott, L. R. 9 Ex. 125.

[89] Smith v. Look, 108 Mass. 139.

[90] Nelson v. Denison, 17 Vt. 73.

[91] Stevens v. Gourley, 7 C. B. (N. S.) 99; O'Brien v. Dillon, 9 Ir. C. L. (N. S.) 318; Cope v. Rowlands, 2 Mees. & W. 149; Clark v. Protection Ins. Co., 1 Story, 109, Fed. Cas. No. 2,832; Skelton v. Bliss, 7 Ind. 77; Bacon v. Lee, 4 Iowa, 490; Lewis v. Welch, 14 N. H. 294; Hallett v. Novion, 14 Johns. 273; Mitchell v. Smith, 1 Binn. 110.

"Every contract made for or about any matter or thing which is prohibited and made unlawful by any statute is a void contract, although the statute itself doth not mention that it shall be so, but only inflicts a penalty on the offender; because a penalty implies a prohibition, though there are no prohibitory words in the statute." [92] The fundamental principle of public policy on which this rule rests is expressed in the maxim "ex dolo malo non oritur actio." For example, where a statute imposes a penalty on any person who practises the profession of surgery without being duly admitted, this is a prohibition against such practising by an unlicensed person, and it disables him from recovering for work and labor done as such. [93] And especially where the statute is made with a view to the protection of the public health or morals, or to the prevention of frauds by the seller of a given article, though there be nothing but a penalty prescribed, a contract which infringes the statute cannot be supported. Thus, when the statute prohibits the sale of intoxicating liquors except by a person holding a license or permit, or prohibits the sale altogether, a sale made by a person not so protected, or made under any other circumstances amounting to a violation of law, is void, and the seller cannot maintain an action against the purchaser for the price or value. [94] And on the same principle, no action can be maintained on a promissory note given for the price of liquors sold by the payee in violation of law. [95] But here it is necessary for the reader to remember that if a contract, thus tainted with illegality, has been executed, the law will leave the parties where it finds them, and will not allow the person who has parted with a consideration for the illegal act to recover it back, unless it be by the help of a statute. [96]

Statutory Grant of Powers or Privileges.

Whenever powers, privileges, or property are granted by a statute, everything indispensable to their enjoyment or exercise is

---

[92] Bartlett v. Vinor, Carth. 251.

[93] D'Allex v. Jones, 2 Jur. (N. S.) 979.

[94] Griffith v. Wells, 3 Denio, 226; Cobb v. Billings, 23 Me. 470; Bancroft v. Dumas, 21 Vt. 456; Jones v. Surprise, 64 N. H. 243, 9 Atl. 384; Loranger v. Jardine, 56 Mich. 518, 23 N. W. 203.

[95] Turck v. Richmond, 13 Barb. 533; Glass v. Alt, 17 Kans. 444.

[96] Ellsworth v. Mitchell, 31 Me. 247; Holman v. Johnson, Cowp. 341.

impliedly granted also, as it would be in a grant between private persons.[97] This rule finds an important application in relation to the powers of corporations. It has been said: "In this country, all corporations, whether public or private, derive their powers from legislative grant, and can do no act for which authority is not expressly given or may not be reasonably inferred. But if we were to say that they can do nothing for which a warrant could not be found in the language of their charters, we should deny them, in some cases, the power of self-preservation as well as many of the means necessary to effect the essential objects of their incorporation. And therefore it has been an established principle in the law of corporations that they may exercise all the powers within the fair intent and purpose of their creation which are reasonably proper to effect the powers expressly granted."[98] It has even been held, in England, that a corporation may be created by implication. Thus, where trustees were appointed by statute, to perform duties which would necessarily continue without limit of time, it was held that, from the nature of the powers given to them, they were impliedly made a corporation.[99] Whenever the statute grants power to do an act, with an unrestricted discretion as to the manner of executing the power, all reasonable and necessary incidents in the manner of executing the power are also granted.[100] For instance, where a municipal corporation has lawfully created a debt, it has the implied power, unless restrained by its charter or a statute, to evidence the same by bill, bond, note, or other instrument. The power to contract the debt implies the right to issue the proper acknowledgment therefor.[101] So, when a statute directs a thing to be done, it authorizes the performance of whatever is necessary to execute its commands. Thus, an act increasing the salaries of municipal officers imposes upon the municipality the increased burden consequent thereon, though in terms no provision to meet it is made.[102] And again, the concession of privileges or powers often

---

[97] Endlich, Interp. § 418; Stief v. Hart, 1 N. Y. 20, 30.

[98] City of Bridgeport v. Housatonic R. Co., 15 Conn. 475, 501.

[99] Ex parte Newport Marsh Trustees, 16 Sim. 346.

[100] People v. Eddy, 57 Barb. 593.

[101] City of Williamsport v. Comm., 84 Pa. St. 487.

[102] Green v. Mayor, etc., of New York, 2 Hilt. (N. Y.) 203.

carries with it implied obligations. For instance, an act which gives a power to dig up the soil of streets for a particular purpose, such as making a drain or sewer, impliedly casts on those thus empowered the duty of filling up the ground again and of restoring the street to its original condition.[103] So also, authority given by statute to build and maintain a bridge virtually implies an obligation to keep the bridge in good travelling and business condition, so long as the proprietors are in the use and enjoyment of the privileges of the grant.[104]

Statutory Grant of Jurisdiction.

Jurisdiction may be created or conferred by implication. "While an unfounded assumption by the legislature that a particular jurisdiction existed might not alone be sufficient to create it, yet where the jurisdiction is assumed to exist, and explicit provisions made as to the form and mode of its exercise, the authority to proceed in that form and mode carries with it, by necessary implication, jurisdiction of the proceedings."[105] And where an act confers a jurisdiction, it impliedly grants also the power of doing all such acts, or employing such means, as are essentially necessary to its execution. "Cui jurisdictio data est, ea quoque concessa esse videntur sine quibus jurisdictio explicari non potuit."[106] Thus, the authority to punish for contempt is granted as a necessary incident in establishing a tribunal as a court.[107] And where a statute gives to an inferior court the power to issue the writ of injunction, it must be understood as impliedly carrying with it the power to punish disobedience to the writ by commitment.[108] So also, the power to grant temporary alimony belongs to the courts as an incident to their jurisdiction over divorces.[109] And a grand jury, in execution of their general powers, and without special authority therefor, have the power, when a witness who was duly summoned

103 Gray v. Pullen, 5 Best & S. 970.

104 People v. Cooper, 6 Hill (N. Y.) 516.

105 State v. Miller, 23 Wis. 634.

106 Dig. 2, 1, 2; People v. Hicks, 15 Barb. 153.

107 U. S. v. New Bedford Bridge, 1 Woodb. & M. 401, 440, Fed. Cas. No. 15,867.

108 Ex parte Martin. L. R. 4 Q. B. Div. 212.

109 Goss v. Goss, 29 Ga. 109.

appears before them, but refuses to be sworn and behaves in a dis-
respectful manner towards the jury, to require the officer in attendance upon them to take the witness before the court, in order to
obtain its aid and direction in the matter.[110]   But in giving judicial
powers to affect prejudicially the rights of persons or property, a
statute is understood as silently implying, when it does not expressly provide, the condition or qualification that the power is to
be exercised in accordance with the fundamental rules of judicial
procedure, such, for instance, as that which requires that, before
its exercise, the person sought to be prejudicially affected shall
have an opportunity of defending himself.[111]   And so, where the
legislature prescribes the mode by which private property may be
taken for public use, the court will presume that it intends that
notice of the appropriation shall be given to the parties to be affected, although the statute may not have said so in express terms.
This requirement will be read in by implication.   For it will not be
supposed that the legislature designed to violate the principles of
right and justice.[112]

Subsidiary and Collateral Implications.

All those minor directions and details which are not specified in
the statute, but are involved in its general terms, will be filled in,
by implication, whenever it is necessary in order to give the law
an effective operation.   This is not adding to the act provisions which
the legislature did not contemplate, but evolving from its broad
terms those particular provisions which are necessarily included
within its general purpose and tenor.   Thus, for example, when a
statute requires a notice to be given, or any other similar thing to
be done, but does not specify the period of time within which it
must be done, it will be construed to mean a reasonable time, depending upon the situation of the parties and the nature of the
thing to be performed.[113]   So, again, when the statute directs notice of facts to be published in a newspaper, the courts will presume,
in the absence of any legislative intimation to the contrary, that
the notice is to be given in English, that being the ordinary lan-

---

[110] Heard v. Pierce, 8 Cush. 338.

[111] Maxwell, Interp. (2d edn.) 443; Bagg's Case, 11 Coke, 93b.

[112] City of Boonville v. Ormrod, 26 Mo. 193.

[113] Burden v. Stein, 25 Ala. 455; Moore v. Fields, 1 Oreg. 317.

guage of the state, and in a newspaper published in the same tongue.[114]

Limitations of Doctrine of Implications.

The extension, or evolution, of a statute by implication is to be confined to its strictly necessary incidents or logical consequences. When, for instance, an act requires the performance of a public service, it implies no provision that the person performing it shall be remunerated.[115] So, where the legislature specifies, as compensation for acts to be done by a public officer of a certain county, less than the usual amount, this raises no presumption that the claim for that compensation is to have precedence of others.[116] Again, a statute which empowers married women to contract debts for necessaries does not validate a bond and warrant of attorney to confess judgment made by a married woman for such a debt.[117] And where a statute exempts a husband from liability for his wife's antenuptial debts, and provides that she may be sued therefor and that her separate property shall be liable for such debts, this gives no jurisdiction or authority to adjudicate her a bankrupt.[118] And a statute which merely authorizes a judge to refer matters to arbitration does not confer upon the arbitrators power to administer oaths.[119] In these cases, it will be observed, none of the provisions sought to be added by implication were necessary to make the statute effective or to accomplish the objects which it was designed to subserve; nor were they necessarily involved in the general terms of the statute, in any such sense as to make it logically necessary to suppose that the legislature foresaw and intended them. But it is also a rule that no limitation is to be inferred or implied which would have the effect to defeat the object of the law. For instance, if a certain sum of money is appropriated for the erection of public buildings which must necessarily cost several times that amount,

---

[114] City Publishing Co. v. Mayor, etc., of Jersey City, 54 N. J. Law, 437, 24 Atl. 571; Wilson v. Inhabitants of Trenton (N. J. Sup.) 29 Atl. 183; Road in Upper Hanover, 44 Pa. St. 277.

[115] Jones v. Carmarthen, 8 Mees. & W. 605.

[116] People v. Williams, 8 Cal. 97.

[117] Glyde v. Keister, 32 Pa. St. 85.

[118] Ex parte Holland, L. R. 9 Ch. App. 307.

[119] Regina v. Hallett, 2 Den. & P. C. C. 237.

this is not to be construed into a limitation as to the expenditure.[120] And again, every legislative grant is understood to be made with the implied reservation that it shall not work injury to the property or rights of other persons.[121]

GRAMMATICAL INTERPRETATION.

34. Primarily, a statute is to be interpreted according to the ordinary meaning of its words and the proper grammatical effect of their arrangement in the act. But if there is any ambiguity, or if there is room for more than one interpretation, the rules of grammar will be disregarded where a too strict adherence to them would raise a repugnance or absurdity or would defeat the purpose of the legislature.[122]

It is to be presumed, in the first instance, that the legislature understood the rules of grammar and the use of language, and that they have expressed their will in apt and well-chosen terms. But this presumption will be abandoned whenever it becomes apparent that the result of adhering to it would be to make the act absurd, extravagant, or repugnant to other provisions of law. No such intention can be charged to the legislature, if it can be escaped by construction. Hence, in such cases, grammatical rules and the propriety of language must yield to the intention of the law-making body, to be ascertained by a rational interpretation of the enactment. "It is a rule in the construction of statutes that, in the first instance, the grammatical sense of the words is to be adhered to. If that is contrary to or inconsistent with any expressed intention, or any declared purpose of the statute, or if it would involve any absurdity, repugnance, or inconsistency in its different provisions, the grammatical sense must then be modified, extended, or abridged, so far as to avoid such inconvenience, but no further."[123] "The

---

[120] Cook v. Comm'rs of Hamilton Co., 6 McLean, 112, Fed. Cas. No. 3,157.

[121] Pittsburg & C. R. Co. v. South West Penn. R. Co., 77 Pa. St. 173.

[122] Garby v. Harris, 7 Exch. 591; Metropolitan Board of Works v. Steed, L. R. 8 Q. B. Div. 445; George v. Board of Education, 33 Ga. 344; State v. Heman, 70 Mo. 441; State v. Brandt, 41 Iowa, 592.

[123] Warburton v. Loveland, 1 Huds. & B. 623, 648.

grammatical construction of a statute is one mode of interpretation. But it is not the only mode, and it is not always the true mode. We may assume that the draftsman of an act understood the rules of grammar, but it is not always safe to do so." [124] It was an old and well-recognized rule of the common law, applicable to all written instruments, that "verba intentioni, non e contra, debent inservire;" that it to say, words ought to be made subservient to the intent, not the intent to the words. [125] Hence, in the construction of statutes, when the intention of the legislature can be gathered from the statute, words may be modified, altered, or supplied to give to the enactment the force and effect which the legislature intended. [126] As an example of departing from the strict grammatical sense, we may cite cases in which the future tense has been read as including the present and the past, where that was necessary to carry out the meaning of the legislature. Thus, an enabling act relating to married women who "shall come into the state" may apply to one who came into the state before the passage of the law. [127] So, where an act provided that certain land "shall be allotted for, and given to," an individual named, it was held that the words were words of absolute donation and passed an immediate interest. [128] In another case, the phrase "current expenses of the year" was made to read "expenses of the current year," it being evident that the latter form of words more correctly expressed the legislative intent. [129]

But it is very necessary to remember that all construction and interpretation has for its sole object to ascertain the meaning and intention of the legislature; that it is never allowable thus to defeat that meaning and intention; and that the meaning of the legislature is primarily to be sought in the words of the law. Hence, the rule which we are now considering is to be taken in connection with that fundamental rule stated in the beginning of this chapter,

---

[124] Fisher v. Connard, 100 Pa. St. 63, 69.

[125] Fox's Case, 8 Coke, 93b. See, also, Singer Manuf. Co. v. McCollock, 24 Fed. 667.

[126] Quin v. O'Keeffe, 10 Ir. C. L. (N. S.) 393; Lyde v. Barnard, 1 Mees. & W. 101; Territory v. Clark (Okl.) 35 Pac. 882.

[127] Maysville & L. R. Co. v. Herrick, 13 Bush, 122.

[128] Rutherford v. Greene, 2 Wheat. 196.

[129] Babcock v. Goodrich, 47 Cal. 488.

that if the words of the enactment are free from all doubt and ambiguity, and express a single, definite, and sensible meaning, that meaning is conclusively presumed to be the one which the legislature intended to convey.

Following out the radical idea that the intention of the law-makers is the thing to be sought for and applied, we easily deduce a corollary to the rule immediately under consideration, which may be thus stated: Neither bad grammar nor bad English will vitiate a statute, if the meaning of the legislature can be clearly discovered. Awkward, slovenly, or ungrammatical phrases and sentences may yet convey a definite meaning; and if they do, the courts must accept it as the meaning of the law-makers.[130]   For example, an act provided that townships might issue bonds when "the consent of a majority of the tax payers appearing upon the last assessment roll as shall represent a majority of the landed property of the township" should be obtained. Hereupon the court observed: "The only difficulty that is or can be suggested is from the awkward and ungrammatical construction of the sentence in using the word 'as' without any proper antecedent.   The draftsman was evidently a bad grammarian, or lacked clearness of conception sufficient to enable him to carry out the idea with which he began a sentence until he got to the end of it.   In the next preceding sentence, the phrase 'such sum of money' is used without anything to which 'such' refers; but the sentence is intelligible and explicit, and its meaning cannot be changed by interlarding at conjecture some words to amend the grammar or construction."[131]

[130] Kelly's Heirs v. McGuire, 15 Ark. 555; Murray v. State, 21 Tex. App. 620.

[131] Lane v. Schomp, 20 N. J. Eq. 82.

INAPT AND INACCURATE LANGUAGE.

35. The use of inapt, inaccurate, or improper terms or phrases in a statute will not defeat the act, provided the real meaning of the legislature can be gathered from the context or from the general purpose and tenor of the enactment. In such cases, the words in question will be interpreted according to that meaning which the legislature actually intended to express, although this may involve a departure from their literal signification.

Where the intent of the legislature, and the object and purpose of a law, are plainly apparent, and such manifest intent and purpose are not inconsistent with, or outside the terms of, the law, it is not allowable to permit the intent and purpose to be defeated merely because not defined and declared in the most complete and accurate language.[132] "It is generally true that where words used in a statute are clear and unambiguous there is no room left for construction; but when it is plainly perceivable that a particular intention, though not precisely expressed, must have been in the mind of the legislator, that intention will be enforced and carried out, and made to control the strict letter."[133]   For example, a statute provided

[132] State v. Whealey (S. Dak.) 59 N. W. 211; Crocker v. Crane, 21 Wend. 211; McLorinan v. Overseers of the Poor, 49 N. J. Law, 614, 10 Atl. 187.

[133] State v. King, 44 Mo. 283. "It has indeed been asserted that no modification of the language of a statute is ever allowable in construction, except to avoid an absurdity which appears to be so, not to the mind of the expositor merely, but to that of the legislature; that is, when it takes the form of a repugnancy. In such cases, the legislature shows in one passage that it did not mean what its words signify in another; and a modification is therefore called for and sanctioned beforehand, as it were. by the author. But the authorities do not appear to support this restricted view. They would seem rather to establish that the judicial interpreter may deal with careless and inaccurate words and phrases in the same spirit as a critic deals with an obscure or corrupt text, when satisfied, on solid grounds, from the context or history of the enactment, or from the injustice, inconvenience, or absurdity of the consequences to which it would lead, that the language thus treated does not really express the intention, and that his amendment probably does." Maxwell, Interp. (2d edn.) 305.

that "no execution shall issue against the body of the defendant * * * unless he shall have been held to bail upon a writ of capias ad satisfaciendum." Now there is no such thing known in the law as a defendant being held to bail under a capias of this character. But on the other hand, if a capias ad respondendum had been specified, the statute would have been intelligible and consistent. The court therefore held that it was evidently a legislative mistake, consisting in the use of an improper term; that the real intention of the legislature would be carried into effect by the substitution of the proper term; and consequently that the statute should be read as thus amended.[134] In another case, the statute spoke of "preferred stockholders" in a corporation, and of the payment to them of "dividends." To take these words literally would have led to absurd consequences, as shown by the context and the whole purpose of the act, and would have made the statute unconstitutional. The court therefore held that "preferred stockholders" must be read "mortgage creditors," and "dividends" must be read "interest." It was said: "A mortgage creditor, although denominated a 'preferred stockholder,' is a mortgage creditor nevertheless, and interest is not changed into a dividend by calling it a 'dividend.' Nothing is more common in the construction of statutes and contracts than for the court to correct such self-evident misnomers by supplying the proper words."[135] Again, an act was entitled "An act to authorize the governor to appoint a district attorney for the Third district." But the body of the statute provided that the governor should "appoint some person learned in the law as attorney general for the Third judicial district." As a literal construction would render the act nugatory, it was held that it should be read as if "district attorney" were substituted for "attorney general."[136] In an English case, where the word "rent" occurred many times in a statute, without further specification, the court read it as sometimes meaning "rent charge" and sometimes "rent reserved," according to the intent of the legislature, as shown by the context, and the propriety of language.[137]

[134] People v. Hoffman, 97 Ill. 234.
[135] Burt v. Rattle, 31 Ohio St. 116.
[136] Territory v. Ashenfelter, 4 N. Mex. 85, 12 Pac. 879.
[137] Angell v. Angell, 9 Ad. & El. (N. S.) 328.

STATUTE DEVOID OF MEANING.

36. If a statute is devoid of meaning,—if the language employed, though clear and precise, directs an impossibility or is incapable of bearing any reasonable signification, or if an ambiguity exists which cannot be cleared up,—so that it is not possible to ascertain the object to which the legislature intended the act to apply or the result which it was expected to accomplish, the act is inoperative. In such a case, the courts cannot revise and amend it, on mere conjecture as to the intention of the legislature, but it is their duty to pronounce it incapable of effectual operation.

"A statute must be capable of construction and interpretation, otherwise it will be inoperative and void. The court must use every authorized means to ascertain and give it an intelligible meaning; but if, after such effort, it is found to be impossible to solve the doubt and dispel the obscurity, if no judicial certainty can be settled upon as to the meaning, the court is not at liberty to supply or make one. The court may not allow conjectural interpretation to usurp the place of judicial exposition. There must be a competent and efficient expression of the legislative will." [138] "Whether a statute be a public or private one, if the terms in which it is couched be so vague as to convey no definite meaning to those whose duty it is to execute it, either ministerially or judicially, it is necessarily inoperative. The law must remain as it was, unless that which professes to change it be itself intelligible." [139] "We are bound," says Lord Denman, "to give to the words of the legislature all possible meaning which is consistent with the clear language used. But if we find language used which is incapable of a meaning, we cannot supply one. To give an effectual meaning [in the present case] we must alter, not only 'or' into 'and,' but 'issued' into 'levied.' It is extremely probable that this would express what the

[138] State v. Partlow, 91 N. Car. 550; State v. Boon, Tayl. (N. Car.) 246; Comm. v. Bank of Pennsylvania, 3 Watts & S. 173.
[139] Drake v. Drake, 4 Dev. (N. Car.) L. 110.

legislature meant. But we cannot supply it. Those who used the words thought that they had effected the purpose intended. But we, looking at the words as judges, are no more justified in introducing that meaning than we should be if we added any other provision." [140] To illustrate further, in a case in Texas, it appeared that a statute authorized appeals from interlocutory judgments thereafter rendered in the district courts, and required that such appeals "be regulated by the law regulating appeals from final judgments in the district courts, so far as the same may be applicable thereto." The statutes regulating appeals from final judgments were entirely inapplicable to appeals from interlocutory judgments, and for this reason it was held that the act was nugatory and void.[141] Again, a statute prohibited the sale of liquor "within three miles of Mt. Zion church in Gaston county." There were two churches of that name in that county, several miles apart. It was held that no effect or operation could be given to the statute.[142] And so, where a statute divided a county into two judicial districts, and provided for the holding of terms of court therein, but enacted that the same court should be held by the same judge in the two different districts on the same day, it was held that the law remained the same as before this enactment, for it was incapable of operation.[143]

[140] Green v. Wood, 7 Ad. & El. (N. S.) 178.
[141] Ward v. Ward, 37 Tex. 389.
[142] State v. Partlow, 91 N. Car. 550.
[143] Ex parte Jones, 49 Ark. 110, 4 S. W. 639.

CORRECTION OF CLERICAL ERRORS AND MISPRINTS.

37. Clerical errors or misprints, which, if uncorrected, would render the statute unmeaning or nonsensical, or would defeat or impair its intended operation, will not vitiate the act; they will be corrected by the court and the statute read as amended, provided the true reading is obvious and the real meaning of the legislature is apparent on the face of the whole enactment.

A good illustration of this rule is found in the case of In re Frey.[144] A statute of Pennsylvania, relating to the apportionment of the expense of certain local improvements between a city and the county in which it was situated, provided that when the balance of expenditures should be against the city, any further expenditures should "be payable out of the treasury of said county, and be reimbursable out of the county treasury only when the balance shall be in favor of said city, and to the extent of such balance." It was held that the word "county," in the clause "be payable out of the treasury of said county," must be read as "city," for there was plainly a clerical error, by which "county" was substituted for "city." It was said by the court: "The obvious meaning and purpose of the act is plain from the context. It needs no argument to show that the word 'county' was mistakenly written for 'city.' It is a mistake apparent on the face of the act, which may be rectified by the context. In making this correction we are not to be understood as correcting the act of the legislature. We are enabled to carry out the intention of the legislature from the plain and obvious meaning of the context, in which the real purpose or intention of the legislature is manifest. It falls within the province of the courts to correct a merely clerical error, even in an act of assembly, when, as it is written, it involves a manifest absurdity, and the error is plain and obvious. The power is undoubted, but it can

---

[144] 128 Pa. St. 593, 18 Atl. 478; Lancaster County v. City of Lancaster, 160 Pa. St. 411, 28 Atl. 854. And see In re Clearfield County License Bonds, 10 Pa. Co. Ct. R. 593.

only be exercised when the error is so manifest, upon an inspection of the act, as to preclude all manner of doubt, and when the correction will relieve the sense of the statute from an actual absurdity, and carry out the clear purpose of the legislature." So again, a statute provided that "the district court shall have and exercise all the civil and criminal jurisdiction heretofore vested in the county court and *not* divested by this act." The intention of the statute was perfectly plain, but it would be entirely defeated by the retention of the word "not" in this clause. It was accordingly held that, as the word must have been inserted by mistake, it might be disregarded and the statute construed as if it were not present.[145] In another case, the words of the statute were: "All persons performing labor, or furnishing machinery or boilers, or castings, or other materials for the construction, or repairing, or carrying on of any mill or manufactory, shall have a lien on such mill or manufactory for such work or labor done on such machinery, or boilers, or castings, or other material furnished by each respectively." It was held that the word "on" in the last clause was a clerical error for "or," and the act should be read as corrected.[146] Another statute, as printed, provided that "any person who alters and publishes as true, and with intent to defraud, any falsely altered, forged, or counterfeited bank-bill * * * is guilty of forgery." The court held that the fourth word of this section, "alters," was a misprint or clerical error for "utters," as shown by the context, and accordingly read the statute as thus corrected.[147] Again, a statute enacted a penalty against all persons gambling or betting in a public place with any "card, token, or other article used as an instrument or means of such wagering on gaming." It was held that the word "on" was evidently, by a clerical error, substituted for "or" and the statute should be read as if the word were "or."[148] A statute which declares that "the officers of the board of health in cities to which this act is applicable, and also all officers created by the council or under legislative act," etc., "are hereby abolished," should be construed as abolishing the offices held by the officers men-

---

[145] Chapman v. State, 16 Tex. App. 76.
[146] Gould v. Wise, 18 Nev. 253, 3 Pac. 30.
[147] Bostick v. State, 34 Ala. 266.
[148] Tollett v. Thomas, L. R. 6 Q. B. 514.

tioned.[149]   The word "acts," in a statute, may be read "act," in the singular, when that is necessary to make the statute sensible and effective.[150]   And when it is enacted that the "venire" in actions against railroads shall be laid in some county wherein the track of the company is situated, this may be held to mean the "venue," as otherwise the law would be unmeaning.[151]   So, where the statute declared that "all penal judgments in the district court may be examined, and affirmed, reversed, or modified by the supreme court," it was held that it should be read "final judgments," instead of "penal judgments."[152]   In a statute of Tennessee, creating a new county, instead of a decimal point between figures describing the boundary, the sign of a degree was used.   The calls would have been meaningless unless the sign were taken as a decimal point. And it was held that it should be so taken.[153]

But it must be remembered that the courts are not at liberty to indulge in corrections and emendations of the written laws, unless it is perfectly plain that there is a clerical error or misprint, and unless the text, as it stands, with the error uncorrected, would be devoid of sensible meaning or contrary to the evident legislative intent.   This was the position taken by the court in Maryland with regard to a revenue law which provided that all property within the state, of every description, except certain property therein particularly named, should be "exempt" from taxation for state or local purposes.   It was almost incredible that the legislature meant what the words imported.   The obvious intention was to say that all property except that mentioned should be subject to taxation.   Yet the court refused to correct the mistake, saying that the language used was perfectly plain and unambiguous, and must be taken in its natural import; and this, although they were obliged, taking the act as it read on its face, to pronounce it unconstitutional.[154]   In another case, it appeared that a statute provided that "whenever an answer has been filed in a suit in which the defendant has had personal service made upon him to appear and file his answer, or

[149] State v. Covington, 29 Ohio St. 102, 117.
[150] Jocelyn v. Barrett, 18 Ind. 128.
[151] Graham v. Charlotte & S. C. R. Co., 64 N. Car. 631.
[152] Moody v. Stephenson, 1 Minn. 401 (Gil. 289).
[153] Brown v. Hamlett, 8 Lea, 732.
[154] Maxwell v. State, 40 Md. 273.

when a judgment has been rendered in a case after answer filed by the defendant or his counsel, the party cast in the suit shall be considered duly notified of the judgment by the fact of its being signed by the judge." It was insisted that the act contained a manifest misprint, and that it should read "whenever no answer has been filed," etc. For as it stood it provided for two cases, in the alternative, which were in fact identical, viz., judgment signed after answer filed.' And the court admitted that the first clause of the statute, as it stood, was surplusage, but held that this would not justify them in changing a word, by way of correction, as that would give an exactly opposite meaning to the clause.[155] And so again, under a statute providing that a demand against an estate in the probate court, if exhibited within two years, might be proved within three years, it was held that, though "three" was substituted by mistake for "two," yet the court could not construe away the plain words of the law.[156]

EFFECT OF MISDESCRIPTIONS AND MISNOMERS.

38. A misdescription or misnomer in a statute will not vitiate the enactment or render it inoperative, provided the means of identifying the person or thing intended, apart from the erroneous description, are clear, certain, and convincing.

It is an ancient maxim of the law, applicable to all written instruments alike, that "falsa demonstratio non nocet cum de corpore constat." [157] Accordingly, in the case of a statute, "the court will inspect the whole act. and if the true intention of the legislature can be reached, the false description will be rejected as surplusage, or words substituted, in the place of those wrongly used, which will give effect to the law." [158] For example, a word in a statute defining the boundaries of a county may be read "north" instead of "south," if it is clear that "north" was really intended.[159]

---

[155] Sentmanat v. Soule, 33 La. Ann. 609.

[156] Hicks v. Jamison, 10 Mo. App. 35.

[157] Broom, Max. 629; State v. Mayor, etc., of Orange, 32 N. J. Law, 49.

[158] Palms v. Shawano County, 61 Wis. 211, 21 N. W. 77.

[159] Palms v. Shawano County, 61 Wis. 211, 21 N. W. 77.

On the same principle, a mistake in the date of passage, or the title, of an act of the legislature referred to by a subsequent amendatory act will not prevent the operative effect of the amendatory act, provided the latter so particularly refers to the subject-matter of the former as clearly to indicate the act intended to be amended.[160] And if a later statute expressly refers to a designated section of an earlier act, to which it can have no application, but there is another section of the prior statute to which, and to which alone, in view of the subject-matter, the later act can properly refer, it will be read according to the manifest purpose of the legislature, and the misdescription will not vitiate.[161] Moreover, a case of erroneous description may sometimes be helped out by extraneous evidence, provided it is adequate and convincing. Thus, in a case in New Jersey, an act of the legislature authorized the managers of a meadow draining scheme to purchase a property known as the "Dennis Mill" property, consisting of a designated quantity of land, with the water power, and the mills and other buildings thereon. In a private action, growing out of the operations of the managers under this statute, it was shown that there was no "Dennis Mill" property in the vicinity, but that "Dunn's Mill" property answered the description in the act and was the one intended by it. Hereupon, an injunction, granted on filing a bill to restrain the purchase of the Dunn's Mill property, was dissolved.[162] But it is important to observe that there is a very material difference between a misdescription and an ambiguous or inadequate description. In the case of the former, the descriptive words are not applicable to the object which the legislature had in mind, but that object is capable of being otherwise identified. In the case of the latter, the descriptive words may be applicable to the legislative object, but that object cannot be identified. This distinction is well illustrated by a comparison of the case last adverted to with the case of State v. Partlow,[163] wherein the act in question forbade the sale of liquor "within

[160] Madison, W. & M. Plankroad Co. v. Reynolds, 3 Wis. 287; School Directors of District No. 5 v. School Directors of District No. 10, 73 Ill. 249; In re Clearfield County License Bonds, 10 Pa. Co. Ct. R. 593.

[161] People v. King, 28 Cal. 266; Stoneman v. Whaley, 9 Iowa, 390; People v. Hill, 3 Utah, 334, 3 Pac. 75; Comm. v. Marshall, 69 Pa. St. 328.

[162] Lindsley v. Williams, 20 N. J. Eq. 93.

[163] 91 N. Car. 550.

three miles of Mt. Zion church in Gaston county," and it was held inoperative and void because there were two churches of that name in that county, several miles apart.   In the former case, there was a misdescription, but when the object was identified, the statute was held to apply to it.   In the latter case, there was no misdescription, but the descriptive words were equally applicable to two different objects, and on account of the latent ambiguity, the act was held inoperative.   It is also said that when the descriptive words constitute the very essence of the act, unless the description is so clear and accurate as to refer to the particular subject intended, and to be incapable of being applied to any other, the mistake is fatal.[164]

The same general rule covers the case of misnomers in a statute. In a legislative act, as in any private writing, a misnomer, whether it be of a person, a corporation, or a locality, will not be allowed to defeat the operation of the act, if it is quite evident that it is a misnomer, and the actual meaning of the legislature is clear.[165] For instance, where an act names "Lewis Mankel" as entitled to a sum of money, the fact that the claimant's name is "Louis Mankel" should not deprive him of the right to receive it.[166]

[164] Blanchard v. Sprague, 3 Sumn. 279, Fed. Cas. No. 1,517.

[165] Chancellor of Oxford's Case, 10 Coke, 53a; State v. Timme, 56 Wis. 423, 14 N. W. 604; Nazro v. Merchants' Mut. Ins. Co., 14 Wis. 295; Attorney General v. Chicago & N. W. R. Co., 35 Wis. 425, 557.

[166] Mankel v. U. S., 19 Ct. Cl. 295.

REJECTION OF SURPLUSAGE.

39. It is the duty of the courts to give effect, if possible, to every word of the written law. But if a word or clause be found in a statute which appears to have been inserted through inadvertence or mistake, and which is incapable of any sensible meaning, or which is repugnant to the rest of the act and tends to nullify it, and if the statute is complete and sensible without it, such word or clause may be rejected as surplusage.

In giving construction to a statute, the courts are bound, if it be possible, to give effect to all its several parts. No sentence, clause, or word should be construed as unmeaning and surplusage, if a construction can be legitimately found which will give force to and preserve all the words of the statute.[167] "It is a canon of construction that, if it be possible, effect must be given to every word of an act of parliament, but that, if there be a word or phrase therein to which no sensible meaning can be given, it must be eliminated."[168] But while the endeavor of the courts should be in the direction of harmonizing and making operative the whole statute, in all its words and parts, yet, in proper cases, the construction of a statute, as of any private writing, is governed by the maxims "utile per inutile non vitiatur" and "surplusagium non nocet." And if it clearly appears, from all the proper sources of interpretation, that a clause or provision of a statute was inserted through inadvertence, especially if it conflicts with the rest of the act and would tend to limit or impair its application, it will be disregarded.[169] For example, an act of congress provided that if any person should attempt to bribe a revenue officer of the United States to commit or connive at a fraud upon the revenue "and be thereof convicted," such person should "be liable to indictment," etc. It was held that the words "and be thereof convicted" must be rejected as surplusage, because their retention in the statute would render it entirely

---

[167] Hagenbuck v. Reed, 3 Neb. 17; Leversee v. Reynolds, 13 Iowa, 310.

[168] Stone v. Mayor, etc., of Yeovil, L. R. 1 C. P. Div. 691, 701.

[169] Pond v. Maddox, 38 Cal. 572.

meaningless and inoperative, whereas, this phrase being exscinded, the statute remained complete, sensible, and operative.[170] So again, a statute of New Hampshire provided that whenever an assignment should be made under its terms. "all attachments shall be void except such as have been made three months previous to such assignment, and all payments, pledges, mortgages, conveyances, sales, and transfers made within three months next before such assignment, and after the passage of this act, and before the 1st of September next, and also all payments, etc., whenever made, if fraudulent as to creditors, shall be void." It was considered that no effect consistent with the plain intent of the statute could possibly be given to the words "before the 1st of September next," and consequently they must be rejected as without meaning.[171] So, also, the word "such," frequently used in statutes, when it is apparent that it has no reference to anything preceding it, may be rejected.[172] In an act of Missouri, it was provided that "if any guardian of any white female under the age of eighteen years, or of any other person to whose care or protection any such female shall have been confided, shall defile her by carnally knowing her," he should be liable to a punishment. It was held that the word "of" before "any other person" must be rejected, as it limited the applicability of the statute contrary to the obvious purpose of the legislature.[173]

INTERPOLATION OF WORDS.

40. Words may be interpolated in a statute, or silently understood as incorporated in it, where the meaning of the legislature is plain and unmistakable, and such supplying of words is necessary to carry out that meaning and make the statute sensible and effective.

The language used in a statute must, if possible, be so construed as to give it some force and effect, ut res magis valeat quam pereat; and consequently, when the language is elliptical, the words which

---

[170] U. S. v. Stern, 5 Blatchf. 512, Fed. Cas. No. 16,389.
[171] Leavitt v. Lovering, 64 N. H. 607, 15 Atl. 414.
[172] State v. Beasley, 5 Mo. 91.
[173] State v. Acuff, 6 Mo. 54.

are obviously necessary to complete the sense will be supplied.[174] But words should never be supplied or changed in a statute, unless to effect a meaning clearly shown by the other parts of the statute, and to carry out an intent somewhere expressed.[175] Where a word is evidently omitted by mistake in one section of a statute, which omission is explained in another part of the same statute by a reference to such section, the defective section may be enforced according to such explanation.[176] Where a law fixed the penalty for a certain act at "not less than one nor more than three hundred dollars," it was held that the minimum penalty was one hundred dollars. In effect, this was interpolating the word "hundred" after "one" in accordance with the evident meaning of the legislature, though contrary to the literal sense of the law.[177] Again, if the law prescribes that a person convicted of crime shall be imprisoned not less than two nor more than five years, and a statute adds the words "or by fine and imprisonment, one or both, at the discretion of the jury," it is the duty of the court to supply the words "be punished" after the word "or" where it first appears in the amendment.[178] So, when an enrolled act limits taxation to "one half of percentum," and the act, as published by authority, expresses the limitation to be "one half of one per centum," the two expressions will be held to mean the same thing.[179] Again, where a statute denounced a penalty against "every person who shall buy, sell, or receive from any slave any commodity," etc., it was held that it must be read as if the word "to" were inserted after "sell."[180] A statute of Minnesota provided for an action by any person in possession of land against any person claiming "an estate, interest, or lien therein adverse," and by any person out of possession against one claiming "an estate or interest therein adverse," etc. It was considered that the word "lien" having been added to the first clause by amendment, its omission from the second was an oversight, and not intentional, and

[174] Nichols v. Halliday, 27 Wis. 406; City of Philadelphia v. Ridge Avenue Pass. Ry. Co., 102 Pa. St. 190; In re Wainewright, 1 Phillips, Ch. 258.

[175] Lane v. Schomp, 20 N. J. Eq. 82.

[176] Brinsfield v. Carter, 2 Ga. 143.

[177] Worth v. Peck, 7 Pa. St. 268.

[178] Turner v. State, 40 Ala. 21.

[179] Goldsmith v. Augusta & S. R. Co., 62 Ga. 468.

[180] Worrell v. State, 12 Ala. 732.

that a "lien" was an estate or interest litigable by a person out of possession.[181] In an English case, a statute made it penal "to be in possession" of game after a certain day. If construed literally, this would apply to the case of one who had lawfully come into possession of game before that day and continued to have it in possession after that day. To avoid this injustice, it was construed as applying only where the possession did not begin until after the close of the season. This, in effect, amounted to interpolating the words "to begin" before "to be in possession."[182] In Ohio, an act passed May 3, 1852, provided that it should take effect "from and after the fifteenth day of May next." It was contended that this meant May 15, 1853. But the court found, from an examination of the legislative journals, that the bill was passed by the concurrent vote of the two houses on April 28, though it was not signed until six days later. And it was considered to be evident that the act, in the mind of the legislature, spoke from the 28th of April, and consequently it should be read as if it declared that it should take effect on the "fifteenth of May next hereafter." This last word was in effect supplied by the court.[183]

---

[181] Donohue v. Ladd, 31 Minn. 244, 17 N. W. 381.

[182] Simpson v. Unwin, 3 Barn. & Ad. 134.

[183] State v. Mayor, etc., of Perrysburg, 14 Ohio St. 472.

CHAPTER IV.

STATUTORY CONSTRUCTION; PRESUMPTIONS.

PRESUMPTIONS IN AID OF INTERPRETATION.

41. In construing a doubtful or ambiguous statute, the courts will presume that it was the intention of the legislature to enact a valid, sensible, and just law, and one which should change the prior law no further than may be necessary to effectuate the specific purpose of the act in question. The construction should be in harmony with this assumption whenever possible. But presumptions of this kind cannot prevail against the clear and explicit terms of the law. And if there is no room for doubt as to the meaning of the legislature, the courts must take the law as it stands, without any regard to the consequences.

It would not be consistent with the respect which one department of the government owes to another, nor with the good of the state, for the courts to impute to the legislature any intention to exceed the rightful limits of their power, to violate the restraints which the constitution imposes upon them, to disregard the principles of sound public policy, or to make a law leading to absurd, unjust, inconvenient, or impossible results, or calculated to defeat its own object. On the contrary, it is the bounden duty of the judicial tribunals to assume that the law-making power has kept within the proper sphere of its authority, and has acted with integrity, good faith, and wisdom. Consequently, if the words of the law are doubtful or ambiguous, or if the statute is susceptible of more than one construction, the courts will lean in favor of that interpretation which will reconcile the enactment with the limitations of legislative power and with the dictates of justice and expediency. At the same time, as we have already remarked, the object of all construction and interpretation is to ascertain the meaning and intention of the legislature. If the meaning is obscure, or the intention doubtful, the courts should seek it out. And in this search they will be aided by the presumptions which we have mentioned. But if the meaning and intention are clear upon the face of the enactment, there is no room for construction. In that event, the literal sense of the statute is to be taken as its intended sense, and the judiciary have nothing to do with considerations of justice, reason, or convenience. "The consequences of evil and hardship may properly exert an influence in giving a construction to a statute when its language is ambiguous or uncertain and doubtful, but not when it is plain and explicit. The same may be said of the consideration of convenience, and in fact of any consequences. If the intention is expressed so plainly as to exclude all controversy, and is one not controlled or affected by any provision of the constitution, it is the law, and courts have no concern with the effects and consequences; their simple duty is to execute it." [1]

And here it is necessary to call the attention of the reader to an important distinction between the office of the judiciary in determining the constitutional validity of a statute, and their duty in construing a statute ascertained or assumed to be constitutional. In order to adjudge that an act of the legislature is in violation of the constitution, it is necessary to be able to show, clearly, how and in what particular it is inconsistent with the organic law; it is not enough to show that it is impolitic, unwise, or even absurd. In passing upon the question of its constitutional validity, the courts

---

[1] Sutherland, Stat. Constr. § 324; U. S. v. Kirby, 7 Wall. 482.

have nothing to do with considerations of expediency, wisdom, or justice.[2] But if the law is ascertained to be constitutionally valid (or if the question of its constitutionality is not raised), and the only doubt is as to its proper construction, the courts may listen to arguments drawn from considerations of public policy, or reason, justice, and propriety, and be guided thereby in deciding in favor of one or the other of two permissible interpretations.

PRESUMPTION AGAINST EXCEEDING LIMITATIONS OF LEGISLATIVE POWER.

42. It is presumed that the legislature does not design any attempt to transcend the rightful limits of its authority, to violate the principles of international law, or to give exterritorial effect to its statutes. In case of doubt or ambiguity, the construction will be such as to avoid these consequences.

It must be assumed that the legislature has intended to keep within the prescribed limits of its authority, and to enact a valid law. Hence, if a statute is fairly susceptible of two interpretations, one of which would make it transcend the boundaries of legislative competence, and the other would make it valid, the latter interpretation is to be adopted.[3] And a construction involving the exercise of a doubtful power will not readily be adopted in the absence of direct words, when the words used admit of another construction which steers clear of all questions in regard to power.[4] The principle of the separation of the powers of government into three co-ordinate departments requires that each of these should be independent of the others, and that neither should usurp the functions nor encroach upon the lawful powers of the others. Hence any act of legislation which should amount to an unlawful assumption of either executive or judicial powers, or which should arrogate to the legislative department duties or prerogatives which the fundamental law confides to the other branches of the government, would be, for that reason, invalid and of no effect. But an inten-

---

[2] Black, Const. Law, 61.

[3] Ferguson v. Borough of Stamford, 60 Conn. 432, 22 Atl. 782.

[4] Mardre v. Felton, Phill. (N. Car.) L. 279.

tion thus to exceed the limits of its rightful power is never to be imputed to the legislature. On the contrary, the presumption is that it has kept within those limits. And in case of a doubtful or ambiguous law, the construction should be such as will reconcile the expressed will of the legislature with the limits fixed for the sphere of its action and with the proper jurisdiction of the other departments. Another consequence of the presumption against any abuse of power by the legislature is that any facts, the existence of which is necessary to the validity of an act of the legislature, are to be taken for true, as an inference from the statute itself.[5] And the correctness or incorrectness of a legislative opinion whereon an act is founded, is not a question within the province of the courts to determine; they must assume the fact to be as the legislature states or assumes it.[6]

Violation of International Law.

In case of doubt, a statute should be so construed as to harmonize and agree with the rules and principles of international law, and to respect rights and obligations secured by treaties, rather than to violate them.[7] But this presumption is admissible only when there is opportunity to choose between two or more possible interpretations. "If the legislature of England in express terms applies its legislation to matters beyond its legislatorial capacity, an English court must obey the English legislature, however contrary to international comity such legislation may be. But unless there be definite express terms to the contrary, a statute is to be interpreted as applicable and as intended to apply only to matters within the jurisdiction of the legislature by which it is enacted."[8] "If the language of an act of parliament, unambiguously and without reasonably admitting of any other meaning, applies to foreigners abroad, or is otherwise in conflict with any principle of international law, the courts must obey and administer it as it stands, whatever

[5] Erie & North-East R. Co. v. Casey, 26 Pa. St. 287; State v. Noyes, 47 Me. 189.

[6] People v. Lawrence, 36 Barb. 177.

[7] Queen v. Anderson, L. R. 1 C. C. R. 161; Bloxam v. Favre, L. R. 8 P. D. 101; Lau Ow Bew v. U. S., 144 U. S. 47, 12 Sup. Ct. 517.

[8] Niboyet v. Niboyet, L. R. 4 P. D. 1, 20; Cail v. Papayanni (The Amalia), 1 Moore P. C. (N. S.) 471.

may be the responsibility incurred by the nation to foreign powers in executing such a law." [9]   And these principles are equally applicable in our own country, with this limitation, in respect to the acts of the legislatures of the states, that if they encroach upon the powers confided to congress in relation to our international concerns, or if they violate the terms of a treaty (which is the "supreme law of the land"), they are unconstitutional and void, and hence no question can arise as to their interpretation.

Exterritorial Operation of Statutes.

Prima facie, every statute is confined in its operation to the persons, property, rights, or contracts, which are within the territorial jurisdiction of the legislature which enacted it.   The presumption is always against any intention to attempt giving to the act an exterritorial operation and effect.[10]   Said Chief Justice Marshall: "It is so unusual for a legislature to employ itself in framing rules which are to operate only on contracts made without their jurisdiction, between persons residing without their jurisdiction, that courts can never be justified in putting such a construction on their words if they admit of any other interpretation which is rational and not too much strained." [11]   Thus, although a legislature may provide remedies within the state for the collection of claims or enforcement of personal liabilities arising out of the state, it is not within the competency of the legislative power, upon grounds of public policy, to create personal liabilities and impose them on persons and property out of the jurisdiction of the state and on account of transactions occurring beyond its territorial limits.[12]   Again, it is a maxim of general law, recognized by all nations, that the criminal and penal laws of a country do not reach, in their effects, beyond the jurisdiction where they are established.[13]   Consequently, it was early decided in this country that the crime of robbery committed by a person who is not a citizen of the United States, on the high

[9] Maxwell, Interp. (2d edn.) 179; The Marianna Flora, 11 Wheat. 40.

[10] Noble v. Steamboat St. Anthony, 12 Mo. 261; Ex parte Blain, L. R. 12 Ch. Div. 522; Jefferys v. Boosey, 4 H. L. Cas. 815; Hendrickson v. Fries, 45 N. J. Law, 555.

[11] Bond v. Jay, 7 Cranch, 350.

[12] Steamboat Ohio v. Stunt, 10 Ohio St. 582.

[13] Comm. v. Green, 17 Mass. 515.

seas, on board of a ship belonging exclusively to subjects of a foreign state, is not piracy under the act of congress defining and punishing that crime, although such an offense might be brought within the broad general terms of the statute.[14] On a similar principle it is held that the civil damage laws,—giving a right of action against liquor-sellers to innocent parties who sustain injury by the intoxication of persons supplied with liquor by the defendants, or by the consequences of such intoxication or the acts of intoxicated persons, or by the furnishing of liquor to minors or drunkards after warning given not to do so,—have no exterritorial operation or effect.[15] And in regard to the statutes, now quite common in the United States, which give a right of action for damages to the surviving family, or the personal representatives, of a person who has been killed by the wrongful act, omission, or default of another, it is generally held that they have no exterritorial force. On the general principle of the limits of political jurisdiction and of the force of municipal law, it is considered that such acts are intended to regulate the conduct of persons and corporations only within the state enacting the law. If a citizen of the state leaves it and goes into another state, he is left to the protection of the laws of the latter state. Hence an action will not lie in the courts of one state, under such a statute enacted by that state, for death caused by a wrongful act or negligence occurring within the limits of another state.[16] It should be observed that this is not a question of legislative power so much as of interpretation. Again, in view of the well settled general rule that real property is subject exclusively to the laws of the state within whose territorial limits it is situated, any statute dealing in general terms with the real property of a bankrupt would not be construed as applying to or affecting his lands in foreign jurisdictions.[17] Neither can the revenue laws of a state have any exterritorial operation.[18] And as it is not competent for the legislature of a state to impose taxation on lands situ-

[14] U. S. v. Palmer, 3 Wheat. 610; U. S. v. Howard, 3 Wash. C. C. 340, Fed. Cas. No. 15,404.

[15] Goodwin v. Young, 34 Hun, 252; Black, Intox. Liq. § 280.

[16] Tiffany, Death by Wr. Act, § 195; Beach v. Bay State Steamboat Co., 30 Barb. 433; Whitford v. Panama R. Co., 23 N. Y. 465.

[17] Selkrig v. Davis, 2 Rose, 291.

[18] State Tax on Foreign-Held Bonds, 15 Wall. 300.

ated in another state, the presumption is against any attempt on their part to bring about this result, and tax laws will not be construed as authorizing such taxation, if it is possible to avoid that consequence.[19]

PRESUMPTION AGAINST UNCONSTITUTIONALITY.

43. Every act of the legislature is presumed to be valid and constitutional until the contrary is shown. All doubts are resolved in favor of the validity of the act. If it is fairly and reasonably open to more than one construction, that construction will be adopted which will reconcile the statute with the constitution and avoid the consequence of unconstitutionality.

Legislators, as well as judges, are bound to obey and support the constitution, and it is to be understood that they have weighed the constitutional validity of every act they pass. Hence the presumption is always in favor of the constitutionality of a statute; every reasonable doubt must be resolved in favor of the statute, not against it; and the courts will not adjudge it invalid unless its violation of the constitution is, in their judgment, clear, complete, and unmistakable.[20] Hence it follows that the courts will not so con-

[19] Drayton's Appeal, 61 Pa. St. 172.

[20] Tonnage Tax Cases, 62 Pa. St. 286; Kerrigan v. Force, 68 N. Y. 381; Hartford Bridge Co. v. Union Ferry Co., 29 Conn. 210; Kellogg v. State Treasurer, 44 Vt. 356; Flint River Steamboat Co. v. Foster, 5 Ga. 194; Mayor, etc., of Baltimore v. State, 15 Md. 376; Osburn v. Stealey, 5 W. Va. 85; Stewart v. Sup'rs of Polk Co., 30 Iowa, 9. A statute can be declared unconstitutional only where specific restrictions upon the power of the legislature can be pointed out, and the case shown to come within them, and not upon any general theory that the statute is unjust or oppressive or impolitic, or that it conflicts with a spirit supposed to pervade the constitution, but not expressed in words. Sawyer v. Dooley (Nev.) 32 Pac. 437; Wadsworth v. Union Pac. Ry. Co., 18 Colo. 600, 33 Pac. 515; Black, Const. Law, 61, 62. In determining the validity of a statute, the courts will not pass upon the motives of the legislature in its enactment. Parker v. State, 132 Ind. 419, 31 N. E. 1114; Fletcher v. Peck, 6 Cranch, 87; Ex parte McCardle, 7 Wall. 506; Ex parte Newman, 9 Cal. 502; State v. Fagan, 22 La. Ann. 545; Williams v. Nashville, 89 Tenn. 487, 15 S. W. 364.

strue the law as to make it conflict with the constitution, but will rather put such an interpretation upon it as will avoid conflict with the constitution and give it full force and effect, if this can be done without extravagance. If there is doubt or uncertainty as to the meaning of the legislature, if the words or provisions of the statute are obscure, or if the enactment is fairly susceptible of two or more constructions, that interpretation will be adopted which will avoid the effect of unconstitutionality, even though it may be necessary, for this purpose, to disregard the more usual or apparent import of the language employed.[21] "It is the duty of the court to uphold a statute when the conflict between it and the constitution is not clear; and the implication which must always exist, that no violation has been intended by the legislature, may require the court, in some cases, where the meaning of the constitution is in doubt, to lean in favor of such a construction of the statute as might not at first view seem most obvious and natural. Where the meaning of the constitution is clear, the court, if possible, must give the statute such a construction as will enable it to have effect."[22] "If, upon the construction we have been considering, the law in question would be void, or even of doubtful validity, it is our duty to find, if we are able, some other construction that will relieve it of this difficulty. If a law can be upheld by a reasonable construction, it ought to be done, and it is to be presumed that the legislature, in passing it, intended to enact a reasonable and just law, rather than an unreasonable and unjust one."[23] A few illustrations will suffice to explain the application of these rules. In 1891, the legislature of California passed an act authorizing the organization and creation of sanitary districts throughout the state, and empowering such districts to issue bonds for the construction of sewers and drains. It was contended that the act might include cities and towns, and that, if this were the case, it would be in violation of a clause of the

[21] Parsons v. Bedford, 3 Pet. 433; Grenada Co. v. Brogden, 112 U. S. 261, 5 Sup. Ct. 125; Inkster v. Carver, 16 Mich. 484; Newland v. Marsh, 19 Ill. 376; Roosevelt v. Godard, 52 Barb. 533; Singer Manuf. Co. v. McCollock, 24 Fed. 667; State v. Haring (N. J.) 26 Atl. 915; Duncombe v. Prindle, 12 Iowa, 1; Iowa Homestead Co. v. Webster County, 21 Iowa, 221; Winter v. Jones, 10 Ga. 190; Cotten v. Comm'rs of Leon Co., 6 Fla. 610.

[22] Slack v. Jacob, 8 W. Va. 612.

[23] Camp v. Rogers, 44 Conn. 291. And see Huggins v. Ball, 19 Ala. 587.

constitution which prohibited the legislature from interfering with the municipal functions of the different cities and towns of the state. But the court refused to assume that the statute must necessarily include municipal corporations, and therefore held it valid and constitutional.[24] An act of New Jersey provided that whenever a corporation created under it should desire to extend any existing railway or to build a new line, it should, before beginning work, file with the secretary of state a description and map of the route, and thereupon such corporation should thereby secure the "exclusive right to build such extension or new line" for a certain period, provided it first obtained the consent of the body having control of the highways as to the location of such route   There was no purpose apparent on the face of the act to attempt to resume any previously granted franchise, to repeal any charter, or to interfere with chartered rights.   And the court held that it could not assume any such intention on the part of the legislature (which would have had the effect of invalidating the act) merely because of an inconsistency between this statute and certain prior laws.[25]   So again, where an act setting off a county may be construed to create it in præsenti, in which case the act would be unconstitutional, or may fairly be construed to provide for the future creation of a county, in which case it would be constitutional, it should receive the latter construction.[26]

But it must be observed that the presumption of constitutionality, like all the other presumptions of this class, is available only in case of doubt or ambiguity   The courts cannot revise or correct an act of the legislature in order to make it conform to the constitution.   If it is plainly and palpably invalid, it is their duty to so declare it.   Where the language is not ambiguous, and the meaning is clear and obvious, an unconstitutional consequence cannot be avoided by forcing upon the language of the act a meaning which, upon a fair test, is repugnant to its terms.[27]

[24] Woodward v. Fruitvale Sanitary Dist., 99 Cal. 554, 34 Pac. 239.

[25] West Jersey Traction Co. v. Camden Horse R. Co. (N. J.) 29 Atl. 333.

[26] Palms v. Shawano County, 61 Wis. 211, 21 N. W. 77.

[27] French v. Teschemaker, 24 Cal. 518, 554; Attorney General v. City of Eau Claire, 37 Wis. 400.

Partial Unconstitutionality.

Where part of a statute is unconstitutional, but the remainder is valid, the parts will be separated, if possible, and that which is constitutional will be sustained.[28]   It frequently happens that some parts, features, or provisions of a statute are invalid, by reason of repugnancy to the constitution, while the remainder of the act is not open to the same objections.   In such cases, it is the duty of the courts not to pronounce the whole statute unconstitutional, if that can be avoided, but, rejecting the invalid portions, to give effect and operation to the valid portions.   The rule is, that if the invalid portions can be separated from the rest, and if, after their excision, there remains a complete, intelligible, and valid statute, capable of being executed, and conforming to the general purpose and intent of the legislature, as shown in the act, it will not be adjudged unconstitutional in toto, but sustained to that extent.[29]   The constitutional and unconstitutional provisions may even be contained in the same section, and yet be perfectly distinct and separable, so that the former may stand although the latter fall.[30] But when the parts of the statute are so mutually dependent and connected, as conditions, considerations, inducements, or compensations for each other, as to warrant a belief that the legislature intended them as a whole, and that if all could not be carried into effect, the legislature would not pass the residue independently, then, if some parts are unconstitutional, all the provisions which are thus dependent, conditional, or connected, must fall with them.[31]   To illustrate, the fact that a state statute, providing for the election of presidential electors, conflicts with the act of congress in that it fixes a different date for the electors to meet and

[28] Black, Const. Law, 62.

[29] Presser v. Illinois, 116 U. S. 252, 6 Sup. Ct. 580; Mobile & O. R. Co. v. State, 29 Ala. 573; State v. Exnicios, 33 La. Ann. 253; People v. Kenney, 96 N. Y. 294; Attorney General v. Amos, 60 Mich. 372, 27 N. W. 571; People v. Whiting, 64 Cal. 67, 28 Pac. 445; In re Assessment of Taxes (S. D.) 54 N. W. 818; In re Groff, 21 Neb. 647, 33 N. W. 426; Lyman v. Martin, 2 Utah, 136.

[30] Comm. v. Hitchings, 5 Gray, 482; Mayor, etc., of Hagerstown v. Dechert, 32 Md. 369; State v. Clarke, 54 Mo. 17.

[31] Warren v. Mayor, 2 Gray, 84; Campau v. Detroit, 14 Mich. 276; State v. Dousman, 28 Wis. 541; Slauson v. Racine. 13 Wis. 398; W. U. Tel. Co. v.

give their votes, does not vitiate the whole act.[32] Again, an act providing that cities of a certain class may incur bonded indebtedness to an amount not exceeding four per cent. of their assessed valuation, though it conflicts with a clause of the constitution providing that such cities may become indebted only three per cent. of the value of the taxable property therein, is void only to the extent of the repugnancy in fixing the amount at four instead of three per cent.[33] An act providing that every grand jury shall consist of twelve persons is not rendered invalid by the insertion therein of an unconstitutional provision that the assent of eight of that number shall be sufficient for the finding of an indictment.[34] But on the other hand, an act apportioning the state into senate and assembly districts, according to the number of inhabitants, is so closely connected as a whole that if the senate districts are based upon an absolutely unconstitutional enumeration, and to such an extent that it can be judicially seen that great injustice to many of the inhabitants of the state is the necessary result, the assembly districts cannot be separated from the senate districts, but the whole act is void.[35]

The constitutions of many of the states provide that the subject of every statute shall be expressed in its title. Where this is the case, if a statute embraces several distinct subjects, some of which are included in the title and others not, it does not necessarily follow that the act is void in toto. If possible, those portions which are unconstitutional, because not expressed in the title, will be separated from the rest, and the valid portions of the act sustained. But in order to justify the courts in thus dealing with a statute, it is necessary that the remaining portions of the act, after the matters not indicated by the title shall have been pruned away, be sufficient

State, 62 Tex. 630; Eckhart v. State, 5 W. Va. 515; Willard v. People, 5 Ill. 461; Comm. v. Potts, 79 Pa. St. 164; Baker v. Braman, 6 Hill (N. Y.) 47; State v. Comm'rs of Perry Co., 5 Ohio St. 497; Brooks v. Hydorn, 76 Mich. 273, 42 N. W. 1122; Ex parte Jones, 49 Ark. 110, 4 S. W. 639; Wadsworth v. Union Pac. Ry. Co., 18 Colo. 600, 33 Pac. 515.

[32] McPherson v. Blacker, 146 U. S. 1, 13 Sup. Ct. 3.

[33] Dunn v. City of Great Falls, 13 Mont. 58, 31 Pac. 1017.

[34] English v. State, 31 Fla. 356, 12 South. 689.

[35] People v. Rice, 135 N. Y. 473, 31 N. E. 921.

in themselves to constitute a complete, intelligible, and sensible law, and one capable of being executed, and that they should be so independent of the rejected portions that it may fairly be presumed that the legislature would have enacted the restricted statute by itself, without making the rejected portions a condition to the passage of the whole act.[36]

PRESUMPTION AGAINST INCONSISTENCY.

44. The mind of the legislature is presumed to be consistent; and in case of a doubtful or ambiguous expression of its will, such a construction should be adopted as will make all the provisions of the statute consistent with each other and with the preexisting body of the law.

"An author must be supposed to be consistent with himself; and therefore, if, in one place, he has expressed his mind clearly, it ought to be presumed that he is still of the same mind in another place, unless it clearly appears that he has changed. In this respect, the work of the legislature is treated in the same manner as that of any other author." [37]   Thus, for example, where one statute made it the duty of a certain officer to prosecute for certain offenses, and provided that for neglect of such duty he might be removed, and another statute provided that he should prosecute such offenders as he might be requested to, and for default he should be removed, it was held that these two laws might be so construed, and should be so construed, as to avoid any inconsistency between them.[38]   And where two statutes were passed on the same day, one providing for the more convenient giving of certain affidavits, and to go into effect immediately, and the other apparently dispensing with the most of them, but to go into effect at a future day, it was held that they were not inconsistent, and that full effect might be

---

[36] Black, Const. Law, 288; People v. Briggs, 50 N. Y. 553; Bradley v. State, 99 Ala. 177, 13 South. 415; Powell v. State, 69 Ala. 10; Lowndes Co. v. Hunter, 49 Ala. 507; Muldoon v. Levi, 25 Neb. 457, 41 N. W. 280; Trumble v. Trumble, 37 Neb. 340, 55 N. W. 869.

[37] Maxwell, Interp. (2d edn.) 186.

[38] Shaw v. Mayor, etc., of Macon, 21 Ga. 280.

given to the apparent meaning of the latter, without imputing foolishness to the legislature.[39]

PRESUMPTION AGAINST IMPOSSIBILITY.

45. A statute is never to be understood as requiring an impossibility, if such a result can be avoided by any fair and reasonable construction.

It is an ancient and well-known maxim of the law that "lex non cogit ad impossibilia;"[40] or, as it is elsewhere expressed, "lex non intendit aliquid impossible."[41] And these maxims are declared to be applicable in the construction of statutes.[42] "The law itself," said an English court, "and the administration of it, must yield to that to which everything must bend,—to necessity. The law, in its most positive and peremptory injunctions, is understood to disclaim, as it does in its general aphorisms, all intention of compelling them to impossibilities; and the administration of law must adopt that general exception in the consideration of all particular cases."[43] "The law is not so unreasonable as to require the performance of impossibilities as a condition to the assertion of acknowledged rights; and when legislatures use language so broad as apparently to lead to such results, the courts must say, as they have always said, that the legislature cannot have intended to include those cases in which, by the act of God, a literal obedience to their mandate has become impossible."[44] Hence if a statute apparently requires the performance of things which cannot be performed, or apparently bases its commands upon the assumption of an impossible state of affairs, the courts must seek for some interpretation of its terms, not too strained or fantastic, which will avoid these results. But yet they are not at liberty to reconstruct the statute, or to import into it, on merely conjectural grounds, a meaning which its terms will not warrant. If the legislature does direct or

[39] Fouke v. Fleming, 13 Md. 392.
[40] Broom, Max. 242.
[41] 12 Coke, 89a.
[42] Potter v. Douglas County, 87 Mo. 239.
[43] The Generous, 2 Dods. Adm. 322.
[44] People v. Admire, 39 Ill. 251.

require an impossibility, in language too plain to be mistaken or to be explained away, the act will simply be rendered inoperative thereby, and it becomes the duty of the courts to pronounce accordingly. For instance, a statute of Texas directed that appeals from interlocutory judgments should be regulated by the law regulating appeals from final judgments, so far as the same might be applicable thereto. But the law governing appeals from final judgments was not at all capable of being applied to appeals from interlocutory determinations. And it was held that the act was inoperative and void.[45]

PRESUMPTION AGAINST INJUSTICE.

46. It is presumed that the legislature never intends to do injustice. If a statute is doubtful or ambiguous, or fairly open to more than one construction, that construction should be adopted which will avoid this result.

"In construing statutes, it is not reasonable to presume that the legislature intended to violate a settled principle of natural justice or to destroy a vested right to property. Courts, therefore, in construing statutes, will always endeavor to give such an interpretation to the language used as to make it consistent with reason and justice."[46] For example, to quote from a decision in Missouri, "although the constitution may not require notice to be given of the taking of private property for public use, yet when the legislature prescribes a mode by which private property may be taken for such purpose, we will, out of respect to it, suppose that it did not contemplate a violation of that great rule, recognized and enforced in all civil governments, that no one shall be injuriously affected in his rights by a judgment or decree resulting from a proceeding of which he had no notice and against which he could make no defense."[47] Again, if, in a statute, a clause creating a new offense and inflicting a penalty is so defectively drawn that in one part it appears that it shall be executed summarily, and in another, in the

---

[45] Ward v. Ward, 37 Tex. 389.

[46] Varick v. Briggs, 6 Paige, 323; Plumstead Board of Works v. Spackman, L. R. 13 Q. B. Div. 878; Ham v. McClaws, 1 Bay, 93.

[47] City of Boonville v. Ormrod's Adm'r, 26 Mo. 193.

usual way, the latter is to be preferred.[48]   The same principle governed the decision of a case in Alabama, where the statute to be construed provided that the widow and minor children of any deceased husband or father, who had had set aside to them a homestead of the property of the decedent, should not be held to have forfeited the same to the claims of heirs or creditors by a removal therefrom, so long as such widow and minor children should continue to reside in the state, and that the provisions of the act should apply to homesteads theretofore set apart as fully as to those set apart thereafter.   It was held that the statute did not apply where the homestead had been abandoned prior to the act, since by such abandonment the title vested in the heirs, subject to the rights of creditors, and the legislature had no power to divest such title.[49] Again, a construction will not be adopted which would disfranchise a considerable number of voters, or deprive a county of representation in the legislature, unless such construction is rendered necessary by the express and unequivocal language of the law.[50]   And "on the general principle of avoiding injustice and absurdity, any construction should be rejected, if escape from it were possible, which enabled a person to defeat or impair the obligation of his contract by his own act, or otherwise to profit by his own wrong." [51] For example, a statute relating to corporations required an annual report to be made by every company organized under its provisions, and provided that, in case of failure to make such report, the trustees should be jointly and severally liable "for all the debts of the company then existing and for all that shall be contracted before such report shall be made."   This language was broad enough to include debts due from the corporation to individual trustees.   But it was held that "the fundamental rule, which lies at the very foundation of all law, that no person, by his own transgression, can create a cause of action in his own favor against another, must be applied to trustees of these corporations," and that debts of that nature were not within the provisions of the statute.[52]

---

[48] Bennett v. Ward, 3 Caines, 259.
[49] Banks v. Speers, 97 Ala. 560, 11 South. 841.
[50] State v. Van Camp, 36 Neb. 9, 91, 54 N. W. 113.
[51] Maxwell, Interp. (2d edn.) 249.
[52] Briggs v. Easterly, 62 Barb. 51.

But "it is to be borne in mind that the injustice and hardship which the legislature is presumed not to intend is not merely such as may occur in individual and exceptional cases only. Laws are made 'ad ea quæ frequentius accidunt;' and individual hardship not infrequently results from enactments of general advantage." [53] Moreover, it is only when the construction is doubtful that the argument from injustice or failure of justice is of force. The presumption that the legislature intends to deal justly is, in a sense, rebuttable; and it is of no value whatever when the language of the act is clear and explicit. In that case, it is the duty of the court to take the statute as it finds it, and if injustice results, it is the legislature which must give a remedy, not the judicial tribunals. [54] Of course, if the injustice took the form of a violation of any rights secured by constitutional guaranties, the question of the validity of the statute would arise; but that is not a question of interpretation.

PRESUMPTION AGAINST INCONVENIENCE.

47. It is presumed that the legislature never intends its enactments to work public inconvenience or private hardship; and if a statute is doubtful or ambiguous, or fairly open to more than one construction, that construction should be adopted which will avoid such results.

It is always to be presumed that the legislature intends the most reasonable and beneficial construction of its enactments, when their design is obscure or not explicitly expressed, and such as will avoid inconvenience, hardship, or public injuries. [55] Hence if a law is couched in doubtful or ambiguous phrases, or if its terms are such as to be fairly susceptible of two or more constructions, the courts, having this presumption in mind, will attach weight to arguments drawn from the inconvenient results which would follow from putting one of such constructions upon the statute, and will

---

[53] Maxwell, Interp. (2d edn.) 247.
[54] Pitman v. Flint, 10 Pick. 504.
[55] Richards v. Daggett, 4 Mass. 534; Somerset v. Dighton, 12 Mass. 383; Gibson v. Jenney, 15 Mass. 205.

therefore adopt the other.[56]   "While it is quite true that where the language of a statute is plain and admits of but one construction, the courts have no power to supply any real or supposed defects in such statute, in order to avoid inconvenience or injustice, inasmuch as that is exclusively within the domain of the legislative department, yet, where the terms of the statute are not plain, but admit of more than one construction, one of which leads to great inconvenience and injustice, and possibly to the defeat or obstruction of the legislative intent, then the court may, with a view to avoid such results, adopt some other construction more in accordance with the legislative intent."[57]   "If words are ambiguous, and one construction leads to enormous inconvenience, and another construction does not, the one which leads to the least inconvenience is to be preferred."[58]   Thus, if it is apparent that, by a particular construction of a statute in a doubtful case, great public interests would be endangered or sacrificed, it ought not to be presumed that such construction was intended by the legislature.[59]   This would be the case, for instance, where one proposed interpretation would prevent the state from exercising the power of eminent domain over lands pending the administration of the estate of their deceased owner.[60]

But if there is no doubt, obscurity, or ambiguity on the face of the law, but its meaning is plain and explicit, the argument from inconvenience has no place.[61]   "It may be proper, in giving a construction to a statute, to look to the effects and consequences when its provisions are ambiguous, or the legislative intent is doubtful. But when the law is clear and explicit, and its provisions are susceptible of but one interpretation, its consequences, if evil, can be avoided only by a change of the law itself, to be effected by legis-

---

[56] Langdon v. Potter, 3 Mass. 215; Gore v. Brazier, Id. 523; Ayers v. Knox, 7 Mass. 306; Rogers v. Goodwin, 2 Mass. 475; Associates of Jersey Co. v. Davison, 29 N. J. Law, 415; Smith v. People, 47 N. Y. 330; U. S. v. Fisher, 2 Cranch, 358; King v. Beeston, 3 Durn. & E. 592.

[57] Carolina Sav. Bank v. Evans, 28 S. Car. 521, 6 S. E. 321.

[58] Reid v. Reid, L. R. 31 Ch. Div. 402.

[59] People v. Board of Comm'rs of Ill. & Mich. Canal, 4 Ill. 153.

[60] Kane v. Kansas City, F. S. & M. Ry. Co., 112 Mo. 34, 20 S. W. 532.

[61] In re Alma Spinning Co., L. R. 16 Ch. Div. 681; Queen v. Overseers of Tonbridge Parish, L. R. 13 Q. B. Div. 339; U. S. v. Fisher, 2 Cranch, 358.

lative and not judicial action." [62]   To give a single illustration of this branch of the rule,—where a statute gives to a husband the power, by his last will, to extinguish the common-law rights of his widow, unless she thinks proper to renounce the will, and if she desires to defeat the testator's provisions it is required of her to do so by an express dissent, and where the language of the act is not ambiguous, and is sufficiently comprehensive to include every widow, whether sane or insane, and the act makes no exception in favor of the latter, the courts cannot make any such exception, from considerations of the hardship and inconvenience which may result. [63]

PRESUMPTION AGAINST ABSURDITY.

48. It is presumed that the legislature does not intend an absurdity, or that absurd consequences shall flow from its enactments. Such a result will therefore be avoided, if the terms of the act admit of it, by a reasonable construction of the statute. [64]

By an "absurdity," as the term is here used, is meant anything which is so irrational, unnatural, or inconvenient that it cannot be supposed to have been within the intention of men of ordinary intelligence and discretion. The presumption against absurd consequences of legislation is therefore no more than the presumption that the legislators are gifted with ordinary good sense. It is applicable, like all the other presumptions which we are considering, only where there is room for construction by reason of the obscurity or ambiguity of the law. For example, where the act relates to the boundary between counties, and its terms, if taken literally, would have the effect of attaching to one county a tract of land which is entirely separated from that county by an intervening space of several miles, it cannot be supposed that this was intended by the

[62] Bosley v. Mattingly, 14 B. Mon. 89.

[63] Collins v. Carman, 5 Md. 503.

[64] Oates v. National Bank, 100 U. S. 239; State v. Clark, 29 N. J. Law, 96; Henry v. Tilson, 17 Vt. 479; Gilkey v. Cook, 60 Wis. 133, 18 N. W. 639; Mayor of Jeffersonville v. Weems, 5 Ind. 547; Foley v. Bourg, 10 La. Ann. 129. "Lex semper intendit quod convenit rationi." Co. Litt. 78b.

legislature, and a more reasonable construction will be put upon the act if its terms will warrant it.[65]   Again, a statute of Massachusetts forbade any person to disinter a human body, "not being authorized by the selectmen of any town in this commonwealth."   In a prosecution under this act, it was held sufficient for the indictment to aver that the defendant was not authorized by the selectmen of the town where the body had been buried.   The statute was thus construed to avoid an absurd and inconvenient result.   For, said the court, as oral testimony can alone be admitted on criminal trials, where the facts are provable by witnesses, the consequence of a different construction would be "that the officers of every town, to the number of 300 or 400, must be summoned and give their personal attenuance in the court where the prosecution is pending. We hazard nothing in saying that the legislature never intended such an absurdity."[66]   So again, a requirement in an act relating to a turnpike road that the "width" of the macadam shall not be less than 8 inches, nor more than 15 inches, will be construed as a requirement that the "depth" of the macadam shall be as specified, as a literal interpretation would lead to an absurdity.[67]

But it must be observed that if the legislature will enact an absurdity in clear and specific terms, the courts are not at liberty to divert the statute from its intended object by any process of construction.   If the absurdity is an impossibility, the act will be inoperative; otherwise, it must be executed exactly as it stands.   It has been said by Jervis, C. J.:   "If the precise words used are plain and unambiguous, in our judgment we are bound to construe them in their ordinary sense, even though it should lead, in our view of the case, to an absurdity or manifest injustice.   Words may be modified or varied when their import is doubtful or obscure; but we assume the functions of legislators when we depart from the ordinary meaning of the precise words used, merely because we see, or fancy we see, an absurdity or manifest injustice from an adherence to their literal meaning."[68]

---

[65] Perry County v. Jefferson County, 94 Ill. 214.

[66] Comm. v. Loring, 8 Pick. 370.

[67] Bird v. Board of Comm'rs of Kenton County (Ky.) 24 S. W. 118.

[68] Abley v. Dale, 20 L. J. C. P. (N. S.) 233. And see Woodward v. Watts, 2 El. & Bl. 452.

PRESUMPTION AGAINST INEFFECTIVENESS.

49. It is presumed that the legislature intends to impart to its enactments such a meaning as will render them operative and effective, and to prevent persons from eluding or defeating them. Accordingly, in case of any doubt or obscurity, the construction will be such as to carry out these objects.

In construing a statute, of whatever class it may be, an interpretation must never be adopted which will defeat the very purpose of the act, if it will admit of any other reasonable construction; for "interpretatio fienda est ut res magis valeat quam pereat." [69] And on the same principle, the construction should not be such as will enable persons to elude the provisions of the law, or escape its consequences, or defeat the objects for which it was ordained, if this can be avoided.[70] For example, where a literal construction of certain words in an act imposing a tax on dividends of a corporation would place it in the power of the directors of the corporation to declare dividends in such a manner as to escape all taxation, such construction will not be adopted, if the act is reasonably susceptible of another construction whereby a revenue is secured.[71]

But yet, if the act is expressed in plain terms without ambiguity, the construction indicated by the face of it is not to be rejected merely because it may render it possible for persons to practice frauds upon the act; such consequences are never to be presumed; and no presumption against the existence or grant of a power can be drawn from the fact that it may possibly be abused.[72] As remarked by the court in New York, in a case where this principle was involved: "It is said that this renders the statute inoperative, and that this result must be avoided. This is a plausible but not a valid or sound position. There is nothing in the constitution, or in any legal principle, to prevent the legislature from passing an

[69] The Emily and The Caroline, 9 Wheat. 381; Simmons v. California Powder Works, 7 Colo. 285, 3 Pac. 420.

[70] Thompson v. State, 20 Ala. 54.

[71] City of Philadelphia v. Ridge Ave. Pass. Ry. Co., 102 Pa. St. 190.

[72] Opinion of the Justices, 22 Pick. 571.

act with provisions which render it inoperative. When different constructions may be put upon an act, one of which will accomplish the purpose of the legislature, and the other render the act nugatory, the former should be adopted; but when the provisions of the act are such that to make it operative would violate the declared meaning of the legislature, courts should be astute in construing it inoperative." [73] To the same effect is a saying of Lord Tenterden, in a case often referred to in this connection. "Our decision," said this learned judge, "may in this particular case operate to defeat the object of the act, but it is better to abide by this consequence than to put upon it a construction not warranted by the words of the act, in order to give effect to what we may suppose to have been the intention of the legislature." [74]

PRESUMPTION AS TO PUBLIC POLICY.

50. It is presumed that the legislature intends its enactments to accord with the principles of sound public policy and the interests of public morality, not to violate them; and due weight should be given to this presumption in the construction of a doubtful or ambiguous statute.

It must always be supposed that the legislative body designs to favor and foster, rather than to contravene, that public policy which is based upon the principles of natural justice, good morals, and the settled wisdom of the law as applied to the ordinary affairs of life. Consequently, if the statute is so worded as to admit of more than one interpretation, that construction should be put upon it which will carry out this presumed intent. [75] For example, a statute should not be so construed, if it can reasonably be avoided, as to authorize or permit a man to be a judge in his own cause, or to determine his right to an office of profit or trust. [76] As it has been

---

[73] Farmers' Bank v. Hale, 59 N. Y. 53.

[74] King v. Barham, 8 Barn. & C. 99.

[75] Aicardi v. State, 19 Wall. 635.

[76] Comm. v. McCloskey, 2 Rawle, 369; Day v. Savadge, Hob. 85; Queen v. Owens, 2 El. & El. 86. But although it is contrary to the general rules of law to make a person a judge in his own cause, it has been intimated that

said by the supreme court of Massachusetts, the language of a statute is to be taken in its natural import, "unless the intention resulting from the ordinary import of the words be repugnant to sound,
acknowledged principles of national policy.[77] And if that intention be repugnant to such principles of national policy, then the
import of the words ought to be enlarged or restrained so that it
may comport with those principles, unless the intention of the legislature be clearly and manifestly repugnant to them. For although
it is not to be presumed that the legislature will violate principles
of public policy, yet an intention of the legislature repugnant to
those principles, clearly, manifestly, and constitutionally expressed,
must have the force of law." [78] In an important case before the
supreme court of the United States, that tribunal declared that it
was historically true that the American people are a religious people, as shown by the religious objects expressed by the original
grants and charters of the colonies, and the recognition of religion
in the most solemn acts of their history, as well as in the constitutions of the states and of the nation; and therefore the courts, in
construing statutes, should not impute to any legislature a purpose
of action against or in derogation of religion.[79]

But it should be remembered that considerations of public policy
are not to be taken into account in determining the validity of a
statute, but only in its construction. If it does not violate any provision of the constitution, it cannot be declared void merely because
it contravenes some rule or principle of public policy. But if the
statute is ascertained or admitted to be constitutionally valid, then
the question of interpretation may arise, and in the solution of this
question it is permissible to consider its effect with reference to
the settled principles of public policy.[80]

---

the legislature, in a proper case, might depart from this rule, and in that event
it would be the duty of the courts to sustain the enactment. But an intention of the legislature to bring about such a result should not be inferred except from very clear and explicit provisions. Mersey Docks Trustees v.
Gibbs, L. R. 1 H. L. 93, 110.

[77] The context shows that the "public policy" of the state is here meant,
and not that of the nation in the wider sense.

[78] Opinion of the Justices, 7 Mass. 523.

[79] Rector, etc., of Holy Trinity Church v. U. S., 143 U. S. 457, 12 Sup. Ct. 511.

[80] Baxter v. Tripp, 12 R. I. 310.

PRESUMPTION AGAINST IRREPEALABLE LAWS.

51. It is always to be presumed, in case of doubt or ambiguity, that the legislature does not intend to derogate from the authority of its successors, to make irrepealable laws, or to divest the state of any portion of its sovereign powers.

"Acts of parliament derogatory from the power of subsequent parliaments bind not." [81] This maxim is not capable in all cases of being applied to the acts of congress or of the state legislatures; but there is, in this country, a presumption that no legislative body intends to fetter the hands of its successors by the enactment of laws which cannot be repealed or modified by them. In a case in Wisconsin, it appeared that a charter of a city declared that none of its provisions should be considered as repealed by any general law contravening them, unless the purpose to repeal them should be expressly set forth in such law. It was held, nevertheless, that the charter might be repealed by implication by a general law; for, it was said, one legislature cannot, by such a provision, bind a future legislature to a particular mode of repeal. [82]

This rule finds its most important application in those cases where it is claimed that a statute or charter involves the surrender, to an individual or corporation, of some portion of the sovereign power of the state, in such a manner as to be irrevocable by any future legislature; as, for instance, where it is alleged that there has been a grant of exemption from taxation, made in such a shape as to constitute a contract, and therefore to be beyond the reach of subsequent legislation, or a grant, similarly made, of a monopoly or exclusive franchise. In these cases the legal doctrine is clear and well settled. It will never be presumed that the legislature intends to make such an irrevocable contract. On the contrary, the presumption is always against such an intention. All doubts will be resolved in favor of the state. No such irrepealable grant can

---

[81] 1 Bl. Comm. 90.
[82] Kellogg v. City of Oshkosh, 14 Wis. 623.

be sustained except upon the clearest and plainest terms, unequivocally manifesting the legislative intention claimed.[83]

PRESUMPTION AGAINST UNNECESSARY CHANGE OF LAWS.

52. It is presumed that the legislature does not intend to make unnecessary changes in the pre-existing body of law. The construction of a statute will therefore be such as to avoid any change in the prior laws beyond what is necessary to effect the specific purpose of the act in question.[84]

"The intention of the legislature in enacting a particular statute is not to be ascertained by interpreting the statute by itself alone, and according to the mere literal meaning of its words. Every statute must be construed in connection with the whole system of which it forms a part, and in the light of the common law and of previous statutes upon the same subject. And the legislature is not to be lightly presumed to have intended to reverse the policy of its predecessors or to introduce a fundamental change in long-established principles of law."[85] Thus, for example, a statute authorizing married women to hold, convey, and devise real property the same as if

[83] Gilman v. City of Sheboygan, 2 Black (U. S.) 510; Providence Bank v. Billings, 4 Pet. 514; Delaware Railroad Tax, 18 Wall. 206; Pennsylvania R. Co. v. Canal Comm'rs, 21 Pa. St. 9; Detroit v. Detroit & H. P. R. Co., 43 Mich. 140, 5 N. W. 275; Probasco v. Town of Moundsville, 11 W. Va. 501; Bennett v. McWhorter, 2 W. Va. 441; Mayor, etc., of Mobile v. Stein, 54 Ala. 23.

[84] Manuel v. Manuel, 13 Ohio St. 458; Bear's Adm'r v. Bear, 33 Pa. St. 525; Thompson v. Mylne, 4 La. Ann. 206; Childers v. Johnson, 6 La. Ann. 634. "One of these presumptions is that the legislature does not intend to make any change in the law beyond what it explicitly declares, either in express terms or by unmistakable implication, or, in other words, beyond the immediate scope and object of the statute. In all general matters beyond, the law remains undisturbed. It is in the last degree improbable that the legislature would overthrow fundamental principles, infringe rights, or depart from the general system of law, without expressing its intention with irresistible clearness; and to give any such effect to general words, simply because, in their widest and perhaps natural sense, they have that meaning, would be to give them a meaning in which they are not really used." Maxwell, Interp. (2d edn.) 96.

[85] Robinson's Case, 131 Mass. 376.

sole, will not empower a married woman to convey to her husband, by deed, her dower rights in his real estate. The supreme court of New York, in making this decision, said that the legislature could not have intended "so violent an innovation upon the existing law;" the safer and more reasonable construction would restrict the right of a married woman to convey to persons other than her husband.[86] So it is held that an act containing no negative words, and providing that all former deeds shall have a certain effect if such and such requisites are observed, does not prevent the deeds from being used as evidence in the same manner as they might have been used before the act was passed.[87]   And where a corporation, incorporated as a road and bridge company, was permitted, by a subsequent act of the legislature, to form itself into two distinct companies, one designated a turnpike company, and the other a bridge company, it was held that it did not exonerate the officers of the road company from the penalties imposed by the original act, it being manifest that the legislature did not intend to relieve them from their liabilities.[88]   So again, a California act in relation to the taking of lands by water companies provided that the proceedings should be conducted as prescribed for railroad companies under the act of 1853. The railroad act was repealed by a subsequent law passed in 1861. It was held that proceedings for the taking of land by water companies were not affected by the change.[89]

[86] Graham v. Van Wyck, 14 Barb. 531.
[87] Jackson v. Bradt, 2 Caines, 169.
[88] Kane v. People, 8 Wend. 203.
[89] Spring Valley Water Works v. San Francisco, 22 Cal. 434.

PRESUMPTION AGAINST IMPLIED REPEAL OF LAWS.

53. Repeals by implication are not favored. A statute will not be construed as repealing prior acts on the same subject (in the absence of express words to that effect) unless there is an irreconcilable repugnancy between them, or unless the new law is evidently intended to supersede all prior acts on the matter in hand and to comprise in itself the sole and complete system of legislation on that subject.

The presumption being, as just stated, against any intention to make unnecessary changes in the laws, it follows that there is also a presumption against repeals by implication. Every new statute should be construed in connection with those already existing in relation to the same subject-matter, and all should be made to harmonize and stand together, if that can be done by any fair and reasonable interpretation, and if the new act does not expressly declare the repeal of an earlier statute, it will not be construed as effecting such repeal unless there is such a repugnancy or conflict between the provisions of the two acts as to show that they could not have been designed to remain equally in force.[90] "Repeals by

[90] Robbins v. State, 8 Ohio St. 131, 191; Casey v. Harned, 5 Iowa, 1; Selman v. Wolfe, 27 Tex. 68; Morris v. Delaware & S. Canal, 4 Watts & S. 461; Crouch v. Hayes, 98 N. Y. 183; Peyton v. Moseley, 3 T. B. Mon. 77; Barringer v. City Council of Florence (S. Car.) 19 S. E. 745. "It is a rule founded in reason as well as in abundant authority, that in order to give an act not covering the entire ground of an earlier one, nor clearly intended as a substitute for it, the effect of repealing it, the implication of an intention to repeal must necessarily flow from the language used, disclosing a repugnancy between its provisions and those of the earlier law so positive as to be irreconcilable by any fair, strict, or liberal construction of it, which would, without destroying its evident intent and meaning, find for it a reasonable field of operation, preserving at the same time the force of the earlier law, and construing both together in harmony with the whole course of legislation upon the subject." Endlich, Interp. § 210. "A revenue law, like any other statute, may be repealed by implication. But there is always a presumption, more or less strong according to circumstances, that a statute is not intended to repeal a prior statute on the same subject, unless it does so in express terms. Without a repealing clause, the two may stand and have effect together, unless they are

implication," says the court in Maryland, "are things disfavored by law, and never allowed but when the inconsistency and repugnancy are plain and unavoidable; and if laws and statutes seem contrary to one another, yet if, by interpretation, they may stand together, they shall stand; and when two laws only so far disagree or differ as that by any other construction they may both stand together, the rule that 'leges posteriores priores contrarias abrogant' does not apply, and the latter is no repeal of the former."[91] "Where a new act is couched in general affirmative language, and the previous law can well stand with it, and if the language used in the later act is all in the affirmative, there is nothing to say that the previous law shall be repealed, and therefore the old and the new laws may stand together. There the general affirmative words of the new law would not of themselves repeal the old."[92] For instance, it is a well settled rule of construction, applicable to all remedial laws, that where a new remedy or mode of proceeding is authorized, without an express repeal of a former one relating to the same matter, it is to be regarded as merely cumulative, creating a concurrent remedy, and not as abrogating the former mode of procedure.[93] Thus, if a statute provides that appeals from the judgments of the county courts in certain cases "may" be taken to the supreme court, it is not to be construed as imperative, and therefore it does not repeal by implication the provisions of an earlier statute which gave an appeal in such cases to the circuit courts.[94] And "even if a subsequent statute, taken strictly and grammatically, is contrariant to a previous statute, yet if, at the same time, the intention of the legislature is apparent that the previous statute should not be repealed, it has been in several cases held that the previous statute is to remain unaffected by the subsequent one."[95]

But if the two acts are positively repugnant, and to such an extent

---

inconsistent; and in that case, to the extent of the inconsistency, the later will repeal the earlier; but even then the two must be given effect so far as practicable." Cooley, Taxn. 294.

[91] Mayor, etc., of Cumberland v. Magruder, 34 Md. 381. And see McAfee v. Southern R. Co., 36 Miss. 669.

[92] Hardcastle, Stat. Law (2d edn.) 346.

[93] Raudebaugh v. Shelley, 6 Ohio St. 307.

[94] Fowler v. Pirkins, 77 Ill. 271.

[95] Hardcastle, Stat. Law (2d edn.) 356.

that they cannot be reconciled and made to stand together by any fair and reasonable construction, then the one last passed will control and will repeal the earlier law.[96] In this case, the rule is, "Leges posteriores priores contrarias abrogant."[97] "If two inconsistent acts be passed at different times, the last is to be obeyed, and if obedience cannot be observed without derogating from the first, it is the first which must give way. Every act of parliament must be considered with reference to the state of the law subsisting when it came into operation and when it is to be applied; it cannot otherwise be rationally construed. Every act is made either for the purpose of making a change in the law, or for the purpose of better declaring the law, and its operation is not to be impeded by the mere fact that it is inconsistent with some previous enactment."[98] Thus, if the legislature grants the same power over a particular matter to two public bodies (as, to the trustees of a public canal and also to a city) and the grants are repugnant, so that the concurrent exercise of the power by the two bodies is impossible, the last expressed will of the legislature must control.[99] Again, acts which, although in pari materia, grant a right conditioned on different things, are inconsistent, and by reason of this inconsistency the later will repeal the earlier.[100] So, where there are two statutes imposing a penalty for the same offense, and the penalty imposed by the one is not the same as that imposed by the other, the later statute repeals the earlier; for the intention to inflict two punishments for the same offense is not to be imputed to the legislature.[101] And again, if a subsequent statute requires the same and more than a former statute prescribed, this is a repeal of the earlier law, so far as the subsequent statute renders more necessary than the first required.[102]

[96] State v. Miskimmons, 2 Ind. 440; Swinney v. Ft. Wayne, M. & C. R. Co., 59 Ind. 205; Comm'rs of Highways v. Deboe, 43 Ill. App. 25; Branagan v. Dulaney, 8 Colo. 408, 8 Pac. 669; Branham v. Long, 78 Va. 352; Pease v. Whitney, 5 Mass. 380.

[97] Broom, Max. 27.

[98] Dean and Chapter of Ely v. Bliss, 5 Beav. 574.

[99] Korah v. City of Ottawa, 32 Ill. 121.

[100] Gwinner v. Lehigh & D. G. R. Co., 55 Pa. St. 126.

[101] Gorman v. Hammond, 28 Ga. 85.

[102] Gorham v. Luckett, 6 B. Mon. 146.

If one statute enacts something in general terms, and afterwards another statute is passed on the same subject, which, although expressed in affirmative language, introduces special conditions or restrictions, the subsequent statute will usually be considered as repealing by implication the former; for "affirmative statutes introductive of a new law do imply a negative."[103] More especially when the later act is expressed in negative terms, as where, for example, it prohibits a certain thing from being done, or where it declares that a given act shall be performed in a certain manner "and not otherwise," it is usually impossible to escape the conclusion that earlier acts are repealed by it. And if the co-existence of the two sets of provisions would be destructive of the object for which the later act was passed, it is clear that there must be an implied repeal. A provision in a general law may be repealed, pro tanto, by a provision in a charter of a municipal corporation, granted after the enactment of the law; and such repeal will be held to have been intended where the two provisions are in direct conflict, or where the intention of the legislature to that effect is plainly expressed.[104] "Not only statutes passed at different sessions of the legislature may thus affect each other, but a repeal by implication has been effected where two inconsistent enactments have been passed at the same session, even while the earlier act was in its progress to become a law, but before it had become so by the executive approval; it being said that the parliamentary rule that an act shall not be repealed at the session at which it was passed has no reference to repeal by implication."[105]

Where it is necessary to hold an earlier statute impliedly repealed by a later one, on account of the repugnancy between them, the extent of the repeal will be measured by the extent of the necessary conflict or inconsistency between them; and if there are any parts or provisions of the earlier law which may stand as unaffected by the later act, they will not be held repealed thereby.[106]

[103] Hardcastle, Stat. Law (2d edn.) 353. And see Isham v. Bennington Iron Co., 19 Vt. 230.

[104] Tierney v. Dodge, 9 Minn. 166 (Gil. 153).

[105] Endlich, Interp. § 188, citing Southwark Bank v. Comm., 26 Pa. St. 446; Spencer v. State, 5 Ind. 41. And see Heilig v. City Council of Puyallup, 7 Wash. 29, 34 Pac. 164; Planters' Bank v. Black, 11 Smed. & Mar. 43.

[106] State v. Grady, 34 Conn. 118; Wood v. U. S., 16 Pet. 342; Putnam v. Ruch, 54 Fed. 216.

Even where there is no direct repugnancy or inconsistency between the earlier and the later law, there may in some cases be an implied repeal. This result follows where the later act revises, amends, and sums up the whole law on the particular subject to which it relates, covering all the ground treated of in the earlier statute, and adding new or different provisions, and thus plainly shows that it was intended to supersede any and all prior enactments on that subject-matter, and to furnish, for the future, in itself alone, the whole and only system of statute law applicable to that subject.[107] "Every statute," says the court in New Jersey, "must be considered according to what appears to have been the intention of the legislature, and even though two statutes relating to the same subject be not, in terms, repugnant or inconsistent, if the later statute is clearly intended to prescribe the only rule which should govern the case provided for, it will be construed as repealing the original act. The rule does not rest strictly upon the ground of repeal by implication, but upon the principle that when the legislature makes a revision of a particular statute, and frames a new statute upon the subject-matter, and from the framework of the act it is apparent that the legislature designed a complete scheme for this matter, it is a legislative declaration that whatever is embraced in the new law shall prevail, and whatever is excluded is discarded. It is decisive evidence of an intention to prescribe the provisions contained in the later act as the only ones on that subject which shall be obligatory."[108] Where a statute is revised, or one act framed from another, some parts being omitted, the parts omitted are not to be revived by construction, but are to be considered as annulled.[109]

General and Special Statutes.

As a corollary from the doctrine that implied repeals are not favored, it has come to be an established rule in the construction of statutes that a subsequent act, treating a subject in general terms,

[107] U. S. v. Tynen, 11 Wall. 88; Oleson v. Green Bay & L. P. Ry. Co., 36 Wis. 383; Fox v. Comm., 16 Gratt. 1. The common law is constructively repealed by a statute which revises the whole subject and is inconsistent with its continued operation. State v. Wilson, 43 N. H. 415.

[108] Roche v. Mayor, etc., of Jersey City, 40 N. J. Law, 257.

[109] Ellis v. Paige, 1 Pick. 43.

and not expressly contradicting the provisions of a prior special statute, is not to be considered as intended to affect the more particular and specific provisions of the earlier act, unless it is absolutely necessary so to construe it in order to give its words any meaning at all.[110] This rule is founded upon, or expressed by, the maxim "Generalia specialibus non derogant." Thus, when the provisions of a general law, applicable to the entire state, are repugnant to the provisions of a previously enacted special law, applicable in a particular locality only, the passage of such general law does not operate to modify or repeal the special law, either wholly or in part, unless such modification or repeal is provided for in express words, or arises by necessary implication.[111] "A local statute, enacted for a particular municipality, for reasons satisfactory to the legislature, is intended to be exceptional and for the benefit of such municipality. It has been said that it is against reason to suppose that the legislature, in framing a general system for the state, intended to repeal a special act which the local circumstances made necessary."[112] So, again, a special act exempting certain property from taxation is not to be considered as impliedly repealed by a subsequent general statute imposing taxes generally, although the

---

[110] Fosdick v. Perrysburg, 14 Ohio St. 472; Gage v. Currier, 4 Pick. 399; Maysville Turnpike Co. v. How, 14 B. Mon. 426; Waldo v. Bell, 13 La. Ann. 329; State v. Bishop, 41 Mo. 16; Brown v. County Comm'rs, 21 Pa. St. 37; Gregory's Case, 6 Coke, 19b. "The reason and philosophy of the rule is that when the mind of the legislator has been turned to the details of a subject, and he has acted upon it, a subsequent statute in general terms, or treating the subject in a general manner, and not expressly contradicting the original act, shall not be considered as intended to affect the more particular or positive previous provisions, unless it is absolutely necessary to give the latter act such a construction, in order that its words shall have any meaning at all." Sedgwick, Stat. Constr. 98. Where there are two acts or provisions, one of which is special and particular, and certainly includes the matter in question, and the other general, which, if standing alone, would include the same matter, and thus conflict with the special act or provision, the special act must be taken as intended to constitute an exception to the general act, as the legislature is not to be presumed to have intended a conflict. Crane v. Reeder, 22 Mich. 322.

[111] State v. Mills, 34 N. J. Law, 177.

[112] Malloy v. Reinhard, 115 Pa. St. 25, 7 Atl. 790, citing Brown v. County Comm'rs, 21 Pa. St. 37. And see Wood v. Board of Election Comm'rs, 58 Cal. 561; Burke v. Jeffries, 20 Iowa, 145.

language of the later act is broad enough to cover the property exempted by the previous law.[113]   Where an act incorporating a turnpike company required the rates of tolls to be written on sign-boards in "large or capital letters," and a general act was afterwards passed, requiring the rates of toll on turnpike roads to be written in capital letters, it was held that the private act was not suspended or repealed by the general act.[114]   Even where two statutes are passed upon the same day, one of which relates to a particular class of cases, and the other is of a more general character, their provisions being repugnant, it is the former which must prevail as to the particular class of cases therein referred to.[115]

But "there is no rule of law which prohibits the repeal of a special act by a general one, nor is there any principle forbidding such repeal without the use of express words declarative of the legislative intent to repeal the earlier statute.   The question is always one of intention, and the purpose to abrogate the particular enactment by a later general enactment is sufficiently manifested when the provisions of both cannot stand together, and it is a cardinal doctrine in the construction of statutes that, if possible, full effect shall be given to all their parts."[116]   Hence a general statute will repeal prior special or local acts, without expressly naming them, where they are inconsistent with it, and where it can be seen from the whole enactment that it was the intention of the legislature to sweep away all local peculiarities, though sanctioned by special acts, and to establish one uniform system.[117]   For instance, where a clause in the charter of a private corporation is entirely inconsistent with a clause in a subsequent general statute relating to the same matter, it is repealed thereby.[118]

[113] Williams v. Pritchard, 4 Durn. & E. 2; Blain v. Bailey, 25 Ind. 165.

[114] Nichols v. Bertram, 3 Pick. 342.

[115] Mead v. Bagnall, 15 Wis. 156; St. Martin v. New Orleans, 14 La. Ann. 113.

[116] State v. Williamson, 44 N. J. Law, 165.

[117] Bramston v. Mayor of Colchester, 6 El. & Bl. 246.

[118] Great Central Gas Consumers' Co. v. Clarke, 13 C. B. (N. S.) 838; Water Comm'rs v. Conkling, 113 Ill. 340.

WHEN GOVERNMENT IS BOUND BY STATUTES.

54. General words in a statute do not include nor bind the government by whose authority the statute was enacted, where its sovereignty, rights, prerogatives, or interests are involved. It is bound only by being expressly named or by necessary implication from the terms and purpose of the act.

This is a very ancient rule of the English law, and is equally applicable to the national and state governments in this country. It is said that laws are supposed to be made for the subjects or citizens of the state, not for the sovereign power. Hence, if the government is not expressly referred to in a given statute, it is presumed that it was not intended to be affected thereby, and this presumption, in any case where the rights or interests of the state would be involved, can be overcome only by clear and irresistible implications from the statute itself.[119] Generally speaking, therefore, the state is not bound by the provisions of any statute, however generally it may be expressed, by which its sovereignty would be derogated from, or any of its prerogatives, rights, titles, or interests would be divested, save where the act is specifically made to extend to the state, or where the legislative intention in that regard is too plain to be mistaken.[120] For example, where a statute enacts that "costs shall follow the event of every action or petition, unless otherwise directed by law or by the court," no costs can be recovered against the state by a party prevailing against it in any civil action.[121] So also, a claim of the government against a private person is not affected by his discharge in bankruptcy, although the bankrupt law provides in general terms that the discharge shall release the bankrupt "from all debts, claims, liabilities, and demands," and that it may be pleaded "as a full and complete bar of any such debts,"

[119] Crooke's Case, 1 Shower, 208; Attorney General v. Donaldson, 10 Mees. & W. 117; U. S. v. Hewes, Crabbe, 307, Fed. Cas. No. 15,359; State v. Milburn, 9 Gill, 105; Cole v. White County, 32 Ark. 45.

[120] Magdalen College Case, 11 Coke, 66b; Perry v. Eames (1891) 1 Chanc. 658; Lambert v. Taylor, 4 Barn. & C. 138; State v. Kinne, 41 N. H. 238.

[121] State v. Kinne, 41 N. H. 238.

etc.[122] For the same reason, it is well settled that the provisions of a statute of limitations do not run against the state, as they do against a private suitor, unless the state is expressly named in the statute and its rights waived.[123] Neither is the state affected by tax laws unless expressly named; that is to say, statutes imposing taxation in general terms are not understood as authorizing the assessment of taxes upon the property of the state, real or personal, or of its municipal subdivisions.[124] On the same principle, a grant of power to a private corporation to take lands for its uses under the power of eminent domain will not be construed as authorizing it to appropriate property belonging to the state or a municipality, or such as is already held and used for another public purpose, unless such a construction is required by the very words of the grant or by necessary implication.[125]

But there are also some cases in which the sovereign will be bound by a statute without express words. In the early and leading case called the "Magdalen College Case,"[126] Lord Coke specified three kinds of statutes which would bind the crown although not specially named in them. These were, first, "general statutes which

---

[122] U. S. v. Herron, 20 Wall. 251.

[123] Glover v. Wilson, 6 Pa. St. 290; Alexander v. State, 56 Ga. 478; City of Jefferson v. Whipple, 71 Mo. 519; Josselyn v. Stone, 28 Miss. 753. This specific rule is expressed in the maxim "nullum tempus occurrit regi." The statute of limitations of a state does not run against the United States. U. S. v. Hoar, 2 Mason, 311, Fed. Cas. No. 15,373.

[124] "The immunity of the property of a state, and of its political subdivisions, from taxation, does not result from a want of power in the legislature to subject such property to taxation. The state may, if it sees fit, subject its property and the property of its municipal divisions to taxation, in common with other property within its territory. But inasmuch as taxation of public property would necessarily involve other taxation, for the payment of the taxes so laid, and thus the public would be taxing itself in order to raise money to pay over to itself, the inference of law is that the general language of statutes prescribing the property which shall be taxable is not applicable to the property of the state or its municipalities. Such property is therefore, by implication, excluded from the operation of laws imposing taxation, unless there is a clear expression of intent to include it." Trustees of Public Schools v. City of Trenton, 30 N. J. Eq. 667.

[125] Comm. v. Erie R. Co., 27 Pa. St. 339; Little Miami, C. & X. R. Co. v. Dayton, 23 Ohio St. 510; State v. Montclair R. Co., 35 N. J. Law, 328.

[126] 11 Coke, 66b.

provide necessary and profitable remedy for the maintenance of religion, the advancement of good learning, and the relief of the poor." Second, statutes for the suppression of wrong. "The king shall not be exempted by construction of law out of the general words of acts made to suppress wrong, because he is the fountain of justice and common right." Third, statutes of such a nature that their general words must be held to include the king, in order to perform the will of a founder or donor. These rules have never been authoritatively disavowed by the courts.[127] But the modern tendency is to draw the line of distinction at the point where the sovereign powers or the legal rights of the government begin to be affected. "It is said," observes Maxwell, "that the rule does not apply when the act is made for the public good, the advancement of religion and justice, the prevention of fraud, or the suppression of injury and wrong. But it is probably more accurate to say that the crown is not excluded from the operation of a statute where neither its prerogative, rights, nor property are in question."[128] Thus, in general, the rule does not apply to acts of legislation which lay down general rules of procedure in civil actions.[129] And the government is bound by statutes which are designed to prevent tortious usurpations and to regulate and preserve the right of elections.[130] And in Georgia it has been held that the state is bound by acts of the legislature exempting certain articles of property from levy and sale on execution, for the benefit of the family of the debtor; and

---

[127] A recent writer, after reviewing several cases, observes: "These are the principal cases in which it has been held that the crown is bound by statutes without being named in them. These cases are scarcely sufficient in number or variety to justify the very general adoption of the propositions propounded by Lord Coke in the Magdalen College Case, with regard to the kinds of statutes by which the crown is bound without being named; at the same time there does not seem to be any case in which Lord Coke's propositions are either denied or overruled." Hardcastle, Stat. Law (2d edn.) 419.

[128] Maxwell, Interp. (2d edn.) 166.

[129] Green v. U. S., 9 Wall. 655. But in Schuyler Co. v. Mercer Co., 9 Ill. 20, it is said that ordinarily a statute which, in general terms, speaks of plaintiffs or defendants, applies to persons only, and not to states, counties, or municipal corporations.

[130] Comm. v. Garrigues, 28 Pa. St. 9.

such property cannot be seized and sold under execution to pay the taxes due by the debtor.[131]

It must also be observed that although the state is not to be bound without express words or necessary implication, the same reasons do not apply when the question is as to the right of the state to take the benefit of a new law not expressly made for its advantage. Here the presumption is rather the other way; and the courts incline to give the government the benefit of new rights and remedies wherever applicable. When general rights are declared or remedies given by statute, the government is generally to be included, though not named. "If a new mode were provided by law for securing or recovering a debt, for getting possession of real estate, or the like, the commonwealth would have the benefit of such new remedy, when applicable, though expressed in general terms."[132] So also, the state is within a statute which makes it a criminal offense to make or alter a public record, falsely or fraudulently, with the intent that any "person" may be defrauded; that is, if it is done with intent to defraud the state, it is punishable under the act.[133]

Municipal Corporations.

In the absence of express statutory provisions to the contrary, the statute of limitations will run against the municipal corporations of a state, the same as against a natural person, at least so far as regards all matters which are not of a purely public nature or connected with the public trusts which the municipality is to administer; as to the latter, there is some doubt.[134]

---

[131] Gladney v. Deavors, 11 Ga. 79.

[132] Comm. v. Boston & Maine R. Co., 3 Cush. (Mass.) 25.

[133] Martin v. State, 24 Tex. 61.

[134] See City of Wheeling v. Campbell, 12 W. Va. 36; Evans v. Erie Co., 66 Pa. St. 222; County of St. Charles v. Powell, 22 Mo. 525; City of Pella v. Scholte, 24 Iowa, 283; Houston & T. C. Ry. Co. v. Travis County, 62 Tex. 16; City of Jefferson v. Whipple, 71 Mo. 519; 2 Dillon, Munic. Corp. (4th edn.) § 675.

PRESUMPTION AS TO JURISDICTION OF COURTS.

**55. A statute will not be construed as ousting or restrict-
ing the jurisdiction of the superior courts, or as vesting a new jurisdiction in them, unless there be express words or a necessary implication to that effect.**

Statutes which merely give affirmatively jurisdiction to one court
do not oust that previously existing in another court; and the jurisdiction of courts of equity, or of the higher courts proceeding according to the course of the common law, is never taken away except by plain words or by an equally plain intendment.[135] "It is,
perhaps, on the general presumption against an intention to disturb the established state of the law, or to interfere with the vested
rights of the subject, that the strong leaning now rests against construing a statute as ousting or restricting the jurisdiction of the
superior courts; although it may owe its origin to the pecuniary interests of the judges in former times, when their emoluments depended mainly on fees. It is supposed that the legislature would
not make so important an innovation without a very explicit expression of its intention."[136] Hence a statute which merely enlarges
the powers of courts of law in respect to usury does not take away
the jurisdiction of the chancery courts.[137] And a statute which authorizes an action at law on a lost note does not deprive the court
of equity of its jurisdiction in such cases.[138] But while this rule is
well established, yet it is equally true that when the object and
intent of the statute manifestly require it, words that appear to be
permissive only may be construed as obligatory, and will then have
the effect of ousting the courts of their jurisdiction.[139] As a general rule, statutes which confer jurisdiction in certain cases upon
inferior tribunals are not understood as affecting the power of con-

---

135 Barnawell v. Threadgill, 5 Ired. (N. Car.) Eq. 86; Cates v. Knight, 3
Durn. & E. 442; Earl of Shaftesbury v. Russell, 1 Barn. & C. 666; Overseers
of the Poor v. Smith, 2 Serg. & R. 363.

136 Maxwell, Interp. (2d edn.) 152.

137 McKoin v. Cooley, 3 Humph. 559.

138 Crawford v. Childress, 1 Ala. 482; Tindall v. Childress, 2 Stew. & P. 250.

139 Crisp v. Bunbury, 8 Bing. 394.

trol and supervision which the superior courts may exercise over the proceedings of such tribunals. This matter is more fully explained by Lord Mansfield in an opinion from which we quote as follows: "If a new offense is created by statute, and a special jurisdiction out of the course of the common law is prescribed, it must be followed. If not strictly pursued, all is a nullity and coram non judice. In such case, there is no occasion to oust the common law courts, because, not being an offense at common law, but punishable only sub modo, in the particular manner prescribed, they never could have jurisdiction. But where a new offense is created and directed to be tried in an inferior court established according to the course of the common law, such inferior court tries the offense as a common law court, subject to be removed by writs of error, habeas corpus, certiorari, and to all the consequences of common law proceedings. In that case, this court [the king's bench] cannot be ousted of its jurisdiction without express negative words."[140]

And "as it is presumed the legislature would not effect a measure of so much importance as the ouster or restriction of the jurisdiction of the superior courts without an explicit expression of its intention, so it is equally improbable that it would create a new, especially a new and exclusive, jurisdiction with less explicitness, and therefore a construction which would impliedly have this effect is to be avoided."[141] Thus, where one statute expressly excludes certain cases from the jurisdiction of a particular court, a subsequent statute which indicates that the court is then supposed to have jurisdiction of them is insufficient to confer it.[142] But "although an unfounded assumption by the legislature that a particular jurisdiction existed might not alone be sufficient to create it, yet when the jurisdiction is assumed to exist, and explicit provision is made as to the form and mode of its exercise, the authority to proceed in that form and mode carries with it, by necessary implication, jurisdiction of the proceedings."[143]

---

[140] Hartley v. Hooker, 2 Cowp. 523.

[141] Endlich, Interp. § 155.

[142] Ludington v. U. S., 15 Ct. Cl. 453. And see In re Contested Election of McNeill, 111 Pa. St. 235, 2 Atl. 341.

[143] State v. Miller, 23 Wis. 634; Cullen v. Trimble, L. R. 7 Q. B. 416.

CHAPTER V.

STATUTORY CONSTRUCTION; WORDS AND PHRASES.

CONSTRUING TERMS WITH REFERENCE TO SUBJECT.

56. The words of a statute are to be construed with reference to its subject-matter. If they are susceptible of several meanings, that one is to be adopted which best accords with the subject to which the statute relates.

There is no rule of construction which requires the same meaning always to be given to the same word, when used in different connections in the same statute or in different statutes.[1] On the contrary, such is the flexibility of language and the want of fixity in many of our commonest expressions, that a word or phrase may bear very different meanings according to the connection in which it is found. Hence the rule that the terms of a statute are always to be interpreted with reference to the subject-matter of the enactment.[2] For example, the word "piracy" may have at least two

---

[1] Rupp v. Swineford, 40 Wis. 28.

[2] See Smith v. Helmer, 7 Barb. 416; Comm. v. Council of Montrose, 52 Pa. St. 391; Wyman v. Fabens, 111 Mass. 77; Hubbard v. Wood, 15 N. H. 74; Hartnett v. State, 42 Ohio St. 568.

meanings. But if this word were found in a statute relating to copyright on literary productions, no one could suppose that it meant robbery committed on the high seas. Conversely, in an act defining and punishing offenses against the law of nations, it could not be understood as meaning the unlawful appropriation of the literary property of another. So again, "stock" might mean a very different thing, when used in relation to husbandry, or to the allowance to a widow of a year's maintenance out of her husband's "stock, crop, and provisions," from what it would mean if used in a statute relating to corporations.[3] So it is also with the common phrase "legal representatives." This term frequently means "executors or administrators." But when found in an act for the relief of landholders, it may mean representatives in the land itself, as, by a purchase under a sheriff's sale on a judgment against the landholder.[4] The word "misdemeanor," as used in a statute providing that if a sheriff shall have been guilty of "any default or misdemeanor in his office" the party aggrieved may apply for leave to prosecute on his official bond, does not denote a criminal offense, but refers to a trespass done by a sheriff in his official capacity.[5] Again, an English statute imposing an inheritance tax made mention of "a successor who shall have been competent to dispose by will of a continuing interest in such property." It was held that the words "competent to dispose by will" referred to the interest in the property and not to the personal capacity; and hence one having a sufficient estate or interest was affected by the act, although a lunatic or a married woman, and therefore not "competent" in the other sense.[6] So also, in some instances, by judicial construction, the extent and force of the term "void," when used in statutes, have been limited so as to make it mean "voidable," or to be made void by some plea or act of the party in whose favor the statutes are set up.[7] Again, it is held that the legal meaning of the term "destroy," as used in the act of congress providing for the punishment of a party destroying a vessel, is to unfit the vessel for serv-

[3] Van Norden v. Primm, 2 Hayw. (N. Car.) 149.
[4] Comm. v. Bryan, 6 Serg. & R. 81.
[5] State v. Mann, 21 Wis. 684.
[6] Attorney General v. Hallett, 2 Hurl. & N. 368.
[7] Green v. Kemp, 13 Mass. 515; Smith v. Saxton, 6 Pick. 483.

ice, with intent to defraud the underwriters, beyond the hope of recovery by ordinary means.[8]   On the same principle, under a statute which imposes a fine upon any person who, in the night-time, shall wilfully disturb "any neighborhood or family," an indictment will lie for disturbing a woman who occupies a dwelling house alone.[9]   A statute authorizing the courts, in certain cases, to render such judgment as substantial justice shall require, means that they shall render substantial legal justice, ascertained and determined by fixed rules and positive statutes, and not the abstract varying notions of equity entertained by each individual.[10]

These illustrations will suffice to show the application of the rule under consideration.   It is based (as all valid rules of interpretation are based) upon the effort to ascertain the real meaning and intention of the legislature, correlating with the well-known rule of language that words invariably take their color from the terms with which they are associated and the subject in reference to which they are used.   It should be mentioned, as a corollary from this rule, that where a statute is divided into separate subjects or articles, having appropriate headings, it must be presumed that the provisions of each article are controlling upon the subject thereof, and operate as a general rule for settling such questions as are embraced therein.[11]   Moreover, when a statute has been enacted with special reference to a particular subject, and by another statute its provisions are directed in general terms to be applied to another subject of an essentially different nature, the adopting statute must be taken to mean that the provisions of the original statute shall be restrained and limited to such only as are applicable and appropriate to the new subject.[12]

[8] U. S. v. Johns, 1 Wash. C. C. 363, Fed. Cas. No. 15,481.
[9] Noe v. People, 39 Ill. 96.
[10] Stevens v. Ross, 1 Cal. 94.
[11] Griffith v. Carter, 8 Kans. 565.
[12] Jones v. Dexter, 8 Fla. 276.

TECHNICAL AND POPULAR MEANING OF WORDS.

57. The words of a statute are to be taken in their ordinary and popular meaning, unless they are technical terms or words of art, in which case they are to be understood in their technical sense. But popular words may bear a technical meaning, and technical words may have a popular signification, and they should be so construed when that is the evident intention of the legislature, or when it is necessary in order to make the statute operative.

"It is a familiar rule in the construction of legal instruments," says the court in South Carolina, "alike dictated by authority and common sense, that common words in the instrument are to be extended to all the objects which, in their usual acceptation, they describe or denote, and that the technical terms are to be allowed their technical meaning and effect; unless, in either case, the context indicates that such a construction would frustrate the real intention of the draughtsman." [13]   As the first part of this rule, there-

---

[13] De Veaux v. De Veaux, 1 Strobh. Eq. 283. "Words are generally to be understood in their usual and most known signification, not so much regarding the propriety of grammar as their general and popular use." But "terms of art, or technical terms, must be taken according to the acceptation of the learned in each art, trade, and science." 1 Bl. Comm. 59. A statute of Kentucky provides that "all words and phrases shall be construed and understood according to the common and approved usage of language; but technical words and phrases, and such others as may have acquired a peculiar and appropriate meaning in law, shall be construed and understood according to such meaning." In relation to this statute, the supreme court of that state says that it is "only declaratory of a part of the common law on that subject. Words in a statute are always to be understood according to the approved use of language. But there are other rules of construction, of equal dignity and importance, which must not be overlooked, and which, although not incorporated in our statute, are as binding upon the courts as if embodied in it. One of these rules is that every statute ought to be expounded, not according to the letter, but according to the meaning; and another, that every interpretation that leads to an absurdity ought to be rejected; and still another, that a law ought to be interpreted in such manner as that it may have effect and not be found vain and illusive." Bailey v. Comm., 11 Bush, 688.

fore, we may state that, in the interpretation of statutes, words of common use are generally to be taken in their natural, plain, and ordinary signification, as they are familiarly employed in the every-day speech of the people.[14]   For example, in a statute defining and punishing aggravated assaults, the word "child" is to be construed in the sense in which it is understood in common language, and it is not necessarily synonymous with the word "minor."[15]   So again, in their ordinary and familiar signification, the words "sell" and "give" have not the same meaning, but are commonly used to express different modes of transferring the right to property from one person to another.   A sale means a transfer for a valuable consideration, while a gift signifies a gratuitous transfer.   And these terms should be so construed in a statute, unless there is something in the act to indicate that the legislature meant to use them otherwise.[16]   Again, a vessel lying at a wharf in process of construction, being yet unfinished, and for that reason not yet fit for navigation, cannot be deemed within a statute provision or exception relating to vessels "engaged in navigation."[17]   And particularly, it is said, "when particular terms are used to describe the objects of taxation, they should be construed according to their popular acceptation, not by any refined or strained analogies, and especially when that acceptation corresponds with the use of those terms in recent legislative enactments."[18]

But "verba artis ex arte,"—terms of art should be explained from their usage in the art to which they belong.   Where a word used in a statute has a fixed technical meaning, the legislature must be understood as employing it in that sense, unless there is something in the context which shows that it was intended to be used in a dif-

---

[14] Bridge Proprietors v. Hoboken Co., 1 Wall. 116; Chartered Mercantile Bank v. Wilson, L. R. 3 Ex. Div. 108; New Orleans Canal & B. Co. v. Schroeder, 7 La. Ann. 615; Schriefer v. Wood, 5 Blatchf. 215, Fed. Cas. No. 12,481; Quigley v. Gorham, 5 Cal. 418; Gross v. Fowler, 21 Cal. 392; Parkinson v. State, 14 Md. 184; Green v. Weller, 32 Miss. 650; Mayor of Wetumpka v. Winter, 29 Ala. 651; Favers v. Glass, 22 Ala. 621; Engelking v. Von Wamel, 26 Tex. 469; Neilson v. Lagow, 12 How. 98.

[15] McGregor v. State, 4 Tex. App. 599.

[16] Parkinson v. State, 14 Md. 184.

[17] The Vermont, 6 Bened. 115, Fed. Cas. No. 16,917.

[18] Deitz v. Beard, 2 Watts, 170; Nix v. Hedden, 39 Fed. 109.

ferent sense.[19]   Where, however, a word which has both a technical and a common or popular meaning is used in a constitution or a statute, the courts will accord to it its popular signification, unless the very nature of the subject indicates, or the context suggests, that it is used in its technical sense.[20]   For instance, although the strictest legal propriety may perhaps require us to speak of "actions at law" and "suits in equity," yet in common use, these two terms are indifferently applied to any proceeding in either forum; and hence the word "action" in a statute will be held to include suits in chancery.[21]   So again, where a statute declares that an unrecorded deed shall not be valid "at law," it does not mean simply that it shall be held invalid in a court of law only, but in all courts.   "At law" is not an expression which, in a statute, signifies merely a legal tribunal as distinguished from an equitable jurisdiction, but it means the system of jurisprudence generally, whether legal or equitable.[22]

Technical Legal Terms.

The technical terms and phrases of the law, when found in a statute, must be taken in their proper technical signification, unless there is something in the context to show that they were intended to bear a different meaning.[23]   Especially on subjects relating to courts and legal process, the legislature are to be considered as speaking technically, unless, from the statute itself, it appears that they used the terms in a more popular sense.[24]   Where a word or phrase has a clear, definite, and settled meaning at common law, it is to have the same meaning in the construction of a statute in which it is found, unless it is plainly apparent that such was not the legislative intention.[25]   And when an act of congress uses a technical term, which is known, and its meaning clearly ascertained,

[19] State v. Smith, 5 Humph. 394.   "Where technical words are used in reference to a technical subject, they are primarily interpreted in the sense in which they are understood in the science, art, or business in which they have acquired it."   Maxwell, Interp. (2d edn.) 69.

[20] Weill v. Kenfield, 54 Cal. 111.

[21] Coatsworth v. Barr, 11 Mich. 199.

[22] Fleming v. Burgin, 2 Ired. Eq. 584.

[23] Laird v. Briggs, L. R. 19 Ch. Div. 22.

[24] Merchants' Bank v. Cook, 4 Pick. 405.

[25] Adams v. Turrentine, 8 Ired. L. 147; McCool v. Smith, 1 Black (U. S.) 459;

by the common or the civil law, from one or the other of which it is obviously borrowed, it is proper to refer to the source from which it is taken, for its meaning.[26] Further, words or phrases in a statute, which have received a judicial construction before its enactment, are to be understood according to that construction, unless the statute clearly requires a different one.[27]

A few illustrations will help to make plain the application of these principles. "Land," for instance, is a technical term of the law, and when it is used in a statute, it is to be given its accepted legal meaning, unless restrained by the context. Hence, when a statute grants to a railroad company the right to appropriate "land" for its uses, this includes the right to remove a dwelling house.[28] The term "property," as applied to lands, includes every species of title, inchoate and complete, and it embraces those rights which lie in contract, executory as well as executed.[29] Again, the word "murder" connotes the idea of premeditation or malice aforethought.[30] And the word "wilful," when used in a statute creating a criminal offense, implies the doing of the act purposely and deliberately, in violation of law.[31] "Purchaser" has a well-defined technical signification, and embraces every holder of the legal title to real or personal property, where such title has been acquired by deed, including a mortgagee.[32] So again, "due process of law" requires that a party shall be properly brought into court, and when

Buckner v. Real Estate Bank, 5 Ark. 536; State v. Engle, 21 N. J. Law, 347. Some of the terms to which this rule was applied, in the cases cited, were "negligent escape," "next of kin," and "heir."

[26] U. S. v. Jones, 3 Wash. C. C. 209, Fed. Cas. No. 15,494. Where congress adopts or creates a common-law offense, and, in so doing, uses terms which have acquired a well-understood meaning by judicial interpretation, the presumption is that the terms were used in that sense, and courts may properly look to prior decisions, interpreting them, for the meaning of the terms and the definition of the offense, where there is no other definition in the act. U. S. v. Trans-Missouri Freight Ass'n, 7 C. C. A. 15, 58 Fed. 58.

[27] McKee v. McKee, 17 Md. 352.

[28] Brocket v. Ohio & Pa. R. Co., 14 Pa. St. 241.

[29] Figg v. Snook, 9 Ind. 202.

[30] State v. Phelps, 24 La. Ann. 493.

[31] State v. Whitener, 93 N. Car. 590.

[32] Halbert v. McCulloch, 3 Met. (Ky.) 456. "In the construction of registry acts, the term 'purchaser' is usually taken in its technical legal sense. It

there, shall have the right to set up any lawful defense to any proceeding against him.[33] Where criminal prosecutions, under a statute, are to be instituted "on complaint," a complaint under oath or affirmation is implied, as a part of the technical meaning of the term.[34] In a statute of distribution, the words, "the ancestor from whom the estate came," designate the last ancestor from whom it came.[35] Again, the word "crime," in its popular sense, means a criminal offense of a deeper or more heinous description, while smaller faults are designated as "misdemeanors." But "crime," as a legal term, includes both felonies and misdemeanors. Hence, where a statute provided that any person brought before a justice of the peace on a charge of having "committed a crime" should not be required to pay the costs where the charge should appear to be unfounded, it was held that the word, in this connection, included any felony or misdemeanor within the jurisdiction of a justice.[36] But it is said that the word "grant" is not a technical term like "enfeoff;" it may import a grant of a naked power, as well as of an interest or title.[37]

Limitations of the Rule.

Although common words are primarily to be taken in their popular sense, and technical words in their technical sense, yet this rule is subordinate to the great fundamental rule that the real intention of the legislature must in all cases prevail. Hence a popular word may have the force and effect of a technical word, if the legislature so designed. For example, an act provided that half of the rights of a husband or wife to property held in common, upon the death of either "shall go" to the survivor; and it was held that this meant that such property "shall vest" in the survivor.[38] And per contra, a technical word, capable of bearing a popular meaning also, shall be taken in the latter sense, if the obvious design of the act requires

means a complete purchaser, or, in other words, a purchaser clothed with the legal title." Steele's Lessee v. Spencer, 1 Pet. 552.

[33] Wright v. Cradlebaugh, 3 Nev. 341.

[34] Campbell v. Thompson, 16 Me. 117.

[35] Clayton v. Drake, 17 Ohio St. 367.

[36] County of Lehigh v. Schock, 113 Pa. St. 373, 7 Atl. 52.

[37] Rice v. Railroad Co., 1 Black (U. S.) 358.

[38] Broad v. Broad, 40 Cal. 493.

it.   Thus, the term "purchaser" may be understood, when the intention disclosed by the context requires it, in its ordinary commercial sense as equivalent to "buyer." [39]   In determining the construction of a statute, even of one which authorizes the confiscation of property for an offense by its owner, technical words are not to be confined to a strict technical sense, when so doing will defeat the evident intent of the statute.   Hence the federal statute declaring private property used in promoting insurrection to be "lawful subject of prize and capture" is not to be restricted to property taken at sea (though that is the technical meaning of the words), when it was the evident design of congress to make it apply equally to such property seized on land.[40]   To take another illustration, the St. 15 & 16 Vict. c. 86, § 40, provides for the cross-examination of "any party having filed an affidavit to be used or which shall be used" in a proceeding in chancery.   In order to make the act operative and intelligible, it was found necessary to construe the word "party," not in its proper legal sense, but in the decidedly colloquial usage in which it is made the equivalent of "person." [41]   Again, if the effect of construing the words of a statute according to their technical signification would be to render it inoperative, but it would have a reasonable operation by construing them according to their common meaning, the latter mode of construction should be adopted.[42]   For example, a statute of Alabama provided that when any person should be assassinated or murdered "by any outlaw, or person in disguise, or mob," his next of kin should have an action for damages against the county.   Now the word "outlaw" has a well-defined meaning at common law and in English statutes.   But the court considered it impossible that the legislature could have meant to use it in this sense, as common-law outlawry was unknown in the state and could not be pronounced by an act of the legislature. But looking at the condition of the country at the time the act was passed, and considering another statute designed to remedy the same evil, they concluded that the word should be taken in a more

[39] Ex parte Hillman, L. R. 10 Ch. Div. 622; Cummings v. Coleman, 7 Rich. Eq. 509.

[40] Union Ins. Co. v. U. S., 6 Wall. 759; U. S. v. Athens Armory, 2 Abb. U. S. 129, Fed. Cas. No. 14,473.

[41] In re Quartz Hill Co., L. R. 21 Ch. Div. 642.

[42] Robinson v. Varnell, 16 Tex. 382.

popular sense, and as denoting a desperado or lawless person accustomed to go about in disguise working violence and outrage.[43]

COMMERCIAL AND TRADE TERMS.

58. Words of commerce or trade, in a statute relating to those subjects, are primarily to be taken in their accepted commercial or trade signification.

Thus, for example, words used in a tariff act are generally to be interpreted according to their meaning in the trade and commerce of the country at the time of the passage of the act.[44] In a leading case in the supreme court of the United States, the controversy being as to the meaning of the term "Bohea tea," as used in a revenue act, it was said by Mr. Justice Story: "Congress must be understood to use the word in its known commercial sense. The object of the duty laws is to raise revenue, and for this purpose to class substances according to the general usage and known denominations of trade. Whether a particular article were designated by one name or another, in the country of its origin, or whether it were a simple or mixed substance, was of no importance in the view of the legislature. It did not suppose our merchants to be naturalists, or geologists, or botanists. It applied its attention to the description of articles as they derived their appellations in our own markets, in our domestic as well as our foreign traffic."[45] Hence, in the construction of such acts, the vocabulary of merchants is to be adopted in preference to that of mechanics; and to authorize the entry of small pieces of bolt iron under the name of "chain links," it must be proved that they have been previously known in commerce by that name.[46] But where it appears that a word used in the tariff law had, at the time of the passage of the act, a special and technical trade meaning, but the language of the section in which the word is used shows clearly that such technical meaning

---

[43] Dale County v. Gunter, 46 Ala. 118.

[44] McCoy v. Hedden, 38 Fed. 89.

[45] Two Hundred Chests of Tea, 9 Wheat. 430. And see Roosevelt v. Maxwell, 3 Blatchf. 391, Fed. Cas. No. 12,034; Elliott v. Swartwout, 10 Pet. 137; U. S. v. Breed, 1 Sumn. 159, Fed. Cas. No. 14,638.

[46] U. S. v. Sarchet, Gilp. 273, Fed. Cas. No. 16,224.

could not have been the one which congress placed upon the word, such technical meaning cannot be adopted by the court in construing the statute.[47]

ASSOCIATED WORDS.

59. Associated words explain and limit each other. When a word used in a statute is ambiguous or vague, its meaning may be made clear and specific by considering the company in which it is found and the meaning of the terms which are associated with it.

This rule is analogous to that which requires the words of a statute to be construed with reference to the subject-matter of the act, but is not identical with it. That rule directs us to seek the exact meaning of a doubtful word or phrase by a consideration of the tenor of the whole law and the object and purpose of the legislature in enacting it; but the present rule is rather one of verbal criticism, and applies to the case of several terms grouped together and mutually qualifying each other. It is expressed in the maxim "noscitur a sociis."[48] To illustrate, an English act required licenses for "houses, rooms, shops, or buildings, kept open for public refreshment, resort, and entertainment." It was adjudged that the word "entertainment," in this connection, did not necessarily mean a concert, dramatic performance, or other divertisement, nor did it necessarily imply the furnishing of food or drink, but that, judged from its associations, it meant the reception and accommodation of the public.[49] So where a policy of marine insurance is specified to protect the assured against "arrests, restraints, and detainments of all kings, princes, and people," the word "people" means the ruling or governing power of the country, this signification being impressed upon it by its association with the words "kings" and "princes."[50] Again, in a statute relating to imprisonment for debt, which speaks of debtors who shall be charged with "fraud, or undue

---

[47] In re Salomon, 48 Fed. 287.
[48] Broom, Max. 588; Bear v. Marx, 63 Tex. 298.
[49] Muir v. Keay, L. R. 10 Q. B. 594.
[50] Nesbitt v. Lushington, 4 Durn. & E. 783.

preference to one creditor to the prejudice of another," the word "undue" means fraudulent.[51] A statute of bankruptcy, declaring that any fraudulent "gift, transfer or delivery" of property shall constitute an act of bankruptcy, applies only to such deliveries as are in the nature of a gift,—such as change the ownership of the property, to the prejudice of creditors; it does not include a delivery to a bailee for safe keeping.[52] So also, the term "proceeding," in a statute which declares that "no action or proceeding," commenced before its adoption, shall be affected by its provisions, does not include a judgment, for that is an entire act and cannot, in any proper sense, be said to be "commenced" before a certain day.[53] On the same principle, the language of an act conferring equity jurisdiction in "all cases of trust arising under deeds, wills, or in the settlement of estates," applies only to express trusts arising from the written contracts of the deceased, not to those implied by law, or growing out of the official situation of an executor or administrator.[54]

GENERAL AND SPECIAL TERMS.

60. **General terms in a statute are to receive a general construction, unless restrained by the context or by plain inferences from the scope and purpose of the act.**

61. **General terms or provisions in a statute may be restrained and limited by specific terms or provisions with which they are associated.**

62. **Special terms in a statute may sometimes be expanded to a general signification by the consideration that the reason of the law is general.**

General Terms Construed Generally.

It is a well-recognized principle of statutory construction that general terms and expressions are primarily to be accorded their

51 Bulwinkle v. Grube, 5 Rich. 286.

52 Cotton v. James, Mood. & M. 273.

53 Daily v. Burke, 28 Ala. 328.

54 Given v. Simpson, 5 Me. 303. The court said: "It is certainly very vague and indefinite language, but we must give it a reasonable construction. In

natural, full, and general significance. It is only when the context, or some other admissible consideration, shows that the legislature intended to use them in a more limited sense, that their meaning can be restrained within narrower limits.[55] It is mentioned as an illustration of the force of the rule that general terms are to be understood in their full extent, unless thus restrained, that the statute of wills (St. 32 Hen. VIII., c. 1) having authorized "all and every person or persons" to devise their lands, it was feared that it might enable infants and insane persons to do so, and consequently the St. 34 Hen. VIII., c. 5, § 14, was passed to introduce these exceptions.[56] Power given by the legislature to purchase "any property" for a designated purpose will, on this principle, include real as well as personal property.[57] But general terms are to receive such reasonable interpretation as will leave the other provisions of the statute in practical operation and effect.[58] And they are often to be restrained by considerations drawn from the subject-matter of the enactment and its general scope and purpose. Thus, it is said that the word "all" is frequently and carelessly used in all writings, lay as well as legal, and the generality of the term is often to be restrained in an act, not only by the context, but also by the general form and scheme of the statute, as indicative of the intention of the legislature.[59] A statute providing that any person who has been convicted of certain offenses shall not be entitled "for any of the following causes" to a new trial or arrest of judgment, should be construed as though the provision read "for any one of the following causes." [60]

cases somewhat similar, the rule of construction 'noscitur a sociis' is found useful and is consequently adopted. Now it is clear that the legislature begins by speaking of trusts created by those having the ownership or legal control of the property. Such is the case of trusts created by deeds or wills, and according to the before mentioned rule, it is reasonable to suppose that they intended, by the words 'or in the settlement of estates,' trusts created by the same authority."

[55] Torrance v. McDougald, 12 Ga. 526.

[56] Beckford v. Wade, 17 Ves. 88.

[57] DeWitt v. San Francisco, 2 Cal. 289.

[58] Electro-Magnetic Mining & Development Co. v. Van Auken, 9 Colo. 204, 11 Pac. 80.

[59] Phillipps v. State, 15 Ga. 518. And see People v. Hoffman, 37 N. Y. 9.

[60] Thurston v. State, 3 Coldw. 115.

"Person" including "Corporation."

The word "person" is a general or generic term. Hence, when used in a statute, it embraces not only natural persons but also artificial persons, such as private corporations, unless the context indicates that it was used in a more limited sense, or the subject-matter of the act leads to a different conclusion; ·that is to say, it applies to corporations in all circumstances where it can reasonably and logically so apply.[61] For example, a statute providing that "if any person shall convey any real estate, . . . and shall not at the time have the legal estate in such lands, but shall afterwards acquire the same, the legal or equitable title afterwards acquired shall immediately pass to the grantee," applies as well to corporations as to individuals.[62] So also, a statute giving a right of action for damages against any "person" whose wrongful act, neglect, or default shall cause the death of a human being, applies equally to corporations as to private persons.[63] But still there are many cases in which the legislature does not mean that the word "person" shall include corporations. This is always a question of intention; and the intention must be sought for and determined, in each case, by the aid of the context, the general scope and purpose of the act, and other pertinent considerations.[64] Very often the

---

[61] Planters' & Merchants' Bank v. Andrews, 8 Port. (Ala.) 404; Trenton Banking Co. v. Haverstick, 11 N. J. Law, 171; U. S. v. Amedy, 11 Wheat. 392; Cary v. Marston, 56 Barb. 27; In re Fox, 52 N. Y. 530; Miller's Exr. v. Comm., 27 Gratt. 110; People v. Utica Ins. Co., 15 Johns. 358; Douglass v. Pacific Mail Steamship Co., 4 Cal. 304; Louisville & N. R. Co. v. Comm., 1 Bush, 250. Per contra, see School Directors v. Carlisle Bank, 8 Watts, 289.

[62] Jones v. Green, 41 Ark. 363.

[63] Chase v. American Steamboat Co., 10 R. I. 79.

[64] In the case of Pharmaceutical Society v. London & P. S. Ass'n, L. R. 5 App. Cas. 857, Lord Selborne said: "There can be no question that the word 'person' may, and I should be disposed myself prima facie to say, does, in a public statute, include a person in law, that is, a corporation, as well as a natural person. But although that is a sense which the word will bear in law, and which, as I said, perhaps ought to be attributed to it in the construction of a statute, unless there should be any reason for a contrary construction, it is never to be forgotten that in its popular sense and ordinary use it does not extend so far. Statutes, like other documents, are constantly conceived according to the popular use of language, and it is certain that this word is often used in statutes in a sense in which it cannot be intended to

legislature, to preclude any uncertainty on this point, will incorporate in the statute an explicit declaration that it shall or shall not apply to bodies politic.   Moreover, in some cases, the word "person" could not be construed in this extensive sense without doing violence to language or defeating the purpose or intended effect of the act.   For instance, where a statute provides that a certain number of persons may organize themselves into a corporation, it cannot be understood as including corporations; that is, it does not authorize corporations, to the prescribed number, to organize themselves into a new corporation distinct from themselves.   The word "persons" here obviously means only natural persons,—individuals capable of contract and association.[65]

General Terms Associated with Specific Terms.

When the particular provisions of a statute indicate its object and purpose, general language will be confined to those alone, unless a more extended application is clearly intended.[66]   So again, "when two words or expressions are coupled together, one of which generically includes the other, it is obvious that the more general term

---

extend to a corporation.   That accounts for the frequent occurrence in some statutes, in interpretation clauses, of an express declaration that it shall extend to a body politic or corporate."

"It is evident," says Endlich, "that the word 'person' may or may not include corporations, according to the intention of the legislature in the use of the term, and that, in ascertaining the intention, in the absence of determining features in the context, in other parts of the statute, in acts in pari materia, and the like, the subject-matter and object of the enactment are recognized as furnishing the only guide.   If any general rule can be drawn from the decisions, it would seem to be this, that where the act imposes a duty towards, or for the protection of, the public or individuals, or grants a right properly common to all, and from participation in which the limited character of corporate franchises and the absence of any natural rights in corporations do not, by any policy of the law, debar them, the term 'persons' will in general include them, whether the act be a penal or a remedial one.   But in cases of enactments having a different object in view, and especially of the class preeminently requiring a construction in accordance with common and popular usages of the language (tax laws), it would seem that corporations would not, in general, be included."   Endlich, Interp. § 89.

[65] Factors' & Traders' Ins. Co. v. New Harbor Protection Co., 37 La. Ann. 233.

[66] U. S. v. Crawford, 6 Mackey, 319.

is used in a meaning excluding the specific one. Though the words 'cows,' 'sheep,' and 'horses,' for example, standing alone, comprehend heifers, lambs, and ponies, respectively, they would be understood as excluding them if the latter words were coupled with them. The word 'land,' which, in its ordinary legal acceptation, includes buildings standing upon it, is evidently used as excluding them, when it is coupled with the word 'buildings.' " [67]   And again, when a legislative act contains two sets of provisions, one giving specific and precise directions to do a particular thing, and the other in general terms prohibiting certain acts which would, in the general sense of the words used, include the particular act before authorized, the general clause does not control or affect the specific enactment.[68]   And when general terms are used, and the statute enumerates the particulars under a videlicet, this shows the intention of the legislature to limit the comprehensiveness of the general phraseology to the particulars enumerated and those of the same class or kind.   Thus, an act of a state legislature laying a tax on all real estate, to wit, on various sorts of real estate specified by the act, and as such shown to be private property, does not include property of any sort of the United States within its territory.[69] General words in one clause of a statute may also be restrained, according to these principles, by the particular words in a subsequent clause of the same statute.[70]

Special Terms Expanded by Construction.

"Quando verba statuti sunt specialia, ratio autem generalis, statutum generaliter est intelligendum," [71] that is to say, when the words or expressions used in a statute are special, but the reason, or spirit, or purpose, of the law is general, it should be read as if correspondingly general expressions had been used.   On this principle, the word "child," as used in a statute relating to the distribution of intestates' estates, may be taken to include grandchildren.[72]

[67] Maxwell, Interp. (2d edn.) 396.
[68] State v. Inhabitants of City of Trenton, 38 N. J. Law, 64.
[69] U. S. v. Weise, 2 Wall. Jr. 72, Fed. Cas. No. 16,659.
[70] Covington v. McNickle, 18 B. Mon. 262; Felt v. Felt, 19 Wis. 193; State v. Goetze, 22 Wis. 363.
[71] Beawfage's Case, 10 Coke, 99b, 101b.
[72] Eshleman's Appeal, 74 Pa. St. 42.

GENERAL TERMS FOLLOWING SPECIAL TERMS.

63. It is a general rule of statutory construction that where general words follow an enumeration of persons or things, by words of a particular and specific meaning, such general words are not to be construed in their widest extent, but are to be held as applying only to persons or things of the same general kind or class as those specifically mentioned. But this rule must be discarded where the legislative intention is plain to the contrary.

This rule is commonly called the "ejusdem generis" rule, because it teaches us that broad and comprehensive expressions in an act, such as "and all others," or "any others," are usually to be restricted to persons or things "of the same kind" or class with those specially named in the preceding words.[73] It is of very frequent use and application in the interpretation of statutes. For example, where a statute gave certain property and business rights to "any married woman whose husband, either from drunkenness, profligacy, or any other cause, shall neglect or refuse to provide for her," it was held that the words "any other cause" must be understood of causes ejusdem generis with those enumerated, and hence would not include mere poverty, sickness, intellectual inferiority, or physical inability of the husband, not caused by vice.[74] So a statute which gives to county supervisors the authority to remove superintendents of houses of correction from office "for incompetency, improper conduct, or other cause satisfactory to the board," must be construed as meaning "other cause" of the same general nature with those causes specified, that is, such cause as shows that it is improper

[73] King v. Manchester & S. Waterworks, 1 Barn. & C. 630; King v. Wallis, 5 Durn. & E. 375; Countess of Rothes v. Kirkcaldy Waterworks Comm'rs, L. R. 7 App. Cas. 694; Chegaray v. Mayor, etc., of New York, 13 N. Y. 220; Stone v. Stone, 1 R. I. 425; In re Swigert, 119 Ill. 83, 6 N. E. 469; McIntyre v. Ingraham, 35 Miss. 25; City of Lynchburg v. Norfolk & W. R. Co., 80 Va. 237; Roberts v. Savannah, F. & W. R. Co., 75 Ga. 225; Bevitt v. Crandall, 19 Wis. 581; City of St. Louis v. Laughlin, 49 Mo. 559.

[74] Edson v. Hayden, 20 Wis. 682.

that the incumbent should be retained in the office.[75]   Again, this
rule has been applied to a statute authorizing the correction of
"clerical or other errors" in tax assessments; the words "clerical
or other" refer to some error of form in the assessment-roll, and not
to an error of the assessors in making the assessment, nor any substantial error of judgment or of law.[76]   Another statute provided
that "every person who shall set fire to any building, or to any other
material, with intent to cause any such building to be burned, or
shall by any other means attempt to cause any building to be burned," should be punished.   It was held that this would not support
an indictment for an attempt based on solicitation alone, for, under
the rule in question, the statute must be held to contemplate the
employment of means similar to those enumerated, that is, physical
means.[77]   Again, a statute relating to the navigation of the river
Thames with "any wherry, lighter, or other craft," was held not to
apply to a steam tug of 87 tons burden, employed in moving another
vessel, because it was not ejusdem generis with wherries and light-
ers.[78]   And so, where a statute prohibited all persons from hauling
on turnpike roads "any timber, stone, or other thing," unless upon
wheeled carriages, it was held that the other things prohibited were
of the same nature with timber and stone, that is, heavy and likely
to injure the road if hauled otherwise than upon wheels, and that
the act did not apply to the transportation of a quantity of straw.[79]
Again, a statute authorized actions to be brought in the name of
the state to recover "money, funds, credits, and property" held by
public corporations for public purposes and wrongfully converted
or disposed of.   It was held that an action to recover real property
was not within the purview of the act; for the word "property," associated with the preceding words of specific description in the act,
is to be construed as referring to property of the same general character.[80]   A statute provided that "whenever the exigencies of any
army in the field are such as to make impressments of forage, articles of subsistence, or other property absolutely necessary, then

[75] State v. McGarry, 21 Wis. 496.

[76] In re Hermance, 71 N. Y. 481.

[77] McDade v. People, 29 Mich. 50.

[78] Reed v. Ingham, 3 El. & Bl. 889.

[79] Radnorshire County Roads Board v. Evans, 3 Best & S. 400.

[80] People v. New York & M. B. Ry. Co., 84 N. Y. 565.

such impressment may be made." This did not authorize the impressment of a hotel or a drug-store for hospital purposes.[81] On the same principle, when a civil damage act gives to "every wife, child, parent, guardian, husband, or other person" a right of action against a liquor-seller for injury done the plaintiff by reason of the intoxication of any person, it does not give the intoxicated person himself a right of action against the seller for money stolen from him while drunk.[82]

But the rule of construction, that general and unlimited terms are restrained and limited by particular recitals, when used in connection with them, does not require the rejection of general terms entirely, and it is to be taken in connection with other rules of construction, not less important, such as that an act should be so construed as to carry out the declared intention of the legislature. "The doctrine of ejusdem generis is but a rule of construction to aid in ascertaining the meaning of the legislature, and does not warrant a court in confining the operation of a statute within narrower limits than was intended by the lawmakers. The general object of an act sometimes requires that the final general term shall not be restricted in meaning by its more specific predecessors." [83] For example, where a statute prohibited judicial officers from exacting fees, except as expressly allowed in the act, from "any guardian, executor, administrator, or other person," and there was nothing in the context to show an intention to restrict the operation of the statute to probate business, the court thought it plainly evident that the legislature designed to put a stop to the taking of excessive fees

[81] White v. Ivey, 34 Ga. 186.

[82] Brooks v. Cook, 44 Mich. 617.

[83] Willis v. Mabon, 48 Minn. 140, 50 N. W. 1110; State v. Williams, 2 Strobh. 474. Speaking of this rule, Sutherland says: "This rule can be used only as an aid in determining the legislative intent, and not for the purpose of controlling the intention or of confining the operation of a statute within narrower limits than were intended by the law-maker. It affords a mere suggestion to the judicial mind that where it clearly appears that the law-maker was thinking of a particular class of persons or objects, his words of more general description may not have been intended to embrace any other than those within the class. The suggestion is one of common sense. Other rules of construction are equally potent, especially the primary rule which suggests that the intent of the legislature is to be found in the ordinary meaning of the words of the statute." Sutherland, Stat. Constr. § 279.

in all cases before the courts, and hence the law was applied where an illegal fee had been taken in a criminal case, though that was not at all ejusdem generis with those enumerated.[84]   In another case, where a statute imposed a punishment for resisting a "sheriff, constable, or other officer," it was held that, as a supervisor of roads is completely within the term "officer," he must be deemed within the protection of the statute, unless the context indicated that the legislature intended to include only that particular class of officers who are ministerially connected with the courts.[85]   So again, where a statute made it a penal offense to obtain signatures to a written instrument "by color of any false token or writing, or by any other false pretense," it was held that the statute did not attempt to enumerate the false pretenses in particular terms, so that the term "any other false pretense" was not limited to a particular kind of pretense, and the rule in question would not apply.[86]   On similar principles, the court in South Carolina ruled that the act imposing a penalty on any person who wilfully put into any bale of cotton any "stone, wood," or "any matter or thing whatsoever," embraced the putting in of an undue quantity of water.   This decision was rested on the ground that the plain and evident purpose of the legislature was to punish frauds in packing cotton, without regard to the character of the material used.[87]   It is further to be remarked that this principle or rule applies only where the specific words preceding the general expression are all of the same nature.   "Where they are of different genera, the meaning of the general word remains unaffected by its connection with them.   Thus, where an act made it penal to convey to a prisoner, in order to facilitate his escape, any 'mask, dress, or disguise, or any letter, or any other article or thing,' it was held that the last general terms were to be understood in their primary and wide meaning, and as including any article or thing whatsoever which could in any manner facilitate the escape of a prisoner, such as a crowbar."[88]

[84] Foster v. Blount, 18 Ala. 687.

[85] Woodworth v. State, 26 Ohio St. 196.

[86] Higler v. People, 44 Mich. 299, 6 N. W. 664.

[87] State v. Holman, 3 McCord, 306.   And see State v. Solomon, 33 Ind. 450.

[88] Maxwell, Interp. (2d edn.) 413, citing Queen v. Payne, L. R. 1 C. C. 27.

Superior not Classed with Inferior.

There is an important branch of the foregoing rule which may be stated in the following terms: A statute which enumerates persons or things of an inferior rank, dignity, or importance, is not to be extended, by the addition of general words, to persons or things of a higher rank, dignity, or importance than the highest enumerated, if there are any of a lower species to which the general words can apply.[89] For example, a statute avoiding conveyances by masters and fellows of colleges, deans and chapters of cathedrals, parsons, vicars, and "others having any spiritual or ecclesiastical living," would not include bishops, because they are of a higher rank than any of those mentioned.[90] So again, the St. 31 Hen. VIII., c. 43, discharged from the payment of tithes all lands which should come to the crown by the dissolution of monasteries or colleges, or by renouncing, relinquishing, forfeiture, giving up, or "by any other means." But it was held that the general words closing the enumeration could not be understood to include the vesting of lands in the crown by act of parliament, "which is the highest manner of conveyance that can be;" they referred only to other inferior means of a nature similar to those specified.[91] Again, a statute imposed certain duties on articles exported and imported at a certain harbor. Under the head of "metals," certain specified duties were imposed on copper, brass, pewter, tin, and "all other metals not enumerated." It was held that the latter words did not include gold and silver, the decision being based partly on the ground that, taking the words in their ordinary sense, these would not be included, because they are always spoken of either by name or as the "precious metals," and partly on the rule that general words following a particular enumeration should not be held to include things superior to those enumerated.[92] But while this rule will generally hold good, yet there are certain cases in which it cannot be followed, without violating the great fundamental principle that the intention of the legislature is always to be sought out and followed. If, for instance,

---

[89] Woodworth v. Paine's Adm'rs, 1 Ill. 374; Bishop, Wr. Laws, § 246b; 1 Bl. Comm. 88.

[90] Archbishop of Canterbury's Case, 2 Coke, 46a.

[91] Idem.

[92] Casher v. Holmes, 2 B. & Ad. 592.

all those things which are of an inferior degree or rank are specifically mentioned and enumerated, and there are still general words
added, the latter must be applied to things of a higher degree or
rank than those named, because, if this were not done, there would
be nothing for the general words to operate upon, and this result
must always be avoided, for it is not to be presumed that the legislature would add to the terms of its enactment words which could
have no value or significance.[93] Thus, it is a general rule that
where, in a statute relating to the courts, one or more courts are
named, and the words "and other courts" follow, those words must
be taken as applying only to courts inferior to those named.   But
if the specific enumeration exhausts all the inferior courts, or if
there are none lower than those named, the superior courts must
necessarily be included in the general words, for otherwise those
words would be entirely without effect.[94]

EXPRESS MENTION AND IMPLIED EXCLUSION.

**64. It is a general rule of statutory construction (to be ap-
plied under proper conditions and with important
limitations) that the express mention of one person,
thing, or consequence is tantamount to an express
exclusion of all others.**

The maxim "expressio unius est exclusio alterius" is of very important, though limited, application in the interpretation of statutes.   It is based upon the rules of logic and the natural workings
of the human mind.   But it is not to be taken as establishing a Pro-
crustean standard to which all statutory language must be made to
conform.   On the contrary, it is useful only as a guide in determining the probable intention of the legislature, and if it should be
clearly apparent, in any particular case, that the legislature did not
in fact intend that its express mention of one thing should operate
as an exclusion of all others, then the maxim must give way.   It
has indeed been said that, at least in the construction of criminal
statutes, this rule is too general and subject to too many exceptions

---

[93] Ellis v. Murray, 28 Miss. 129.   [94] Chapman v. Woodruff, 34 Ga. 91.

in its application, to be allowed to govern.[95] But though it must be applied with great caution, there are still many cases in which it undoubtedly helps the interpreter to a clear understanding of the legislative design. It is particularly applicable in the construction of such statutes as create new rights or remedies, derogate from the common law, impose penalties or punishments, or otherwise come under the rule of strict construction. For instance, where a statute enlarging the powers of married women specifically enumerates the cases in which they may sue in their own names, this maxim applies, and they cannot maintain an action in any other cases.[96] So where a statute defining an offense designates one class of persons as subject to its penalties, it is to be understood that all other persons are not made liable.[97] Again, when a statute assumes to specify the effects of a certain provision, it is to be presumed that no others are intended than those described.[98] And so, if there is an enumeration of the cases in which creditors shall be allowed to recover interest on their demands, it may safely be assumed that it was not the legislative intention to allow it in any other cases.[99] In an act forming a new county out of portions of old ones, a provision for the transfer of suits pending against defendants from the courts of the old counties into those of the new, without referring to administrations pending in the former, is to be construed as an expression of legislative intent that such administrations should not be removable.[100] Again, a law of Texas, enacted in 1846, provided that collectors of taxes should receive in payment thereof "all coins made current by the laws of the United States and the exchequer bills of the republic." By previous laws

[95] State v. Connor, 7 La. Ann. 379. "Whether the expression of one thing is to operate as the exclusion of another is clearly a mere question of intention, to be gathered from the statute by the usual means and rules of interpretation. As an auxiliary rule, the maxim expressio unius, etc., becomes an important aid. It means that the special mention of one thing indicates that it was not intended to be covered by a general provision which would otherwise include it." Endlich, Interp. § 399.

[96] Miller v. Miller, 44 Pa. St. 170.

[97] Howell v. Stewart, 54 Mo. 400.

[98] Perkins v. Thornburgh, 10 Cal. 189.

[99] Watkins v. Wassell, 20 Ark. 410.

[100] Paige v. Bartlett (Ala.) 13 South. 768.

they had been authorized to receive certain certificates issued by the republic.   It was held that they were not bound to receive these certificates after the passage of the act mentioned.[101]   Particularly when a statute gives a new right or a new power, and provides a specific, full, and adequate mode of executing the power or enforcing the right given, the fact that a special mode is prescribed will be regarded as excluding, by implication, the right to resort to any other mode of executing the power or of enforcing the right.[102]   A statute granting pieces of land to Indians, and prescribing a specific mode in which they may sell the same, impliedly forbids a sale in any other mode.[103]   So, an act of congress conferring on the secretary of war the power to discharge enlisted minors on certain conditions, must be construed as having provided a mode by which persons improperly enlisted can be discharged, and as having forbidden other modes of obtaining their discharge.[104]   Another case in which this maxim may almost invariably be followed is that of a statute which makes certain specific exceptions to its general provisions. Here we may safely assume that all other exceptions were intended to be excluded.   For instance, where a law imposing taxes generally makes an express exception in favor of a certain class of persons, this exception excludes all others, and negatives the idea that any other exception was intended.[105]

But there are many cases in which it would obviously be inappropriate to judge the statute solely by the maxim in question. For one thing, "the maxim does not apply to a statute the language of which may fairly comprehend many different cases, in which some only are expressly mentioned by way of example merely, and

[101] Bryan v. Sundberg, 5 Tex. 418.

[102] Johnston v. Louisville, 11 Bush, 527. Where a statute, which confers special privileges, also imposes specified duties, and provides a remedy for the neglect of them, that remedy alone must be pursued by persons who would seek redress for such neglect. Bassett v. Carleton, 32 Me. 553; Calking v. Baldwin, 4 Wend. 667. A statute incorporating the proprietors of a canal having prescribed a particular remedy for all damages occasioned by the opening of the canal, all other modes of remedy are excluded by necessary implication. Spring v. Russell, 7 Me. 273.

[103] Smith v. Stevens, 10 Wall. 321.

[104] Matter of O'Connor, 48 Barb. 258.

[105] Miller v. Kirkpatrick, 29 Pa. St. 226; State v. Inhabitants of Trenton, 40 N. J. Law, 89.

not as excluding others of a similar nature." [106]   Again, where the statute is plainly directed to one particular thing, and there is no reason why its terms should in any manner affect other related or similar things lying outside its specific purpose, the rule of "expressio unius" would be an unsafe guide.   Thus, a law prescribing what shall be an appearance for a certain purpose does not preclude an appearance in a different manner for other purposes. [107]   And although a statute provides that a certain thing shall prove a certain fact, this does not render other proof of the fact incompetent, unless it is explicitly so provided. [108]

It is sometimes said that the converse of this rule is equally available in statutory construction; that is, that the express exclusion of one thing will operate as the inclusion of all others. Thus, if a statute explicitly provides that a court, in certain cases, shall not impose a fine of less than $100, this implies the power to impose a fine of $100 or more. [109]   But this inversion of the rule is to be applied with even greater caution than the rule itself.   We should not infer the inclusion of one thing from the exclusion of another, unless such an inference is very clearly in accordance with the intention of the legislature, or unless it is necessary to give the statute effect and operation.   Particular care should be observed in resisting the conclusion that the express shutting out of one thing will necessarily let in its opposite.   For example, if a statute declares that husband and wife shall not be competent or compellable to give evidence for or against each other in any criminal proceeding, this does not make them competent in civil cases. [110]

[106] Sutherland, Stat. Constr. § 329.
[107] State v. McCullough, 3 Nev. 202.
[108] Town of Bethlehem v. Town of Watertown, 51 Conn. 490.
[109] Hankins v. People, 106 Ill. 628.
[110] Barbat v. Allen, 7 Exch. 609.

RELATIVE AND QUALIFYING TERMS.

65. As a general rule, relative, qualifying, or limiting words or clauses in a statute are to be referred to the next preceding antecedent, unless the context, or the evident meaning of the enactment, requires a different construction.

This grammatical rule is of use only in cases where there is ambiguity or doubt on the face of the statute. If there is difficulty in interpreting the qualifying words of a sentence, the rule is to apply the relatives "which," "said," and other relative or limiting words or phrases, to such terms or clauses as shall immediately precede them, rather than to such as are more remote.[111] But the rule that a relative or qualifying word refers to its last antecedent is not invariable. It will yield to the evident sense and meaning of the statute. It is a rule of grammar, and a statute is presumed to be grammatically expressed. But this will not be held in the face of the apparent and rational interpretation of the act.[112] "It is true that in strict grammatical construction, the relative ought to apply to the last antecedent; but there are numerous examples in the best writers to show that the context may often require a deviation from this rule, and that the relative may be connected with nouns which go before the last antecedent, and either take from it or give to it some qualification."[113] Particularly where a relative or qualifying phrase cannot be applied to its immediate antecedent without producing absurd results, or violating the evident purpose of the legislature, the rule requiring such reference must be rejected; and in such a case, the phrase may be made to qualify any other part of the statute to which the intention of the legislature, so far as it can be discovered, would seem to make it applicable.[114] For instance, a statute provided that certain officers

---

[111] Gaither v. Green, 40 La. Ann. 362, 4 South. 210; Cushing v. Worrick, 9 Gray, 382; Fowler v. Tuttle, 24 N. H. 9.

[112] Fisher v. Connard, 100 Pa. St. 63; Gyger's Estate, 65 Pa. St. 311; State v. Stoller, 38 Iowa, 321.

[113] Staniland v. Hopkins, 9 Mees. & W. 178, per Lord Abinger. See, also, Great Western R. Co. v. Swindon & C. E. R. Co., L. R. 9 App. Cas. 787.

[114] State v. Zanesville & M. Turnpike Road Co., 16 Ohio St. 308.

should not be "liable to military or jury duty, nor to arrest on civil process, or to service of subpœnas from civil courts, whilst actually on duty." According to the usual rules of English composition, the qualifying phrase "whilst actually on duty" would apply only to the last antecedent, "service of subpœnas," etc. But it was held that this would not carry out the plain and evident intention of the legislature, and consequently the act should be read as exempting these persons, whilst actually on duty, both from arrest and from the service of process.[115]   Again, a statute authorized exterritorial service of process on nonresident defendants in suits in equity "concerning goods, chattels, lands, tenements, or hereditaments, or for the perpetuating of testimony concerning any lands, tenements, and so forth, situate or being within the jurisdiction of such court." It was held that the qualifying phrase "situate or being within the jurisdiction" referred not merely to the last antecedent, "perpetuating of testimony," etc., but also to the first clause of the sentence quoted.[116]   So again, a statutory authority to levy a tax to defray the "current expenses of the year" has been held equivalent to "the expenses of the current year," because the adjective could properly be made to qualify only the last word.[117]   Also it is said that general words occurring at the end of a sentence are presumed to refer to and qualify the whole, but if they occur in the middle of a sentence, and obviously apply to a particular portion of it, they are not to be extended to what follows them.[118]

REDDENDO SINGULA SINGULIS.

66. **Where a sentence in a statute contains several antecedents and several consequents, they are to be read distributively; that is to say, each phrase or expression is to be referred to its appropriate object.**

"The different portions of a sentence, or different sentences, are to be referred respectively to the other portions or sentences to which we can see they respectively relate, even if strict grammat-

---

[115] Hart v. Kennedy, 14 Abb. Pr. 432.
[116] Eby's Appeal, 70 Pa. St. 311.
[117] Babcock v. Goodrich, 47 Cal. 488.
[118] Coxson v. Doland, 2 Daly (N. Y.) 66.

ical construction should demand otherwise. The maxim of construction, 'reddendo singula singulis,' is well established." [119]   "It is one
of the best settled rules of construction that words in different parts
of a statute must be referred to their appropriate connection, giving to each in its place its proper force, reddendo singula singulis,
and, if possible, rendering none of them useless or superfluous." [120]
To illustrate, a question having arisen as to the construction of the
words "for money or other good consideration paid or given," in
an English statute, it was decided that the consequent "paid" should
be referred to the antecedent "money" and the consequent "given"
to the antecedent "consideration;" that is, the sentence should be
read as if it spoke of "money paid or other good consideration
given." [121]   Again, a statute provided for its adoption by cities and
towns "at a legal meeting of the city council or the inhabitants of
the town called for that purpose."   It was held, on this principle,
that only in the case of a town need a meeting be called for the
specific purpose. [122]   An act of congress declared that all fines, penalties, and forfeitures accruing under the laws of Maryland and Virginia, in the District of Columbia, should be recovered by indictment or information in the name of the United States, or by action
of debt in the name of the United States and of the informer.   It
was held that a proceeding for a penalty under the law of one of
those states, which, by such law, could not have been taken by indictment, but by a private action, should be, not by indictment in
the name of the United States, but by an action of debt. [123]   Again,
"where several words importing power, authority, and obligation,
are found at the commencement of a clause containing several
branches, it is not necessary for each of those words to be applied
to each of the different branches of the clause; it may be construed
reddendo singula singulis; the words giving power and authority
may be applicable to some branches, and those of obligation to
others."   Thus, in the case from which this quotation is made, it
appeared that an act of parliament provided "it shall and may be

[119] Comm. v. Barber, 143 Mass. 560, 10 N. E. 330.
[120] McIntyre v. Ingraham, 35 Miss. 25.
[121] Potter's Dwarris on Stat. 230.
[122] Quinn v. Lowell Electric Light Co., 140 Mass. 106, 3 N. E. 200.
[123] U. S. v. Simms, 1 Cranch, 252.

lawful for the said directors, and they are hereby authorized and required to form a new common sewer" in a certain direction, "and also to alter or reconstruct all or any of the sewers of the city at the mouths."   It was held, taking the language distributively, that the directors were "required" to construct a new common sewer, and "authorized" to alter or reconstruct the existing ones.[124]

CONJUNCTIVE AND DISJUNCTIVE PARTICLES.

67. The word "and," in a statute, may be read "or," and vice versa, whenever the change is necessary to give the statute sense and effect, or to harmonize its different parts, or to carry out the evident intention of the legislature.[125]

This rule is based upon the assumption that the legislature could not have intended to produce an absurd or unreasonable result, or to express itself in terms which would defeat the very objects of the enactment; and consequently, when such effects would follow a literal construction of the statute, the conjunctive particle may be read as disjunctive, or vice versa, on the theory that the word to be corrected was inserted by inadvertence or clerical error.   For instance, where a statute defined the common law offense of burglary, and made it a felony to "break or enter" a dwelling-house in the night-time, it was held that it should be read "break and enter."[126]   Where a statute provided that a person libelled, in certain cases, might proceed against the author of the libel by indictment "or" bring an action at law for his damages, it was held that it could not possibly have been the intention of the legislature to give the plaintiff merely his choice between these two remedies, and consequently the word "or" must be read "and."[127]   So a statute providing that any person violating "the first and second sections of this

---

[124] King v. Bristol Dock Co., 6 Barn. & C. 181.

[125] Metropolitan Board of Works v. Steed, L. R. 8 Q. B. Div. 445; Comm. v. Harris, 13 Allen, 534; Comm. v. Griffin, 105 Mass. 185; State v. Brandt, 41 Iowa, 593; McConkey v. Superior Court of Alameda County, 56 Cal. 83; O'Connell v. Gillespie, 17 Ind. 459.

[126] Rolland v. Comm., 82 Pa. St. 306.

[127] Foster v. Comm., 8 Watts & S. 77.

act" shall be liable to a penalty, renders a person liable for a violation of either section.[128]   Even in a penal statute, and when it will
operate against the accused, it has sometimes been held that con-
junctions which connect different sentences describing different
branches of the same offense will be construed as conjunctive or
disjunctive, as the objects and sense of the law most distinctly require.[129]   Thus, where a statute imposed a punishment upon any
person who should place obstructions in a watercourse, whereby
the flow of water should be lessened "or" navigation should be impeded, it was held that the word "or" should be read "and." [130]

NUMBER AND GENDER OF WORDS.

**68. Words in a statute importing the plural number may
be made applicable to single persons or things, and
vice versa, and words importing the masculine gender may include females, whenever, in either case,
such a construction is in accord with the evident
meaning and purpose of the legislature.**

It is a general rule, as above stated, that words or phrases in a
statute expressed in the plural may be taken as including the singular, and words in the singular may be extended to several.   But
it is held that this rule is to be applied only when the plain and
evident sense and meaning of the words, derived from the context,
render such a construction necessary to effect the intention of the
legislature.[131]   A statute, for example, enacted that it should be
a felony to steal any "bank notes," and it was adjudged that it was
a felony to steal one single note.[132]   So, where an act provided for
the prosecution of any person who should keep "houses of bawdry

[128] People v. Sweetser, 1 Dak. Ter. 308, 46 N. W. 452.

[129] State v. Myers, 10 Iowa, 448.   But compare U. S. v. Ten Cases of Shawls,
2 Paine, 162, Fed. Cas. No. 16,448.   Where a statute directs a fine and imprisonment, as a punishment for an offense, the court is bound to inflict both, if
the defendant is found guilty.   U. S. v. Vickery, 1 Har. & J. 427, Fed. Cas. No.
16,619.

[130] State v. Pool, 74 N. Car. 402.

[131] Garrigus v. Board of Comm'rs of Parke County, 39 Ind. 66; Jocelyn v.
Barrett, 18 Ind. 128.

[132] King v. Hassel, 1 Leach Cr. L. 1.

and ill fame," it was held that a person might be convicted who kept but one such house.[133]   And the word "persons," in the plural, may sometimes be construed as applicable to a single person.[134] Where a statute imposed penalties for a failure "to comply with the conditions of" the section, it was considered that a disobedience of any one of the provisions subjected the delinquent to the penalty.[135]   Conversely, the word "party," in a statute regulating applications for a change of venue, was held to signify all of the defendants or all of the plaintiffs in an action.[136]

For similar reasons, and under the same conditions, and for the same purposes, words importing the masculine gender, such as "he," "his," or "man," may be held applicable to a woman.   In some states, this rule of construction is enacted in the code.   Such is the case, for example, in Arkansas; and in that state, where a statute of distribution provided for the case where "any man shall die, leaving minor children and no widow," the provision was held to be applicable to the case of a woman dying and leaving minor children and no husband.[137]

PERMISSIVE AND MANDATORY TERMS.

69. **Words in a statute importing permission or authorization may be read as mandatory, and words importing a command may be read as permissive or enabling only, whenever, in either case, such a construction is rendered necessary by the evident intention of the legislature or the rights of the public or of private persons under the statute.**

The word "may," according to the ordinary uses of language, is a term of authorization only.   It confers a power, faculty, or discretion, but does not impose a positive command.   Yet there are cases, not infrequently occurring, in which it is necessary to understand that this term was used in an imperative sense, this necessity

---

[133] State v. Main, 31 Conn. 572.
[134] Hill v. Williams, 14 Serg. & R. 287.
[135] State v. Kansas City, Ft. S. & G. R. Co., 32 Fed. 722.
[136] Rupp v. Swineford, 40 Wis. 28.
[137] Smith v. Allen, 31 Ark. 268.

arising from the fact that the plain meaning of the legislature, as gathered from the whole statute or from the general scope and purpose of the enactment, was to impose a positive command, instead of a mere permission. Moreover, the word must sometimes be taken as mandatory in order to sustain public or private rights. Thus, it is well settled that "may," in any statute, is to be construed as equivalent to "shall" or "must" when the public interests or rights are concerned, and when the public or third persons have a right de jure to claim that the power granted should be exercised.[138] "The result seems to be," says a learned writer, "that when a public power for the public benefit is conferred in enabling terms, a duty is impliedly imposed to exercise it whenever the occasion arises. These terms are then, in effect, invariably invested with a compulsory force; and when a judicial discretion is found to be involved in the exercise of the power, this is not owing to the circumstance that the power is couched in the language of authorization only, and not of command, but because, according to the construction of the act, it is intended by the legislature that the power shall be exercised only when some fact is found to exist which can, from its nature, be ascertained only by the judicial discretion."[139] "But where there is no design manifest to do something required by the purposes of justice; where the public has no interest or concern with the execution of the powers conferred; and where no private rights are affected by its failure, there is no room for an inference that the legislature, in using permissive language, intended that it should be given a compulsory signification, but it is even reasonable to suppose that in using language mandatory in its strict grammatical sense, it attached to it the meaning and effect of permissive words only."[140] For example, where a statute provides that the court "may appoint three commissioners" to settle a disputed boundary line between towns, the word "may" is equivalent to "shall,"

---

[138] Alderman Backwell's Case, 1 Vern. 152; Blake v. Portsmouth & C. R. Co., 39 N. H. 435; Nave v. Nave, 7 Ind. 122; Bansemer v. Mace, 18 Ind. 27; Ex parte Banks, 28 Ala. 28; Schuyler County v. Mercer County, 9 Ill. 20; Supervisors v. U. S., 4 Wall. 435; Tarver v. Commissioners' Court, 17 Ala. 527; Newburgh Turnpike Road v. Miller, 5 Johns. Ch. 101; Minor v. Mechanics' Bank of Alexandria, 1 Pet. 46; Cutler v. Howard, 9 Wis. 309.

[139] Maxwell, Interp. (2d edn.) 303.

[140] Endlich, Interp. § 312.

because the public interest is involved. Hence, in such a case, the towns cannot agree that two commissioners only may be appointed.[141] So, where a statute provided that the commissioners of highways, after giving reasonable notice, "may" remove any fence or other obstruction from the highway, it was held that "may" should here be construed as "shall;" that is, that the law was intended to impose upon the commissioners the imperative duty of removing obstructions from the public highway.[142] Again, where an act provides that the judge of the probate court "may" set apart a homestead for the widow and minor children of a decedent, it is meant that, in a proper case, he "must" do so, because the persons mentioned have a right to claim that the power shall be exercised.[143]

But it is said that the word "may," in a statute, is to be construed as mandatory only for the purpose of sustaining or enforcing a right, and never for the purpose of creating one. This rule is illustrated by the interpretation of the statutes providing for the grant of licenses to liquor sellers. These acts generally provide that the authorities "may" grant such licenses, under certain circumstances, to persons who are properly qualified, or who bring certain recommendations, or otherwise comply with the conditions of the act. But it is held that the word is one of permission or authorization only, and that, although an applicant may bring himself fully within the terms of the law, yet a license may be refused by the authorities in the exercise of a sound judicial discretion. In other words, it would not be sound interpretation to read the word as equivalent to "shall" in this connection.[144]

Substantially the same rules are applicable to the construction of the phrase "it shall be lawful." These words primarily grant permission only, but they may, in proper cases, be understood as importing a command. On this point it has been said by Lord Cairns: "The question has been argued, and has been spoken of by some of the learned judges of the courts below, as if the words 'it shall be lawful' might have a different meaning and might be dif-

---

[141] Monmouth v. Leeds, 76 Me. 28.

[142] Brokaw v. Comm'rs of Highways, 130 Ill. 482, 22 N. E. 596.

[143] Estate of Ballentine, 45 Cal. 696.

[144] State v. Justices of Holt County Court, 39 Mo. 521; Ailstock v. Page, 77 Va. 386; Batters v. Dunning, 49 Conn. 479; In re Raudenbusch, 120 Pa. St. 328, 14 Atl. 148.

ferently interpreted in different statutes or in different parts of the same statute. I cannot think that this is correct. The words 'it shall be lawful' are not equivocal. They are plain and unambiguous. They are words merely making that legal and possible which there would otherwise be no right or authority to do. They confer a faculty or power, and they do not of themselves do more than confer a faculty or power. But there may be something in the nature of the thing empowered to be done, something in the object for which it is to be done, something in the conditions under which it is to be done, something in the title of the person or persons for whose benefit the power is to be exercised, which may couple the power with a duty, and make it the duty of the person in whom the power is reposed to exercise that power when called upon to do so. Whether the power is one coupled with a duty, such as I have described, is a question which, according to our system of law, speaking generally, it falls to the court of queen's bench to decide on an application for a mandamus." [145]   In all cases where these words, "it shall be lawful," are used in a statute with reference to a court of justice, and are not otherwise controlled, they give the court a jurisdiction, leaving it to the court to exercise its discretion according to the requirements of justice in each particular case.[146]

The converse of the rule thus far considered is equally valid; that is, an imperative word, such as "shall," may sometimes be read as permissive or enabling only, when the legislature plainly designed that it should not be taken in the strictest sense, or when such a construction is necessary to effectuate justice or secure the rights of parties. In a subsequent chapter it will be more fully shown that the word "shall," although, in its primary sense, it imports a positive command, is often to be construed as directory only; that is to say, that while the direction introduced by this term is meant to be followed, yet the neglect or disregard of it will not be attended by consequences entirely fatal to the action or proceeding.

[145] Julius v. Bishop of Oxford, L. R. 5 App. Cas. 214.
[146] In re Bridgman, 1 Drew. & S. 164.

ADOPTED AND RE-ENACTED STATUTES.

70. Where a statute of a foreign jurisdiction, which had there received a settled judicial construction, is adopted, wholly or in part, and enacted as a law of the state adopting it, it is presumed that the construction previously put upon it is adopted with it, and it should be interpreted according to such construction. This rule applies equally to a re-enacted statute; and it is likewise applicable to single words or phrases borrowed from another enactment.

Statutes from Other States.

If the legislature of a state, in enacting a statute, literally or substantially copies the language of a statute previously existing in another state, or borrows from such statute a provision, clause, or phrase, the same having received a settled judicial interpretation in the state of its origin, it is presumed that the enactment was made with knowledge of such interpretation, and that it was the design of the legislature that the act should be understood and applied according to that interpretation.[147] But the interpretation, to be thus considered as adopted with the statute, must have been made before the adoption. Afterwards, decisions rendered in the state from which the law was taken may be entitled to respectful

[147] Metropolitan R. Co. v. Moore, 121 U. S. 558, 7 Sup. Ct. 1334; Stutsman County v. Wallace, 142 U. S. 293, 12 Sup. Ct. 227; Freese v. Tripp, 70 Ill. 496; Coulter v. Stafford, 48 Fed. 266; Rigg v. Wilton, 13 Ill. 15; Fisher v. Deering, 60 Ill. 114; Campbell v. Quinlin, 4 Ill. 288; Nicollet Nat. Bank v. City Bank, 38 Minn. 85, 35 N. W. 577; Drennan v. People, 10 Mich. 169; Harrison v. Sager, 27 Mich. 476; Greiner v. Klein, 28 Mich. 12; Daniels v. Clegg, Id. 32; Westcott v. Miller, 42 Wis. 454; Kilkelly v. State, 43 Wis. 604; Draper v. Emerson, 22 Wis. 147; State v. Macon County Court, 41 Mo. 453; Clark v. Jeffersonville R. Co., 44 Ind. 248; Fall v. Hazelrigg, 45 Ind. 576; Everding v. McGinn, 23 Oreg. 15, 35 Pac. 178; State v. Robey, 8 Nev. 312; Lindley v. Davis, 6 Mont. 453, 12 Pac. 118. An act of congress adopted and put in force in the Indian Territory the body of the statutes of the state of Arkansas. It was held that it would be presumed that the construction placed on those statutes by the supreme court of the state prior thereto was adopted at the same time. Sanger v. Flow, 1 C. C. A. 56, 48 Fed. 152.

consideration, but they are in no sense authoritative.[148] This is because the only reason for holding the construction of the statute to have been adopted with it is that the legislature may be presumed to have known of the construction and to have approved of it, and intended it to be followed. Moreover, the rule is not invariable. If the original construction of the adopted statute is not in harmony with the spirit and policy of the laws of the state adopting it, or would make it conflict with existing laws of that state or with the settled practice under them, it will not be followed, but the courts will work out a construction for themselves.[149] For example, a certain section of the Nevada insolvent act, denying to depositaries of public funds, and to other persons of a fiduciary character, the benefit of the act, was adopted from the insolvent law of California, where it had previously been construed as denying to the insolvency court jurisdiction over insolvents of the class therein specified. The California construction was based on the policy of its laws, which was to procure the discharge of insolvent debtors. But the main purpose of the Nevada insolvency law was the ratable distribution of the insolvent's property among his creditors, and hence the reason for the California construction of that section did not exist in Nevada. It was therefore held that the adoption of the statute was not an adoption of this construction, and the court was not thereby denied jurisdiction over insolvents of the class named.[150] Again, it must be remembered that if a foreign construction is thus adopted, it is the settled interpretation of the statute as fixed by the authoritative deliverances of the courts, and not a practical construction put upon it by executive or administrative officers.[151]

British Statutes.

On the same general principle, when congress or a state legislature adopts a British statute (such, for example, as the statute of frauds), it is presumed to be adopted with reference to the set-

[148] Stutsman County v. Wallace, 142 U. S. 293, 12 Sup. Ct. 227; Myers v. McGavock, 39 Neb. 843, 58 N. W. 522.

[149] Jamison v. Burton, 43 Iowa, 282; Gage v. Smith, 79 Ill. 219; McCutcheon v. People, 69 Ill. 601; Cole v. People, 84 Ill. 216.

[150] Frankel v. Creditors, 20 Nev. 49, 14 Pac. 775.

[151] Gray's Lessee v. Askew, 3 Ohio, 466.

tled construction put upon it by the English courts, and hence it should be interpreted in the same manner by our courts, whenever practicable, because that will accord with the presumed intention of the legislature in adopting it.[152]   For example, in the third section of the "Interstate Commerce Act," congress adopted the language of the English traffic act of 1854, in respect to "undue preferences."   Hence it is to be presumed that it was intended also to adopt the construction given to these words by the English courts, and they are so construed.[153]   But here also, as in the case of a statute adopted from another state, the construction which is to be followed is that which was put upon the act before its adoption. In one of the cases, Chief Justice Marshall is reported to have said: "By adopting them [English statutes] they become our own as entirely as if they had been enacted by the legislature of the state. The received construction in England at the time they are admitted to operate in this country, indeed, to the time of our separation from the British empire, may very properly be considered as accompanying the statutes themselves, and forming an integral part of them.   But however we may respect subsequent decisions,—and certainly they are entitled to great respect,—we do not admit their absolute authority.   If the English courts vary their construction of a statute which is common to the two countries, we do not hold ourselves bound to fluctuate with them." [154]

Re-enacted Statutes.

Where a statute has received a settled judicial construction, and is afterwards re-enacted by the same legislative power, in the same terms, or in substantially the same language, for the same purpose and object, it will be presumed that the legislature intended that the re-enacted law should bear the same interpretation which was given to its original, and it will be construed accordingly, unless a

---

[152] Interstate Commerce Commission v. Baltimore & O. R. Co., 145 U. S. 263, 12 Sup. Ct. 844; Pennock v. Dialogue, 2 Pet. 1; Kirkpatrick v. Gibson. 2 Brock. 388, Fed. Cas. No. 7,848; Kennedy v. Kennedy, 2 Ala. 571; Tyler v. Tyler, 19 Ill. 151; Adams v. Field, 21 Vt. 256; Marqueze v. Caldwell, 48 Miss. 23.

[153] McDonald v. Hovey, 110 U. S. 619, 4 Sup. Ct. 142; Interstate Commerce Commission v. Baltimore & O. R. Co., 145 U. S. 263, 12 Sup. Ct. 844.

[154] Cathcart v. Robinson, 5 Pet. 264.

contrary intention is very clearly shown.[155] So also, when terms or modes of expression are employed in a new statute, which had acquired a definite meaning and application in a previous statute on the same subject, or one analogous to it, they are generally supposed to be used in the same sense, and in settling the construction of the new statute, regard should be had to the known and established interpretation of the former.[156] Thus, in the federal bankruptcy act of 1841, it was provided that a discharge should not release debts which had been contracted by the bankrupt in a "fiduciary capacity." The same provision was repeated in the bankruptcy act of 1867, and it was held that these words were intended by congress to bear, and should be construed by the courts to bear, the same meaning which had been given to them by the judicial interpretations under the earlier law.[157]

COMPUTATION OF TIME.

71. Where a statute requires an act to be performed a certain number of days prior to a day named, or within a definite period after a day or event specified, or where time is to be computed either prior or subsequent to a day named, the usual rule is to exclude one day of the designated period and to include the other.[158]

72. The word "month," in a statute, means a calendar month.

73. A "day," as this term is used in statutes, means a period of twenty-four hours, beginning and ending (usually but not invariably) at midnight.

[155] The Abbotsford, 98 U. S. 440; Woolsey v. Cade, 54 Ala. 378; Ex parte Matthews, 52 Ala. 51; O'Byrnes v. State, 51 Ala. 25; Cota v. Ross, 66 Me. 161; Tuxbury's Appeal, 67 Me. 267; Comm. v. Hartnett, 3 Gray, 450; McKenzie v. State, 11 Ark. 594; State v. Swope, 7 Ind. 91; Harvey v. Travelers' Ins. Co., 18 Colo. 354, 32 Pac. 935; Greaves v. Tofield, L. R. 14 Ch. Div. 563.

[156] Whitcomb v. Rood, 20 Vt. 49.

[157] Woolsey v. Cade, 54 Ala. 378.

[158] Stebbins v. Anthony, 5 Colo. 348; Odiorne v. Quimby, 11 N. H. 224; Spencer v. Haug, 45 Minn. 231, 47 N. W. 794. Compare Dousman v. O'Malley, 1 Dougl. (Mich.) 450.

Computing Number of Days.

The rule stated above for the computation of a prescribed number of days, or a designated period, by which one day is excluded (generally the first) and the other included, is of very general application, and the courts are nearly all agreed in adopting it. But expressions in regard to time are sometimes found in statutes which require a different interpretation, by reason of the peculiarity of the language used. Thus, where a statute provides that it shall take effect "from and after" its passage, in computing the time when it takes effect, the day of its passage is to be excluded.[159] So, where notice of an official meeting is required to be given "three weeks before the time of meeting," three successive publications of the notice, made within less than three weeks before the meeting, are not a sufficient compliance.[160] Where a statute requires a notice to be given "ten clear days" before a certain time, this means ten perfect intervening days, both days being excluded; and hence a notice given on the 9th, to expire on the 19th, is not in time.[161] A statute requiring an inspection for public security to be made "once in six months" should be construed as meaning that not more than six months should elapse between two inspections. It is not satisfied by dividing time into periods of six months, and making one inspection early in one period and another late in the next.[162]

"Month."

It was the rule of the English common law that the term "month," as used in a statute, meant a lunar month, that is, a period of twenty-eight days or four weeks.[163] This rule was applied in the common law courts, but was not recognized by the ecclesiastical courts. According to the usage of the latter, and also in the custom of merchants and by the mercantile law, a month was a calendar month; that is, a month reckoned according to the calendar, and containing a greater or less number of days according to the particular month intended. This latter doctrine was established as the law of Eng-

---

[159] Parkinson v. Brandenburg, 35 Minn. 294, 28 N. W. 919.

[160] In re North Whitehall Tp., 47 Pa. St. 156.

[161] King v. Justices of Herfordshire, 3 Barn. & Ald. 581; Zouch v. Empsey, 4 Barn. & Ald. 522.

[162] Virginia Steam Nav. Co. v. U. S., Taney, 418, Fed. Cas. No. 16,973.

[163] Rives v. Guthrie, 1 Jones (N. Car.) 84.

land, so far as concerned the interpretation of this word in future acts of parliament, by the St. 13 & 14 Vict. c. 21.   In this country, either by statutory enactment, or by judicial interpretation without the aid of statutes, it has come to be the settled rule that a month, in an act of congress or of a state legislature, always means a calendar month, unless there is something clearly showing a contrary intention.[164]   The theory is that the word "month" is not a technical term, but a word in popular and common use, and it should therefore be taken in its usual, common, and accepted meaning, and according to that meaning, it always denotes a calendar month, not a lunar month.[165]

"Day."

In statutory language a "day" means twenty-four hours.   But whether it begins at midnight, or at sunrise, or at some other time, depends upon the intention of the legislature in each particular case, to be gathered from the context and from the general purpose and subject of the act.[166]   It is also a general rule that the law does not regard fractions of a day.   Hence when something is required to be done within a certain number of days from a given event or action, the day upon which the event occurs or the act is done must either be excluded entirely or else counted in as a whole day.[167]   Where a statute gives to the owner of lands sold for nonpayment of taxes the privilege of redeeming them within two years from the sale, an offer of redemption is in time if made on the second anniversary of the day of the sale; that is, in computing the time, the day of the sale must be excluded, and the owner must be allowed the whole of the last day in which to redeem.   "A day is always an indivisible point of time," says the court in Pennsylvania, "except where it must be cut up to prevent injustice.   In the sense of these statutes, it has neither length nor breadth, but simply position with-

---

[164] Sheets v. Sheldon's Lessee, 2 Wall. 177; Guaranty Trust Co. v. Green Cove Springs & M. R. Co., 139 U. S. 137, 11 Sup. Ct. 512; Brown v. Williams, 34 Neb. 376, 51 N. W. 851; Strong v. Birchard, 5 Conn. 357; Churchill v. Merchants' Bank, 19 Pick. 532; Bartol v. Calvert, 21 Ala. 42; Brudenell v. Vaux, 2 Dall. 302, Fed. Cas. No. 2,049.

[165] Gross v. Fowler, 21 Cal. 392.

[166] Comm. v. Wentworth, 15 Mass. 188; Zimmerman v. Cowan, 107 Ill. 631.

[167] Brown v. Buzan, 24 Ind. 194.

out magnitude. If the time for redemption were fixed at one day after the sale, that day could not be the day of the sale; for it might be made at the last moment of the day, and the owner, being thus prevented from tendering on that day, would lose his right. The time mentioned must therefore be the following day. So of one year, and of two years." [168]

[168] Cromelian v. Brink, 29 Pa. St. 522; Hare v. Carnall, 39 Ark. 196.

CHAPTER VI.

INTRINSIC AIDS IN STATUTORY CONSTRUCTION.

74. Statute to be Construed as a Whole.
75. Context.
76. Title.
77. Preamble.
78. Chapter and Section Headings.
79–81. Punctuation.
82–83. Use of Same Language and Change of Language.
84. Interpretation Clause.

STATUTE TO BE CONSTRUED AS A WHOLE.

74. In the construction of a statute, in order to determine the true intention of the legislature, the particular clauses and phrases should not be studied as detached and isolated expressions, but the whole and every part of the statute must be considered in fixing the meaning of any of its parts.

There are two principal reasons for this rule. In the first place, the force and significance of particular expressions will largely depend upon the connection in which they are found and their relation to the general subject-matter of the law. The legislature must be understood to have expressed its whole mind on the special object to which the legislative act is directed; but the vehicle for the expression of that meaning is the statute, considered as one entire and continuous act, and not as an agglomeration of unrelated clauses. Each clause or provision will be illuminated by those which are cognate to it and by the general tenor of the whole statute, and thus obscurities and ambiguities may often be cleared up by the most direct and natural means. In the second place, effect must be given, if it is possible, to every word and clause of the statute, so that nothing shall be left devoid of meaning or destitute of force. It must be so construed "ut res magis valeat quam pereat." To this end, each provision of the statute should be read in the light of the whole. For the general meaning of the legislature, as gathered from the entire act, may often prevail over that construction which would appear to be the most natural and obvious on the face of a particular clause. It is by this means that contradictions and repugnancies between the different parts of the statute may be avoided. The rule stated is therefore one of primary importance, and it is well established upon the authorities.[1] "The office of a good expositor of an act of parliament," says Lord Coke in the Lincoln College Case,[2] "is to make construction on all the parts together, and not of one part only by itself; nemo enim aliquam partem recte intelligere possit antequam totum iterum atque iterum perlegerit." "The key to the opening of every law is the reason and spirit of the law,—it is the 'animus imponentis,' the intention of the law-maker expressed in the law itself taken as a whole. Hence, to arrive at the true meaning of any particular phrase in a statute, that particular expression is not to be viewed detached from its context in the statute; it is to be viewed in connection with its whole context,—meaning by this as well the title and preamble as the purview or enacting part of the statute."[3] "One clause of a statute, apparently conclusive as to some particular thing, may be enlarged or limited by other provisions of the instrument upon the same subject; and in such a case, the intent must be gathered from all the provisions considered together, the interpreter having his eye on the subject-matter of the instrument, and giving effect to each clause of the latter, when it can be done."[4] "In construing acts of parliament," says Lord Tenterden, "we are to look not only at the language of the preamble, or of any particular clause, but

---

[1] Co. Litt. 381a; 1 Bl. Comm. 89; Comm. v. Alger, 7 Cush. 53, 89; Matter of New York & Brooklyn Bridge, 72 N. Y. 527; Comm. v. Duane, 1 Binn. 601; City of Philadelphia v. Barber, 160 Pa. St. 123, 28 Atl. 644; State v. Mayor, etc., of Paterson, 35 N. J. Law, 196; Mayor, etc., of Baltimore v. Howard, 6 Har. & J. 383; State v. Atkins, 35 Ga. 315; Gas Co. v. Wheeling, 8 W. Va. 320; Crawfordsville & S. W. Turnpike Co. v. Fletcher, 104 Ind. 97, 2 N. E. 243; Thompson v. Bulson, 78 Ill. 277. This was also the rule of the expositors of the Roman law. Thus, it is said by Celsus, in the Digest: "Incivile est, nisi tota lege perspecta, una aliqua particula ejus proposita judicare vel respondere." Dig. 1, 3, 24.

[2] 3 Coke, 59b.

[3] Brett v. Brett, 3 Add. Eccl. 210.

[4] City of San Diego v. Granniss, 77 Cal. 511, 19 Pac. 875.

at the language of the whole act.   And if we find in the preamble, or in any particular clause, an expression not so large and extensive in its import as those used in other parts of the act, and upon a view of the whole act we can collect, from the more large and extensive expressions used in other parts, the real intention of the legislature, it is our duty to give effect to the larger expressions, notwithstanding the phrases of less extensive import in the preamble or in any particular clause." [5]

In construing a statute containing a general enactment and also a particular enactment, the effort must be, in the first instance, to harmonize all the provisions of the statute, by construing all parts together, and it is only when, on such a construction, the repugnancy of specific provisions to the general language is plainly manifested, that the intent of the legislature as declared in the general enacting part is made to give way.[6]   But it is a general rule that where there is an irreconcilable conflict between different sections or parts of the same statute, the last words stand, and those in conflict with them are repealed.[7]   If, however, the first clause is clear and explicit, and the latter incoherent, the former, notwithstanding its position, will prevail over the latter.[8]   And again, if the last clause of one section of a statute is plainly inconsistent with the first portion of the same section and with another preceding section of the statute, and this section and part of a section conform to the obvious policy and intent of the legislature, the last clause, if operative at all, must be so construed as to give it an effect consistent with the other parts of the statute and with the policy which they indicate.[9]   In the interpretation of a statute

[5] Bywater v. Brandling, 7 Barn. & C. 643; Burke v. Monroe Co., 77 Ill. 610; Torrance v. McDougald, 12 Ga. 526. And see Hagenbuck v. Reed, 3 Neb. 17; Frank v. San Francisco, 21 Cal. 668; People v. Burns, 5 Mich. 114.

[6] State v. Comm'rs of Railroad Taxation, 37 N. J. Law, 228.

[7] Albertson v. State, 9 Neb. 429, 2 N. W. 742; Ryan v. State, 5 Neb. 276; Quick v. White Water Tp., 7 Ind. 570.

[8] State v. Williams, 8 Ind. 191. In California it is provided (Pol. Code Cal. § 4484) that if conflicting provisions are found in different sections of the same chapter or article of the code, the provisions of the sections last in numerical order must prevail; but it is held that this has no application where the sections were passed at different times. People v. Dobbins, 73 Cal. 257, 14 Pac. 860.

[9] Sams v. King, 18 Fla. 557.

which remains in force, resort may be had to a proviso to it, although the proviso is repealed.[10]

CONTEXT.

75. **Sections, clauses, and provisions of a statute, as well as the particular words and phrases employed, are not to be considered in themselves alone and construed as if isolated from the rest, but they are to be interpreted with reference to the language surrounding and accompanying them,—the context; and if there is any ambiguity or doubt as to their intended meaning, the context must be consulted as a means of removing the obscurity.[11]**

When we speak of the "context," it is not meant merely that different words or clauses in the same sentence must be compared with each other, or successive sentences be read together. But in a wider sense, one section of a statute may stand as context to another, whether it immediately precedes or follows it or is more widely separated from it, provided it bears upon the same general subject-matter. Thus, for example, where one section of an act provides that a certain notice shall be published for ten days in succession, and another section provides that all notices under the act shall be published daily, Sundays excepted, these two sections must be read together, and they mean that the Sundays shall be included for enumeration, but not for publication.[12] If a statute, in one part of it, makes use of a word which is susceptible of two meanings, and in another place the same word is used in a single and definite sense, it is to be understood throughout in the latter sense, unless the object to which it applies, or the connection in which it stands,

[10] Bank for Savings v. Collector, 3 Wall. 495.

[11] Blackwood v. Queen, L. R. 8 App. Cas. 82; U. S. v. Pirates, 5 Wheat. 184; Cooper v. Shaver, 101 Pa. St. 547; Ruggles v. Washington Co., 3 Mo. 496; State v. Judge of Ninth District, 12 La. Ann. 777; McIntyre v. Ingraham, 35 Miss. 25; Crone v. State, 49 Ind. 538. "Ex antecedentibus et consequentibus fit optima interpretatio." 2 Co. Inst. 317.

[12] Taylor v. Palmer, 31 Cal. 240

requires it to be differently understood in the two places.[13] It also follows that particular words ought not to be permitted to control the evident meaning of the context. Thus, in a case in Wisconsin, the word "jury" was construed, not according to its common-law signification, but as meaning a board of assessors, because the context made it evident that the latter was the meaning intended by the legislature.[14] Further, in construing a statute, if there is a mistake apparent upon the face of the act, which may be corrected by other language in the act itself, the mistake is not fatal.[15]

Bi-Lingual Texts.

The early laws of Louisiana were promulgated in both French and English; and it is held that, in construing those portions of the code of that state which re-enact provisions originally enacted in both languages, both texts may be taken into consideration to aid in ascertaining their meaning as parts of one law, and obscurities or ambiguities in the English text may be cleared up by referring to the greater precision of the French text. But if the two texts cannot be reconciled, it is the English which must prevail.[16]

TITLE.

76. The title of a statute cannot control or vary the meaning of the enacting part, if the latter is plain and unambiguous. But if there is doubt or obscurity in the body of the act, the title may be consulted, as a guide to the probable meaning of the legislature, and should be accorded some weight in the interpretation. Especially is this the case in those states whose constitutions require the subject of the act to be expressed in the title.

The English judges, in most of the earlier cases, refused to take the titles of the statutes into consideration in aid of their interpre-

---

[13] James v. DuBois, 16 N. J. Law, 285.

[14] Williams v. McDonal, 4 Chand. (Wis.) 65.

[15] Blanchard v. Sprague, 3 Sumn. 279, Fed. Cas. No. 1,517.

[16] Viterbo v. Friedlander, 120 U. S. 707, 7 Sup. Ct. 962; Hudson v. Grieve, 1 Mart. 143; State v. Dupuy, 2 Mart. 177; Parish of Lafourche v. Parish of Terrebonne, 34 La. Ann. 1230; State v. Ellis, 12 La. Ann. 390.

tation. They held that reference to the title was not permissible, because it was not a part of the statute. "The title of an act of parliament," said Chief Justice Holt, "is no part of the law or enacting part, no more than the title of a book is part of the book; for the title is not the law, but the name or description given to it by the makers."[17] So also, Lord Hardwicke observed: "The title is no part of the act, and has often been determined not to be so, nor ought it to be taken into consideration in the construction of this act; for originally there were no titles to the acts, but only a petition and the king's answer; and the judges thereupon drew up the act into form and then added the title; and the title does not pass the same forms as the rest of the act, only the speaker, after the act is passed, mentions the title and puts the question upon it. Therefore the meaning of this act is not to be inferred from the title, but we must consider the act itself."[18] But this doctrine has been of late years silently abandoned. In the later volumes of reports we find many cases in which the title of a statute has been consulted as an aid in determining the meaning of the statute, and that, as a matter of course and without discussion.[19] And Huddleston, B., now says: "I think there is ample authority for saying that the title of an act may be looked at in order to remove any ambiguity in the words of the act."[20]

The earlier English doctrine on this point never gained any considerable recognition in this country. On the contrary, with us, it has been almost universally held that if the provisions contained in the body of the statute are expressed in ambiguous or doubtful

[17] Mills v. Wilkins, 6 Mod. 62. And see Chance v. Adams, 1 Ld. Raym. 77.

[18] Attorney General v. Lord Weymouth, 1 Ambl. 20. See, also, Hunter v. Nockolds, 1 Macn. & G. 640; King v. Williams, 1 W. Bl. 93; Jefferys v. Boosey, 4 H. L. Cas. 815, 982; Morant v. Taylor, L. R. 1 Ex. Div. 188. This doctrine was followed in a few American cases. See State v. Welsh, 3 Hawks, 404; Bradford v. Jones, 1 Md. 351; Cohen v. Barrett, 5 Cal. 195.

[19] Rawley v. Rawley, L. R. 1 Q. B. Div. 460; King v. Inhabitants of Gwenop, 3 Durn. & E. 133; King v. Cartwright, 4 Durn. & E. 490; King v. Wright, 1 Ad. & El. 434; Taylor v. Newman, 4 Best & S. 89.

[20] Coomber v. Justices of Berks, L. R. 9 Q. B. Div. 17, 33. And see Bentley v. Rotherham Board of Health, L. R. 4 Ch. Div. 588; Brett v. Brett. 3 Add. Eccl. 210.

language, or so as to be fairly susceptible of more than one inter·pretation, then it is permissible and proper to consider the title of the act, as a clue or guide to the intention and meaning of the leg·islature, and in this manner and to this extent it may be allowed to aid in the construction of the law.[21] But while this much is admitted, it is also firmly held that the meaning apparent upon the face of the act, if clear, sensible, and free from ambiguity, cannot be modified or varied by any considerations drawn from the title. The court in Georgia, in an early case, remarked: "The great diffi·culty which has been felt in the minds of some in the construction of this statute, it is believed, has been in giving too much attention to the title and preamble, without carefully examining the enacting clause. The title of the act and the preamble are, strictly speak·ing, no parts of it. It is true they may assist in removing am·biguities where the intent is not plain, but where the words of the enacting clause are clear and positive, recourse must not be had

[21] U. S. v. Palmer, 3 Wheat. 610, 631; Hadden v. Collector, 5 Wall. 107; Myer v. Car Co., 102 U. S. 1; Coosaw Min. Co. v. South Carolina, 144 U. S. 550, 12 Sup. Ct. 689; U. S. v. Union Pac. Ry. Co., 37 Fed. 551; Wilson v. Spaulding, 19 Fed. 304; U. S. v. McArdle, 2 Sawy. 367, Fed. Cas. No. 15,653; People v. Abbott, 16 Cal. 358; Bell v. Mayor, etc., of New York, 105 N. Y. 139, 11 N. E. 495; People v. O'Brien, 111 N. Y. 1, 59, 18 N. E. 692; Hines v. Wilmington & W. R. Co., 95 N. Car. 434; City of Rushville v. Rushville Natural Gas Co., 132 Ind. 575, 28 N. E. 853; Field v. Gooding, 106 Mass. 310; State v. Archer, 73 Md. 44, 20 Atl. 172; State v. Stephenson, 2 Bail. (S. Car.) 334; Comm. v. Slifer, 53 Pa. St. 71; Bradford v. Jones, 1 Md. 351; Cohen v. Barrett, 5 Cal. 195; Burgett v. Burgett, 1 Ohio, 469; Allor v. Wayne County Auditors, 43 Mich. 76, 4 N. W. 492; Deddrick v. Wood, 15 Pa. St. 9; Torreyson v. Board of Examiners, 7 Nev. 19. In Ogden v. Strong, 2 Paine, 584, Fed. Cas. No. 10,460, it is said that the English doctrine that the title of an act is no part of it, because added by the clerk, does not apply in the United States, where the legislature makes the title; but even though the title may not, strictly speaking, be a part of the act, yet it may serve in doubtful cases to explain and show the general purport of the act and the inducement which led to its passage. In truth, the question whether or not the title of the act is a part of the act is really not of the least importance in connection with the subject of construction. For if the statute is not ambiguous, there is no room for construction and neither the title nor anything else can be resorted to to vary its meaning. And if the act is ambiguous, there is no rule of law which restricts the court to the statute itself in the search for the meaning of the legislature.

to either of them." [22]   It follows, therefore, that the title of a statute cannot be used to extend or to restrain any of the provisions
contained in the body of the act; that is, cases which are clearly
not within the contemplation of the enacting clause cannot be
brought within it merely because the title appears to include them,
nor can cases which are plainly covered by the provisions of the
statute be excluded from its operation on the mere ground that the
title does not embrace them, unless, in the latter case, the statute
fails to conform to the constitutional requirement of correspond-
ence between the title and subject-matter.[23]   Thus, where the
words of the enacting clause of a statute, even a penal statute, are
more general than the title, it is the enacting clause which must
govern.[24]

In further elucidation of the proper influence of the title in statutory construction, we shall now cite a few of the most conspicu-
ous illustrations found in the reports.   A recent case before the
supreme court of the United States involved the interpretation of
the "alien contract labor law."   The title of this act is "An act to
prohibit the importation and migration of foreigners and aliens under contract or agreement to perform labor in the United States,
its territories, and the District of Columbia."   The enacting clause
prohibits the importation of "any" foreigners under contract to
perform "labor or service of any kind."   The question was whether
the statute applied to the case of a foreign clergyman imported by
an ecclesiastical society to serve as the rector of its church.   The
court said: "Obviously, the thought expressed in this [title] reaches
only to the work of the manual laborer, as distinguished from that
of the professional man.   No one reading such a title would suppose that congress had in its mind any purpose of staying the coming into this country of ministers of the gospel, or, indeed, of any
class whose toil is that of the brain.   The common understanding
of the terms 'labor' and 'laborers' does not include preaching and
preachers, and it is to be assumed that words and phrases are used

[22] Eastman v. McAlpin, 1 Ga. 157. And see Matter of Boston Mining &
Milling Co., 51 Cal. 624.

[23] U. S. v. Fisher, 2 Cranch, 358, 386; Hadden v. Collector, 5 Wall. 107;
People v. Abbott, 16 Cal. 358; State v. Cazeau, 8 La. Ann. 109; Auditor General v. Lake George & M. R. R. Co., 82 Mich. 426, 46 N. W. 730.

[24] U. S. v. Briggs, 9 How. 351.

in their ordinary meaning. So, whatever of light is thrown upon the statute by the language of the title indicates an exclusion from its penal provisions of all contracts for the employment of ministers, rectors, and pastors." On this and other grounds it was therefore held that the statute did not apply to the case at bar.[25] A leading English case involved the construction of "Lord Campbell's Act." The important question in the case was whether the jury, in giving damages apportioned to the injury resulting from the death of the decedent to the parties for whose benefit the action was brought, were confined to injuries capable of pecuniary estimation, or might add a solatium to the plaintiffs in respect to the mental sufferings occasioned by such death. On this question, the title of the act was consulted and was allowed some weight. It was "An act for compensating the families of persons killed by accidents," and from this Coleridge, J., inferred that it was not the design of parliament to allow for solacing their wounded feelings, but only for compensating their pecuniary losses.[26] So again, where a statute "relative to the revenue of the state," the principal object of which is taxation, authorizes the treasurer to collect sums to be paid by curators of vacant successions, it will be construed to apply to sums which go into the treasury as a revenue, and not those which, being deposited there for absent heirs, constitute no part of the revenue.[27]

But the reader should bear in mind that the argument drawn from the title is not entitled to the greatest weight in solving questions of statutory construction. It is a clue, rather than a criterion. It may aid in ascertaining the legislative intention, but does not fix it absolutely. It is not a rule that the construction of an ambiguous statute must be determined by the title; but the title may be called in aid. In point of fact, courts very seldom decide a question of statutory interpretation upon one consideration alone. They are wont to consider many things bearing upon the probable intention of the legislature, such as the relation of the statute to other existing legislation, the collocation and arrangement of the words, their character, as being technical or otherwise, the spirit

[25] Rector, etc., of Holy Trinity Church v. U. S., 143 U. S. 457, 12 Sup. Ct. 511.
[26] Blake v. Midland Ry. Co., 18 Q. B. 93.
[27] Succession of D'Aquin, 9 La. Ann. 400.

and reason of the law and the scope and purpose of the act, the circumstances which led to its enactment or the evil which it was designed to remedy, the presumptions against unconstitutionality, injustice, and absurdity, executive and legislative constructions put upon the act, contemporary history and usage, and so on. If considerations drawn from all or many of these sources conduce to the support of one theory as to the meaning of the law, the fact that the consideration of the title leads to the same conclusion will have some persuasive force and will strengthen the argument. But if the inference drawn from the title contradicts the inference drawn from a consensus of other arguments (entitled to greater weight), it should not be allowed to prevail against them.

Effect of Title under Constitutional Provisions.

Where the constitution of the state provides that each act of the legislature shall relate to but one subject, which shall be expressed in the title, the effect is to make the title a part of the enactment, so that any provisions of the act which lie outside the title will be rejected by the courts as unconstitutional, if that can be done without destroying the entire law. In this case, it is very clear that the title may be resorted to as an aid in the interpretation of the statute, and that it will be entitled to greater weight than belongs to it in the absence of this constitutional provision; since it must be presumed that the mind of the legislature was directed to the title no less than to the provisions of the enacting clause.[28] As already indicated, the real reason why the title is not ordinarily entitled to very great weight is that it is not always or necessarily subject to the scrutiny and thought of the members of the legislature with the same care as the enacting clause, and hence may not truly disclose the meaning of the legislature and the purpose of the statute. But if the constitution requires it to express the subject of the act, this objection is removed. "The constitutional mandate that the object of every law shall be expressed in its title has given

---

[28] People v. Wood, 71 N. Y. 371; Garrigus v. Board of Comm'rs of Parke County, 39 Ind. 66; Nazro v. Merchants' Ins. Co., 14 Wis. 295; Attorney General v. Central R. Co., 50 N. J. Eq. 52, 24 Atl. 964; Pennsylvania R. Co. v. Riblet, 66 Pa. St. 164; Coosaw Min. Co. v. South Carolina, 144 U. S. 550, 12 Sup. Ct. 689; Halderman's Appeal, 104 Pa. St. 251; Orvis v. Board of Park Comm'rs (Iowa) 56 N. W. 294.

the title of an act a two-fold effect. It has added additional force to the title as an indication of legislative intent in aid of the construction of a statute couched in language of doubtful import, and it also operates as a constitutional limitation upon the enacting part of the law. The enacting part of a statute, however clearly expressed, can have no effect beyond the object expressed in the title. To maintain any part of such a statute, those portions not embraced within the purview of the title must be exscinded, and if the superaddition to the declared object cannot be separated and rejected, the entire act must fail." [29] But it must not be supposed that, even under such a constitutional provision, the title of the statute may be considered, as an aid to its construction, unless there is need of interpretation by reason of obscurity or doubt in the body of the act. Says the supreme court of Indiana: "It is not said, by any writer that we know of, that the constitutional provisions in reference to the title of an act have so changed the rules of construction that the title may be looked to when the words of the statute are plain and unambiguous, and we do not think that such rules have been so changed. The only effect of such provisions in reference to titles of acts is to give greater weight and consideration to the title, in ascertaining the mind of the legislature, than was formerly given to titles, when the language of the act is ambiguous and doubtful." [30]

PREAMBLE.

77. The preamble to a statute can neither expand nor control the scope and application of the enacting clause, when the latter is clear and explicit. But if the language of the body of the act is obscure or ambiguous, the preamble may be consulted, as an aid in determining the reason of the law and the object of the legislature, and thus arriving at the true construction of the terms employed.

The preamble to a statute is an introductory clause which sets forth the reasons which have led to the enactment, by reciting the

[29] Dobbins v. Township Committee of Northampton, 50 N. J. Law, 496, 14 Atl. 587.

[30] Garrigus v. Board of Comm'rs of Parke County, 39 Ind. 66.

state of affairs intended to be changed, the evils designed to be remedied, the advantages sought to be secured or promoted by the new law, or the doubts as to the prior state of the law which it is meant to remove. It is thus an exposition of the motives of the legislature, and in some sense a key to the meaning of the terms which they have employed to express their avowed intention. But it is not an essential part of the statute, and is by no means universally found in modern laws. It is in the form of a statement of facts, and is usually prefaced by the word "whereas."[31] In an ancient case, it was said by Dyer, J., that, the better to understand the purview, the preamble of the act is to be considered; that the preamble is a key to open the minds of the makers of the act and the mischiefs which they intend to remedy, the which the preamble recites.[32] And it is now settled by the authorities, without any important dissent, that when any doubt or ambiguity is found to exist in the enacting clause, it is permissible and proper to resort to the preamble, as a clue or guide to the true interpretation.[33] "In construing an act of parliament," says Lord Blackburn, "where the intention of the legislature is declared by the preamble, we are to give effect to that preamble to this extent, namely, that it shows us what the legislature are intending; and if the words of enactment have a meaning which does not go beyond that preamble, or which may come up to the preamble, in either case we prefer that meaning to one showing an intention of the legislature which would not answer the purposes of the preamble or which would go beyond them."[34] It is sometimes said that the preamble is not a part of the statute. This is true in a measure. The preamble is no part of the enactment; it does not proprio vigore make the law; in it-

---

[31] "It is to the preamble, more especially, that we are to look for the reason or spirit of every statute, rehearsing, as it ordinarily does, the evils sought to be remedied, or the doubts purported to be removed, by the statute, and so evidencing, in the best and most satisfactory manner, the object or intention of the legislature in making and passing the statute itself." Brett v. Brett, 3 Add. Eccl. 210.

[32] Stowell v. Lord Zouch, Plowd. 369.

[33] Beard v. Rowan, 9 Pet. 301, 317; Mayor of Baltimore v. Moore, 6 Har. & J. 375; Edwards v. Pope, 4 Ill. 465; Sussex Peerage Case, 11 Cl. & Fin. 85, 143.

[34] Overseers of West Ham v. Iles, L. R. 8 App. Cas. 386.

self it has no constraining force upon the citizen or subject. But nevertheless it is for some purposes, and to a limited extent, a part of the statute. More especially, if it be referred to in the enacting clause to identify the subject-matter of the law, or to explain the motive or the meaning of the legislature, it can be used for this purpose.[35]

But while the uses of the preamble in cases of doubt or ambiguity are admitted, it is equally well settled that if the enacting clause is clear, sensible, and explicit, it cannot be controlled in its operation, nor extended or abridged, by any considerations drawn from the preamble; for, in such cases, there is no room for construction and no need to resort to the preamble.[36] And an act which is clear and specific in its enacting part will not be rendered inoperative or void by a defective or repugnant preamble.[37] Moreover, it should be remembered that the preamble to a statute does not invariably recite the real reason for its enactment. Its statements of facts are neither infallible nor conclusive. This should operate as a restraint upon the disposition to attach too great weight to the preamble as evidencing the purpose and intention of the law-makers. Barrington, in his Observations on the Statutes, remarks that "it is frequently said that the preamble to a statute is the best key to its construction; it often, however, dwells upon a pretense, which was not the real occasion of the law, when, perhaps, the proposer had very different views in contemplation. The most common recital for the introduction of any new regulation is to set forth that 'doubts have arisen at common law,' which frequently never existed; and such preambles have therefore much weakened the force of the common law in several instances."[38]

---

[35] Comm. v. Marshall, 69 Pa. St. 328.

[36] Yazoo & M. V. R. Co. v. Thomas, 132 U. S. 174, 10 Sup. Ct. 68; Emanuel v. Constable, 3 Russ. 436; Mason v. Armitage, 13 Ves. 25; U. S. v. Webster, Daveis, 38, Fed. Cas. No. 16,658; James v. DuBois, 16 N. J. Law, 285; Laidler v. Young, 2 Har. & J. 69; Blue v. McDuffie, Busb. L. 131; Clark v. Bynum, 3 McCord, 298; Jackson v. Gilchrist, 15 Johns. 89; Lucas v. McBlair, 12 Gill & J. 1; Tripp v. Goff, 15 R. I. 299, 3 Atl. 591; Eastman v. McAlpin, 1 Ga. 157.

[37] Erie & N. E. R. Co. v. Casey, 26 Pa. St. 287, 323; Salters' Co. v. Jay, 3 Q. B. 109.

[38] Barringt. Obs. Stat. (4th edn.) 394.

There are two classes of cases in which a conflict may arise between the preamble of a statute and its enacting clause, and in which, therefore, it is necessary to determine the force of the preamble in fixing the construction of the law.   The first case is where the words of the enacting clause are more broad and comprehensive than the words of the preamble.   The second case is where the words of the preamble are more broad and comprehensive than the words of the enacting clause.   In the first place, it is well settled, by the decided preponderance of authority, that general words in the body of the statute, if free from ambiguity, are not to be restrained or narrowed down by particular, or less comprehensive, recitals in the preamble.[39]   This is the general rule.   It is, perhaps, subject to exceptions; but such exceptions always arise out of the language of the particular act or the consequences which would attend its construction in a particular manner.   Thus, it was said by Lord Ellenborough: "It cannot by any means be regarded as a universal rule that large and comprehensive words in the enacting clause of a statute are to be restrained by the preamble.   In a vast number of acts of parliament, although a particular mischief is recited in the preamble, yet the legislative provisions extend far beyond the mischief recited; and whether the words shall be restrained or not must depend on a fair exposition of the particular statute in each particular case, not upon any universal rule of construction."[40]   And in another case, Lord Chancellor Cowper declared: "I can by no means allow of the notion that the preamble shall restrain the operation of the enacting clause, and that, because the preamble is too narrow or defective, therefore the enacting clause, which has general words, shall be restrained from its full latitude and from doing that good which the words would otherwise, and of themselves, import."[41]   It appears, however, that

---

[39] Fellowes v. Clay, 4 Q. B. 313; Mace v. Cammel, Lofft, 782; Colehan v. Cooke, Willes, 393; Holbrook v. Holbrook, 1 Pick. 248; Treasurers v. Lang, 2 Bail. (S. Car.) 430; Bywater v. Brandling, 7 Barn. & C. 643; Salkeld v. Johnson, 2 Exch. 256.

[40] King v. Peirce, 3 Maule & S. 62.   See, also, King v. Athos, 8 Mod. 136; Trueman v. Lambert, 4 Maule & S. 234.

[41] Copeman v. Gallant, 1 P. Wms. 314.   "The true meaning of the statute is generally and properly to be sought from the purview, providing part, or body of the act.   The preamble of a statute is no more than a recital of some

if the refusal to narrow down the general words of the enacting part of the law to a scope commensurate with the particular recitals of the preamble would lead to absurd or inconvenient consequences, or would result in harm or mischief in particular cases, then the generality of the enacting clause should be restrained by the preamble.[42]

In the second place, detailed and specific provisions in the body of the statute cannot be expanded beyond their proper scope by the use of more general expressions in the preamble. Thus, where the preamble refers to several matters or things, and only some of these, not all, are expressly mentioned in the enacting part of the statute, its terms cannot be extended to those things not provided for, merely in virtue of the larger recital in the preamble. For instance, in a case in Virginia, it was said: "The enacting clauses of the statute making provision only with regard to coupons detached from bonds of the commonwealth issued under the act of 1871, and making no provision with regard to coupons detached from bonds issued under the act of 1879, the circumstance that the latter are mentioned in the preamble, and though the representation, by way of recital, of a state of things as inducements to the act which follows might be applied to the latter as well as the former, the latter not being within the enacting clauses, to bring them within the purview of the act would be to go beyond what the legislature did, and to give to the preamble the province of enlarging and extending the act of legislation beyond the purview of the statute, and of conferring powers per se, which is warranted by no decision that has ever been made, but is contrary to the settled doctrine on the subject, as declared in judicial decisions and maintained by the

---

inconveniences, which by no means excludes any others, for which a remedy is given by the enacting part of the statute. Great doubts have existed how far the preamble should control the enacting part of the statute; but abundant cases have established that where the words in the enacting part are strong enough to take in the mischief intended to be prevented, they shall be extended for that purpose, though the preamble does not warrant it; in other words, the enacting part of the statute may extend the act beyond the preamble." Potter's Dwarris on Stat. 109.

[42] Seidenbender v. Charles, 4 Serg. & R. 151, 166; Ryall v. Rolle, 1 Atk. 165. See, also, Halton v. Cave, 1 B. & Ad. 538.

most eminent sages of the law in their published works.   It would
be to assume legislative power by the court." [43]

CHAPTER AND SECTION HEADINGS.

**78. Headings prefixed to the titles, chapters, and sections of
a statute or code may be consulted in aid of the interpretation, in case of doubt or ambiguity; but inferences drawn from such headings are entitled to
very little weight, and they can never control the
plain terms of the enacting clauses.**

"It would seem," says Endlich, "that the fact that a particular
provision is placed in a group prefaced by a particular heading
should not give the latter any very great weight in either extending
or restricting the plain language of the provision, nor prevent a construction of it in connection with, and in the light of, other provisions in other parts of the statute, classed under different headings, where, in the absence of such a division and classification, a comparison of all such provisions would be proper. It may be regarded
as the sound view that the grouping of provisions in an extended
statute, a code, or a revision of laws, is, in general, designed for
convenience of reference, not intended to control the interpretation;
or, at most, it may be regarded as indicating the opinion of the
draftsman, the legislators, or the codifiers, as to the proper classification of the various branches of the enactment, which may or may
not be accurate." [44]   In a case in Kansas, it is said that where a
statute is divided into separate subjects or articles, having appropriate headings, it must be presumed and held that the provisions
of each article are controlling upon the subject thereof and operate
as a general rule for settling such questions as are embraced therein.[45]   But the rule accepted by the most of the authorities is that
if the chapter or section heading has been inserted merely for convenience of reference, and not as an integral part of the statute,
it should not be allowed to control the interpretation.[46]   And while

---

[43] Comm. v. Smith, 76 Va. 477; Wilson v. Knubley, 7 East, 128.
[44] Endlich, Interp. § 70.
[45] Griffith v. Carter, 8 Kans. 565.
[46] Union Steamship Co. v. Melbourne Harbor Comm'rs, L. R. 9 App. Cas. 365.

it is not improper to refer to such headings, when it becomes necessary to ascertain the true meaning of ambiguous or doubtful expressions found in the body of the act,[47] yet such a resort is neither
necessary nor permissible when the language of the enacting part
is plain and clear.   Thus, in an English case, where the section of
the statute which was in question was prefaced by a short sentence
which might be taken as a kind of preamble or section-heading, it
was said by Kelly, C. B.: "Although we may refer to the introductory words of the section to put a construction upon a doubtful part
of the statute, yet if the language of the enactment is clear, and includes in express terms such an instrument as this [the deed in
controversy], we should not be justified in limiting that sense by
the introductory words."[48]

In some few of the states it is held that when a code or revision
of the statutes is passed or adopted by the legislature at one time

[47] Hammersmith & C. Ry. Co. v. Brand, L. R. 4 H. L. 171, 203.

[48] Latham v. Lafone, L. R. 2 Ex. 115.   But there are some English cases
in which considerable weight has been given to the section headings, as an
indication of the legislative intent.   Thus, in Shiel v. Mayor, etc., of Sunderland, 6 Hurl. & N. 796, it appeared that an ordinance of a local board of
health was headed "width and level of new streets."   It provided for the
width of new streets, dividing them into front streets, cross streets, and back
streets.   In a subsequent paragraph it provided that "no dwelling house shall
be built immediately adjoining any back street without the special permission of the board."   It was held that this provision applied only to new back
streets, and not to a new building in an old back street.   Again, the British
statute called the "Lands Clauses Consolidation Act" is divided into different subjects by headings, which are accompanied by corresponding words
in the margin.   One of these divisions is marked by the words "intersected
lands" in the margin.   In the body of the statute is a line containing these
words as a heading, "And with respect to small portions of intersected land,
be it enacted as follows."   Then follow two sections, the first of which (§ 93
of the act) begins thus: "If any lands not being situated in a town," etc.
The other section (§ 94 of the act) begins: "If any such land shall be so
cut through and divided," etc.   It was contended, in the case of the Eastern Counties, etc., R. Co. v. Marriage, 9 H. L. Cas. 32, that the rule that a
relative term refers to the next preceding antecedent should here be applied.
But it was held, principally in view of the headings, that the word "such"
was not confined to "lands not being situate in a town" as described in § 93,
but applied to the words in the general heading "small portions of intersected land."

and as one statute, the headings to the parts, titles, chapters, and sections are also enacted as and for a part of the law, and hence they are not to be considered, in construction, as the titles of ordinary statutes, but as parts of the act, defining and limiting its provisions.[49] But in others of the states which have adopted codes, very much less reliance is placed upon these headings. The decisions in these states proceed upon the reasonable ground that the actual worth of chapter and section headings as guides to the meaning of the law depends entirely upon their accuracy and the precision with which they are employed; if they are found, in numerous instances, to be misplaced or inaccurate, their value throughout the whole code or revision is depreciated. Thus, in Georgia, it is held that an act providing that judgments shall become dormant, in certain circumstances, is not to be read and construed as a "statute of limitations" merely because it appears in a chapter of the code bearing that heading. The court said that the classifications of the code were not law, nor were they at all accurate, and the only inference that could be drawn from the position of the act in question was that it was the opinion of the codifiers that it might fairly be classed as a statute of limitations.[50] So also in Maryland, "in arriving at the true construction of any particular section of the code, very little reliance can be placed upon the heading under which it may be found. There are many instances in which sections relating to different subjects are placed under the same head, and in some cases such sections are found in the same article. * * * In short, we have found that the only satisfactory and safe rule of construction to be adopted is to read and construe together all sections of the code relating to the same subject-matter, without reference to the particular article or heading under which they may be placed."[51] In the Revised Statutes of the United States, it is provided that "the arrangement and classification of the several sections of the revision have been made for the purpose of more convenient and orderly arrangement of the same, and therefore no inference or presumption of a legislative construction is to be drawn

---

[49] People v. Molyneux, 40 N. Y. 113; Barnes v. Jones, 51 Cal. 303.

[50] Battle v. Shivers, 39 Ga. 405.

[51] State v. Popp, 45 Md. 432. And see Huff v. Alsup, 64 Mo. 51.

by reason of the title under which any particular section is placed." [52]

Marginal Notes.

In the English statutes, the marginal notes are brief abstracts of the matter to which the section relates, or a word or phrase descriptive of the subject-matter, much resembling section-headings. In American statutes, marginal notes, when used at all, are of the same character, or, in codes and revisions, they are used for the purpose of referring to the statute compiled, the place where it may be found in full, and the date of its enactment. The rule is settled, both in England and in this country, that such notes are not available as a means of determining the interpretation to be put upon the body of the statute. The marginal note is no part of the statute, not being considered or passed upon by the legislature. It is nothing more than an abstract of the clause intended to catch the eye, and inserted merely to facilitate reference to the statute and promote the convenience of the reader in examining it. Nor are such notes always accurate or reliable. Hence they should never be allowed to control the construction of the statute, and it is doubtful whether they may be at all considered for that purpose. [53]

[52] Rev. St. U. S. § 5600.   See U. S. v. Fehrenback, 2 Woods, 175, Fed. Cas. No. 15,083.

[53] Attorney General v. Great Eastern Ry. Co., L. R. 11 Ch. Div. 449; Sutton v. Sutton, L. R. 22 Ch. Div. 511; Birtwhistle v. Vardill, 7 Cl. & Fin. 895, 929; Claydon v. Green, L. R. 3 C. P. 511; Cook v. Federal Life Ass'n, 74 Iowa, 746, 35 N. W. 500; Nicholson v. Mobile & M. R. Co., 49 Ala. 205. Compare King v. Inhabitants of Milverton, 5 Ad. & El. 841, 854.

PUNCTUATION.

79. **The punctuation marks in the published copies of an act are not allowed to control, enlarge, or restrict the plain and evident meaning of the legislature as disclosed by the language employed.**

80. **If there is no doubt as to the meaning of the legislature, other than such as is created by the defective or erroneous punctuation of the statute, the courts will disregard the punctuation marks and read the statute as if correctly punctuated.**

81. **If the statute is equally open to two constructions, and there is nothing to show which of them was intended by the legislature, except the punctuation, and if the punctuation would support one of such constructions but would be inconsistent with the other, the punctuation will govern.**

The British statutes, on the original rolls of parliament, are not punctuated at all, and although more or less marks of punctuation appear in the printed transcripts of the acts of parliament, they are not inserted by authority and are not regarded as an essential part of the law. In the legislative bodies of this country, the punctuation marks are usually inserted, with a greater or less approach to correctness, by the member who drafts and introduces the bill, are sometimes changed by the engrossing clerks, and are frequently reformed by the printer. They very seldom receive the attentive consideration of the legislature, and no great importance is ever attached to them during the progress of the bill through the house. For this reason it has come to be recognized as a settled legal doctrine that the punctuation marks are no part of the statute. Hence, in the matter of interpretation, they are never allowed a controlling force as against the obvious meaning of the act. The words used by the legislature to express its meaning are first to be considered, and if these convey a clear, definite, and sensible meaning, without any doubt or ambiguity, their significance cannot be enlarged, restricted, or perverted by any considerations flowing merely from the character and position of the stops.[54] "In the interpretation of written instruments, very little consideration is given by the courts to the punctuation, and it is never allowed to interfere with or control the sense and meaning of the language used. The words employed must be given their common and natural effect, regardless of the punctuation or grammatical construction;" and considerations based on the punctuation alone must never be allowed to "violate the well-settled rule that, where it is possible, effect must be given to every sentence, phrase, and word, and the parts must be compared and considered with reference to each other."[55] "Punctuation," says Baldwin, J., "is a most fallible standard by which to interpret a writing; it may be resorted to when all other means fail; but the court will first take the instrument by its four corners, in order to ascertain its true meaning; if that is apparent on judicially inspecting the whole, the punctuation will not be suffered to change it."[56]

If, therefore, the words of the act, taken in themselves alone, or compared with the context and read in the light of the spirit and reason of the whole act, convey a precise and single meaning, they are not to be affected by the want of proper punctuation or by the insertion of incorrect or misplaced marks. In that event, the court will disregard the existing punctuation, supply such stops as may be missing, transpose those which are erroneously placed, eliminate those which are superfluous, reform such as are incorrectly used, and read the act as if correctly punctuated.[57] For instance, where effect may be given to all the words of a statute by transposing a comma, the alternative being the disregard of a material or significant word, or grossly straining and perverting it, the former

[54] Hammock v. Loan & Trust Co., 105 U. S. 77; Stephenson v. Taylor, 1 Best & S. 101; Queen v. Oldham, 21 L. J. M. C. 134; State v. McNally, 34 Me. 210; Matter of Olmstead, 17 Abb. New Cas. 320; Murray v. State, 21 Tex. App. 620; Morrill v. State, 38 Wis. 428; State v. Payne, 22 Or. 335, 29 Pac. 787; Cushing v. Worrick, 9 Gray, 382; Martin v. Gleason, 139 Mass. 183, 29 N. E. 664; Archer v. Ellison, 28 S. Car. 238, 5 S. E. 713.

[55] O'Brien v. Brice, 21 W. Va. 704.

[56] Ewing's Lessee v. Burnet, 11 Pet. 41; Albright v. Payne, 43 Ohio St. 8, 1 N. E. 16.

[57] U. S. v. Lacher, 134 U. S. 624, 10 Sup. Ct. 625; Doe v. Martin, 4 Durn. & E. 39, 65; Gyger's Estate, 65 Pa. St. 311; Hamilton v. Steamboat R. B. Hamilton, 16 Ohio St. 428; Allen v. Russell, 39 Ohio St. 336; Shriedley v. State, 23 Ohio St. 130.

course is to be adopted.[58]   So, to take another illustration, an act of congress required a stamp to be placed upon every "memorandum, check, receipt, or other written or printed evidence of an amount of money to be paid."   The court, considering the act as a whole, and finding a change of punctuation necessary to make the statute harmonious and sensible and to avoid useless repetitions, decided that the comma after "memorandum" must have been erroneously printed there instead of a hyphen, so that the section should be construed as if it read "memorandum-check, receipt," etc.[59]   In an English case, a question arose upon the interpretation of an act of parliament which provided that it should not repeal any statute then in force "concerning aliens duties customs and impositions."   The question was whether this act should be read as if the word "aliens" were followed by a comma or by an apostrophe.   It is apparent that this would make an important difference in its meaning.   The master of the rolls compared two printed editions of the act, and found that they differed in the punctuation at this point.   The original roll of parliament had no punctuation at all.   He therefore considered the general spirit and object of the act, and found that its intention was to leave undisturbed the laws relating to taxes.   Hence he concluded that it should be read "aliens' duties, customs, and impositions." [60]   Especially is the existing punctuation to be disregarded or reformed where the marks, as they stand, would make the statute absurd or unmeaning, but a change of the punctuation would render it clear and intelligible.[61]

Nevertheless, punctuation often determines the meaning of a sentence.[62]   It is entirely possible to select words which are clear and specific in themselves, and place them in such an order and arrangement in a sentence that it shall be equally open to two constructions, each of which is perfectly consistent with the rules of grammar and the ordinary use of language.   In such a case, the choice between the two constructions cannot be determined in any other

[58] Comm. v. Shopp, 1 Woodw. Dec. (Pa.) 123; Albright v. Payne, 43 Ohio St. 8, 1 N. E. 16.

[59] U. S. v. Isham, 17 Wall. 496.

[60] Barrow v. Wadkin, 24 Beav. 327.

[61] Bradstreet Co. v. Gill, 72 Tex. 115, 9 S. W. 753; Randolph v. Bayue, 44 Cal. 366.

[62] Squires' Case, 12 Abb. Pr. 38.

way than by the marks of punctuation which may be inserted. Hence, while punctuation is ordinarily a weak and unreliable guide in questions of interpretation, it does not follow that it is to be disregarded altogether. While it is never permissible to make the construction depend upon the punctuation in cases where there is no real ambiguity other than that which the punctuation itself creates, and in such cases it will not be allowed to confuse a construction otherwise clear,[63] yet in other cases it may serve as an indication of the legislative intention, and may even, under peculiar circumstances, determine the question.[64] "Punctuation is the least reliable guide to the construction of a statute, but cannot properly be said to be without any force. In itself it is ordinarily insufficient to fix the sense of a statute where that is disputable, especially when the question is one of the force of a comma; but when the punctuation is strictly consistent with one of two senses, equally grammatical, and inconsistent with the other, it should be allowed the force of opening the question of construction to receiving aid from the context and from the nature of the purpose the statute has in view. It is certainly competent to cancel the equally weak argument that arises from the relative position in the sentence of the two clauses."[65] And if the two constructions between which the choice is to be made are equally consistent with the rules of grammar and the ordinary meaning of the words, and if no light upon the meaning of the legislature can be derived from the context or from admissible extraneous considerations, then the construction must be governed by the punctuation alone. For example, an act of congress prescribes fees for witnesses in the following terms: "For each day's attendance in court, or before any officer pursuant to law, one dollar and fifty cents." And it is held that the phrase "pursuant to law," on account of the punctuation, applies only to the attendance of witnesses before commissioners.[66] Cases of this kind not infrequently arise in the construction of the tariff acts of congress and it has more than once been found necessary to pass

[63] Weatherly v. Mister, 39 Md. 620; Pancoast v. Ruffin, 1 Ohio, 381; Price v. Price, 10 Ohio St. 316.

[64] U. S. v. Three Railroad Cars, 1 Abb. U. S. 196, Fed. Cas. No. 16,513.

[65] Caston v. Brock, 14 S. Car. 104.

[66] Cummings v. Akron Cement & Plaster Co., 6 Blatchf. 509, Fed. Cas. No. 3,473.

special acts to correct the punctuation of such statutes. One of the paragraphs of the tariff act of 1890 reads as follows: "Chocolate, (other than chocolate confectionery, and chocolate commercially known as 'sweetened chocolate') two cents per pound." In a case involving the construction of this clause, it was contended that the parenthesis should have ended after the word "confectionery," and this argument was supported by the official statements of members of the conference committees and by the history of the bill and its amendments. But since the attention of congress had been called to the mistake, and no action was taken thereon, the court held that it was not authorized, when construing the statute, to change the punctuation actually made, in the absence of other evidence that the intent of the statute required such change.[67]

USE OF SAME LANGUAGE AND CHANGE OF LANGUAGE.

82. Where the same language is used repeatedly in a statute in the same connection, it is presumed to bear the same meaning throughout the act; but this presumption will be disregarded where it is necessary to assign different meanings to the same terms in order to make the statute sensible, consistent, and operative.

83. Conversely, where different language is used in the same connection, in different parts of the statute, it is presumed that the legislature intended it to have a different meaning and effect.

Where the same word or phrase is used more than once in the same act in relation to the same subject-matter, and looking to the same general purpose, if in one connection its meaning is clear, and in another it is otherwise doubtful or obscure, it is, in the latter case, to receive the same construction as in the former, unless there is something in the connection in which it is employed plainly calling for a different construction.[68] But the presumption that the

---

[67] In re Schilling, 53 Fed. 81, 3 C. C. A. 440.

[68] Rhodes v. Weldy, 46 Ohio St. 234, 20 N. E. 461; Raymond v. Cleveland, 42 Ohio St. 529; James v. DuBois, 16 N. J. Law, 293; Pitte v. Shipley, 46

same meaning is intended for the same expression in every part of the act is not controlling; and where it appears that, by giving it effect, an unreasonable result will follow, and the manifest object of the statute be defeated, the courts will disregard the presumption, and will attach a meaning which will make the act consistent with itself, and carry out the true purpose and intent of the legislature.[69] Hence, when the general meaning and intention of the act are perfectly plain, it may be necessary to assign different meanings to the same word as used in different sections of the statute, or even in different sentences in the same section. Thus, in an English case, the act repeatedly used the word "rent;" but in order to carry out its meaning and purpose, and make it sensible and intelligible, it was considered necessary to take the word as meaning sometimes "rent charge" and sometimes "rent reserved."[70] Again, an act of parliament provided that "whosoever, being married, shall marry any other person during the life of the former husband or wife, shall be guilty of felony." A case arose in which the second marriage, aside from its bigamous character, would have been void by reason of a legal disability of the parties. It was argued that, in construing this statute, the same effect must be given to the word "marry" in both parts of the sentence, and that, consequently, as the first marriage must necessarily be a perfect and binding one, the second must be of equal efficacy in order to constitute bigamy, or, at least, that the words "shall marry" must be read as meaning "shall marry under such circumstances as that the second marriage would be good but for the existence of the first." But the court refused to accept this reasoning. Looking at the general purpose and meaning of the statute, and the evil which it was intended to prevent or punish, it was adjudged that the word "marry" could not have been intended to be used in the same sense in both parts of the sentence, but that "shall marry" should be taken to mean "shall go through the form and ceremony of marriage with another person," and consequently that a second marriage, the first remain-

---

Cal. 161; In re County Seat of Linn Co., 15 Kans. 500; Queen v. Poor Law Comm'rs, 6 Ad. & El. 56; In re National Savings Bank Ass'n, L. R. 1 Ch. App. 547; Courtauld v. Legh, 4 Exch. 126.

[69] Henry v. Trustees of Perry Tp., 48 Ohio St. 671, 30 N. E. 1122.

[70] Angell v. Angell, 9 Q. B. 328.

ing undissolved, would come within the statute, even though it might otherwise have been void or voidable for diriment impediments or lack of compliance with formal requisites.[71]

The general rule (with its exception) as above stated, is confined to the case of the same language being used in different places in the same statute. "The intention of one legislative body in the use and application of a term, in an act passed by it, is not conclusive as to the intention of another and different legislative body in the use of the term in the passage of another and different act. True, it is proper to look at such a circumstance, in arriving at a correct interpretation of the subsequent law, but still that interpretation must be such as is demanded by the terms of the act itself, if they are clear and unambiguous."[72] And there is no rule of construction requiring the same meaning to be given to the same word used in different connections in different statutes.[73]

If, in a subsequent statute on the same subject as a former one, the legislature uses different language in the same connection, the courts must presume that a change of the law was intended.[74] If a provision in one statute, which has received a judicial construction, is inserted in another, the same construction will be given to it; but if the clause varies, it shows a different intention in the legislature.[75]

INTERPRETATION CLAUSE.

84. The definitions and rules of construction contained in an interpretation clause are a part of the law and are binding on the courts; but they will not be extended beyond their necessary import, nor will they be allowed to defeat the intention of the legislature otherwise clearly manifested in the act.

An "interpretation clause" is a section sometimes incorporated in a statute, prescribing rules for its construction, or defining the

---

[71] Queen v. Allen, L. R. 1 C. C. R. 367.
[72] Feagin v. Comptroller, 42 Ala. 516.
[73] Rupp v. Swineford, 40 Wis. 28.
[74] Lehman v. Robinson, 59 Ala. 219; Rich v. Keyser, 54 Pa. St. 86.
[75] Rutland v. Mendon, 1 Pick. 154.

meaning to be attached to certain words and phrases frequently occurring in the other parts of the act. When a statute contains such a clause, the courts are bound to adopt the construction which it prescribes, and to understand the words in the sense in which they are therein defined, although otherwise the language might have been held to mean something different.[76] A definition incorporated in a statute is as much a part of the act as any other portion. It is imperative. "The right of the legislature to prescribe the legal definitions of its own language must be conceded."[77] "The right of the legislature enacting a law to say in the body of the act what the language used shall, as there used, mean, and what shall be the legal effect and operation of the law, is undoubted. If they have mistaken the meaning of the words they have used, when read in their ordinary and popular sense, or as legally and technically understood, still they may, in terms, declare what the law shall be for the future, under and by virtue of the terms employed."[78] An interpretation clause may have the effect to repeal one or more of the settled and accepted rules of statutory construction, either with reference to the particular act in which it is found, or, if inserted in a code or body of compiled laws, generally for the entire statute law of the state. Thus, in California, the fourth section of the Penal Code provides that "the rule of the common law that penal statutes are to be strictly construed has no application to this code. All its provisions are to be construed according to the fair import of their terms, with a view to effect its objects and to promote justice."[79]

But interpretation clauses, more especially in England, have been regarded with great disfavor, and the courts have manifested a disposition to hold them down to the narrowest possible effects. Says Wilberforce: "Severe censures have been passed upon this section [clause] by some of the judges. It has been said that a very strict construction should be placed upon a section which declares that one thing shall mean another; that interpretation clauses embarrass rather than assist the courts in their decisions, and frequently do a great deal of harm by giving an unnatural sense to words

[76] Smith v. State, 28 Ind. 321; Jones v. Surprise, 64 N. H. 243, 9 Atl. 384.
[77] Herold v. State, 21 Neb. 50, 31 N. W. 258.
[78] Farmers' Bank v. Hale, 59 N. Y. 53, 62.
[79] People v. Soto, 49 Cal. 67.

which are afterwards used in a natural sense without the distinction being noticed." [80]   In the first place, such clauses are strictly construed and not extended a whit beyond their necessary import. Thus, the interpretation clause in an English statute provided that the word "justice" should mean "a justice acting for the county in which the matter requiring the cognizance of such justice shall arise, and who shall not be interested in the matter."   But it was held that the last clause was merely declaratory of the common law, and was inserted only out of abundant caution, and that it was not intended to withhold jurisdiction from a justice who was interested in the matter, where both parties, knowing his interest, waived objections on that ground.[81]   Again, an act of the legislature directing that all statutes made for the suppression of gaming shall be construed remedially, passed when every species of gaming then punishable by law was treated as a misdemeanor, will not be applied to statutes subsequently passed making certain kinds of gaming felonies and infamous.[82]   Further, where an interpretation clause provides that a certain word shall include certain things, this does not necessarily exclude all other things beside those enumerated.   The object of such a definition is to give to the word a more extensive signification than it would otherwise bear; but if there be any other thing, not mentioned, to which the word would ordinarily be applied with propriety, it is not to be excluded.[83]

[80] Wilberforce, Stat. Law, 296.   And see Lindsay v. Cundy, L. R. 1 Q. B. Div. 348, 358.   In Queen v. Justices of Cambridgeshire, 7 Ad. & El. 480, Lord Denman observed: "We cannot refrain from expressing a serious doubt whether interpretation clauses of so extensive a range will not rather embarrass the courts in their decision than afford that assistance which they contemplate.   For the principles on which they themselves are to be interpreted may become matter of controversy, and the application of them to particular cases may give rise to endless doubts."   See also Allsopp v. Day, 7 Hurl. & N. 457.   In Queen v. Pearce, L. R. 5 Q. B. Div. 386, Lush, J., said: "I think an interpretation clause should be used for the purpose of interpreting words which are ambiguous or equivocal, and not so as to disturb the meaning of such as are plain."

[81] Wakefield Local Board of Health v. West Riding & G. Ry. Co., L. R. 1 Q. B. 84.   .

[82] McGowan v. State, 9 Yerg. 184.

[83] Ex parte Ferguson, L. R. 6 Q. B. 280.   A statute made certain provisions for the safe keeping of petroleum and certain dangerous products.   It

"An interpretation clause is not meant to prevent the word from receiving its ordinary, popular, and natural sense, whenever that would be properly applicable, but to enable the word, as used in the act, when there is nothing in the context or the subject-matter to the contrary, to be applied to some things to which it would not ordinarily be applicable." [84] Again, if the definitions contained in the interpretation clause are at variance with the intention of the legislature, as plainly manifested by the language employed in a particular part of the statute, it is that intention which must prevail, and the official definitions which must give way. On this point, an English vice-chancellor is reported as saying: "With regard to all these interpretation clauses, I understand them to define the meaning, supposing there is nothing else in the act opposed to the particular interpretation. When a concise term is used, which is to include many other subjects besides the actual thing designated by the word, it must always be used with due regard to the true, proper, and legitimate construction of the act." [85] And again, "although the meaning of the words is defined by the statute, yet that statute declares (what would have been supplied if it had not been so expressed) that the words are not to have that meaning attached to them in the interpretation clause if a contrary intention appears." [86] And in Louisiana, it is said that where positive enactments of the Civil Code are at variance with the definitions which it contains, the latter must be considered as modified by the clear intent of the former.[87] In the next place, statutory definitions of this character are not to be given any effect beyond the statute in which they are found or statutes in pari materia with it. "Definitions have no meaning beyond that which those who use them intend they should have. When incorporated in a code, they exclusively refer to the positive enactments inserted in that

---

enacted that "petroleum shall include any product thereof that gives off an inflammable vapor at a temperature of less than 100 degrees." Blackburn, J., said: "That means that petroleum shall mean petroleum and also include that which might not otherwise be considered as petroleum, viz., products derived from petroleum." That is, petroleum itself is not excluded by the terms of the act. Jones v. Cook, L. R. 6 Q. B. 505.

[84] Robinson v. Local Board of Barton-Eccles, L. R. 8 App. Cas. 798.

[85] Midland Ry. Co. v. Ambergate, etc., Ry. Co., 10 Hare, 359.

[86] Dean of Ely v. Bliss, 2 DeG. M. & G. 459.

[87] Egerton v. Third Municipality, 1 La. Ann. 435.

code on the subject of which they treat, and have no meaning beyond those enactments." [88] For this reason, an interpretation given in a statute is to be restricted to the purposes and effects of that statute, and not made a general rule of law. Thus, where an act relating to the registration of bills of sale provides that the term "personal chattels" shall be deemed to include fixtures, this does not make fixtures personal chattels for any purpose outside of that statute.[89] So also, a legislative definition in a statute does not govern in an indictment. "The construction of the statutes is governed by legislative definitions, that of indictments is governed entirely by the ordinary use of language." [90]

A distinction has also been taken between interpretation clauses which are incorporated in, and apply to, only one particular act of the legislature, and those which form a part of an entire code, revision, or compiled body of laws and are intended to govern the whole. "Statutory provisions," says Sutherland, "are made in various forms to have effect specially in the interpretation of the law. They are distinguishable, and all are not construed and applied in the same manner. There is a manifest difference between definitive or interpretation clauses which are special and those which are general, the former always having the most controlling effect where it is obvious that the legislature, without misconception of the effect of other legislation, have precisely in view the particular words or provisions to which the clause in question ostensibly applies." [91] To illustrate the operation of interpretation clauses in a general body of laws, we may mention that the code of Illinois provides, in relation to statutes, that "all general provisions, terms, phrases, and expressions shall be liberally construed, in order that the true intent and meaning of the legislature may be fully carried into effect." This provision, it is said, "requires a liberal construction to effectuate the purpose of the legislature, but it does not require the court to bring cases of a like nature, not named in terms or by clear implication, into the statute, nor to give a narrow and restricted meaning to the language employed, but to fairly and reasonably carry out the intention of the legislature as gathered from the entire provision or enactment." [92]

[88] Depas v. Riez, 2 La. Ann. 30.   [90] State v. Adams, 51 N. H. 568.
[89] Meux v. Jacobs, L. R. 7 H. L. 481.   [91] Sutherland, Stat. Constr. § 231.
[92] Hankins v. People, 106 Ill. 628.

CHAPTER VII.

EXTRINSIC AIDS IN STATUTORY CONSTRUCTION.

ADMISSIBILITY OF EXTRINSIC AIDS.

85. In the interpretation of a statute, if a doubt or uncertainty as to the meaning of the legislature cannot be removed by a consideration of the act itself and its various parts, recourse may be had to extraneous facts, circumstances, and means of explanation, for the purpose of determining the legislative intent; but those only are admissible which are logically connected with the act in question, or authentic, or inherently entitled to respectful consideration.

When Resort may be had to Extrinsic Aids.

The cardinal rule of all statutory construction is that the meaning and intention of the legislature are to be sought for. This meaning and intention are to be sought first of all in the statute itself,—in the words which the legislature has chosen to express its purpose. If these words convey a definite, clear, and sensible meaning, that must be accepted as the meaning of the legislature, and it is not permissible to vary it or depart from it by reason of any considerations found outside the statute or based on mere conjecture. In such case, there is no room for construction.[1] But if

---

[1] "Whether we are considering an agreement between parties, a statute, or a constitution, with a view to its interpretation, the thing we are to seek is the thought which it expresses. To ascertain this, the first resort in all

the words of the law are not intelligible, if there arises a substantial doubt as to their meaning or application, or if there is ambiguity on the face of the statute, then the endeavor must be made to ascertain the true meaning and intent of the legislature. And to this end, first of all, the intrinsic aids for the interpretation of the statute are to be resorted to. It should be read and construed as a whole; its various parts should be compared; each doubtful word or phrase is to be read in the light of the context; the interpretation clause, if there is any, should be examined to see if it defines or explains the ambiguous part; and light may be sought from the title of the act, the preamble, and even the headings of the chapters and sections.

But if these intrinsic aids are exhausted without success, if there still remains a substantial doubt or ambiguity, then recourse may be had to extraneous facts, considerations, and means of explanation, always with the same object, to find out the real meaning of the legislature.[2]

But this does not mean that all such extrinsic circumstances are entitled to equal weight in determining the meaning of the statute. Some of them will be of very great authority; others of very little force; some of no value, except as tending to confirm a preconceived view of the construction of the law. Neither does it mean that anything and everything outside the statute may be thus consulted in regard to its meaning. There is a rule on this point, although it has not been clearly formulated by the courts, but has

cases is to the natural signification of the words employed, in the order and grammatical arrangement in which the framers of the instrument have placed them. If, thus regarded, the words embody a definite meaning, which involves no absurdity and no contradiction between different parts of the same writing, then that meaning apparent on the face of the instrument is the one which alone we are at liberty to say was intended to be conveyed. In such a case, there is no room for construction. That which the words declare is the meaning of the instrument, and neither courts nor legislatures have the right to add to or take away from that meaning." Newell v. People, 7 N. Y. 9. "In construing these laws, it has been truly stated to be the duty of the court to effect the intention of the legislature; but this intention is to be searched for in the words which the legislature has employed to convey it." Schooner Paulina's Cargo v. U. S., 7 Cranch, 52, per Marshall, C. J.

[2] See People v. Schoonmaker, 63 Barb. 44.

rather been taken for granted and silently acted on.   It is similar
to the rule which requires the best evidence that is available, for
the proof of any fact in issue in an action or suit.   It may be thus
stated: The extrinsic fact or circumstance which it is permissible
to consider in the construction of an ambiguous statute must be
either logically connected with the act in question, as a statute in
pari materia, or it must be authentic (authoritative), such as a legislative declaration of the meaning of the law, or it must be inherently entitled to respect or to weight, by reason of the universality
of its acceptance or prevalence, or by reason of its official character.[3]   A general usage, a practical construction by the executive
department of the government, and an opinion by the legal adviser
of the executive, are examples of the last class.

It should also be observed that the principle which requires that
the intrinsic aids to the interpretation of the law shall be exhausted
before recourse is had to matters outside the statute does not for-
bid the conjoint consideration of all these matters, when they all
tend to the establishment of one and the same view in regard to
the construction to be adopted.   Very frequently, the courts will
state their opinion as to the proper construction of a statute and
support it by arguments drawn from many diverse sources, sources
outside the words of the act as well as those which are to be found
within it.   But the rule means that if the intrinsic means of determining the will and intention of the legislature are sufficient to
put a clear, definite, and sensible meaning upon the law, this should
be adopted, and it should not be rejected or overthrown on extraneous considerations.

Dictionaries.

Dictionaries, both legal, scientific, and general, may be consulted
by the courts, in proper cases, in the construction of a statute.   It

---

[3] "We are of opinion, on principle as well as authority, that whenever a
question arises in a court of law of the existence of a statute, or of the time
when a statute took effect, or of the precise terms of a statute, the judges
who are called upon to decide it have a right to resort to any source of information which in its nature is capable of conveying to the judicial mind a
clear and satisfactory answer to such question, always seeking first for that
which in its nature is most appropriate, unless the positive law has enacted
a different rule."   Gardner v. Collector, 6 Wall. 499.

is indeed quite customary for the judicial tribunals to turn to the standard lexicons for aid in determining the meaning to be assigned to words of common speech or to technical terms.   They do not recognize these works as binding authorities, which they are imperatively required to follow, but consider their definitions as persuasive evidence in support of the conclusions which they are induced, on other and more weighty considerations, to adopt.[4]   "I am quite aware," says Coleridge, C. J., "that dictionaries are not to be taken as authoritative exponents of the meanings of words used in acts of parliament, but it is a well-known rule of courts of law that words should be taken to be used in their ordinary sense, and we are therefore sent for instruction to these books."[5]   But "the best dictionary is but a guide to the true meaning of a word in a particular context, and can never be an absolute authority on so varied and fluctuating a subject as language.   It facilitates the comparison of the different meanings of a word, and aids the memory of the person in search of the particular meaning, but can rarely anticipate the exact color which will be given to any word or phrase by the context in which it is set."[6]   And "no meaning of a word which has received a construction, by law or uniform custom, can be adopted from the dictionaries in conflict with that construction. And where a word is reconcilable with law or established custom in the particular manner in which it is used, a different meaning cannot be given to it upon the authority of a lexicographer."[7]

Documents and State Papers.

Documentary evidence which is capable of throwing light upon the meaning of a statute is admissible in aid of its interpretation, especially when the evidence is of the character of a public official document or state paper.   This principle is well illustrated in the case of United States v. Webster.[8]   This case involved the construction of an act of congress providing for the payment of the

[4] See Burke v. Monroe Co., 77 Ill. 610; U. S. v. Three Railroad Cars, 1 Abb. U. S. 196, Fed. Cas. No. 16,513; Burnam v. Banks, 45 Mo. 351; Dole v. New England Mut. Ins. Co., 6 Allen, 386.

[5] Queen v. Peters, L. R. 16 Q. B. Div. 636.

[6] Hardcastle, Stat. Constr. (2d edn.) 172.

[7] State v. Hueston, 44 Ohio St. 1, 4 N. E. 471.

[8] Daveis, 38, Fed. Cas. No. 16,658.

expenses of the Florida war, and the question was as to the authority of a quartermaster to pay for property taken by the United States by impressment. Mr. District Judge Ware said: "Looking at the words of the act alone, it is difficult to derive from them an authority for the payment of any other claims than such as the quartermaster is authorized to settle by the general laws and military usage. But there is a paper, among the public documents of that session of congress, which may, like the preamble of a statute, serve to fix and give a more precise and definite meaning to these general terms, by showing the cause and purposes for which the act was passed. It is a paper which was prepared by the war department, submitted to the house of representatives, and by their order printed, before the passage of the law. It contains an abstract of the various claims which were, or would be, preferred against the United States, growing out of the Florida war, for the payment of which there was no authority under the existing laws, and which must therefore be ultimately rejected, unless provision were made for their settlement by a special act. It is a rule in the construction of a statute that recourse may be had to the preamble, though it is in strictness no part of the law, as one element for opening and expounding the meaning and intention of the legislature, although it cannot control the enacting part of the law when the words are clear and explicit, and are manifestly more comprehensive than the preamble. But when the words of the enacting part are ambiguous, or may fairly admit a larger or more restricted signification, then reference may be made to the preamble to determine which sense is intended by the legislature. The reason is that the preamble states the grounds and objects of the law. And when the reasons and grounds of the law are made known in any other manner equally certain and authentic, they are entitled to have the same influence in the construction of the statute as the preamble, if the meaning of the words is doubtful, because every law ought to be carried into effect according to the intention of the law-maker, when the intention can be certainly known. It appears to me that a document, prepared and published as this was, and preserved among the public archives of the country, stating the nature of the claims to be provided for, and the necessity of a special act for that purpose, and which was before the legislature at the time the act was passed, may be fairly invoked in aid of the exposition of the statute, not to control the meaning of the legislature clearly and explicitly expressed, but to give a precise and determinate meaning to words which are ambiguous or expressions which may be taken with a greater or less latitude of signification. If it does not bring before the court the objects and intentions of the law-maker in so solemn and authentic a form as when these intentions are set forth in a preamble, at least it affords a medium of exegesis, against which the court cannot shut its eyes without excluding from its consideration what would have an influence upon every mind studious of ascertaining the real intention of the law-maker." In another case, a statute provided that cities having 14,000 children between the ages of 6 and 21 years, as shown by the official returns of county superintendents made to the state superintendent, should have a board of metropolitan police. There were official reports to which the court could resort for information as to such population. Hence it was held that the act could not be pronounced indefinite and uncertain, in respect to the cities to which it was applicable.[9] So also, when, at the time of the passage of an act, a map was used by the legislature while considering the question, and was referred to in the act itself, it was held that it was thereby incorporated into, and became a part of, the act.[10] Public petitions presented to a legislative body, praying for legislative action, would also be admissible evidence of the meaning and intention, or the scope and effect, of a statute passed in pursuance of them. A memorial address to congress by the legislature of a state is also a document which is entitled to this sort of consideration. But a statement in such a memorial, to the effect that certain lands were not liable to taxation, cannot be admitted to control the judgment of the court, in reference to the construction of the tax laws of that state, when the court is clearly of the opinion that the statement was incorrect and the law was otherwise.[11]

Scientific and Political Writings.

When it becomes necessary to determine the meaning of words or phrases employed in a statute by the aid of extraneous circumstances, recourse may be had, for this purpose, to the published

[9] State v. Kolsem, 130 Ind. 434, 29 N. E. 595.
[10] People v. Dana, 22 Cal. 11.
[11] Ross v. Outagamie Co., 12 Wis. 26.

writings of scientists, publicists, and other authors, conversant with the particular subject-matter, provided that the works consulted are of generally accepted authority. The standard works on medicine, the physical sciences, commerce, political economy, and other subjects, are thus frequently referred to by the courts. Such sources of information are not invested with a controlling authority, but may often furnish valuable assistance to the judicial tribunals in their search for the meaning intended to be conveyed by an obscure or technically worded statute. For example, in a case in Alabama, it appeared that a statute made it a penal offense to play, in public places, "at any game with dice." The question arose as to whether the game called "backgammon" was within this statute, and to determine the nature of the game and solve this question, the court referred to and cited the "American Cyclopædia."[12] So, in a case before the supreme court of the United States involving the construction of the federal constitution, with a view to determine the validity of the income tax law of 1894, and especially with reference to the meaning of the phrase "direct taxes," the judges referred, among other authorities, to the published writings of Albert Gallatin, Alexander Hamilton, James Madison, and others.[13] And the reader need scarcely be reminded of the high measure of respect which is accorded to the opinions of the Federalist on all questions concerning the interpretation of the constitution of the United States.

Legal Text-Books.

The writings of legal authors, while never admitted to be absolutely authoritative, are often of considerable assistance to the courts in the department of statutory construction, as in other branches of the law. Such works may be consulted whenever a resort to extrinsic aids is permissible, and when their remarks are pertinent and well-informed. They serve as persuasive or cumulative evidence of the true meaning of the disputed statute, but the degree of respect to be accorded to their opinions will vary with the learning and reputation of the author, and the measure of care and right reason with which he has elucidated his subject. In an

[12] Wetmore v. State, 55 Ala. 198.
[13] Pollock v. Farmers' L. & T. Co., 15 Sup. Ct. 673.

English case, Jessel, M. R., observed: "The text-writers agree that this is the true view of the act. I should not have any difficulty without the assistance of the text-writers, but it is very satisfactory to find that they have considered it independently in the same way."[14] Lord Brougham, construing a Scotch statute, reinforced his opinion by references to the Scottish text-writers Erskine, Bankton, and Bell, and said: "The authority of all text-writers is in favor of the construction adopted by the court below."[15] So, on the question of the construction of an ancient statute, it was said: "We must look not only to the statute but to the commentary [upon it] of Lord Coke, which has been uncontradicted to the present day. When we see the authority of so great a writer, not only uncontradicted, but adopted in all the digests and text-books, we can scarcely err if we adhere to his opinion."[16]

Official Opinions.

The official opinions rendered by the law officers of the government, on questions of statutory construction, are always received with great respect. Thus, the opinions of the attorneys general of the United States, on questions involving the construction of the public land laws, when they have been accepted and acted upon by the department of the interior, are entitled to the highest respect. "These opinions of very eminent lawyers are worthy of high consideration, especially as, when giving them, they were the official advisers of the government, and their advice was accepted and acted upon by the department of the interior."[17]

Judicial Notice.

All those matters or facts of public and general notoriety of which the courts may take judicial notice may be summoned to their aid, when it is necessary to look beyond the words of a statute in order to determine its meaning and intention, or its proper scope and effect.[18] Thus, for example, for the purpose of putting a construction upon a statute which prohibits or regulates the manufacture or sale of "intoxicating" or "spirituous" liquors, the courts will take

---

[14] In re Warner's Settled Estates, L. R. 17 Ch. Div. 711.

[15] McWilliams v. Adams, 1 Macq. H. L. 120.

[16] Strother v. Hutchinson, 4 Bing. N. C. 83.

[17] Johnson v. Ballou, 28 Mich. 379, per Cooley, J.

[18] Mohawk Bridge Co. v. Utica & S. R. Co., 6 Paige, 554.

judicial notice that such fluids as whisky, brandy, gin, and rum, belong to the class mentioned in the act.[19]

STATUTES IN PARI MATERIA.

86. Statutes in pari materia are to be construed together; each legislative act is to be interpreted with reference to other acts relating to the same matter or subject.[20]

The reasons which support this rule are twofold. In the first place, all the enactments of the same legislature on the same general subject-matter are to be regarded as parts of one uniform system. Later statutes are considered as supplementary or complementary to the earlier enactments. In the course of the entire legislative dealing with the subject we are to discover the progressive development of a uniform and consistent design, or else the continued modification and adaptation of the original design to apply it to changing conditions or circumstances. In the passage of each act, the legislative body must be supposed to have had in mind and in contemplation the existing legislation on the same subject, and to have shaped its new enactment with reference thereto. Hence the same principle which requires us to study the context for the meaning of a particular phrase or provision, and which directs us to compare all the several parts of the same statute, only takes on a broader scope when it bids us read together, and with reference to each other, all statutes in pari materia. Whatever is ambiguous or obscure in a given statute will be best explained by a consideration of analogous provisions in other acts relating to the same sub-

[19] Schlicht v. State, 56 Ind. 173; Fenton v. State, 100 Ind. 598; Comm. v. Peckham, 2 Gray, 514; State v. Munger, 15 Vt. 290; State v. Wadsworth, 30 Conn. 55.

[20] Earl of Ailesbury v. Pattison, 1 Dougl. 28; U. S. v. Freeman, 3 How. 556; Vane v. Newcombe, 132 U. S. 220, 10 Sup. Ct. 60; LeRoy v. Chabolla, 2 Abb. U. S. 448, Fed. Cas. No. 6,267; Grant v. Cooke, 7 D. C. 165; The Harriet, 1 Story, 251, Fed. Cas. No. 6,099; U. S. v. Trans-Missouri Freight Ass'n, 7 C. C. A. 15, 58 Fed. 58; Church v. Crocker, 3 Mass. 17; Manuel v. Manuel, 13 Ohio St. 458; State v. Babcock, 21 Neb. 599, 33 N. W. 247; Kollenberger v. People, 9 Colo. 233, 11 Pac. 101; Billingslea v. Baldwin, 23 Md. 85; Green v. Comm., 12 Allen, 155; Hendrix v. Rieman, 6 Neb. 516.

ject, or by a study of the general policy which pervades the whole system of legislation. Secondly, the rule derives support from the principle which requires that the interpretation of a statute shall be such, if possible, as to avoid any repugnancy or inconsistency between different enactments of the same legislature. To achieve this result, it is necessary to consider all previous acts relating to the same matters, and to construe the act in hand so as to avoid, as far as it may be possible, any conflict between them.[21] Hence, for example, when the legislature has used a word in a statute in one sense and with one meaning, and subsequently uses the same word in legislating on the same subject-matter, it will be under-stood as using the word in the same sense, unless there is something in the context or in the nature of things to indicate that it intended a different meaning thereby.[22]

We are next to inquire when different statutes are to be considered as in pari materia, within the meaning of this rule. According to the supreme court of Connecticut, "statutes are in pari materia which relate to the same person or thing, or to the same class of persons or things. The word 'par' must not be confounded with

---

[21] "The purpose of the rule of construction under discussion is, of course, like that of every other, to elucidate the meaning of a given statute. Its method is to ascertain the meaning of any particular phrase or provision in the light of every direction made upon the subject-matter it refers to by the legislature up to the time when the court is called upon to pronounce its judgment. It requires particular phrases, left doubtful by the act itself, to be construed as synonymous with, or analogous to, the same phrases used in other statutes upon the same subject in such connections or surroundings as define their meaning beyond question, or point emphatically to a certain interpretation. It requires gaps left in the act, not amounting to casus omissi, to be filled from the materials supplied by other statutes upon the same subject and in harmony with them. It requires words capable of several meanings, the choice among which is not determined by the use of words in a definite and unmistakable sense in one of the other statutes, to be so construed, if possible, as to preserve in force and effect, side by side with them, the words of earlier statutes, to the avoidance of an interpretation which would raise a repugnancy between the earlier and later statutes, fatal to the former. The effect is to preserve harmony and consistency in the entire body of the legislation upon a given subject-matter." Endlich, Interp. § 53.

[22] In re County Seat of Linn County, 15 Kans. 500. See, also, Robbins v. Omnibus R. Co., 32 Cal. 472.

the term 'similis.' It is used in opposition to it, as in the expression 'magis pares sunt quam similes,' intimating not likeness merely but identity. It is a phrase applicable to public statutes or general laws, made at different times, and in reference to the same subject. Thus, the English laws concerning paupers and their bankrupt acts are construed together, as if they were one statute and as forming a united system, otherwise the system might, and probably would, be unharmonious and inconsistent. Such laws are in pari materia." [23] To illustrate further, all the statutes of the same state relating to the property rights and contracts of married women, removing their common-law disabilities, authorizing them to manage their separate estates, to engage in business, etc., are to be read and construed together as constituting one system. Though they may have been passed at different times, successively advancing to a standard the opposite of that of the common law, they are all strictly in pari materia, and any doubt or ambiguity in one should be cleared up by reference to the terms, the purpose, and the policy of the rest.[24] Again, an act authorizing married women to dispose of their property by will is in pari materia with the general statute relating to the execution and proof of wills.[25] A statute in relation to attachments against steamboats for debt is in pari materia with the general attachment law of the state, and hence, in so far as the special law is silent as to the modes of proceeding in the execution and return of writs issued under it, they must be regulated by the general rules prescribed by the general law.[26] Again, it is said that the rule of construction by the aid of statutes in pari materia is especially applicable in the case of revenue laws, which though made up of independent enactments, are regarded as one system, in which the construction of any separate act may be aided by the examination of other provisions which compose the system.[27] And the same rule is applicable to the provisions in appropriation acts.[28] An act providing for a homestead and exemption for fam-

---

[23] United Society v. Eagle Bank, 7 Conn. 456.

[24] Perkins v. Perkins, 62 Barb. 531.

[25] Linton's Appeal, 104 Pa. St. 228.

[26] Wallace v. Seales, 36 Miss. 53.

[27] U. S. v. Collier, 3 Blatchf. 325, Fed. Cas. No. 14,833.

[28] Converse v. U. S., 21 How. 463.

ilies of minor children is in pari materia with the laws allowing
dower to the widow and minor children of a decedent, and is to be
construed in harmony therewith.[29] So also, all the laws of the
state, whenever passed, relating to the subject of the regulation of
the liquor-traffic, are in pari materia.[30] In a case in Massachusetts,
it appeared that a statute prohibited discrimination against negroes
in any licensed inn or in any public place of amusement. A later
act prohibited the exclusion of such persons from any public place
of amusement "licensed under the laws" of the state. It was considered that the two acts were in pari materia, and should be read
together, and that the second act showed that the public places of
amusement referred to in the first were such as were licensed.[31]
Again, two statutes requiring certain sums to be paid into the state
treasury by a city gave a certain court jurisdiction to enforce the
payment. A third act required an additional payment, and thereby
increased the aggregate, but was silent as to the mode of enforcement. It was held that the three acts should be construed together,
and that the remedy given by the two former was applicable under
the last.[32] So also, an act providing for convict labor on the state
capitol grounds and one for leasing the penitentiary are in pari
materia.[33] Especially is it the rule that different legislative enactments passed upon the same day or at the same session, and relating to the same subject, are to be read as parts of the same act.[34]
And if one statute refers to another for the power given by the
former, the statute referred to is to be considered as incorporated

[29] Roff v. Johnson, 40 Ga. 555.

[30] Ferguson v. Board of Sup'rs of Monroe County, 71 Miss. 524, 14 South. 81.

[31] Comm. v. Sylvester, 13 Allen, 247.

[32] City of Louisville v. Comm., 9 Dana, 70.

[33] State v. Clark, 54 Mo. 216.

[34] People v. Jackson, 30 Cal. 427; Chandler v. Lee, 1 Idaho, N. S. 349. "It
is to be observed that in the comparison of different statutes passed at the
same session or nearly at the same time, this circumstance has weight; for
it is usually referred to as indicating the prevalence of the same legislative
purpose, as rendering it unlikely that any marked contrariety was intended.
But whether the prior statute is recent or of long standing, it must yield if
there is a conflict. But with a view to ascertain the intent of the legislature
on a given subject at any time, it must all be considered, whether it has
continued in force or been modified by successive changes." Sutherland,
Stat. Constr. § 283.

in the one making the reference.[35]   But, on the other hand, a statute designed to prevent accidents and injury from the reckless driving of vehicles of all sorts is not in pari materia with an act regulating the rates of toll on a local turnpike; and hence the fact that the former statute was held applicable to a bicycle is no reason why the latter act should be held so applicable.[36]   And again, a statute relating to the confinement of cattle, so as to prevent their straying on the premises of others, is not in pari materia with a statute which prescribes the rule of diligence to be observed by railway companies in the running of their trains and defines their liabilities in cases where stock is killed; such acts relate to distinct subjects, and the one should not be interpreted by the other.[37]

In order that one statute should be considered as in pari materia with another, so as to lend its aid on a question of interpretation, it is not necessary that the latter should refer to the former.   Nor is it necessary that the earlier act should still continue in force.   Although it may have expired by its own limitation, or though it may have been expressly or impliedly repealed, still it is to be considered and read as explanatory of the later enactment.[38]   Thus, for example, one section of an act of congress defined the term "Indian country."   It was not re-enacted in the Revised Statutes of the United States, and therefore, by § 5596 thereof, was repealed.   Yet it was held that it may be referred to for the purpose of ascertaining the meaning of the phrase as found in other sections of the Revised Statutes, which were re-enactments of other parts of the original act.[39]   Although a proviso to a statute is unconstitutional, and must therefore be rejected and denied any effectual operation, yet it cannot be disregarded in putting an interpretation upon the remaining portion of the act.[40]   And statutes in pari materia, passed

[35] Nunes v. Wellisch, 12 Bush, 363; Turney v. Wilton, 36 Ill. 385.

[36] Williams v. Ellis, L. R. 5 Q. B. Div. 175.

[37] Central R. Co. v. Hamilton, 71 Ga. 461.

[38] King v. Loxdale, 1 Burr. 445; Medbury v. Watson, 6 Metc. (Mass.) 246; Church v. Crocker, 3 Mass. 17; Daniels v. Comm., 7 Pa. St. 371; Forqueran v. Donnally, 7 W. Va. 114.

[39] Ex parte Crow Dog, 109 U. S. 556, 3 Sup. Ct. 396; U. S. v. Le Bris, 121 U. S. 278, 7 Sup. Ct. 894.   See, also, Attorney General v. Lamplough, L. R. 3 Ex. Div. 214.

[40] Comm. v. Potts, 79 Pa. St. 164.

after the law in question, as well as those enacted before it, may be considered in its interpretation.[41] And it is held that contemporaneous legislation which is of a similar nature, although not precisely in pari materia, is within the reason of the rule, and may be referred to for the same purpose.[42] But amendments to a bill, offered during its passage, but which were not finally incorporated in the statute as passed, cannot be considered in interpreting the statute.[43]

But although the statute under consideration may be one of a series or group, it may still be that the legislature designs to depart from the general purpose or policy of its previous enactments on the general subject; and if such a design is unmistakably apparent on the face of the act, it must be given effect. It would be entirely erroneous, in such a case, to defeat the will of the legislature by undertaking to reconcile the act with prior statutes or to control its terms by theirs. Hence this rule of construction is to be resorted to only in cases of doubt or ambiguity, or where the words, in their ordinary and prima facie signification, would raise an undesigned conflict with previous laws. It is not applicable when the statute is plain and unambiguous and needs no such aid to reconcile it with the existing body of laws. In such cases, there is no occasion to resort to any extrinsic circumstances to determine the meaning of the statute, nor is it justifiable to do so. The legislature must be understood to have expressed its meaning in the words employed. It would be a perversion of the rule to apply it for the purpose of defeating the plainly expressed will of the legislative body.[44] And although statutes relating to the same subject are to be construed together, this rule does not go to the extent of controlling the language of subsequent statutes by any supposed policy of previous ones.[45]

41 Chase v. Lord, 77 N. Y. 1; Smith v. People, 47 N. Y. 330; U. S. v. Freeman, 3 How. 556.

42 Chase v. Lord, 77 N. Y. 1.

43 Lane v. Kolb, 92 Ala. 636, 9 South. 873.

44 State v. Cram, 16 Wis. 343; Chase v. Lord, 77 N. Y. 1; Ex parte Blaiberg, L. R. 23 Ch. Div. 254; Ingalls v. Cole, 47 Me. 530.

45 Goodrich v. Russell, 42 N. Y. 177.

Private Acts in Pari Materia.

The rule which requires the comparison of statutes in pari materia, for the purpose of construction, does not apply to private acts.
A statute conferring special privileges or imposing particular obligations is not to be construed by reference to any other private act,
unless, indeed, the two relate to the very same parties and the
identical subject-matter. Such private statutes stand upon the
same basis with contracts by deed, which, generally, are not to be
affected by evidence aliunde. "It is unquestionably a correct principle," says Mellen, C. J., "that public statutes made in pari materia
should be construed as though their several provisions were embraced in one act, or that one act may be explained and construed
by comparison with another, all having a general relation to the
same subject-matter. It is at least doubtful, even in the construction of public statutes, whether the principle before stated can in
any case be admitted where they relate and extend to subjects distinct and independent of each other, which have been the occasion
of legislation at successive periods. Be this as it may, there is a
manifest distinction between a public statute, which is of universal
concernment and obligation and prescribes a rule of action to all,
and a grant by the legislature, or a private act granting certain
chartered privileges to individuals, or to be executed by persons appointed for the purpose and under bond for their fidelity. The
former is the declaration of the sovereign will, and when constitutionally proclaimed it becomes binding on all citizens, without any
subsequent assent on their part, express or implied. But such is not
the effect of a grant or charter of privileges to individuals, or of any
private act to be executed in the manner before mentioned. Such
an act, though passing with all constitutional sanctions, possesses
no binding force, even on the grantees of such chartered privileges,
unless expressly or by implication accepted by them, or on those
appointed to carry its provisions into execution, until they have
accepted the appointment and subjected themselves to a legal obligation to perform the duties it imposes. Then, and not otherwise,
it is in effectual operation. And why is it not? Simply because
such an act is in the nature of a contract, to the perfection of which
the assent of two or more minds is always necessary. Can an individual, when he receives a grant from the legislature, or when a

private act is passed for his benefit, be bound to look into and carefully examine the language of other grants and private acts, in order to ascertain the true meaning of the grant or act made for his own benefit? This question seems to be of easy solution. If, in the present instance, the condition of the bond had contained a distinct recital of the several duties to be performed by the defendants, without any reference to the act, it would then present the common case of a contract by deed between two parties, in which evidence aliunde could not be admitted to limit or extend the condition, or in any manner be brought in aid of its construction. The same principle must exclude proof aliunde in both cases; for both are cases of contract. In the case at bar, the act itself, being a private act or grant, must be construed by a careful examination of its language, and by no other mode." [46] In pursuance of this principle, it is held that where separate statutes are passed, each chartering a boom company and authorizing the erection of a boom, they must be interpreted separately, though both become the property of one company; and an act consolidating the two companies will not change the liability of either under its act of incorporation.[47]

Constitutional and Statutory Provisions in Pari Materia.

It has sometimes been said that statutory enactments and constitutional provisions, when in pari materia, are to be read and construed together as forming one system.[48] It is true, as already explained, that every statute should be so construed, if possible, as to make it harmonize with the provisions of the constitution and so as to avoid any conflict between them, so that the act, if it can be done, shall be saved from the charge of unconstitutionality. But the question here presented is different. The object of comparing one statute with another statute in pari materia is not solely to

[46] Thomas v. Mahan, 4 Me. 513. "Private acts of the legislature, conferring distinct rights on different individuals, which never can be considered as being one statute or the parts of a general system, are not to be interpreted by a mutual reference to each other. As well might a contract between two persons be construed by the terms of another contract between different persons. The obligation of a contract cannot be impaired by this indirect proceeding." United Society v. Eagle Bank, 7 Conn. 456.

[47] Gould v. Langdon, 43 Pa. St. 365.

[48] Billingsley v. State, 14 Md. 369.

reconcile any apparent differences between them, but also to find the explanation of obscure or ambiguous provisions in the one by the aid of the other. In respect to this latter purpose, it is at least doubtful whether a statute may be compared with the constitution, as it might be compared with another statute. The objections to such a course are well stated by the supreme court of South Carolina, in the following terms: "Where enactments separately made are read in pari materia, they are treated as having formed, in the mind of the enacting body, parts of a connected whole, though considered by such body at different moments of time and under distinct and separate aspects of the common subject. Such a principle is in harmony with the actual practice of legislative bodies, and it is essential to give unity to the laws and a consistent embodiment in a connected system. It is difficult to see how this principle can become the means of connecting, for the purpose of construction, clauses and provisions of a constitution established by an authority distinct from and independent of such legislative body, and proceeding by different methods, with the enactment of a strictly legislative body. As the two bodies cannot in their nature unite to carry out a common purpose, it is difficult to see how their independent enactments can be treated as if they had such capacity and intention." [49]

CONTEMPORARY HISTORY.

87. When a resort to extrinsic evidence becomes necessary, in the construction of a statute, it is proper to consider the facts of contemporary history, and especially the evil which the statute was designed to correct and the remedy intended. [50]

In one of the ancient and most important cases on the subject of statutory construction, we read: "It was resolved by the barons of

---

[49] State v. Williams, 13 S. Car. 546.

[50] King v. Inhabitants of Hodnett, 1 Durn. & E. 96; In re Wahll, 42 Fed. 822; Woods v. Mains, 1 Greene (Iowa) 275; Winslow v. Kimball, 25 Me. 493; Alexander v. Worthington, 5 Md. 471; Sibley v. Smith, 2 Mich. 486; Clark v. City of Janesville, 10 Wis. 136; Big Black Creek Imp. Co. v. Comm., 94 Pa. St. 450; Keith v. Quinney, 1 Oreg. 364; Tonnele v. Hall, 4 N. Y. 140; Fairchild v. Gwynne, 16 Abb. Pr. 23; State v. Nicholls, 30 La. Ann. 980.

the exchequer that for the sure and true interpretation of all statutes in general (be they penal or beneficial, restrictive or enlarging
of the common law) four things are to be discerned and considered:
(1) what was the common law before the making of the act, (2)
what was the mischief and defect for which the common law did not
provide, (3) what remedy the parliament hath resolved and appointed to cure the disease of the commonwealth, (4) the true reason of
the remedy.   And then the office of all the judges is always to make
such construction as shall suppress the mischief and advance the
remedy, and to suppress subtle inventions and evasions for continuance of the mischief and pro privato commodo, and to add force
and life to the cure and remedy, according to the true intent of the
makers of the act, pro bono publico." [51]   "The occasion of the enactment of a law," says another court, "may always be referred to in
interpreting and giving effect to it.   The court should place itself
in the situation of the legislature and ascertain the necessity and
probable object of the statute, and then give such construction to
the language used as to carry the intention of the legislature into
effect, so far as it can be ascertained from the terms of the statute
itself." [52]   "Courts, in construing a statute, may with propriety recur to the history of the times when it was passed; and this is
frequently necessary, in order to ascertain the reason as well as the
meaning of particular provisions in it." [53]   Hence, whenever light
can be derived from such sources, the courts will take judicial notice of the facts of contemporary history, the prior state of the law,
the particular abuse or defect which the act was meant to remedy,
and the application to such state of affairs of the language which it
employs.   They will also, for this purpose, inform themselves as to
such facts and circumstances by any and all available means.[54]
Thus, while the courts cannot recur to the views of individual members of the legislative body expressed in debate on the act, yet they
may advise themselves as to the history of the times and the general state of public, judicial, and legislative opinion at that period.[55]

[51] Heydon's Case, 3 Coke, 7a.   See, also, 1 Bl. Comm. 87.
[52] People v. Supervisors of Columbia Co., 43 N. Y. 130.
[53] U. S. v. Union Pac. R. Co., 91 U. S. 72.
[54] Lake v. Caddo Parish, 37 La. Ann. 788.
[55] U. S. v. Oregon & C. R. Co., 57 Fed. 426.

For instance, in the interpretation of the "alien contract labor law," the supreme court of the United States held that it was justified in looking into contemporaneous events, including the situation as it existed, and as it was pressed upon the attention of congress, while the act was under consideration; and to this end, it considered not only the general historical condition of the times, as showing the abuse against which the statute was directed, but also the petitions presented to congress asking for the enactment of such a law, the testimony given before the congressional committees, and the reports of those committees to their respective houses.[56]

But this rule has its necessary restrictions. Such evidence of the meaning of the legislature is not to be resorted to unless there is substantial need of it; that is, unless there is a real doubt or ambiguity on the face of the enactment. "As has been truly observed, we have nothing to do with the history of the words unless the words in the statute are doubtful and require historical investigation to explain them. If the words are really and fairly doubtful, then, according to well-known legal principles and principles of common sense, historical investigation may be used for the purpose of clearing away the doubts which the phraseology of the statute creates."[57]   It is also said that the intention of the legislature in enacting a statute cannot be determined by reference to any traditional history of the occasion of its passage, unless that results from some known state of embarrassment under the former law.[58] And what is termed the policy of the government with reference to any particular legislation is declared to be too unstable a ground upon which to rest the judgment of the court in the interpretation of statutes.[59]

[56] Rector, etc., of Holy Trinity Church v. U. S., 143 U. S. 457, 12 Sup. Ct. 511.
[57] Queen v. Most, L. R. 7 Q. B. Div. 244.
[58] Barker v. Esty, 19 Vt. 131.
[59] Hadden v. Collector, 5 Wall. 107.

CONTEMPORARY CONSTRUCTION AND USAGE.

88. When the meaning of a statute is doubtful, a practical construction put upon it at the time of its passage, or soon afterwards, and universally acquiesced in for a long period of time, as shown by a general usage, will be entitled to great weight and will be accepted as the true construction, unless there are cogent reasons to the contrary.

Contemporary Construction.

The contemporary construction of an old statute, even though not official or per se authoritative, is entitled to great consideration, more especially if such construction was universally acquiesced in and acted upon; and in view of the inconveniences which would result from overruling it, it will not be reversed or changed by the courts unless it is very manifest that it was altogether erroneous.[60] "Contemporanea expositio," says Coke, "est fortissima in lege." [61] "A contemporaneous construction is that which the statute receives soon after its enactment. This, after the lapse of time, without change of that construction by legislation or judicial decision, has been declared to be generally the best construction. It gives the sense of the community as to the terms made use of by the legislature. If there is ambiguity in the language, the understanding of the application of it when the statute first goes into operation sanctioned by long acquiescence on the part of the legislature

---

[60] Gorham v. Bishop of Exeter, 15 Q. B. 52; Blankley v. Winstanley, 3 Durn. & E. 279; Earl of Buckinghamshire v. Drury, 2 Eden, 60; Bank of United States v. Halstead, 10 Wheat. 51; Stuart v. Laird, 1 Cranch, 299; McKeen v. Delancy, 5 Cranch, 22; Morrison v. Barksdale, 1 Harp. (S. Car.) 101; Rogers v. Goodwin, 2 Mass. 475; Packard v. Richardson, 17 Mass. 122; Opinion of Justices, 3 Pick. 517; Board of Comm'rs of Franklin Co. v. Bunting, 111 Ind. 143, 12 N. E. 151; Fall v. Hazelrigg, 45 Ind. 576; Matter of Warfield's Will, 22 Cal. 51; People v. Loewenthal, 93 Ill. 191; Brown v. State, 5 Colo. 496.

[61] 2 Co. Inst. 11. So, also, in the Roman law. "Si de interpretatione legis quaeratur, in primis inspiciendum est quo jure civitas retro in ejusmodi casibus usa fuisset, optima enim est legum interpres consuetudo." Dig. 1, 3, 37.

and judicial tribunals, is the strongest evidence that it has been rightly explained in practice. A construction, under such circumstances, becomes established law." [62] But if the meaning of the statute is too plain to admit of any reasonable doubt, it cannot be thus overruled. Thus, the contemporary construction given to a statute by an officer intrusted with its execution cannot be adopted by the judiciary if contrary to the judicial construction. [63]

Usage.

The best evidence of a contemporary construction of a statute, and of its universal acceptance, is a general usage, pursuant to such construction. Where the statute is of doubtful import on its face, great weight is due to such a usage, and it will not be disregarded by the courts, unless there are very satisfactory reasons to induce them to such a course of action. [64] A very good illustration of the effect of usage, in this behalf, is found in an early case in Massachusetts. On the interpretation of certain colonial laws of that state, giving to freemen the power to "dispose of" their lands, the court said: "Of these statutes a practical construction early and generally obtained that in the power to dispose of lands was included a power to sell and convey the common lands. Large and valuable estates are held in various parts of the commonwealth, the titles to which depend on this construction. Were the court now to decide that this construction is not to be supported, very great mischief would follow. And although, if it were now res integra, it might be very difficult to maintain such a construction, yet at this day the argumentum ab inconvenienti applies with great weight. We cannot shake a principle which in practice has so long and so extensively prevailed. If the practice originated in error, yet the error is now so common that it must have the force of law. The legal ground on which this provision is now supported is that long and continued usage furnishes a contemporaneous construction which must prevail over the mere technical import of the words." [65]

---

[62] Sutherland, Stat. Constr. § 307.

[63] Union Pac. R. Co. v. U. S., 10 Ct. Cl. 548.

[64] Attorney General v. Bank of Cape Fear, 5 Ired. Eq. 71; Bailey v. Rolfe, 16 N. H. 247; Chesnut v. Shane, 16 Ohio, 599.

[65] Rogers v. Goodwin, 2 Mass. 475.

The "usage" which is entitled to be considered in the construction of a statute is such as is practical, general, and public. It may be the usage of the courts, in regulating matters of practice and procedure without formal decisions; of the executive and administrative officers of the government, in the discharge of their duties; of the legal profession generally, in advising their clients and conducting their business; of the practical men of the community, in conforming their conduct and their contracts to the generally understood meaning of the law; or of some or all of these combined. But it must not be merely theoretical or speculative.

As to the length of time during which a usage must have prevailed, in order to entitle it to be considered in the construction of a statute, there is some difference of opinion in the authorities, and in the nature of things it cannot be very definitely settled. Some of the English cases speak of a period of two or three hundred years. In this country, where no such statutory age is as yet possible, a very much shorter period of time would probably suffice to justify the courts in considering the usage. But it must be remarked that the principle of "contemporanea expositio" is not applicable to laws recently passed. And the degree of force which should attach to the argument from usage will increase with the age of the usage. "Where there are ambiguous expressions in an act passed one or two centuries ago, it may be legitimate to refer to the construction put upon these expressions throughout a long course of years by the unanimous consent of all parties interested, as evidencing what must presumably have been the intention of the legislature at that remote period. But I feel bound to construe a recent statute according to its own terms, when these are brought into controversy, and not according to the views which interested parties may have hitherto taken." [66]

The existence and nature of such a usage is a matter of law. The court will take judicial notice thereof, or will inform itself by any proper and available means. Interested parties are neither required nor permitted to prove it as a fact. Thus, in a case in Connecticut, upon a question as to the validity of the execution of a will, a counsellor, of long experience in the state, was offered as a witness, to show what had been the practice as to requiring the wit-

[66] Trustees of Clyde Navigation v. Laird, L. R. 8 App. Cas. 658.

nesses to a will to subscribe their names in the presence of each other, for the purpose of showing what was the general understanding of the legal profession as to the meaning of the statute of wills on this point. The testimony was rejected, and the appellate court held that this was proper. It was said that the judge, who alone is to decide as to the law, may, if he so desires, ask the advice of those who are learned in the law, but a party has no right to introduce such persons as witnesses.[67]

It is further to be remarked that a general law is not to be interpreted by a special or local usage; for, being of general application, it cannot receive different constructions in different places, according to their varying local usages.[68] But if a statute is applicable only to a particular locality, doubtful words in it may be construed by usage prevailing at that place.[69]

Again, it must not be forgotten that usage, like all other extraneous aids in statutory construction, may be resorted to only when the meaning of the statute is involved in doubt or obscurity. If the act is so plain and clear in its terms as not to admit of any substantial doubt, the courts are bound to put upon it that construction which its terms demand, and to disregard any and all contrariant usages or popular opinions. "As to usage," says Buller, J., "I am clearly of opinion that it ought not to be attended to in construing an act of parliament which cannot admit of different interpretations; where the words of the act are doubtful, usage may be called in to explain them."[70] To the same effect is the following language of Lord Brougham: "Usage can be binding and operative upon the parties only as it is the interpreter of a doubtful law, as affording a contemporary interpretation; but it is quite plain that as against a plain statutory law no usage is of any avail. But this undeniable proposition supposes the statute to speak a language plainly and indubitably differing from the purport of the usage. Where the statute, speaking on some point, is silent as to others, usage may well supply the defect, especially if it is not inconsistent

[67] Gaylor's Appeal, 43 Conn. 82.

[68] King v. Hogg, 1 Durn. & E. 721.

[69] Love v. Hinckley, 1 Abb. Adm. 436, Fed. Cas. No. 8,548; Frazier v. Warfield, 13 Md. 279.

[70] King v. Hogg, 1 Durn. & E. 721.

with the statutory directions, where any are given; or where the statute uses a language of doubtful import, the acting under it for a long course of years may well give an interpretation to that obscure meaning, and reduce that uncertainty to a fixed rule." [71]   A custom, however venerable, must yield to a positive and explicit statute. Thus, for example, where the compensation of a public officer is fixed by statute, the officer cannot recover additional compensation for expenses incurred by him incident to the performance of his official duties; and it is immaterial that, by usage long antedating the statute, such incidental expenses have been paid heretofore without objection.[72] It is not permissible to show that the members of the legislature knew of a custom existing at the time the law was remodelled, in order to argue from their silence that they intended to sanction such custom.[73]

Communis Error Facit Jus.

This maxim, though always regarded with distrust and accepted with great caution, has a certain validity as applied to matters of practice, and indicates the eventual legalization, by inveterate repetition, of that which was at first erroneous or even illegal. But it has no applicability to the interpretation of the written laws. It is sometimes appealed to as if it meant that an erroneous understanding of the law, being universally accepted, will prevail over the true and proper understanding of the law. But this is not correct. The construction of a statute may be influenced, in case of doubt, by the course of practice under it (not the mere abstract understanding of it), especially if general and long continued. But if it is clear that the common understanding of a law is really and unmistakably "error," it cannot be at all regarded.[74]   For example, in

---

[71] Magistrates of Dunbar v. Duchess of Roxburghe, 3 Cl. & Fin. 335.   But in Pease v. Peck, 18 How. 595, it is said that where a law, as published, has been acknowledged by the people, and has received a harmonious interpretation for a long series of years, the propriety may well be doubted of referring to an ancient manuscript to show that the law as published was not an exact copy of the original manuscript.

[72] Allbright v. County of Bedford, 106 Pa. St. 582.

[73] Delaplane v. Crenshaw, 15 Gratt. 457.

[74] "It has been sometimes said, communis error facit jus; but I say communis opinio is evidence of what the law is; not where it is an opinion merely speculative and theoretical, floating in the minds of persons, but where

England, "a general understanding had prevailed, founded on the practice of a long series of years, that if patented inventions were used in any of the departments of the public service, the patentees would be remunerated by the officers or ministers of the crown administering such departments, as though the use had been by private individuals. In numerous instances, payments had been made to patentees for the use of patented inventions in the public service, and even the legal advisers of the crown appeared also to have considered the right as well settled. There was, further, little doubt that on the faith of the understanding and practice, many inventors had, at great expense of time and money, perfected and matured inventions, in the expectation of deriving a portion of their reward from the adoption of their inventions in the public service. It was nevertheless held that the language of the patent should be interpreted according to the legal effect of its terms, irrespective of the practice."[75] It must be admitted, however, that there are some decisions in which a practical construction has been allowed to override the obvious meaning of the law.[76]

EXECUTIVE AND LEGISLATIVE CONSTRUCTION.

89. A practical construction put upon a doubtful or ambiguous statute by the officers of the executive department, who are charged with its execution, if long acted upon and generally acquiesced in, is regarded as strong evidence of the true meaning of the law; and though it is not binding upon the courts, they will not interpret the law differently, unless there are weighty reasons for so doing.

90. A construction put upon a statute by the legislature itself, by a subsequent act or resolution, cannot control the judgment of the courts; but it is entitled to weight and consideration in case of doubt or obscurity.

it has been made the groundwork and substratum of practice." Per Lord Ellenborough, C. J., in Isherwood v. Oldknow, 3 Maule & S. 382, 396.

[75] Broom, Leg. Max. 141, citing Feather v. Queen, 6 Best & S. 257, 289.

[76] See, for instance, Clay v. Sudgrave, 1 Salk. 33.

Executive Construction.

The executive and administrative officers of the government are bound to give effect to the laws which regulate their duties and define the sphere of their activities, and in so doing, they must necessarily put their own construction upon such acts. When the courts shall have interpreted the laws, these officers are of course bound to accept and abide by their decisions. But in advance of such judicial construction, they must interpret the statutes for themselves and to the best of their own abilities.[77] Hence it frequently happens that the judicial tribunals, when called upon to construe the acts of the legislature, will have their attention directed to a uniform practical construction put upon such acts by the executive department for its own guidance, under which official action has been regulated and rights fixed. Now such practical constructions are never binding upon the courts. The courts cannot be controlled by them, for the reason that the courts alone are invested with the power and charged with the duty of putting a final and authoritative interpretation upon the laws. And if the statute to be construed is a recent one,—so that official action cannot be seriously deranged, nor private rights be very much affected, by a change in its interpretation,—the mere fact that subordinate officers have already begun to read it in a certain way and to regulate their actions accordingly will have no weight or influence with the courts in their search for the true meaning of the law.[78] But it is a rule, announced by the supreme court of the United States at an early day, and which has since been followed in numerous cases both in the federal and state courts, that the contemporaneous construction put upon a statute by the officers who have been called upon to carry it into effect, made the basis of their constant and uniform practice for a long period of time, and generally acquiesced in, and not questioned by any suit brought, or any public or private action instituted, to test and settle the construction in the courts, is entitled to great respect, and if the statute is doubtful or ambiguous, such practical construction ought to be accepted as in accordance with the true meaning of the law, unless there are very cogent

[77] U. S. v. Lytle, 5 McLean, 9, Fed. Cas. No. 15,652.
[78] Ewing v. Ainger, 97 Mich. 381, 56 N. W. 767.

and persuasive reasons for departing from it.[79] For example, a
question arose in the federal supreme court as to the construction
of an act of congress providing for the retirement of "officers of the
navy." It was contended that this applied only to commissioned
officers, and not to warrant officers. The court said: "It must be
conceded that, were the question a new one, the true construction
of the section would be open to doubt. But the findings of the court
of claims show that soon after the enactment of the act the President and the navy department construed the section to include
warrant as well as commissioned officers, and that they have since
that time uniformly adhered to that construction, and that under
its provisions large numbers of warrant officers have been retired.
This contemporaneous and uniform interpretation is entitled to
weight in the construction of the law, and, in a case of doubt, ought
to turn the scale."[80] So again, where the secretary of the treasury
gives a certain construction to a statute concerning the distribution of fines, penalties, and forfeitures, and officers interested adversely apparently acquiesce in the decision through a long period
of time, and large sums are accordingly distributed and paid out of
the treasury, the courts will not interfere by giving a different construction to the statute, at least where that adopted by the secretary
is not unreasonable.[81] So, where the language of the tariff acts has
been substantially the same in respect to certain goods, a construction uniformly followed by the treasury department for nearly fifty
years will not be disregarded except for very strong reasons.[82] A
uniform construction put upon a land-grant act by the land office
and the department of the interior for a period of eighteen years,
and under which lands have been put upon the market and sold,

[79] Stuart v. Laird, 1 Cranch, 299; U. S. v. Gilmore, 8 Wall. 330; U. S. v.
Hill, 120 U. S. 169, 182, 7 Sup. Ct. 510; Merritt v. Cameron, 137 U. S. 542,
11 Sup. Ct. 174; Hahn v. U. S., 107 U. S. 402; Robertson v. Downing, 127
U. S. 607, 8 Sup. Ct. 1328; U. S. v. Philbrick, 120 U. S. 52, 7 Sup. Ct. 413;
People v. Loewenthal, 93 Ill. 191; Westbrook v. Miller, 56 Mich. 148, 22 N.
W. 256; Wetmore v. State, 55 Ala. 198; Bank of Utica v. Mersereau, 3 Barb.
Ch. 528.

[80] Brown v. U. S., 113 U. S. 568, 5 Sup. Ct. 648.

[81] Hahn v. U. S., 14 Ct. Cl. 305.

[82] U. S. v. Wotten, 50 Fed. 693.

should have considerable weight in determining the meaning of doubtful language in the statute.[83] For the same reasons, the practical construction given to a state statute by the public officers of the state, although it cannot be admitted as controlling, when the federal courts are called upon to construe the statute, is not to be overlooked, and should perhaps be regarded as decisive in a case of doubt, or where the error of such practical construction is not apparent.[84]

It is only in cases of doubt or ambiguity that the courts may allow themselves to be guided or influenced by an executive construction of a statute. If the words of the law are clear and precise, and the true meaning evident on the face of the enactment, there is no room for construction. In such case, no executive or administrative interpretation of the act should be allowed to defeat the plain meaning and purpose of the statute as the courts understand them. If such an interpretation is plainly erroneous, it is the duty of the courts to disregard it, no matter how long it may have prevailed, or how universally it may have been accepted, or what interests may be affected, and to construe the law according to its real and true meaning.[85]

Legislative Construction.

Although a legislative interpretation of a statute, if clearly wrong, should not be allowed to control the judicial construction of the act, yet if there is substantial doubt as to the meaning of the law, the expression of the opinion of the legislature in regard to it is entitled to consideration.[86] Thus, while the legislature cannot, by resolution, change the obligation of a contract made under a previous act, yet if they instruct a public officer as to his duties under the contract, such legislative expression of opinion as to what has been done, and the resulting duties of the officer, may be resorted

[83] U. S. v. Union Pac. Ry. Co., 148 U. S. 562, 13 Sup. Ct. 724.

[84] Union Ins. Co. v. Hoge, 21 How. 35.

[85] U. S. v. Tanner, 147 U. S. 661, 13 Sup. Ct. 436; U. S. v. Graham, 110 U. S. 219, 3 Sup. Ct. 582; Greely v. Thompson, 10 How. 225; In re Manhattan Savings Institution, 82 N. Y. 142; Comm. v. Owensboro, etc., R. Co. (Ky.) 23 S. W. 868.

[86] Comm. v. Miller, 5 Dana, 320; Philadelphia & E. R. Co. v. Catawissa R. Co., 53 Pa. St. 20, 60.

to in determining the intention of the legislature in passing the act.[87] But the enactment of a specific provision on a given subject does not, of itself, prove that the law on that subject was different before; for such enactment may have been made in affirmance of the existing law, and to remove doubts.[88]

JOURNALS OF LEGISLATURE.

91. In aid of the interpretation of an ambiguous statute, or one which is susceptible of several different constructions, it is proper for the courts to study the history of the bill in its progress through the legislature, by examining the legislative journals.

An obscure or ambiguous law is often rendered clear and intelligible by a consideration of the various steps which led to its final passage, as shown by the journals of the legislative body. The court in Indiana remarks that "it has never been held by this court that, for the purpose of construction or interpretation, and with the view of ascertaining the legislative will and intention in the enactment of a law, the courts may not properly resort to the journals of the two legislative bodies to learn therefrom the history of the law in question, from its first introduction as a bill until its final passage and approval. Where, as in this case, a statute has been enacted which is susceptible of several widely differing constructions, we know of no better means for ascertaining the will and intention of the legislature than that which is afforded, in this case, by the history of the statute, as found in the journals of the two legislative bodies." [89] So also, in Kansas, it is said that the courts will take judicial notice, without proof, of all the laws of the state; and in so doing, they will take judicial notice of what the books of published laws contain, of what the enrolled bills contain, of what the legislative journals contain, and indeed of everything that is allowed to affect the validity, or affect or modify the meaning, of

---

[87] Georgia Penitentiary Co. v. Nelms, 65 Ga. 67.

[88] Inhabitants of Montville v. Haughton, 7 Conn. 543.

[89] Edger v. Randolph County Comm'rs, 70 Ind. 331. See, also, Walter A. Wood Co. v. Caldwell, 54 Ind. 270; Hill's Adm'rs v. Mitchell, 5 Ark. 608.

any law in any respect whatever.[90]   And a learned judge in Ohio says: "In cases of doubt as to the proper interpretation of wills and contracts, it is a familiar rule that evidence is admissible to show the circumstances surrounding the party or parties at the time of the making of the instrument to be interpreted, and thus to place the court upon the standpoint of the party or parties whose intentions are to be ascertained, and to enable the court to see things in the light in which he or they saw them.   And on principle, I know of no good reason why, on a question like this, we may not, in analogy to the rule referred to, look into the history and progress of the bill which finally ripened into this act, during its pendency in, and passage by, the general assembly, as shown by the journals of the two houses of that body." [91]   In the case of Blake v. National Banks,[92] we find an act of congress, apparently contradictory in terms, interpreted by a reference to the journals of congress, whereby it appeared that the peculiar phraseology was the result of an amendment introduced without due reference to the language used in the original bill.   This doctrine does not pass entirely without contradiction.   Some cases there are in the reports which deny that the courts may properly consult the legislative journals in the search for the true meaning of a statute.[93]   But these decisions are opposed to the weight of authority.

It will be observed that this question is an entirely different matter from resorting to the legislative journals to ascertain whether an act was constitutionally passed, that is, passed with the requisite majority, or after the required number of readings, or with a call of the house on its final passage, or otherwise in conformity with the requirements of the constitution.   On this point, the rule set-

---

[90] In re Division of Howard County, 15 Kans. 194.

[91] Fosdick v. Village of Perrysburg, 14 Ohio St. 472.

[92] 23 Wall. 307.   And see Gardner v. Collector, 6 Wall. 499.

[93] Bank of Pennsylvania v. Comm., 19 Pa. St. 144; State v. Under-Ground Cable Co. (N. J. Ch.) 18 Atl. 581.   In Southwark Bank v. Comm., 26 Pa. St. 446, it is said: "The journals are not evidence of the meaning of a statute, because this must be ascertained from the language of the act itself and the facts connected with the subject on which it is to operate."   But the remark was obiter.   And in the same case it was held that the legislative journals are evidence for the purpose of identifying a bill to which another act of the legislature referred.

tled by a majority of the courts is that it is competent to go behind
the enrolled bill and consult the journals, but that the act will not
be declared void for lack of compliance with the constitutional
forms unless their nonobservance is affirmatively shown by the
journals. If the journals are silent as to these matters, it will be
presumed that the legislature complied with all the constitutional
requisites. In any event, no evidence can be received to contradict
the journals.[94]

Reports of Committees.

It is generally agreed, by both the English and American courts,
that reports or recommendations made to the legislative bodies by
their respective committees in relation to a pending measure cannot be accepted as pertinent evidence of the meaning which the
legislature intended to attach to the statute.[95] But mention should
be made of a case in Louisiana, where it was held that a report of
a committee, presented and adopted with an ordinance of a municipal corporation, might be regarded as a preamble showing its reasons, and might therefore be considered in aid of its construction.[96]

OPINIONS OF LEGISLATORS.

**92. Opinions of individual members of the legislature
which passed a statute, expressed by them in debate or otherwise, as to the meaning, scope, or effect of the act, cannot be accepted by the courts as
authority on the question of its interpretation, and,
if received at all, are entitled to but little weight.**

This doctrine has often been asserted by the courts, and in the
most unequivocal terms. Thus, the supreme court of the United
States declares: "In expounding this law, the judgment of the
court cannot in any degree be influenced by the construction placed
upon it by individual members of congress in the debate which took
place on its passage, nor by the motives or reasons assigned by

---

[94] Black, Const. Law, 60, 265.

[95] Steele v. Midland Ry. Co., L. R. 1 Ch. 275; Donegall v. Layard, 8 H. L.
Cas. 460; Bank of Pennsylvania v. Comm., 19 Pa. St. 144.

[96] Second Municipality of New Orleans v. Morgan, 1 La. Ann. 111.

them for supporting or opposing amendments that were offered. The law as it passed is the will of the majority of both houses, and the only mode in which that will is spoken is in the act itself; and we must gather their intention from the language there used, comparing it, when any ambiguity exists, with the laws upon the same subject, and looking, if necessary, to the public history of the times in which it was passed." [97] So, also, the supreme court of Pennsylvania observes: "In giving construction to a statute, we cannot be controlled by the views expressed by a few members of the legislature who expressed verbal opinions on its passage. Those opinions may or may not have been entertained by the more than hundred members who gave no such expressions. The declarations of some, and the assumed acquiescence of others therein, cannot be adopted as a true interpretation of the statute. Keeping in mind the previous law, the supposed evil, and the remedy desired, we must consider the language of the statute, and the fair and reasonable import thereof." [98] So again, "It has been insisted in the argument that the court, with a view to a clearer understanding of the language used in the section, is at liberty to consult the record of the debates in the houses of congress while this section was under discussion. * * * But we have seen no authority that would justify us in appealing to so uncertain a source for guidance as the remarks of members in debate. It is well known that a measure is sometimes advocated by a person upon grounds which another may assign as the cause of his opposition; and in this case there can be no more striking proof of the fallacious character of such evidence than the fact that both sides refer to different portions of the same debate in support of their respective views." [99]

[97] Aldridge v. Williams, 3 How. 9, 24. And see Taylor v. Taylor, 10 Minn. 107 (Gil. 81); Forrest v. Forrest, 10 Barb. 46; McGarrahan v. Maxwell, 28 Cal. 75, 95.

[98] Cumberland County v. Boyd, 113 Pa. St. 52, 4 Atl. 346.

[99] District of Columbia v. Washington Market Co., 3 MacArthur, 559. See, also, as holding the same views, Queen v. Whittaker, 2 Car. & K. 636; Attorney General v. Sillem, 2 Hurl. & C. 431, 521; District of Columbia v. Washington Market Co., 108 U. S. 243, 2 Sup. Ct. 543; U. S. v. Union Pac. R. Co., 91 U. S. 72; Stewart v. Atlanta Beef Co. (Ga.) 18 S. E. 981; City of Richmond v. County of Henrico, 83 Va. 204, 2 S. E. 26; Leese v. Clark, 20 Cal. 387, 425; State v. Burk (Iowa) 56 N. W. 180.

Nevertheless, the courts should not close their eyes to any light which may fall upon the pages of an obscure statute. The opinion of a member of the legislature, if he be a man of learning and of acute and discriminating intelligence, may be of quite as much persuasive force as the opinion of a judge delivered in a court of co-ordinate jurisdiction. But the latter is authority, while the former is not. Hence, if we carefully distinguish between those sources of information as to the meaning of a statute which are in their nature authoritative and those which are entitled only to the force of an argument, such as may combine with other arguments and considerations and tend to lead the mind to a certain conclusion, it may be that place will be found for the opinions of individual legislators in the list of extraneous aids which are available to the courts on questions of statutory construction.[100]   And cases are not wanting which have recognized the admissibility of such opinions, with this restriction and limitation. Thus, in a case in a federal circuit court, where the question was as to the power of the United States court in the Indian Territory to impanel a grand jury, under the act of congress creating the court, the judge allowed himself to be considerably influenced in his decision by the opinion expressed by the chairman of the judiciary committee of the house of representatives in presenting to the house the final conference report.[101]   And in England, during the argument of a case before the court of appeal, counsel proposed to cite as an authority on the interpretation of a statute the opinion of the Lord Chancellor as to its construction, contained in a speech delivered by him during a debate

[100] "How far opinions promulgated in connection with the making of a statute are to be regarded in its interpretation is an inquiry more easily answered on principle than on authority. Practical obscurities arise from the fact that commonly there are two dissimilar aspects from which such opinions are to be viewed. Courts properly look into legal treatises, whose only weight consists in their citation of authorities and the learning of their authors. In like manner they sometimes give attention to opinions of learned lawyers in the various other ways expressed. In this aspect, it is evidently proper for them to look, if they choose, into discussions by lawyers in the legislative body, the views of the draftsman of a bill, of the revisers of statutes, and of the legislature passing an act. As authority, this sort of matter is not admissible. As opinion to persuade, it varies with the particular circumstances." Bishop, Written Laws, § 76.

[101] Ex parte Farley, 40 Fed. 66.

in the house of lords upon the third reading of another act. It was held by two of the judges (the third doubting) that the speech might be read for that purpose.[102] So, in a case in Pennsylvania, Chief Justice Gibson stated that he was a member of the legislature at the time the act under consideration was passed, and that he knew that it was intended to operate in a certain manner.[103] Moreover, it is said that the courts may advert to statements made by individual members of the legislature, as part of the history of the times, and for the purpose of meeting an objection that a word used could have no operation at all, if it were not given a certain meaning contended for.[104]

MOTIVES OF LEGISLATURE.

93. In the interpretation of statutes, it is not proper or permissible to inquire into the motives which influenced the legislative body, except in so far as such motives are disclosed by the statute itself.[105]

"The rule is general, with reference to the enactments of all legislative bodies, that the courts cannot inquire into the motives of the legislators in passing them, except as they may be disclosed on the face of the acts, or inferable from their operation, considered with reference to the condition of the country and existing legislation. The motives of the legislators, considered as the purposes they had in view, will always be presumed to be to accomplish that which follows as the natural and reasonable effect of their enactments. Their motives, considered as the moral inducements for their votes, will vary with the different members of the legislative body. The diverse character of such motives, and the impossibility of penetrating into the hearts of men and ascertaining the truth, precludes all

[102] Queen v. Bishop of Oxford, L. R. 4 Q. B. Div. 525.

[103] Moyer v. Gross, 2 Pen. & W. 171. And see (a somewhat similar case) In re Mew, 31 L. J. (N. S.) Bankruptcy, 89.

[104] U. S. y. Wilson, 58 Fed. 768.

[105] Holme v. Guy, L. R. 5 Ch. Div. 901; Keyport & M. P. Steamboat Co. v. Farmers' Transp. Co., 18 N. J. Eq. 13; Kountze v. Omaha, 5 Dill. 443, Fed. Cas. No. 7,928; City of Richmond v. County of Henrico, 83 Va. 204, 2 S. E. 26; People v. Shepard, 36 N. Y. 285; Fletcher v. Peck, 6 Cranch, 87; Williams v. Nashville, 89 Tenn. 487, 15 S. W. 364; Black, Const. Law, 60.

such inquiries as impracticable and futile."[106]   Hence, for example, it cannot be shown, for the purpose of avoiding an act of the legislature, that the act was passed for insufficient or improper reasons.[107]   Nor, it is said, can the magnitude of the consideration, political or financial, which may operate upon the legislative mind as an inducement for grants and franchises conferred by statute, change the character of the legislation, or vary the rule of construction by which the rights of the grantees must be measured.[108]

[106] Soon Hing v. Crowley, 113 U. S. 703, 5 Sup. Ct. 730.
[107] City of Wichita v. Burleigh, 36 Kans. 34, 12 Pac. 332.
[108] Union Pac. R. Co. v. U. S., 10 Ct. Cl. 548.

CHAPTER VIII.

INTERPRETATION WITH REFERENCE TO COMMON LAW.

94. Common Law in Force in the United States.
95. Construction with Reference to Common Law.
96. Statutes Affirming Common Law.
97. Statutes Supplementing Common Law.
98. Statutes Superseding Common Law.
99. Statutes in Derogation of Common Law.

COMMON LAW IN FORCE IN THE UNITED STATES.

94. The English common law, in so far as it is applicable in this country, and where it has not been abrogated or changed by constitutional or statutory enactments, is in force in the several American states.

Generally speaking, the common law of England, except in so far as it has been repealed or modified by constitutions or statutes, is in force in the several states of the American Union.[1]   Not only do its principles permeate our system of jurisprudence, but its specific rules and doctrines are looked to by the courts as furnishing the grounds for their decisions in cases not otherwise explicitly provided for.   In many of the states, either a clause of the constitution or a statutory provision adopts and continues in force the body of the common law, save as it may have been rejected or changed by positive law.   The American colonists brought this law with them from the home of their race, and adopted it and lived under its precepts as naturally and inevitably as they continued to use their mother-tongue.   But it would be error to suppose that they adopted, or that the legislative and constitutional provisions of which we have spoken continued in force, the entire body of the common law, with every one of its rules, doctrines, and principles.

[1] Marburg v. Cole, 49 Md. 402; Hollman v. Bennett, 44 Miss. 322. But a statute adopting the common law of England as the basis of criminal jurisprudence does not adopt subsequent English enactments. State v. Davis, 22 La. Ann. 77.

It has always been the understanding that that law was accepted and put in force by the founders of the American states, and continued in force by those provisions, only in so far as it was applicable to the conditions and circumstances of this country. There are many particulars in which the common law would be entirely unsuited to the conditions and needs of our country and our life. Where it is inapplicable to the spirit, the genius, or the objects of our political or social institutions; where it does not accord with or suit the habits of our people; where it is rendered inapplicable by the physical conformation or the natural characteristics of the land, in these and similar cases it is not in force. All those features which depend upon the existence of a monarchical form of government have thus been eliminated. The common-law test of the navigability of rivers has been rejected. The common-law doctrine of riparian rights is not in force in those states where mining is the paramount interest and where the arid nature of the land renders such doctrines inapplicable. The rule of the common law requiring the owner of cattle to keep them within fences and prevent their straying on the lands of others has no place in the new and sparsely settled states of the west. These illustrations (which might be indefinitely multiplied) will suffice to show the meaning of the rule that the common law is to be considered as having been adopted and continued in force only so far as it is applicable to the circumstances of the particular state.[2] The courts are never precluded from considering this question of applicability, even where the constitution or a statute specifically adopts the common law as the rule of decision in the courts of the state.[3]

CONSTRUCTION WITH REFERENCE TO COMMON LAW.

95. Statutes are to be read in the light of the common law and construed with reference thereto.

When any question arises as to the meaning or the scope of a statutory enactment, it is a good rule to compare it with the com-

---

[2] See 1 Kent, Comm. 473; 1 Washburn, Real Prop. (4th edn.) 36; Van Ness v. Packard, 2 Pet. 137, 144; Reno Smelting Works v. Stevenson, 20 Nev. 269, 21 Pac. 317; Bogardus v. Trinity Church, 4 Paige, 198; Seeley v. Peters, 5 Gilm. 130; People v. Canal Appraisers, 33 N. Y. 461.

[3] Reno Smelting Works v. Stevenson, 20 Nev. 269, 21 Pac. 317.

mon law on the same subject, and to construe the statute with reference to that law.[4] This is but an extension of the rule, already
noticed in these pages, that a doubtful or ambiguous statute is to
be construed with all acts in pari materia, and adjusted and har-
monized, as far as possible, with the existing laws applicable to
the same subject-matter. No statute enters a field which was before entirely unoccupied. It either affirms, modifies, or repeals
some portion of the previously existing law. In order, therefore, to
form a correct estimate of its scope and effect, it is necessary to
have a thorough understanding of the laws, both common and statutory, which heretofore were applicable to the same subject.
Whether the statute affirms the rule of the common law on the
same point, or whether it supplements it, supersedes it, or displaces
it, the legislative enactment must be construed with reference to
the common law; for in this way alone is it possible to reach a
just appreciation of its purpose and effect. Again, the common law
must be allowed to stand unaltered as far as is consistent with a
reasonable interpretation of the new law. "The general rule in the
exposition of all acts of parliament is this, that in all doubtful
matters, and where the expression is in general terms, they are to
receive such a construction as may be agreeable to the rules of the
common law in cases of that nature; for statutes are not presumed
to make any alteration in the common law further or otherwise
than the act does expressly declare; and therefore in all general
matters the law presumes the act did not intend to make any alteration, for if the parliament had had that design, they would have
expressed it in the act." [5] And again, if a statute makes use of a
word, the meaning of which is well known at common law, the word
should be understood in the statute in the same sense in which it
was understood at common law.[6] Although the federal courts have
no common-law jurisdiction, all their jurisdiction being conferred
by the constitution and the acts of congress, and although their
rules of decision are derived from the laws of the states, yet, in

[4] Scaife v. Stovall, 67 Ala. 237; Howe v. Peckham, 6 How. Pr. 229.

[5] Arthur v. Bokenham, 11 Mod. 148. See, also, Greenwood v. Greenwood,
28 Md. 369; Edwards v. Gaulding, 38 Miss. 118.

[6] Mayo v. Wilson, 1 N. H. 53; Walton v. State, 62 Ala. 197; Apple v Apple,
1 Head, 348.

construing the statutes of congress, the rules of interpretation furnished by the common law are the true guides and have been uniformly followed.[7]

STATUTES AFFIRMING COMMON LAW.

96. A statute which is in affirmance of a rule of the common law is to be construed, as to its incidents and its consequences, in accordance with the common law.[8]

STATUTES SUPPLEMENTING COMMON LAW.

97. A statute which is supplementary to the common law does not displace that law any further than is clearly necessary. The statute is in general considered as merely cumulative, unless the rights or remedies which it creates are expressly made exclusive.

If a statute recognizes a right already existing at common law and merely gives a new remedy for its infringement, without declaring or implying that such remedy shall be exclusive, it is cumulative, and the party injured is at liberty to pursue either the statutory remedy or that previously existing by the common law. If the statute gives the same remedy which the common law gave, it is merely affirmative, and the party has his election whether to proceed at common law or upon the statute. But if the statute denies or withholds the remedy which before existed at common law, the common-law right ceases to exist, and the statute alone is available to the party.[9] Where the statute does not vest a right in a person, but only prohibits the doing of some act under a penalty, the party violating the statute is liable only to the penalty; but where a right of property is vested in consequence of the statute, it may be vindicated at common law, unless the statute confines the remedy to the

---

[7] Rice v. Railroad Co., 1 Black (U. S.) 358.

[8] Baker v. Baker, 13 Cal. 87; Hewey v. Nourse, 54 Me. 256.

[9] Gooch v. Stephenson, 13 Me. 371; Crittenden v. Wilson, 5 Cow. 165; Proprietors of Fryeburg Canal v. Frye, 5 Me. 38.

penalty.[10]   So also, it is a rule of almost universal application that a statute fixing a penalty for an offense, which does not expressly or by implication cut off the common-law prosecution or punishment for the same offense, intends merely a cumulative remedy.[11]   But it is equally well settled that where the legislature has authorized the erection of a public work, by individuals or by a corporation, which may, in its erection or operation, occasion damage to the property of others, and has provided a specific mode of obtaining indemnity, the common-law action on the case, treating such erection as a tort, and regarding the damages given by it as a compensation for an injury done, is taken away, and the party must proceed upon the statute alone.   The reason is that under such statutory authorization, the persons erecting or maintaining the public work are not wrong-doers, and it cannot be treated as a tort.[12]   Statutory regulations, it is said, for the exercise of a pre-existing common-law right should not be construed by the same rigid rules as are sometimes applied to statutes regulating the exercise of a right conferred by statute and in derogation of the common law.[13]   But where a statute provides a remedy unknown to the common law, and by which no personal notice to the person proceeded against is required, it should, for obvious reasons, be strictly construed.[14]

[10] Barden v. Crocker, 10 Pick. 383.

[11] Washington & B. Turnpike Road v. State, 19 Md. 239; People v. Bristol & R. Turnpike Road, 23 Wend. 222, 244.

[12] Proprietors of Sudbury Meadows v. Proprietors of Middlesex Canal, 23 Pick. 36; Dodge v. County Comm'rs of Essex, 3 Met. (Mass.) 380; Elder v. Bemis, 2 Met. (Mass.) 599.

[13] Avery v. Town of Groton, 36 Conn. 304.

[14] Souter v. The Sea Witch, 1 Cal. 162.

STATUTES SUPERSEDING COMMON LAW.

98. The common law gives way to a statute which is inconsistent with it; and when a statute is designed as a revision, consolidation, or codification of the whole body of the law applicable to a given subject, it supersedes the common law so far as it applies to that subject, and leaves no part of it in force.

"Where the common law and a statute differ, the common law gives place to the statute, and an old statute gives place to a new one; and this upon a general principle of universal law, that 'leges posteriores priores contrarias abrogant.'" [15]   Although an immemorial custom may override or control the common law, yet both must give way to a statute introducing a new principle and a new rule sufficient of itself.[16]   Consequently, when it is evident that a statute, or a code or revision of the laws, is not intended merely to be cumulative, or to remedy the defects of the common law, but designed as a complete and comprehensive body of law in relation to a given subject, enacting or consolidating all the laws, new or old, which are for the future to govern the legal aspects of that subject, it supersedes the common law entirely, as to that subject, and leaves no part or branch of it to be governed or determined by the common law.[17]   The theory of this rule is well explained by the supreme court of Alabama, where, in speaking of the revised code of that state, it is said that it "is intended to contain all the statute law of the state of a public nature, designed to operate upon all the people of the state, up to the date of its adoption, unless otherwise directed in the code. This law is not merely cumulative of the common law, and made to perfect the deficiencies of that system, but it is designed to create a new and independent system, applicable to our own institutions and government. In such case,

---

[15] 1 Bl. Comm. 89; State v. Norton, 23 N. J. Law, 33; State v. Boogher, 71 Mo. 631.

[16] Delaplane v. Crenshaw, 15 Gratt. 457.

[17] Hannon v. Madden, 10 Bush, 664; Kramer v. Rebman, 9 Iowa, 114; Comm. v. Cooley, 10 Pick. 37; State v. Wilson, 43 N. H. 415.

where a statute disposes of the whole subject of legislation, it is the only law. Otherwise we shall have two systems, where one only was intended to operate, and the statute becomes the law only so far as a party may choose to follow it. Besides, the mere fact that a statute is made shows that, so far as it goes, the legislature intended to displace the old rule by a new one. On some questions, the common law conflicts more or less with our constitutional law, and is necessarily displaced and repealed by it; and on others, it has, by the lapse of ages, and mistakes inevitably attendant on all human affairs, become uncertain and difficult to reconcile with the principles of justice. Hence the legislature intervenes to remove such difficulties, uncertainties, and mistakes, by a new law. This new law, to the extent that it goes, necessarily takes the place of all others. It would be illogical to contend that the old rule must stand, as well as the new one, because this would not remedy the evil sought to be removed and avoided." [18]

STATUTES IN DEROGATION OF COMMON LAW.

99. It is a rule generally observed (except where prohibited by statute) that acts of the legislature made in derogation of the common law will not be extended by construction; that is, the legislature will not be presumed to intend innovations upon the common law, and its enactments will not be extended, in directions contrary to the common law, further than is indicated by the express terms of the law or by fair and reasonable implications from its nature or purpose or the language employed.

It was formerly accepted, by all the courts, as a rule of universal applicability, that all statutes made in derogation of the common law were to be strictly construed.[19] This rule often led to hardship

[18] Barker v. Bell, 46 Ala. 216.

[19] Melody v. Reab, 4 Mass. 471; Esterley's Appeal, 54 Pa. St. 192; Bailey v. Bryan, 3 Jones L. (N. Car.) 357; Hollman v. Bennett, 44 Miss. 322; Arthur's Appeal, 1 Grant (Pa.) 55; Howes v. Newcomb, 146 Mass. 76, 15 N. E. 123; Dean v. Metropolitan El. Ry. Co., 119 N. Y. 540, 23 N. E. 1054; Cooley, Const. Lim. 61 and note.

and injustice in individual cases, and by means of it the beneficent and progressive purposes of the legislative bodies were frequently balked. But for ages no one thought of questioning its propriety or validity. The rule owes its being to the great regard which was formerly entertained for the system of the common law. "To understand the meaning and present value of the rule that statutes in derogation of the common law are to be strictly construed, we must keep in mind the feelings of our ancestors in regard to that system of jurisprudence. They invariably spoke of it with a reverential awe, blended with a tender attachment."[20] "This has been the language of the courts," says Kent, "in every age; and when we consider the constant, vehement, and exalted eulogy which the ancient sages bestowed upon the common law as the perfection of reason, and the best birthright and noblest inheritance of the subject, we cannot be surprised at the great sanction given to this rule of construction."[21] The judges, in particular, manifested an enthusiastic devotion to the common law, which, it must be remembered, was very largely their own creation, and were prone to regard the interference of parliament, by way of abrogating or modifying its rules, with jealousy and distrust. It was therefore quite natural that they should set up for themselves a rule that all statutes which derogated from the force or applicability of their idolized system should be subjected to a strict interpretation. We shall presently endeavor to show that this rule no longer has any foundation in reason, and that it should be very considerably modified before it is justly applicable to the enactments of our legislative bodies. But before doing so it will be useful to adduce some illustrations to show the meaning of the rule and its application in practice. It has been said, for example, that where a statute abrogates a common-law right or confers a right not vested by the common law, it should not be so construed as to go beyond the letter, nor even to that extent, unless it appears to accord with the spirit and intent of the act.[22] Again, an act conferring summary jurisdiction or authorizing summary proceedings is very much out of

---

[20] Sedgwick, Stat. Constr. (2d edn.) 273.

[21] 1 Kent, Comm. 464.

[22] Dewey v. Goodenough, 56 Barb. 54.

the course of the common law, and ought to be strictly construed.[23] Thus, an act which gives a remedy by motion against public officers on their official bonds is in derogation of the common law.[24] So also, statutes exempting portions of a debtor's property from liability for his debts are in derogation of the common law, and are not to be extended by an equitable construction.[25] Again, the power to take lands of private owners for public purposes is considered in derogation of that system of law, and hence to be strictly construed.[26] A statute which grants to a city rights and powers unknown to the common law, as the power to donate the corporate funds in aid of a railroad, should be strictly construed.[27] And a statute allowing persons to testify in their own cases, being in derogation of the common law, should be subjected to a strict interpretation.[28] So also, "although it is competent to the legislature to alter the rules of evidence so as to compel a party to give testimony against himself, it is nevertheless a power of such transcendent and overwhelming importance that a just regard for the liberties of the citizen should at all times induce the most cautious and jealous exercise of it by the legislature; and especially should courts of justice anxiously and narrowly watch it, and never, under any pretense whatever, extend it beyond the limits to which the strictest interpretation of the language of the legislature confines it in a particular case."[29] So the West Virginia statute known as the "suitors' test-oath" act—providing that if a plaintiff would not take and file an oath of expurgation (an oath asserting his loyalty to the rightful government and his freedom from any participation in the rebellion) in the cases where such oath was required by the act, his suit should be dismissed—was held to be in derogation of the common law, and for that reason not to be extended beyond its express terms.[30] Undoubtedly, many of the foregoing cases were

[23] McMullin v. McCreary, 54 Pa. St. 230.
[24] Hearn v. Ewin, 3 Coldw. 399.
[25] Rue v. Alter, 5 Denio, 119.
[26] Sharp v. Speir, 4 Hill (N. Y.) 76.
[27] Indiana North & South Ry. Co. v. City of Attica, 56 Ind. 476.
[28] Hotaling v. Cronise, 2 Cal. 60; Warner v. Fowler, 8 Md. 25.
[29] Broadbent v. State, 7 Md. 416.
[30] Harrison v. Leach, 4 W. Va. 383.

correctly decided; that is, it was right that the statutes severally before the courts in those cases should be subjected to a strict interpretation. But there was ample reason, in each case, for adopting such a construction, without any reference to the effect of the statute upon the common law.

In fact, as we have already stated, this rule is no longer supported by reason. "It is difficult," says Sedgwick, "if not impossible, now to understand this enthusiastic loyalty to a body of law, the most peculiar features of which the activity of the present generation has been largely occupied in uprooting and destroying."[31] American courts have no reason to attach any peculiar sanctity to the common law. Nor is there any reason why a statute abrogating the common law should be any more strictly construed than a statute abrogating another act of the same legislature. On this point we quote from an eminent authority as follows: "It would seem that modern courts and judges have repeated the rule without any knowledge of its origin and without any thought of the enormous changes in the relations between the courts and the legislature which have taken place since the rule was promulgated. In fact, the reason of the rule, or rather the occasion of it, for there never was any reason for it, has entirely passed away. It is a demonstrable proposition that there is hardly a rule or doctrine of positive practical jurisprudence in England or in the United States to-day which is not the result, in part at least, of legislation; hardly a rule or doctrine of the original common law which has not been abrogated, or changed, or modified by statute. Furthermore, it is conceded that the ancient conception as to the perfection of the common law was absurdly untrue. The great mass of its practical rules as to property, as to persons, as to obligations, and as to remedies, were arbitrary, unjust, cumbersome, and barbarous. For the last generation, the English parliament and our state legislatures have been busy in abolishing these common-law rules and in substituting new ones by means of statutes. That all this remedial work, all this benign and necessary legislative endeavor to create a jurisprudence scientific in form and adapted to the wants of the age, should be hampered, and sometimes thwarted, by a parrot-like repetition and unreflecting application of the old judicial maxim

---

[31] Sedgwick, Stat. Constr. (2d edn.) 273.

that statutes in derogation of the common law are to be strictly construed is, to say the least, absurd." [32]

It has been said that a reason for this rule may still be found in the fact that the common law found its most worthy expression in the safeguards which it threw around the rights of the individual, both in respect to its immediate protection to life, liberty, and property, and in respect to the rules and principles of procedure which it devised with a view to the protection of those rights. But all the rights of persons which it is the duty of a free government to preserve and protect have been adequately guarantied in our constitutions, national and state. Any legislative enactment encroaching upon them to an extent deemed incompatible with the fullest measure of liberty which a republican government can secure will be annulled by the decisions of the courts, not with any reference to the common law, but because it is unconstitutional. And even where the express provisions of the constitution may not enter into the question, a statute infringing upon the just rights of the citizen, either in substance or in matters of procedure, would be subjected to a strict construction, in virtue of certain other rules of interpretation, which will be noticed in a subsequent chapter, and which, unlike the rule now under consideration, rest upon a solid and substantial basis of reason.

In many of the states, this rule has been abolished by statute. Thus, the civil code of California provides that "the rule of the common law, that statutes in derogation thereof are to be strictly construed, has no application to this code. The code establishes the law of this state respecting the subjects to which it relates, and its provisions are to be liberally construed, with a view to effect its objects and to promote justice." [33]   And in other states, a tendency is observable to restrict and modify the rule very greatly before it is considered applicable to modern statutory enactments. As adopted and approved by the best authorities, it may now be stated

[32] From Prof. Pomeroy's note in Sedgwick, Stat. Constr. (2d edn.) 270, 271.
[33] Civ. Code Cal. § 4. And see Code Civ. Proc. N. Y. § 3345; Rev. St. Ohio, § 4948; Code Civ. Proc. Mont. § 3453; 2 McClain Ann. Code Iowa, § 3733; Genl. St. Kans. 1889, § 7281; Code Civ. Proc. Neb. § 1; Bullitt's Civ. Code Ky. § 733; Code Ark. 1894, § 7222; Civ. Code Colo. § 446; Code Civ. Proc. S. Car. § 448; 2 Hill's Code Wash. § 1707; Code Civ. Proc. Idaho, § 3; Rev. St. Wyom. § 2338; Darby v. Heagerty, 2 Idaho, 260, 13 Pac. 85.

as follows: Statutes in modification or derogation of the common law will not be presumed to alter it further than is expressly declared, or further than may be fairly and reasonably inferred from the purpose and nature of the statute or from the language employed in it. Such acts will be liberally construed, if their nature is remedial, but their operation will not be extended by a forced construction. The presumption is that the terms of the statute disclose the extent of the alteration or change it was designed to effect.[34] The whole tendency of modern statutory construction, it should be observed, is to escape from the domination of fixed and unalterable rules, which often are arbitrary and tend only to becloud justice, and to seek, first and always, the actual intention and meaning of the legislature. "It is said," observes the court in Massachusetts, "that statutes made in derogation of the common law are to be strictly construed. This is true; but they are also to be construed sensibly, and with a view to the object aimed at by the legislature." [35] Statutes derogating from the common law cannot, therefore, be properly extended by construction so as to embrace cases not fairly within the scope of the language used.[36] Thus, a charge created by statute on property, as, a landlord's lien on the tenant's crops, will not, unless it is clearly expressed or justly implied, be construed to have a superiority which the common law does not attach to similar charges.[37] There are also numerous cases of statutes which might come under the influence of this rule, but which are also within the equally well settled rule that remedial statutes are to be liberally construed. For instance, an act of the legislature dispensing with the necessity of a seal and giving effect to instruments in writing according to the intention of the grantor, is remedial in its character, and hence should be liberally construed, in order to suppress the mischief intended to be remedied and to effectuate the purpose and intent of the law-makers; but the courts also hold that such a law, being in derogation of the common law,

[34] Cook v. Meyer, 73 Ala. 580; Sullivan v. La Crosse & M. Steam Packet Co., 10 Minn. 386; Shaw v. Railroad Co., 101 U. S. 557; Wilbur v. Crane, 13 Pick. 284.

[35] Gibson v. Jenney, 15 Mass. 205.

[36] Dwelly v. Dwelly, 46 Me. 377.

[37] Scaife v. Stovall, 67 Ala. 237.

should not be extended by construction in respect to its operation.[38]   Where a statute is equally susceptible of two constructions,
one of which is in harmony with a settled principle of the common
law, and the other in derogation of it, the courts will adopt the
former.[39]   But some of the courts, breaking away from the artificial
control of this rule, have established a principle which is much more
in accordance with modern conditions and modern needs.   They
hold that a statute which is penal in its nature and in derogation of
some right existing at common law should not be extended by construction beyond its natural meaning;[40] but that, if these conditions do not exist, they are not bound to put a strict construction
upon any law merely because it conflicts with the previously existing common law.   For example, an act of congress passed in 1851,
entitled "An act to limit the liability of ship owners," declares that
such owners shall not be liable for loss or damage "which may
happen to any goods or merchandise which shall be shipped, taken
in, or put on board any such ship or vessel, by reason or by means
of any fire happening to or on board the said ship or vessel, unless
such fire is caused by the design or neglect of such owner."   It is
held that although this statute changes the rule of the common law,
it is not a penal statute, nor in derogation of natural right, so as
to require a strict interpretation.   It was enacted to modify the
extreme rigor of the common law, and is therefore a remedial act.
Hence it should be construed, if not liberally, at least fairly, to carry
out the policy which it was enacted to promote; and for this reason,
the broad terms "any goods or merchandise" must be held to include
the ordinary baggage of passengers.[41]

This modification of the ancient rule simply places the common
law on a level with the pre-existing statutory law of the state.   As
we have explained in an earlier chapter of this work, there is always a presumption against an intent to change the existing law;
and this presumption applies as well to the common law as to earlier
statutes.   To this extent, and only to this extent, the rule we are

[38] Webb v. Mullins, 78 Ala. 111.

[39] Ryan v. Couch, 66 Ala. 244.

[40] Gunter v. Leckey, 30 Ala. 591.

[41] Chamberlain v. Western Transp. Co., 44 N. Y. 305. And see The Wark-
worth, L. R. 9 P. Div. 20.

considering may be allowed a place and a value. And an attentive examination of the cases in which the stricter form of the rule has been appealed to as justifying the courts in putting a restrictive interpretation upon the statutes before them will generally show that the real reason for such an interpretation lay in the nature of the act itself, and not in any necessity of observing respect for the common law. For example, the statutes authorizing the seizure and sale of land for the nonpayment of taxes are usually subjected to a strict construction. That they are in derogation of the common law has nothing to do with the case, although that consideration is often put forward as the reason for giving them such an interpretation.[42] The true reason is that such laws put the citizen to the danger of being deprived of his property without a judicial investigation, and invest administrative officers with a power to sell and dispose of what they do not own.

Married Women's Property Acts.

A good illustration of the mistaken application of the rule requiring the strict construction of statutes in derogation of the common law, and of the way in which the progress of the law has been hampered by the rule, is found in the case of the statutes enabling married women to deal freely with their separate property and to make contracts respecting the same. In this regard the common law was harsh and unjust. Moreover, it had become utterly unsuited to the modern conditions of life and the modern progress of ideas. Yet when the legislatures began to take steps for the enfranchisement of the feme covert, the courts quite generally held that these remedial and beneficent statutes, because they were in derogation of the common law, must be subjected to a strict construction, and the same rule is laid down in some quite recent cases.[43] In some instances, these decisions were afterwards overruled.[44] In many

[42] See, for example, Sibley v. Smith, 2 Mich. 486; Newell v. Wheeler, 48 N. Y. 486: Dequasie v. Harris, 16 W. Va. 345.

[43] Brown v. Fifield, 4 Mich. 322; Graham v. Van Wyck, 14 Barb. 531; Perkins v. Perkins, 62 Barb. 531; Fitzgerald v. Quann, 109 N. Y. 441, 17 N. E. 354; Bertles v. Nunan, 92 N. Y. 152; Compton v. Pierson, 28 N. J. Eq. 229; Thompson v. Weller, 85 Ill. 197.

[44] For instance, De Vries v. Conklin, 22 Mich. 255, holds that a statute empowering a married woman to deal freely with her separate property, as if

more, it was necessary for the legislature to counteract their effects by additional legislation, extending still further the liberal features of this class of laws.   In some cases the courts have applied to such statutes the modified form of the rule of which we have spoken above.   Thus, the supreme court of Indiana, speaking of such an act, says: "While the provisions of the act must be liberally construed, according to their true intent and meaning, yet, as they are in derogation of the common-law rule, they are not to be enlarged by construction beyond the plain meaning of the language used by the law-making power in their enactment." [45]

Mechanics' Lien Laws.

A similar conflict of authority has attended the construction of the statutes creating mechanics' liens and providing for their enforcement.   Many of the courts have held that these laws are to be construed strictly, because they are in derogation of the common law.[46]   "This court has repeatedly declared in substance that these acts are innovations upon the common law over rights of property, by permitting the institution of private charges on property without or against the owner's assent, and without any judicial or other official sanction, and by authorizing an enforcement of such charges by unusual and summary methods, and that the provisions of these enactments cannot be extended in their operation and effect beyond the plain and fair sense of the terms, and that parties asserting liens or titles resting upon them must bring themselves and their titles plainly and distinctly within these terms, and affirmatively make out that a lien was originally effected regularly and thereafter kept up, and that every essential statutory step either in the creation, continuance, or enforcement of the lien has been duly taken." [47]   But on the other hand, the courts in several

she were sole, and to make contracts respecting it, is a remedial act, and is to be construed liberally to effectuate its purpose, thus overruling Brown v. Fifield, supra.

[45] Haas v. Shaw, 91 Ind. 384. And see Cook v. Meyer, 73 Ala. 580; Moore v. Cornell, 68 Pa. St. 320.

[46] Lynch v. Cronan, 6 Gray, 531; Wade v. Reitz, 18 Ind. 307; Rothgerber v. Dupuy, 64 Ill. 452.

[47] Wagar v. Briscoe, 38 Mich. 587. And see Chapin v. Persse & Brooks Paper Works, 30 Conn. 461.

of the other states have taken an exactly opposite view of these statutes. Thus, for example, the supreme court of Ohio says: "Looking thus at the object of the statute, and perceiving it to be one of an equitable character and beneficent tendency, section seven being directory as to the mode of securing the object of the statute, the same ought to be liberally construed, for the furtherance and attainment of such object." [48]

[48] Thomas v. Huesman, 10 Ohio St. 152. See, also, Oster v. Rabenau, 46 Mo. 595; Collins Granite Co. v. Devereux, 72 Me. 422; Barnes v. Thompson, 2 Swan (Tenn.) 313; Buchanan v. Smith, 43 Miss. 90; Minor v. Marshall (N. Mex.) 27 Pac. 481.

CHAPTER IX.

RETROSPECTIVE INTERPRETATION.

DEFINITION.

100. A retrospective law is one which looks backward or contemplates the past; one which is made to affect acts or transactions occurring before it came into effect, or rights already accrued, and which imparts to them characteristics, or ascribes to them effects, which were not inherent in their nature in the contemplation of the law as it stood at the time of their occurrence.

Every statute which takes away or impairs vested rights acquired under existing laws, or creates a new obligation, imposes a new duty, or attaches a new disability, in respect to transactions or considerations already past, must be deemed to be retrospective.[1] "As the terms are commonly used in the law, prospective legislation is such as provides rules for facts thereafter to transpire; retrospective, for those which have partly or fully occurred. Prospective interpretation restricts the application of the new law to facts arising after its enactment; retrospective, applies it to the past and present facts as well as the future."[2] But a statute cannot properly be called retrospective merely because a part of the requisites for its operation may be drawn from a time antecedent to its passage.[3] Thus, for example, an act is not retrospective which estab-

---

[1] Society for Propagating the Gospel v. Wheeler, 2 Gall. 105, Fed. Cas. No. 13,156.

[2] Bishop, Writ. Laws, § 83.

[3] Queen v. Inhabitants of St. Mary, 12 Q. B. 120, 127.

lishes the death of a husband or wife as the future event on which it is to operate, although, in the particular case, the relation of husband and wife existed before the taking effect of the act.[4]

CONSTITUTIONAL CONSIDERATIONS.

101. If a retrospective statute is in the nature of an ex post facto law or a bill of attainder, or if it impairs the obligation of contracts or divests vested rights, or if all retrospective laws are specifically forbidden by the constitution of the particular state, such an act will be unconstitutional and void, but not otherwise.

102. If giving to a statute a retrospective operation would make it conflict with the constitution, in one or other of the ways above mentioned, such a result will be avoided, if possible, by construction.

Bills of attainder and ex post facto laws are both specifically prohibited by the federal constitution. They are both included in the category of retrospective laws. A bill of attainder or an ex post facto law is always retrospective; but not all retrospective laws are bills of attainder or ex post facto laws. The latter terms, according to the familiar doctrine of constitutional law, relate only to the imposition of pains or penalties or the conduct of criminal trials.[5] Again, all laws which impair the obligation of contracts

---

[4] Noel v. Ewing, 9 Ind. 37.

[5] An ex post facto law is one which makes an action done before the passing of the law, and which was innocent when done, criminal, and punishes such action; or which aggravates a crime, or makes it greater than it was when committed; or which changes the punishment and inflicts a greater punishment than the law annexed to the crime when it was committed; or which alters the legal rules of evidence, and receives less or different testimony than the law required at the time of the commission of the offense, in order to convict the offender. An ex post facto law is necessarily, as the words imply, a retroactive law. If any law is intended to operate only upon future actions or future trials, it cannot be called ex post facto. And again, the term is restricted to penal and criminal proceedings which affect life or liberty or may impose punishments or forfeitures. It has no applicability to purely civil proceedings which affect private rights only, although such proceedings, for

are retroactive.   For if they related only to future contracts, they
could not be said to have this effect, because contracts are made
with reference to existing laws.   Laws which have the effect of di-
vesting vested rights are also of this character; for the phrase
"vested right" implies something settled or accrued in the past, on
which the new statute is to operate.   There are also numerous
classes of retrospective laws which are constitutionally objection-
able for the reason that they exceed the powers of the legislature
or invade the province of one of the other departments of the government.   But unless the law in question belongs to one of the
classes mentioned above, or is open to some one of the objections
described, the mere fact that it is retroactive in its operation will
not suffice to justify the courts in declaring it unconstitutional, unless all laws of that character are prohibited by the constitution
of the particular state.   No such prohibition is found in the federal constitution.   If a state statute does not impair the obligation
of contracts or partake of the nature of a bill of attainder or an
ex post facto law, its retrospective character does not make it inconsistent with the national constitution.[6]

It will therefore be seen that the question of a retrospective interpretation and the question of constitutionality are not coinci-
dent.   The primary question is as to the meaning and intention of the legislature.   When the court is called upon to decide
whether it was intended that a given statute should have a retroactive operation or not, the further question of its constitutional
validity, conceding to it such operation, may or may not be involved.   But when it is seen that the statute, if allowed to retroact,
will impair the obligation of contracts, or violate the rule against
ex post facto laws, or otherwise conflict with the constitution, then
the alternative is between construing it as prospective only and

their retroactive effect, may be unlawful. See, generally, Calder v. Bull, 3
Dall. 390; Kring v. Missouri, 107 U. S. 221, 2 Sup. Ct. 443; Cummings v.
Missouri, 4 Wall. 277; Ex parte Garland, Id. 333; Boston v. Cummins, 16
Ga. 102; Watson v. Mercer, 8 Pet. 88; Baltimore & S. R. Co. v. Nesbitt, 10
How. 395; Caldwell v. State, 55 Ala. 133; Hart v. State, 40 Ala. 32.

[6] Satterlee v. Matthewson, 2 Pet. 380; Reed v. Beall, 42 Miss. 472; Burwell
v. Tullis, 12 Minn. 572 (Gil. 486); Smith v. Van Gilder, 26 Ark. 527; Weister
v. Hade, 52 Pa. St. 474; Bay v. Gage, 36 Barb. 447; People v. Board of
Sup'rs of Ulster Co., 63 Barb. 83.

adjudging it to be void.   In that event, the courts will struggle
hard against the necessity of putting a retrospective interpretation
upon the law.   We have already seen [7] that the courts are bound
to presume all legislative enactments to be valid; that it is never
to be presumed that the law-making authority has exceeded its
rightful powers; and that any conflict between the statute and the
constitution is to be avoided by construction, if that is possible.
Hence if a retrospective interpretation would make the statute unconstitutional, the judges will not so interpret it unless the intention of the legislature in that regard has been expressed in terms
so plain and unmistakable that there is no possibility of any choice
of meanings.   "Courts will not give to a law a retrospective operation, even where they might do so without violation of the constitution, unless the intention of the legislature is clearly expressed
in favor of such retrospective operation. This rule applies with the
greater force when, by giving the law such effect, a serious question
would be raised as to the constitutionality of the act.   Where a
statute can, consistent with the rules of interpretation, be so construed as to harmonize with the constitution, such construction will
be adopted by the courts, rather than one which will raise an apparent conflict between the law and the constitution." [8]

THE GENERAL RULE.

103. **Except in the case of remedial statutes and those
    which relate to procedure in the courts, it is a
    general rule that acts of the legislature will not be
    so construed as to make them operate retrospec-
    tively, unless the legislature has explicitly declared
    its intention that they should so operate, or unless
    such intention appears by necessary implications
    from the nature and words of the act so clearly as
    to leave no room for a reasonable doubt on the sub-
    ject.** [9]

[7] Ante, p. 93.

[8] Town of La Salle v. Blanchard, 1 Ill. App. 635.

[9] Moon v. Durden, 2 Exch. 22; Pardo v. Bingham, L. R. 4 Ch. App. 735;
Queen v. Guardians of Ipswich Union, L. R. 2 Q. B. Div. 269; Gardner v.

The reason for this rule is the general tendency to regard retrospective laws as dangerous to liberty and private rights, on account of their liability to unsettle vested rights or disturb the legal effect of prior transactions. "Retrospective laws being in their nature odious, it ought never to be presumed the legislature intended to pass them, where the words will admit of any other meaning." [10] "Legislation of this character is exceedingly liable to abuse, and it is a sound rule of construction that a statute should have a prospective operation only, unless its terms show clearly a legislative intention that it should operate retrospectively." [11] Generally, when the legislature designs that a statute shall operate upon past

Lucas, L. R. 3 App. Cas. 582; Englehardt v. State, 88 Ala. 100, 7 South. 154; Maxwell v. Commissioners of Fulton Co., 119 Ind. 20, 23, 19 N. E. 617, and 21 N. E. 453; Warren Manuf. Co. v. Etna Ins. Co., 2 Paine, 501, Fed. Cas. No. 17,206; State v. Hill, 32 Minn. 275, 20 N. W. 196; State v. Ferguson, 62 Mo. 77; State v. Hays, 52 Mo. 578; Citizens' Gaslight Co. v. State, 44 N. J. Law, 648; Warshung v. Hunt, 47 N. J. Law, 256; Wood v. Oakley, 11 Paige, 400; U. S. v. Starr, 1 Hempst. 469, Fed. Cas. No. 16,379; Costin v. Corporation of Washington, 2 Cranch, C. C. 254, Fed. Cas. No. 3,266; Aurora & L. Turnpike Co. v. Holthouse, 7 Ind. 59; Barnes v. Mayor, etc., of Mobile, 19 Ala. 707; Pritchard v. Spencer, 2 Ind. 486; Hopkins v. Jones, 22 Ind. 310; Seamans v. Carter, 15 Wis. 548; Saunders v. Carroll, 12 La. Ann. 793; Hastings v. Lane, 15 Me. 134; Guard v. Rowan, 3 Ill. 499; Torrey v. Corliss, 33 Me. 333; Whitman v. Hapgood, 10 Mass. 437; Somerset v. Dighton, 12 Mass. 383; Medford v. Learned, 16 Mass. 215; Brown v. Wilcox, 14 Sm. & Mar. 127; State v. Thompson, 41 Mo. 25; Finney v. Ackerman, 21 Wis. 268; State v. Scudder, 32 N. J. Law, 203; Taylor v. Mitchell, 57 Pa. St. 209; Dewart v. Purdy, 29 Pa. St. 113; Ex parte Graham, 13 Rich. 277; Appeal of Deake, 80 Me. 50, 12 Atl. 790; Jimison v. Adams Co., 130 Ill. 558, 22 N. E. 829; Smith v. Humphrey, 20 Mich. 398; People v. Board of Sup'rs of Columbia Co., 43 N. Y. 130; Wade v. Strack, 1 Hun, 96; Hooker v. Hooker, 10 Sm. & Mar. 599; Bruce v. Schuyler, 9 Ill. 221; Garrett v. Beaumont, 24 Miss. 377; McGeehan v. Burke, 37 La. Ann. 156; State v. Wallis, 57 Ark. 64, 20 S. W. 811.

[10] Underwood v. Lilly, 10 Serg. & R. 97, 101.

[11] Cooley, Const. Lim. 370. This rule against retroactive laws is not only of great antiquity and dignity in the English law, but is also recognized in various foreign systems. It was a part of the imperial Roman law. "Leges et constitutiones futuris certum est dare formam negotiis, non ad facta praeterita revocari, nisi nominatim et de praeterito tempore et adhuc pendentibus negotiis cautum sit." Codex, lib. I, tit. 14, § 7. So, also, the Civil Code of France, art. 2, provides "La loi ne dispose que pour l'avenir; elle n'a point d'effet retroactif."

or present facts or transactions as well as upon future transactions, its intention in that regard will be expressed by apt words. For example, a statute making certain provisions in relation to "all contracts which have been heretofore made or which shall be hereafter made" would be explicitly retroactive. So also would a law regulating the rights and duties of "all persons now or hereafter engaging in the business of common carriers." But the problem of interpretation is presented to the courts, and the rule we have cited is put into operation, in those cases where the language of the statute is so ambiguous or lacking in precision that it is doubtful whether it was designed to apply to future cases only or to include the past as well. It is said that, in the absence of any express declaration in the act, the question whether it is meant to be prospective or retrospective is one of construction upon the statute, considered per se and in connection with the subject-matter.[12] And the occasion of the enacting of the law may be looked to, to assist in determining its character as retroactive or prospective.[13] It has also been laid down that when the legislature fixes a future day for the statute to go into effect, it thereby plainly shows that it is intended to be prospective only. Thus, for instance, in a case in Pennsylvania, the act made certain provisions for "cases of partition of real estate in any court wherein a valuation shall have been made of the whole or parts thereof." It was held that the words "shall have been made" referred only to valuations made after the date when the act was to take effect.[14] And so where the act provides for the giving of notice of injuries caused by defective highways, except in the case of injuries "already sustained," but the statute is not to take effect until a future day, the words quoted must be referred to the time when the act takes effect, and not to the date of its passage; in legal contemplation, the words are spoken when it becomes the law.[15] In New Jersey, an act provided that all judgments "shall be" assignable, and that the assignee might sue thereon in his own name. This might mean either that all judgments recovered before the date of the act, as well as those recov-

---

[12] Bay v. Gage, 36 Barb. 447.

[13] People v. Board of Sup'rs of Essex Co., 70 N. Y. 228.

[14] Dewart v. Purdy, 29 Pa. St. 113.

[15] Jackman v. Inhabitants of Garland, 64 Me. 133.

ered after, should be thereafter capable of assignment, or that assignments of judgments, whether made before or after the act,
should enable the assignee to sue in his own name. But the court,
in accordance with the general rule, held that the statute was prospective only, and that it did not apply to a judgment assigned
before its passage.[16] In another case, the expression in a statute
"when any judgment is obtained," was construed as meaning "when
any judgment is hereafter obtained." It was argued that the statute should be so interpreted as to embrace pre-existing judgments.
But the court said: "The most that can be said in favor of this
construction is that the language used is indefinite as to time. If
it may mean 'when any judgment has been obtained,' it may, at
least as plainly, be understood to mean 'when any judgment shall
be obtained.' For such language in a statute there is a long-established rule of interpretation." [17] Again, a compilation of the
statutes of a state, amending and re-enacting a particular law, providing that every conveyance not recorded should be void as against
creditors, omitted the words "hereafter made" which were in the
re-enacted statute. It was nevertheless held that it did not apply
to conveyances executed prior to the date of the original act.[18] And
again, a statute attempting to validate a void assessment on a lot
in a city, for a street improvement, if it has that effect, does not,
by relation, make the assessment valid as of the date when it was
levied, but only validates it at the date of the passage of the act.[19]

There is a corollary to the main rule stated above, which is based
upon the same reason and is supported by the same considerations.
It is thus stated: "Where the retroactive character of a statute is
clearly indicated on its face, and although it is free from constitutional objections, yet it will always be subjected to the most cir-
cumscribing construction that can possibly be made consistent with
the avowed intention of the legislature. Hence, to a statute explicitly retroactive to a certain extent and for a certain purpose, the
courts will not, by construction, give a retroactive operation to any

---

[16] Lydecker v. Babcock, 55 N. J. Law, 394, 26 Atl. 925.

[17] State v. Connell, 43 N. J. Law, 106.

[18] Gaston v. Merriam, 33 Minn. 271, 22 N. W. 614.

[19] Reis v. Graff, 51 Cal. 86.

greater extent or for any other purpose."[20] It was said by a learned English judge: "It seems to me that even in construing an act which is to a certain extent retrospective, and in construing a section which is to a certain extent retrospective, we ought nevertheless to bear in mind that maxim as applicable whenever we reach the line at which the words of the section cease to be plain. That is a necessary and logical corollary of the general proposition that you ought not to give a larger retrospective power to a section, even in an act which is to some extent intended to be retrospective, than you can plainly see the legislature meant."[21] But there is no reason for the strict application of this rule in cases where the statute is remedial in its nature, and designed to work beneficent results. In that case, as we shall presently see, it is to be construed according to the true intent of the legislature, and liberally if need be.[22]

If the statute is free from all ambiguity, there is no more room for interpretation in this respect than in any other. If the legislature has declared, in terms too plain to be mistaken, that the statute shall be applicable to past facts and transactions, the courts are not at liberty to evade this result by construction. It is then their duty to take the law as they find it, and to give to it that meaning which, alone, on its face, it was intended to bear, even though the consequence should be that they are obliged to pronounce the act void for conflict with the constitution.[23] And the intention of the legislature that the statute should operate retrospectively may be discovered (and may be so plain that the courts cannot allow themselves to disregard it) not only in the use of explicit terms, but in necessary implications from the language used. Such, for instance, would be the case where a retrospective interpretation would make the statute sensible and effective, but any other would render it unmeaning. When such implications show, indubitably and unambiguously, what was the real intention of the legislature, the interpreter is constrained to follow it.[24]

---

[20] Black, Const. Prohib. § 180; Thames Manuf. Co. v. Lathrop, 7 Conn. 550.

[21] Reid v. Reid, L. R. 31 Ch. Div. 402.

[22] See Journeay v. Gibson, 56 Pa. St. 57.

[23] See Baldwin v. City of Newark, 38 N. J. Law, 158.

[24] Young v. Hughes, 4 Hurl. & N. 76.

Retrospective Acts, When Construed as Prospective Also.

Another question of statutory construction, which is directly converse to that which we have been considering, but which arises much less frequently, is whether an act, explicitly made retrospective, is to be confined to past cases, or is to be construed as prospective also. This is of course always a question of legislative intention. If the design of the legislature is expressed in plain words, the courts have no choice but to carry it into effect. For example, a statute of Indiana, designed to legalize the acts of certain boards of municipal officers, made provision for cases in which "the inspectors of elections have failed" to take certain action. It was held that this was, on its face, retrospective and curative only, and that it could have no prospective force.[25] But in the absence of express language, the question must be determined by reference to the nature of the statute and the objects which it is designed to accomplish. Thus, it is a rule that where a statute impairs or abridges the rights of a certain class of people, or deprives the citizens of one part of the state of privileges enjoyed by citizens of other parts of the state, it should be construed strictly. Hence, if it is explicitly made retroactive, but not explicitly made prospective, it will be construed as retrospective only, that thereby its discriminating or penal provisions may be restricted as much as possible. Thus, a statute of Pennsylvania, in reference to tax sales in certain specified counties, to the effect that the oath of the tax collector shall be deemed conclusive evidence that the taxes are unpaid, was held to be retrospective only.[26] But on the other hand, if the statute is beneficial and remedial, it should be liberally construed, and if there is a substantial doubt whether it was meant to be retroactive only or to extend also to future cases, it should be interpreted in the largest sense which the words will properly bear. Thus, a statute provision that an alien "who shall have resided within the state two years" shall be capable of holding and transmitting real estate the same as a citizen, may apply as well to future as to past residence.[27] So also, the operation of a law for regulating "all existing railroad corporations," in respect to requiring them to exer-

---

[25] Lucas v. State, 86 Ind. 180.

[26] Marsh v. Nelson, 101 Pa. St. 51.

[27] Beard v. Rowan, 1 McLean, 135, Fed. Cas. No. 1,181; s. c.. 9 Pet. 301.

cise certain care and take certain precautions for the protection of the public, will extend to and control railroads incorporated after, as well as before, its passage, unless exception is made in their charters.[28] There may also be special and peculiar reasons which will suffice to determine this question in particular cases. For example, in New Jersey, it is held that a statute authorizing cities "already divided into wards" to subdivide the wards when they reach a certain size, is not confined to cities which had been divided into wards before the passage of the statute. It will be observed that there was here a fair choice of constructions. But if the act were construed as retrospective only, it would make it "special legislation," which is forbidden by the constitution of that state. For this reason, the court held it to be prospective also.[29]

STATUTES IMPAIRING VESTED RIGHTS.

104. When the effect of giving to a statute a retrospective construction would be to make it destroy or impair vested rights, or impose new penalties, forfeitures, liabilities, or disabilities, such construction will be avoided, and the statute will be held to apply to future acts and cases only, provided that this can be done by any reasonable interpretation of the language used by the legislature.[30]

"The courts uniformly refuse to give to statutes a retrospective operation, whereby rights previously vested are injuriously affected, unless compelled to do so by language so clear and positive as to leave no room to doubt that such was the intention of the legislature."[31] "The rule is that a statute affecting rights and liabilities should not be so construed as to act upon those already existing,

---

[28] Indianapolis & St. L. R. Co. v. Blackman, 63 Ill. 117.

[29] Wood v. Atlantic City (N. J. Sup.) 28 Atl. 427.

[30] Couch v. Jeffries, 4 Burr. 2460; Moore v. Phillips, 7 Mees. & W. 536; Hannum v. Bank of Tennessee, 1 Coldw. 398; Berley v. Rampacher, 5 Duer, 183; Quackenbush v. Danks, 1 Denio, 128; Thorne v. San Francisco, 4 Cal. 127; Dillon v. Dougherty, 2 Grant (Pa.) 99; State v. Atwood, 11 Wis. 422; Kelley v. Kelso, 5 Ohio St. 198.

[31] Chew Heong v. U. S., 112 U. S. 536, 5 Sup. Ct. 255.

and it is the result of the decisions that although the words of a statute are so general and broad in their literal extent as to comprehend existing cases, they must yet be so construed as to be applicable only to such as may thereafter arise, unless the intention to embrace all is clearly expressed." [32]

Impairing Vested Rights.

We shall not in this place enter upon a discussion of the nature of vested rights, as that subject more properly belongs to the domain of constitutional law, [33] but shall be satisfied with adducing a sufficient number of illustrations from the reported cases to explain the operation of the well-settled rule above stated.   The statutes which have been passed in most of the states, securing to married women the more free and perfect control of their individual property, authorizing them to deal with the same as if sole, and otherwise enlarging their powers over it, and at the same time abridging the husband's rights and interests in such property and his authority to control the disposition of the same, are not construed, unless it is clearly necessary, as having a retroactive effect; that is, in their application to estates of married women already vested, they will not be taken as destroying any rights or estates held by husbands in such property, jure uxoris, if such a construction can be fairly avoided. [34]   Again, where a mortgage is made prior to the passage of the statute which provides for the vesting, upon foreclosure, of the inchoate interest of the mortgagor's wife, her rights are fixed, upon foreclosure, by the law in force when the mortgage was made.   "When a mortgage is executed upon a tract of land, the mortgagee acquires, by contract, a specific lien.   *   *   * The lien thus acquired by the mortgagee becomes by the terms of

[32] In re Protestant Episcopal Public School, 58 Barb. 161; Goillotel v. Mayor, etc., of New York, 87 N. Y. 441.

[33] See Black, Const. Law, pp. 429–434.

[34] Hershizer v. Florence, 39 Ohio St. 516; Quigley v. Graham, 18 Ohio St. 42; Leete v. State Bank, 115 Mo. 184, 21 S. W. 788.   Though a married woman comes into possession of real estate after the passage of an act conferring certain rights on married women, yet if her title is derived through a will which took effect before the passage of such act, her rights in the property are determined by the law as it existed prior to the passage of the act, and the husband's freehold, jure uxoris, cannot be thus divested.   White v. Hilton, 2 Mackey, 339.

CONSTRUC.LAWS—17

the contract a vested right, which the legislature can neither abridge nor diminish by subsequent legislation. Any subsequent enlargement of the inchoate interest of the wife in the mortgaged land would necessarily operate as a diminution of the security afforded by the mortgage, and be an invasion of the vested right which the mortgagee had acquired under it." [35] Again, a statute authorizing administrators to take possession of the real estate of their decedents, not being explicitly retroactive, will not operate to give that right as against the heirs of a person whose estate was in process of administration before the passage of the statute, and whose heirs and devisees had already become vested with the interests to which they were entitled. [36] Where, at the time of the death of a testator, a bequest to a cemetery was void under the rule against perpetuities, and the property bequeathed vested in the testator's next of kin, and a statute was afterwards passed abolishing the rule against perpetuities so far as it affects gifts made to cemetery corporations for designated purposes, before the day for the payment of the legacy, it was held that this did not divest the rights of the next of kin in favor of the cemetery company. [37] So again, the vendor of real estate has a lien upon the property sold for the unpaid purchase-money, independent of the existence of a lien evidenced by a title-bond or mortgage; and hence a statute which provides that no vendor's lien shall be enforced after a conveyance by the vendee, unless the lien is recorded, cannot apply to sales made before the enactment of the statute. [38] So likewise, the statutes which give to occupying claimants, life tenants, and others, in certain cases, the benefit of improvements placed by them upon the land before eviction or before the termination of their estate, are not construed retroactively unless the plain language of the law requires it. [39] Moreover, a right of action, completely accrued under the existing law, may be a vested right which the courts are bound to protect. Thus, a statute passed after the accruing of a cause of action based

[35] Lease v. Owen Lodge, 83 Ind. 498; McGlothlin v. Pollard, 81 Ind. 228. See, also, Baldwin v. Cullen, 51 Mich. 33, 16 N. W. 191.

[36] Van Fleet v. Van Fleet, 49 Mich. 610, 14 N. W. 566.

[37] Hartson v. Elden, 50 N. J. Eq. 522, 26 Atl. 561.

[38] Jordan v. Wimer, 45 Iowa, 65.

[39] Shay's Appeal, 51 Conn. 162; Wilson v. Red Wing School Dist., 22 Minn. 488; Folsom v. Clark, 72 Me. 44.

upon an injury caused by defendant's negligence, limiting the amount of recovery in such cases, will be construed, if possible, as prospective only, and will consequently have no bearing upon plaintiff's right to recover full damages.[40] A statute of limitations is not to be construed retrospectively unless such is the plain and manifest intention of the legislature. More especially is this the rule where the effect of giving it a retrospective operation would be to cut off altogether the remedy on existing causes of action, or to reduce unreasonably the time within which that remedy may be sought.[41] A statute giving exclusive jurisdiction where concurrent jurisdiction has been exercised should not be construed retroactively, unless no other construction can fairly be given.[42] No person can have a vested right in a penalty or forfeiture until it has been judicially ascertained and declared. Hence, if it has not been reduced to judgment before a repeal of the statute which created the right of action, the penalty or forfeiture falls with the law, and cannot afterwards be enforced. But a right to a penalty, forfeiture, or bounty, when once it has become fully vested, should not be held to be divested by a subsequent statute, if the statute can be so construed as to avoid this retroactive effect.[43]

Imposing Penalties and New Liabilities.

A statute imposing a new penalty, or a new liability or disability, or giving a new right of action, should not be construed as having a retroactive operation, if such consequences can fairly be avoided. This is the rule, for example, in regard to the statutes which give a right of action in damages for injuries resulting from negligence or wrongful act and causing the death of a human being,[44] and also in regard to the civil damage acts.[45] So also, a revenue act imposing penalties upon delinquent tax payers should not be so construed as to affect persons who became delinquent before the statute took

[40] Osborne v. City of Detroit, 32 Fed. 36; Gorman v. McArdle, 67 Hun, 484, 22 N. Y. Supp. 479.

[41] State v. Pinckney, 22 S. Car. 484; Smith v. Packard, 12 Wis. 371.

[42] State v. Littlefield, 93 N. Car. 614.

[43] State v. Youmans, 5 Ind. 280; People v. Board of State Auditors, 9 Mich. 327; Breitung v. Lindauer, 37 Mich. 217.

[44] Kelley v. Boston & M. R. Co., 135 Mass. 448; Chicago, St. L. & N. O. R. Co. v. Pounds, 11 Lea, 127.

[45] Reinhardt v. Fritzsche, 69 Hun, 565, 23 N. Y. Supp. 958.

effect.[46]   And a statute authorizing a forfeiture of dower or curtesy "whenever a married man shall be deserted by his wife, or a married woman by her husband, for the space of one year," should be construed as prospective only, and as applying only to cases of desertion beginning after the law takes effect.[47]   On the same principle, a statute providing that no person shall recover any fees or charges for medical or surgical services, unless he shall prove at the trial that he is duly registered under the act, does not apply to an action commenced before the passage of the statute.[48]   And an act prohibiting the intermarriage of a white person with an Indian, enacted after such a marriage, has no bearing upon the validity of the marriage; that is, it should not be construed retroactively so as to invalidate a marriage which was good when contracted.[49]   Again, an act providing that married women shall be bound, like other persons, by estoppels in pais, is not retroactive, and has no application to a mortgage made by a married woman before the enactment.[50]   After an administration bond had been executed, an act was passed providing that ten per cent. damages should be awarded against administrators and their sureties on the bonds.   But it was held that the ten per cent. could not be awarded on the bond mentioned.[51]   It is also said that a statute increasing the rate of interest operates only on future rights.[52]

[46] Bartruff v. Remey, 15 Iowa, 257.
[47] Giles v. Giles, 22 Minn. 348.
[48] Thistleton v. Frewer, 31 L. J. Exch. 230.
[49] Illinois Land & Loan Co. v. Bonner, 75 Ill. 315.
[50] Levering v. Shockey, 100 Ind. 558.
[51] Steen v. Finley, 25 Miss. 535.
[52] Cummings v. Howard, 63 Cal. 503.

REMEDIAL STATUTES.

105. Remedial statutes are to be liberally construed; and if a retrospective interpretation will promote the ends of justice and further the design of the legislature in enacting them, or make them applicable to cases which are within the reason and spirit of the enactment, though not within its direct words, they should receive such a construction, provided it is not inconsistent with the language employed.[53]

"It is undoubtedly the general rule," says the court in Indiana, "that statutes are to be construed and applied prospectively, unless a contrary intent is manifested in clear and unambiguous terms, and it is sometimes held that, to work an exception, the intent favoring retrospective application must affirmatively appear in the words of the statute. The better rule of construction, and the rule peculiarly applicable to remedial statutes, is that a statute must be so construed as to make it effect the evident purpose for which it was enacted; and if the reason of the statute extends to past transactions, as well as to those in the future, then it will be so applied, although the statute does not, in terms, so direct, unless to do so would impair some vested right or violate some constitutional guaranty." [54] To the same general effect is the following language employed by the supreme court of Alabama: "The statutes excluded from judicial favor and subjected to the strictness of judicial construction—statutes which may be properly denominated retrospective—are such as take away or impair vested rights acquired under existing laws, or create a new obligation, impose a new duty, or attach a new disability, in respect to transactions or considerations already past. Such statutes are offensive to the principles of sound and just legislation, and it is of these that the authorities use the term 'odious' and other epithets expressive of judicial opprobrium.

[53] Sturgis v. Hall, 48 Vt. 302; Dobbins v. First Nat. Bank, 112 Ill. 553; Broaddus's Devisees v. Broaddus's Heirs, 10 Bush, 299; People v. Board of Sup'rs of Ulster Co., 63 Barb. 83; Indianapolis v. Imberry, 17 Ind. 175; Augusta Bank v. City of Augusta, 49 Me. 507.

[54] Connecticut Mut. Life Ins. Co. v. Talbot, 113 Ind. 373, 14 N. E. 586.

There are other statutes which, when operating retrospectively, have not incurred judicial condemnation, and to which a liberal construction, for the consummation of the just and beneficent purposes in view, has been freely accorded. Such statutes are intended to remedy a mischief, promote public justice, correct innocent mistakes into which parties may have fallen, cure irregularities, or give effect to the acts or contracts of individuals fairly done and made. These are remedial statutes, conducive alike to individual and public good." [55]

For example, where it clearly appears that the object of the statute is to obviate controversies between innocent parties arising out of defective legislation or the improper conduct of public officers, and to accomplish this object it is necessary to give it a retroactive operation, although there may be no express words in the act giving to it such an effect, it is the duty of the courts so to construe it.[56] For this reason, an act providing that a general devise or bequest shall operate as an execution of a power of appointment, unless a contrary intention appears by the will, is not confined to wills executed after the date of the act, but extends to cases where the testator dies after its enactment.[57] On the same principle, a statute declaring that no words of inheritance shall be necessary to convey a fee by devise may operate retrospectively.[58] And a statute providing that "actions at law may be sustained against any married woman upon any contract made by her upon her personal credit, for the benefit of herself, her family, or her estate," applies to such contracts made before the passage of the act as well as to those made after.[59] A statutory provision that, when mortgaged land is taken for public use under the power of eminent domain, the mortgagor and mortgagee may join in a petition for damages, is remedial in its character, and it will apply to proceedings begun after it took effect, although the land was previously taken.[60] An act authorizing justices of the peace to issue gar-

---

[55] Ex parte Buckley, 53 Ala. 42. See, also, Tilton v. Swift, 40 Iowa, 78.
[56] People v. Spicer, 99 N. Y. 225, 1 N. E. 680.
[57] Aubert's Appeal, 109 Pa. St. 447, 1 Atl. 336.
[58] Adams v. Chaplin, 1 Hill, Ch. (S. Car.) 265.
[59] Buckingham v. Moss, 40 Conn. 461.
[60] Wood v. Inhabitants of Westborough, 140 Mass. 403, 5 N. E. 613.

nishee process may be so construed as to permit the issue of such process upon a judgment rendered before the enactment of the statute, the law being remedial, and no constitutional rule being affected by such construction.[61]   An act giving to the plaintiff suing for the purchase money of land a lien thereon while in the vendee's hands, and authorizing a writ of seizure on the filing of the declaration, and a special execution for the sale of the property in addition to a personal judgment, is remedial in its nature, and may constitutionally be made applicable to causes of action existing at the time of its passage.[62]   Again, a statute which extends the time and releases the conditions prescribed in a former statute in regard to the issuing of executions, may apply to judgments recovered before the passage of the act, without being liable to the objection of affecting vested rights.[63]   And a statutory provision that a judgment against the principal on an injunction bond shall conclude the surety also may be held to apply to a bond executed before the enactment of the statute; the remedy only, not the right, is affected.[64]   Again, an act declaring that marriage between persons within the prohibited degrees of consanguinity shall not be pronounced void after the death of either, if the marriage was followed by cohabitation and the birth of issue, applies to such marriages contracted before the enactment of the statute, as well as to those contracted afterwards.[65]   For similar reasons it is held that a statute which confers upon cities, not previously possessing it, the power to sell real and personal property for delinquent taxes, may apply as well to taxes delinquent before the act was passed as to those becoming delinquent thereafter.[66]   An English statute enacted that "every person convicted of felony shall forever be disqualified from selling spirits by retail, and no license shall be granted to any person who shall have been so convicted."   It was held that this applied to the case of a person who had been convicted of felony before the passage

---

[61] Fisher v. Hervey, 6 Colo. 16.

[62] Excelsior Manuf. Co. v. Keyser, 62 Miss. 155.

[63] Henschall v. Schmidtz, 50 Mo. 454.

[64] Pickett v. Boyd, 11 Lea, 498.

[65] Baity v. Cranfill, 91 N. Car. 293.   See, also, Brower v. Bowers, 1 Abb. App. Dec. 214.

[66] Haskel v. City of Burlington, 30 Iowa, 232.

of the act. The judges considered that the act in question was not so much designed for the punishment of the offender as to protect the public against the dangers which might arise from the keeping of public-houses by convicted felons; and hence the case at bar was within the reason and spirit of the act.[67]   Again, where an act of congress enlarges the jurisdiction of the circuit courts, it will be construed to apply to cases pending and undetermined at the passage of the act, unless excluded by its terms or by necessary implication from the language of the act.[68]   But it is well settled that retrospective curative acts cannot be allowed to interfere with rights of third persons vested at the time of their passage.[69]   And even curative statutes will not be construed as retroactive if they are so expressed as to show that such was not the intention of the legislature.   For instance, an act providing that "any act done by a notary public subsequently to the expiration of his term of office shall be as valid as if done during his term of office," will not retroact so as to make good an unauthorized acknowledgment of a deed taken before the statute was passed.[70]   And it is held that a statute providing that "the contracts of any married woman made for any lawful purpose shall be valid and binding" should be construed as prospective only, and not as applying to promissory notes made before its enactment.[71]

[67] Queen v. Vine, L. R. 10 Q. B. 195.
[68] Larkin v. Saffarans, 15 Fed. 147.
[69] McGehee v. McKenzie, 43 Ark. 156; Black, Const. Law, 545.
[70] Bernier v. Becker, 37 Ohio St. 72.
[71] Bryant v. Merrill, 55 Me. 515.

STATUTES REGULATING PROCEDURE.

106. Statutes regulating the procedure of the courts will be construed as applicable to causes of action accrued, and actions pending and undetermined, at the time of their passage, unless such actions are expressly excepted, or unless vested rights would be disturbed by giving them a retrospective operation.[72]

"The presumption against retrospective construction," says the court in Oregon, "has no application to enactments which affect only the mode of procedure and practice of the courts.   No person has a vested right in any form of procedure.   He has only the right of prosecution or defense in the manner prescribed for the time being, and if this mode of procedure is altered by statute, he has no other right than to proceed according to the altered mode.   Indeed, the rule seems to be that statutes pertaining to the remedy or course and form of procedure, but which do not destroy all remedy for the enforcement of the right, are retrospective, so as to apply to causes of action subsisting at the date of their passage. Statutes which relate to the mode of procedure, and affect only the remedy, and do not impair the obligations of contracts or vested rights, are valid; and it is no objection to them that they are retroactive in their operation.   It is competent for the legislature at any time to change the remedy or mode of procedure for enforcing or protecting rights, provided such enactments do not impair the obligations of contracts, or disturb vested rights, and such remedial statutes take up proceedings in pending causes where they

---

[72] Sampeyreac v. U. S., 7 Pet. 222; Lee v. Buckheit, 49 Wis. 54, 4 N. W. 1077; Kille v. Iron Works, 134 Pa. St. 225, 19 Atl. 547; Lane v. White, 140 Pa. St. 99, 21 Atl. 437; Converse v. Burrows, 2 Minn. 229 (Gil. 191); People v. Herkimer, 4 Wend. 211; Blair v. Cary, 9 Wis. 543; Davidson v. Wheeler, 1 Morris (Iowa) 238.   But this rule is not universally accepted.   See, for example, Boston & M. R. Co. v. Cilley, 44 N. H. 578; Merwin v. Ballard, 66 N. Car. 398.   In New Hampshire, where all retrospective laws are specifically prohibited by the constitution of the state, it is held that statutes which prescribe new rules for the decision of existing causes of action are retrospective, and therefore unconstitutional and inoperative in such cases.   Kennett's Petition, 24 N. H. 139; Smith v. Haines, 58 N. H. 157.

find them; and when the statute under which such proceedings were commenced is amended, the subsequent proceedings must be regulated by the amendatory act." [73]

In this class of statutes are included those which create a new remedy, or enlarge the existing remedy, for existing causes of action. For example, a statute providing a new remedy against persons who place obstructions in public highways may apply as well to the case of obstructions existing at the time of its passage as to those subsequently placed therein.[74] So also, a statute with a proviso that nothing therein contained shall be construed to prevent an action on a judgment after twenty years from its date, and a recovery thereon, in case it shall be established by competent evidence that the judgment, or some part thereof, remains unpaid, may be construed to apply to judgments obtained before its enactment.[75] An act extending the time within which a garnishee may answer in a justice's court will be held to apply to one who was summoned as a garnishee before the passage of the act.[76] So again, statutes which change the rule as to the parties necessary to the determination of controversies will take effect upon prior as well as subsequent contracts and transactions, and the actions arising therefrom.[77] On a similar principle, it is held that a statute giving to a defendant, in certain classes of cases, a right to require the plaintiff to furnish security for costs may be applied to an action commenced before the passage of the statute and pending at that time.[78] And an act of the legislature, prescribing the order of time in which causes are to be tried, is merely remedial, and must apply to all cases not tried at the date of its promulgation.[79] The rules of evidence, it should further be noticed, at least in civil cases, are at all times subject to modification and control by the legislature, and changes in such rules may be made applicable to existing causes of action.[80] In a case in Maryland, it appeared that a bond to the

---

[73] Judkins v. Taffe (Or.) 27 Pac. 221.
[74] Lawrence R. Co. v. Comm'rs of Mahoning Co., 35 Ohio St. 1.
[75] Lawton v. Perry, 40 S. Car. 255, 18 S. E. 861.
[76] Willis v. Fincher, 68 Ga. 444.
[77] Tompkins v. Forrestal, 55 Minn. 119, 55 N. W. 813.
[78] Kimbray v. Draper, L. R. 3 Q. B. 160.
[79] Hoa v. Lefranc, 18 La. Ann. 393.
[80] Howard v. Moot, 64 N. Y. 262; Holmes v. Hunt, 122 Mass. 505.

state was executed at a time when such bonds were required by the revenue laws of the state to be on stamped paper. A suit was brought on this bond, and the court refused to admit it in evidence for want of the stamp. An appeal was taken, and, pending the appeal, the stamp law was repealed, and validity given to all contracts previously made on unstamped paper. It was held that the statute had a retroactive effect, and the judgment was reversed. It might have been supposed that the obligor in the bond had a vested right to object to its admission in evidence, on account of the want of a stamp. But the court observed that the stamp act was passed for the purpose of raising revenue for the state, and did not design or profess to confer upon the citizens of the state, or others, any private benefit or rights, but operated to impose burdens upon them for state purposes. Hence the legislature had full authority to remove such burdens at any time.[81]

But, as has been already stated, statutes which would impair or destroy vested rights will not be allowed to operate retrospectively, if that result can be avoided by any reasonable construction. And this rule is applicable to laws relating to remedies and the course of procedure and practice in the courts, in respect to their applicability to pending suits.[82] Thus, in a case in Alabama, the defendant pleaded a set-off, and the plaintiff, in reply, pleaded the statute of limitations. After these pleadings were interposed, an act was passed excepting cases of set-off from the operation of the statute of limitations, where the set-off was a legal subsisting claim at the time the right of action on the claim in suit accrued to the plaintiff. It was held that this act did not operate retrospectively so as to deprive the plaintiff of the benefit of his replication.[83] Again, a statute of Vermont provided that "the judgment to account in the common-law action of account shall not debar the defendant from making any defense before the auditor which he might have made by special plea in bar of the action if said judgment to account had not been rendered." But it was held that this statute was not retrospective, and did not apply to a case in which judg-

[81] State v. Norwood, 12 Md. 195.

[82] Files v. Fuller, 44 Ark. 273.

[83] Bradford v. Barclay, 42 Ala. 375. But see Campbell v. Holt, 115 U. S. 620, 6 Sup. Ct. 209.

ment to account was rendered, and an auditor appointed, before the passage of the act, but wherein the account was not taken until after that date. The ground of the decision was that, if the statute were allowed to affect the pending case, it would deprive the plaintiff of a substantial right, namely, the right to rely upon the judgment rendered.[84] To take another illustration,—a statute of Iowa provided that pension money should not be liable to be taken for the pensioner's debts. Before this act, a creditor of a pensioner had begun an action to subject the pension money to the satisfaction of his claim. It was held that the statute did not affect the creditor's rights; for he had a vested right of action, and by the institution of his suit he had acquired an equitable lien which the legislature could not divest.[85] So again, under a statute limiting parties to two actions for the recovery of land, and providing that nothing contained therein shall prevent persons from being entitled to two actions after the passage of the act, an action pending at the time the act was passed cannot be considered as one of the actions allowed.[86]

A more difficult question, and one on which the authorities are somewhat divided, is as to the effect of statutes of this kind on cases where a judgment has already been rendered and the case is pending on appeal. Let it be supposed that a judgment has been correctly given in the lower court, for or against one of the parties, on a ground of claim or defense which is afterwards annulled, obviated, or made immaterial by a retrospective statute. In the mean time, the case has been appealed. The question then is whether the appellate court should reverse the judgment (which was correct and in accordance with the law at the time it was rendered) or refuse to give effect to the retrospective statute in this particular case. In some jurisdictions it is maintained that the judgment of the lower court must be tested by the law as it stood at the time the judgment was rendered, and that the question of its affirmance or reversal must be decided solely with reference to the then existing state of the law. Thus, for example, a judgment was rendered declaring a tax levy invalid because the several items

[84] Sturgis v. Hull, 48 Vt. 302.

[85] Goble v. Stephenson, 68 Iowa, 270, 26 N. W. 433.

[86] Duren v. Kee, 41 S. Car. 171, 19 S. E. 492.

of the tax were illegally blended in one assessment roll.   An appeal was taken, and, pending the appeal, a statute was passed legalizing the assessment and assessment roll.   But it was held that this act could not be deemed to operate retrospectively upon the case in which the said judgment had been rendered, and that the judgment must be affirmed on appeal, notwithstanding the act.[87] But on the other hand, there are respectable authorities to the effect that a curative or legalizing act, or one removing a disability or waiving an objection, if applicable to the state of facts on which a judgment was rendered, will go behind the judgment and thereby render it erroneous, so as to require its reversal on appeal.[88]

[87] People v. Moore, 1 Idaho (N. S.) 662. And see Wright v. Graham, 42 Ark. 140; Kingsbery v. Ryan (Ga.) 17 S. E. 689.

[88] King v. Course, 25 Ind. 202; State v. Norwood, 12 Md. 195.

CHAPTER X.

CONSTRUCTION OF PROVISOS, EXCEPTIONS, AND SAVING CLAUSES.

DEFINITIONS.

107. A proviso is a clause added to a statute, or to a section or part thereof, which introduces a condition or limitation upon the operation of the enactment, or makes special provision for cases excepted from the general provisions of the law, or qualifies or restrains its generality, or excludes some possible ground of misinterpretation of its extent.

108. An exception in a statute is a clause similar to a proviso. Specifically, it excepts from the operation of the statute persons, things, or cases which would otherwise have been included in it.

109. A saving clause in a statute is an exemption of a special thing out of the general things mentioned in the enactment. More particularly, it exempts existing rights or causes of action or pending proceedings from the operation of a statute which otherwise would change or destroy them.

Provisos.

A proviso is commonly found at the end of the act or section to which it applies, and it is usually introduced by the word "provided." This, however, is not necessary to determine its character. "It does not necessarily follow that because the term 'provided' is used, that which may succeed it is a proviso, though that is the form in which an exception is generally made to, or a restraint or qualification imposed on, the enacting clause. It is the matter of the succeeding words, and not the form, which determines whether

it is or not a technical proviso." [1]   The office of a proviso is not to
enlarge or extend the act or the section of which it is a part, but
rather to put a limitation or a restraint upon the language which
the legislature has employed. [2]   But while it is a general rule that
a proviso is to be considered as a limitation upon the general words
preceding, or an exception therefrom, yet this rule is not absolute;
but in case of doubt, the meaning of the proviso is to be ascertained
from its language. [3]   The proviso is a subsidiary and dependent
part of the statute, or of the section to which it is appended.   Hence,
when a statute with a proviso is repealed, the proviso will fall with
the statute; it will not continue in force as an independent enactment. [4]   But in interpreting a section of a statute which remains in
force, resort may be had to a proviso to it, although the proviso has
been repealed. [5]

Exceptions.

An exception is commonly incorporated in the body of the act or
section which it modifies.   It is frequently (but not necessarily)
introduced by the word "except."   For example, in the constitution
of the United States it is provided: "Every order, resolution, or
vote to which the concurrence of the senate and house of representatives shall be necessary, except on a question of adjournment, shall
be presented to the President."   Again, if an excise law provides
that it shall be a misdemeanor for "any person not being a licensed
retailer" to sell liquor, the exemption of persons holding licenses is
properly an exception.   When the terms are used with technical
precision, the distinction between a proviso and an exception is this:
an exception exempts absolutely from the operation of an enactment, while a proviso defeats its operation conditionally.   An exception takes out of an enactment something which would otherwise
be part of the subject-matter of it; a proviso avoids it by way of
defeasance or excuse. [6]   There is also a well-known distinction between an exception in the purview of the act and a proviso, in this

[1] Carroll v. State, 58 Ala. 396.

[2] Matter of Webb, 24 How. Pr. 247.

[3] Traders' Nat. Bank v. Lawrence Manuf. Co., 96 N. Car. 298, 3 S. E. 363.

[4] Church v. Stadler, 16 Ind. 463.

[5] Bank for Savings v. Collector, 3 Wall. 495.

[6] Waffle v. Goble, 53 Barb. 517, 522.

respect: If there be an exception in the enacting clause of a statute, it must be negatived in pleading, but a separate proviso need
not be, and that, although it is found in the same section of the act,
if it be not referred to and engrafted on the enacting clause.[7]   This
is a rule of pleading and is not properly germane to the subject of
construction, but is mentioned here as illustrating some of the
differences between provisos and exceptions.

Saving Clauses.

A saving clause is usually placed at or near the end of the act,
and is most commonly introduced by the words "nothing in this act
shall be held," etc.   Such clauses are often found in repealing statutes, where their specific use is to exempt from the effect of the repeal proceedings inaugurated or rights vested under the law to be
repealed.   For example, ordinarily, a right to a statutory penalty
or forfeiture may be destroyed at any time before a recovery has
been had, by the repeal of the law which gave it.   But if it is desired to make an exception in favor of those who had already begun
their actions when the repealing act is passed, this may be done by
a saving clause.   So also, when a new act makes changes in the
jurisdiction of the courts, or in the rules of practice or evidence, a
saving clause is often introduced in order to except from the operation of the act proceedings which may be pending and undetermined
at the time of its passage.   When a new statute on the same subject as a prior one repeals the former law, with a saving clause in
the repealing section as to existing suits or litigation, the saving
in such case is in legal effect a limitation on the repealing clause,
and operates to continue in force the old law as to existing suits or
proceedings.[8]

[7] Sedgwick, Stat. Constr. (2d edn.) 50; Trustees of First Baptist Church v.
Utica & S. R. Co., 6 Barb. 313; Vavasour v. Ormrod, 6 Barn. & C. 430.

[8] Dobbins v. First Nat. Bank, 112 Ill. 553.

PROVISO LIMITED TO PRECEDING MATTER.

110. The natural and appropriate office of a proviso to a statute, or to a section thereof, is to restrain or qualify the provisions immediately preceding it. Hence it is a rule of construction that it will be confined to that which directly precedes it, or to the section to which it is appended, unless it clearly appears that the legislature intended it to have a wider scope.[9]

Although, as just stated, the appropriate function of a proviso in a statute is to restrain or modify the enacting clause, and it should be confined to what precedes it, yet when, from the context, and from a comparison of all the provisions relating to the same subject-matter, it is manifest that the object and intent were to give the proviso a scope extending beyond the section, and an effect beyond the phrase immediately preceding, it will be construed as restraining and qualifying preceding sections relating to the subject-matter of the proviso, or as tantamount to an enactment in a separate section, without regard to its position and connection.[10] Hence the proviso may qualify the whole or any part of the act, or it may stand as an independent proposition or rule, if such is clearly seen to be the meaning of the legislature as disclosed by an examination of the entire enactment.[11] From the character or purpose of a proviso, it may even be evident that it was intended to qualify statutes which might thereafter be passed, being designed as a substantive rule of law or a continuing limitation in a class of cases. Thus, in a case in Maryland, the charter of a city granted certain powers

[9] Rawls v. Doe, 23 Ala. 240; Pearce v. Bank of Mobile, 33 Ala. 693; Carroll v. State, 58 Ala. 396; Gast v. Board of Assessors, 43 La. Ann. 1104, 10 South. 184; Callaway v. Harding, 23 Gratt. 542; Cushing v. Worrick, 9 Gray, 382; Lehigh County v. Meyer, 102 Pa. St. 479; Spring v. Collector of City of Olney, 78 Ill. 101.

[10] Wartensleben v. Haithcock, 80 Ala. 565, 1 South. 38; Appeal of Mechanics' & Farmers' Bank, 31 Conn. 63; Friedman v. Sullivan, 48 Ark. 213, 2 S. W. 785; King v. Inhabitants of Threlkeld, 4 Barn. & Ad. 229; King v. Inhabitants of Newark-upon-Trent, 3 Barn. & C. 59.

[11] United States v. Babbit, 1 Black (U. S.) 55.

to the mayor and council, with the following proviso: "That they shall not have power to pledge the credit or faith of the city for any sum exceeding $10,000, without first submitting the question to the voters of said city." A subsequent statute authorized them to issue bonds of the city for the purpose of building a public bridge, and to levy and collect extraordinary taxes to pay the bonds and the interest thereon. It was held that the power thus given was subject to the proviso in the charter. It was said that the proviso, being engrafted upon the effective part of the charter, was a comprehensive and definite restriction upon the exercise of any power to pledge the faith or credit of the city beyond the limited sum, and that the effect of the later statute was merely to place the powers thereby granted among those previously granted, subject to all the conditions and limitations imposed by the original law. To preserve a restrictive proviso of this character, the court said, liberal application would be made of the settled rules of construction that repeals by implication are disfavored, that apparently contradictory statutes shall stand together if by interpretation they may, and that when two laws only so far differ or disagree as that by any other construction they may both stand together, the latter is no repeal of the former.[12] As a rule, however, and unless the contrary intent is clearly apparent, the proviso is to be strictly limited. Thus, in another case, it appeared that the charter of a bank was to continue in force until 1859, and allowed it to take seven per cent. discount. In 1852, the legislature passed an act to extend the privileges of the bank for twenty years beyond the expiration of its charter, with a proviso that it should not take more than six per cent. It was held that this proviso applied only to the privileges granted by the extension, and did not affect loans made while the original charter was in force.[13]

[12] Mayor, etc., of Cumberland v. Magruder, 34 Md. 381.
[13] Pearce v. Bank of Mobile, 33 Ala. 693.

CONSTRUCTION OF PROVISOS.

111. A proviso in a statute, where the enacting clause is general in its terms and objects, must ordinarily be construed strictly.

"Where the enacting clause is general in its language and objects, and a proviso is afterwards introduced, that proviso is construed strictly, and takes no case out of the enacting clause which does not fall fairly within its terms. In short, a proviso carves special exceptions only out of the enacting clause; and those who set up any such exception must establish it as being within the words as well as within the reason thereof." [14] For example, an act of congress limited the liability of shipowners for loss or damage to merchandise carried by them caused by fires. One of the sections (being in the nature of an exception or proviso) provided that the act should not apply to the owners of vessels "used in rivers or inland navigation." A question arose as to whether the act was applicable to a case where the vessel was employed in navigating the Great Lakes. The court held that the owner could claim the benefit of the act. This was, in effect, construing the statute liberally (as it was remedial) and giving a strict construction to the exception, which removed certain cases from its operation. [15] Again, an act regulating actions against sheriffs for not returning executions declared that "all rights of action secured by existing laws may be prosecuted in the manner provided in this act," and repealed inconsistent provisions. It was held that the damages were to be regulated by this act, although the right of action accrued before. [16] So, where a municipal ordinance forbidding the sale of fresh meat within certain limits, except by licensed persons, contains a proviso in favor of farmers, authorizing them to sell meats which are the produce of their own farms, one who follows the business of a butcher and sells meats without a license, is not within the proviso,

[14] United States v. Dickson, 15 Pet. 141; Roberts v. Yarboro, 41 Tex. 449; Bragg v. Clark, 50 Ala. 363; McRae v. Holcomb, 46 Ark. 306; Looker v. Davis, 47 Mo. 140; Epps v. Epps, 17 Ill. App. 196; Appeal of Clark, 58 Conn. 207, 20 Atl. 456.

[15] Moore v. American Transportation Co., 24 How. 1.

[16] Collier v. State, 10 Ind. 58.

although his meats come from his farm, if the farm is only an appendage to his business as a butcher.[17]

But this rule is not invariably applicable. There are cases in which a proviso to a statute should be liberally construed. This is the case when it is necessary to extend the proviso to persons or cases which come within its equity, though not its strict letter, in order to effectuate justice or secure the benefits or remedies which the proviso had in contemplation, and especially when the statute is penal in its nature.[18] For example, a statute of Pennsylvania declared that any money or thing bet on the result of an election should be forfeited to the directors of the poor, "provided that suit is brought within two years from the time of making such bet." It was held that the proviso operated as a condition and not as a statute of limitations which must be pleaded against a suit by the directors. It will be observed that the forfeiture here was in the nature of a penalty and the statute was therefore a penal act. It followed that the statute must be construed strictly and the proviso liberally. The construction given to the proviso in this case was liberal, because if it had been held a statute of limitations, the right of the directors to recover would not be cut off in two years unless the lapse of time were pleaded and proven.[19] Again, an act of the legislature which disposes of state property, excepting that portion "known as the government reservation," will except all lands known by that name, whether the reservation had any legal existence or not.[20] So, where a statute changing school districts saved rights in favor of parties holding contracts, obligation rights, or liens, it was held that a right of action for trespass in taking a building for a school-house was saved.[21] Where a city ordinance appropriated money for the ensuing year, but before the issue of warrants, an act of the legislature amended the city charter, restricting its right to make appropriations, but providing that nothing in the act should in any measure affect or impair any proceeding had under previous existing acts, or any rights or privileges

[17] Trustees of Rochester v. Pettinger, 17 Wend. 265.
[18] Bank of U. S. v. McKenzie, 2 Brock. 393, Fed. Cas. No. 927.
[19] Forscht v. Green, 53 Pa. St. 138.
[20] People v. Dana, 22 Cal. 11.
[21] Gould v. Sub-District Number Three, 7 Minn. 203 (Gil. 145).

acquired thereunder, it was held that the city auditor was bound to issue the warrants according to the terms of the ordinance.[22] Where a criminal statute is changed between the time of the commission of an offense and a conviction therefor, but the later act contains a saving clause, to the effect that it shall not apply to the trial of offenses committed prior to the amending act, the punishment of the prisoner must be regulated by the old law.[23] Where a repealing statute contains a special saving clause, the general saving clause of the general statutes has no application, and no rights or remedies will be saved except such as are saved by the special saving clause.[24]

The introduction of an exception or saving clause may have an important bearing on the construction of the enacting part of the statute, for it may show it to be more comprehensive than would appear merely from the words used, on the principle that when certain exceptions are specified, no others are intended. This rule is alike applicable to grants inter partes and to public laws. Thus, it is said: "When first there are general words, and after, an exception of some particular, all that is not within the particular shall be within the general; what is not excepted is within the grant; and this rule holds where the general words by themselves will not pass a thing; there by intendment of the exception they shall pass. As if a man grant all trees, yet fruit trees do not pass; but a grant of all trees except apple trees will pass all other kinds of fruit trees."[25] When, by a declaratory provision, the legislature enacts that a thing may be done, which before that time was lawful, and adds a proviso that nothing therein contained shall be so construed as to permit some other matter embraced in the general provision to be done, this is an implied prohibition of such act, though before that time it was lawful.[26]

22 Beatty v. People, 6 Colo. 538.
23 People v. Gill, 7 Cal. 356.
24 State v. Showers, 34 Kans. 269, 8 Pac. 474.
25 Viner's Abr. "Grants," H. 13, 61.
26 State v. Eskridge, 1 Swan (Tenn.) 413.

REPUGNANT PROVISOS AND SAVING CLAUSES.

112. A saving clause which is repugnant to the enacting part of the statute is void; but a proviso which is repugnant to the purview of the act will override and control the latter.

It is well settled that a saving clause in a statute which is inconsistent with the body of the act is to be rejected and disregarded as void and of no effect.[27]   As an example of this rule Blackstone cites the following: "If an act of parliament vests lands in the king and his heirs, saving the rights of all persons whatsoever, or vests the land of A. in the king, saving the right of A., in either of these cases the saving is totally repugnant to the body of the statute, and, if good, would render the statute of no effect or operation; and therefore the saving is void, and the land vests absolutely in the king."[28]   And a saving clause in a general act has no operation if it is inconsistent with the express provisions of a subsequent special act.[29]   On the other hand, if a proviso in a statute is directly contrary to the purview of the statute, the proviso is good and not the purview; the proviso must stand as the last expression of the legislative will.[30]   In one of the earliest cases applying this rule, it was said: "Where the proviso of an act of parliament is directly repugnant to the purview, the proviso shall stand and be a repeal of the purview, as it speaks the last intention of the makers; and it was compared at the bar to a will, in which the latter part, if inconsistent with the former, shall supersede and revoke it."[31] The distinction between provisos and saving clauses, in this respect, is thus explained in a case in New York: "It is said the second section should be regarded as a saving clause or a proviso, and that,

---

[27] Case of Alton Woods, 1 Coke, 40b, 47a; Walsingham's Case, 2 Plowd. 547, 565; Jackson v. Moye, 33 Ga. 296.

[28] 1 Bl. Comm. 89.

[29] Corporation of Yarmouth v. Simmons, L. R. 10 Ch. Div. 518.

[30] Townsend v. Brown, 24 N. J. Law, 80; White v. Nashville & N. W. R. Co., 7 Heisk. 518; Waffle v. Goble, 53 Barb. 517, 522; Farmers' Bank v. Hale, 59 N. Y. 53.

[31] Attorney General v. Governor, etc., of Chelsea Waterworks, Fitzgibbon, 195.

if repugnant to the purview of the act, it is void.   There is a distinction between the effect of a repugnant saving clause and a repugnant proviso.   Whether any sound reason exists for the distinction or not, it seems to be recognized as a settled rule.   A saving clause is only an exception of a special thing out of the general things mentioned in the statute, and, if repugnant to the purview, is void.   The office of a proviso is more extensive.   It is used to qualify or restrain the general provisions of the act, or to exclude any possible ground of interpretation as extending to cases not intended by the legislature to be brought within its purview; and if repugnant to the purview it is not void, but stands as the last expression of the legislature." [32]   Hence, for example, where the statute forbids the doing of a certain act, except upon a condition precedent which it is impossible to perform, the condition is valid and the prohibition absolute.   So, if the statute forbids the doing of the act without a license, and provides that no license shall issue therefor, this would prohibit the act entirely.[33]   But it is held that a saving clause, if in the form of a proviso, restricting the operation of the general language of the enacting clause, is not void because the language of the two clauses is repugnant.[34]

The distinction drawn between saving clauses and provisos, in this particular, has been much criticised.   It is certainly no longer true that the mere position of the proviso at the end of the statute, or of the section, shows it to be a later or reconsidered expression of the meaning of the legislative body.   And on principle, it is difficult to see why a subordinate or subsidiary provision, whether in the nature of a saving or a proviso, should not be disregarded if its retention would destroy the effect of the main features of the enactment.   On this point, Kent speaks as follows: "There is a distinction in some of the books between a saving clause and a proviso in the statute, though the reason of the distinction is not very apparent.   * * * It may be remarked that a proviso repugnant to the purview of the statute renders it equally nugatory and void as a repugnant saving clause, and it is difficult to see why the act should be destroyed by the one and not by the other, or why

32 Farmers' Bank v. Hale, 59 N. Y. 53.
33 State v. Douglass, 5 Sneed, 607.
34 Savings Institution v. Makin, 23 Me. 360.

the proviso and the saving clause, when inconsistent with the body of the act, should not both of them be equally rejected." [35]   There are also some few cases to be found in the books which have been decided in accordance with this more reasonable rule.   Thus, in a case in Pennsylvania, it was said that the distinction laid down in the earlier reports, between a saving clause and a proviso, was never founded in right reason, was no longer tenable, and had been rejected by good authority, and it was consequently held that a proviso repugnant to the enacting clause of the statute was void.[36] And so, in a decision of the supreme court of that state, it was intimated that the true principle is that a proviso inconsistent with the purview of the statute is to be treated as void, though at the same time it was held that this did not apply to an act constituting a private corporation; for any ambiguity in such an act must be taken against the corporation and in favor of the public.[37]   It is also said that a proviso which is so obscurely or defectively worded as to be entirely unintelligible or devoid of meaning will be disregarded, but its invalidity will not affect the other provisions of the statute.[38]

The courts will always endeavor, if it be possible, to put such a construction upon a proviso or a saving clause as will remove any apparent inconsistency with the main body of the act.   The supreme court of Ohio, speaking of the rule that a repugnant proviso nullifies the body of the act, says: "It is a rule of necessity and of last resort.   To apply it in any case is to stultify the legislature."

---

[35] 1 Kent, Comm. 463. But compare the following: "Considering the particular natures of saving clauses and provisos, we shall practically find that, since a saving clause is only an exemption of a special thing out of the general things mentioned in the purview, if it stands and the purview is rejected, the whole statute is destroyed, not even the saving clause itself being of any effect. Hence necessarily it must yield to the purview. But a proviso is somewhat different, and under various circumstances it may prevail over the purview without working the destruction of the entire enactment. When this is so, the question of precedence cannot be one of rule, but it must depend on considerations special to the individual case." Bishop, Wr. Laws, § 65.

[36] In re District Court, 4 Clark (Pa.) 501.

[37] Dugan v. Bridge Co., 27 Pa. St. 303.

[38] Paterson Ry. Co. v. Grundy (N. J. Ch.) 26 Atl. 788.

Hence repugnancy will be avoided by construction if possible.[39] Thus, to avoid any repugnancy, the terms of a proviso may be limited by the general scope of the enacting clause.[40]   There are also cases in which it may be feasible to construe the proviso as merely suspending the operation of the statute until such time as the inconsistency shall be removed.   For example, a statute of Texas changed the time of holding the district courts in a certain district, and, in an emergency clause, was declared to take effect from its passage.   But there was a proviso which required that the first term should be held in a designated county, and this, under certain other provisions of the act, could not be done until six months afterwards.   It was held that the antecedent act controlling the subject remained in force until such term could be held.[41]

[39] Renner v. Bennett, 21 Ohio St. 431; Dollar Savings Bank v. United States, 19 Wall. 227; Ihmsen v. Monongahela Nav. Co., 32 Pa. St. 153; Folmer's Appeal, 87 Pa. St. 133.

[40] Treasurer of Vermont v. Clark, 19 Vt. 129.

[41] Graves v. State, 6 Tex. App. 228.

CHAPTER XI.

STRICT AND LIBERAL CONSTRUCTION.

GENERAL PRINCIPLES.

113. Strict construction of a statute is that which refuses to expand the law by implications or equitable considerations, but confines its operation to cases which are clearly within the letter of the statute as well as within its spirit or reason, not so as to defeat the manifest purpose of the legislature, but so as to resolve all reasonable doubts against the applicability of the statute to the particular case. Liberal construction, on the other hand, expands the meaning of the statute to embrace cases which are clearly within the spirit or reason of the law, or within the evil which it was designed to remedy, provided such an interpretation is not inconsistent with the language used; it resolves all reasonable doubts in favor of the applicability of the statute to the particular case.

Where strict construction is called for, the particular case, to come under the statute, must be within both its letter and its spirit and reason. Though the letter of the law may include it, that is not enough unless the spirit and reason of the law also include it; and although the case may be within the spirit and reason of the

statute, that is not enough unless it is also within its letter.   For
a statute of this kind cannot be extended, by intendment or analogy, to cases for which it does not expressly provide.   "The letter
of remedial statutes may be extended to include cases clearly within the mischief which the statute was intended to remedy, unless
such construction does violence to the language used; but a consideration of the old law, the mischief, and the remedy, is not enough
to bring cases within the purview of penal statutes.   They must
be expressly included by the words of the statute.   This is all the
difference between a liberal and a strict construction of a statute.
A case may come within the one unless the language excludes it,
while it is excluded by the other unless the language includes it." [1]
Moreover, where a strict construction is appropriate, the courts,
standing upon the letter of the statute, will accept it as they find
it, and will not undertake to amend or reform the language which
the legislature has seen fit to employ.   They will not put a forced
or strained interpretation upon the words of the law in order to
avoid penal consequences, but neither will they correct grammatical errors, wrest the words from their usual signification in search
of a supposed legislative intent, nor supply apparent omissions or
oversights.   Thus, in a penal statute, "and" cannot be read as "or,"
however much the sense may seem to require it; and words apparently omitted by inadvertence or inattention cannot be supplied by
intendment.[2]

But the rule that certain classes of statutes are to be construed
strictly and other classes liberally is not a fixed and absolute rule
to be resorted to in all cases.   It is a rule which is applicable only

[1] State v. Powers, 36 Conn. 77.

[2] U. S. v. Ten Cases of Shawls, 2 Paine, 162, Fed. Cas. No. 16,448.   In
Rice v. U. S., 4 C. C. A. 104, 53 Fed. 910, it is said: "Undoubtedly 'and' is
not always to be taken conjunctively.   It is sometimes read as if it were 'or'
and taken disjunctively and distributively, but this is only done where that
reading is necessary to give effect to the intention of the legislature, as
plainly expressed in other parts of the act, or deducible therefrom.   In a case
of doubtful construction 'and' would probably be used disjunctively to prevent the imposition of pains and penalties, but it would not be so used for the
purpose of imposing them; and so, in a doubtful case, it will not be used
disjunctively for the purpose of imposing a tax or charge upon the citizen."
See, ante, p. 153.

in cases of substantial doubt. If the meaning and intention of the legislature are plainly expressed, or indubitably discoverable, they must prevail, without any regard to the character of the statute or the view which the interpreter may take of it. In that event there is no room for construction, and this rule, like all others, is simply unnecessary to be considered.[3] The rule does not mean that in one class of cases the court must somewhat abridge the legislative will and in other cases must somewhat expand it. But it means that where the statute is so expressed that the legislative will is not perfectly discoverable, but there arises a reasonable and substantial doubt as to whether or not the act should be applied to the case in question, then, if the statute is penal in its nature (and in some other cases) it will not be so applied, and if it is remedial in its nature (and in some other cases) it will be so applied. And if the words used are capable of being understood in a larger or a narrower sense, in the one case they will be restricted and in the other extended. But the doubt as to the application of the statute must be a substantial one and founded in reason. The courts have no dispensing power, nor should they be unfaithful in their interpretations merely because the particular measure is a harsh or severe one. Judges will not be justified, in the case of penal statutes more than in any other case, in imagining ambiguities merely that a lenient construction may be adopted.[4] "The court is not to find or make any doubt or ambiguity in the language of a penal statute, where such doubt or ambiguity would clearly not be found or made in the same language in any other instrument."[5] "We are not to invent doubts or magnify quibbles, but are diligently to seek the legislative intent as expressed in the words of the statute, aided by all other rules of interpretation, and when satisfied beyond all reasonable doubt of what that intent really is, it is our duty to apply and enforce it."[6] As an instance of the application of this princi-

[3] Nicholson v. Fields, 7 Hurl. & N. 810.

[4] Comm. v. Martin, 17 Mass. 359.

[5] Dyke v. Elliott, L. R. 4 P. C. 184.

[6] State v. McCrystol, 43 La. Ann. 907, 9 South. 922. "All statutes, whether remedial or penal, should be construed according to the apparent intention of the legislature, to be gathered from the language used, connected with the subject of legislation, and so that the entire language shall have effect if it can, without defeating the obvious design and purpose of the law. And in

ple, we may cite a case in which the statute provided that "if a brother shall marry his brother's wife," the marriage should be dissolved and the parties punished. It was held that marrying the brother's widow was an offense within the statute, since that was the evident meaning of the legislature and since any other construction would have rendered the law nugatory.[7] Again, during the civil war, congress passed an act for the confiscation of property used in aid of the rebellion, declaring it to be "lawful subject of prize and capture." In strict technical propriety, these words relate only to seizures made at sea. But since it was the plain and obvious purpose of congress not to restrict the provisions of the act to property taken at sea, but to extend it also to property seized on land, the courts refused to construe the statute as narrowly as the technical signification of the words would seem to require.[8]

Again, the rule of strict and liberal construction combines with others. For instance, it is presumed that the legislature never intends an absurdity; and if this consequence would result from giving to the statute the kind of interpretation contended for (strict or liberal), that consideration may largely influence the construction. Again, effect must be given to all the different parts of the act, and it must be read in the light of other statutes in pari materia.[9] So also, since the endeavor must first be made, in all cases, to discover the real meaning of the legislature, for this end the other rules of construction which we have heretofore studied may be resorted to. Considerations drawn from these other rules may point the court in a certain direction, while considerations drawn from the nature of the statute may incline it in another direction.

doing this, the application of common sense to the language is not to be excluded. This rule is not inconsistent with the principle that penal statutes are to be construed strictly. By this is meant only that they are not to be so extended, by implication, beyond the legitimate import of the words used in them, as to embrace cases or acts not clearly described by such words, and so as to bring them within the prohibition or penalty of such statutes. And there can be no rule which requires courts so to understand a penal law as to involve an absurdity or frustrate the evident design of the law-giver." Rawson v. State, 19 Conn. 292.

[7] Comm. v. Perryman, 2 Leigh (Va.) 717.

[8] U. S. v. Athens Armory, 35 Ga. 344, 2 Abb. U. S. 129, Fed. Cas. No. 14,473.

[9] The Schooner Harriet, 1 Story, 251, Fed. Cas. No. 6,099.

In such a case, the result would be determined by a compromise or by a preponderance of the arguments.

Moreover, "strict construction is not a precise but a relative expression; it varies in degree of strictness according to the character of the law under construction. The construction will be more or less strict according to the gravity of the consequences flowing from the operation of the statute or its infraction; if penal, the severity of the penalty; if in derogation of common right, or capable of being employed oppressively, the extent and nature of the innovation and the consequences; and in any case, according to the combined effect and the reciprocal influence of all relevant principles of interpretation." [10] It is also said that where the provisions of an act are adopted by a general reference, the act will receive a more liberal construction than if originally passed with reference to the particular subject. [11]

PENAL STATUTES.

114. Penal statutes are to be construed strictly, but not so strictly as to defeat the manifest purpose and intention of the legislature.

Strict Construction of Penal Statutes.

It is a familiar and well-settled rule that penal statutes are to be construed strictly, and not extended by implications, intendments, analogies, or equitable considerations. [12] Thus, an offense

[10] Sutherland, Stat. Constr. § 347.   And see Bishop, Writ. Laws, § 199.

[11] Jones v. Dexter, 8 Fla. 276.

[12] Raynard v. Chase, 1 Burr. 2; U. S. v. Morris, 14 Pet. 464; U. S. v. Sheldon, 2 Wheat. 119; U. S. v. Beaty, Hempst. 487, Fed. Cas. No. 14,555; In re McDonough, 49 Fed. 360; U. S. v. Wilson, 1 Baldw. 78, Fed. Cas. No. 16,730; U. S. v. Starr, Hempst. 469, Fed. Cas. No. 16,739; Andrews v. U. S., 2 Story, 202, Fed. Cas. No. 381; The Enterprise, 1 Paine, 32, Fed. Cas. No. 4,499; Huffman v. State, 29 Ala. 40; State v. Lovell, 23 Iowa, 304; Irish v. Elliott, Add. (Pa.) 238; Lair v. Killmer, 25 N. J. Law, 522; Ferrett v. Atwill, 1 Blackf. 151; Rawson v. State, 19 Conn. 292; Steel v. State, 26 Ind. 82; Simms v. Bean, 10 La. Ann. 346; Gunter v. Leckey, 30 Ala. 591; Myers v. State, 1 Conn. 502; City of St. Louis v. Goebel, 32 Mo. 295; Hall v. State, 20 Ohio, 7; Horner v. State, 1 Oreg. 267; Warner v. Comm., 1 Pa. St. 154; State v. Solomons, 3 Hill (S. Car.) 96; Bettis v. Taylor, 8 Port. (Ala.) 564.

cannot be created or inferred by vague implications.[13] And a court cannot create a penalty by construction, but must avoid it by construction unless it is brought within the letter and the necessary meaning of the act creating it.[14] And where a statute may be so construed as to give a penalty, and also, and as well, so as to withhold the penalty, it will be given the latter construction.[15] A penal statute will not be extended by implication or construction to cases which may be within the mischief which the statute was designed to cure, if they are not at the same time within the terms of the act fairly and reasonably interpreted.[16] Hence an act not expressly prohibited by such a statute cannot be reached by it merely because it resembles the offenses provided against, or may be equally and in the same way demoralizing or injurious.[17] "In construing such laws, we should be careful to distinguish between what may have been desirable in the enactment in order that it should effectually accomplish its purpose, and what has been really prohibited or commanded by it. Before conduct hitherto innocent can be adjudged to have been criminal, the legislature must have defined the crime, and the act in question must clearly appear to be within the prohibitions or requirements of the statute, that being reasonably construed for the purpose of arriving at the legislative intention as it has been declared. It is not enough that the case may be within the apparent reason and policy of the legislation upon the subject, if the legislature has omitted to include it within the terms of its enactments. What the legislature has from inadvertence or otherwise omitted to include within the express provisions of a penal law, reasonably construed, the courts cannot supply."[18] Further, in its application to a case which clearly does come within its terms, such a law must be strictly construed. Many examples of this principle will be given in the following pages. But at present we desire to call the attention of the reader to a striking instance men-

[13] Mayor, etc., of Atlanta v. White, 33 Ga. 229.

[14] Western Union Tel. Co. v. Axtell, 69 Ind. 199.

[15] Renfroe v. Colquitt, 74 Ga. 618.

[16] Verona Cent. Cheese Co. v. Murtaugh, 50 N. Y. 314; Lair v. Killmer, 25 N. J. Law, 522; Jenkinson v. Thomas, 4 Durn. & E. 665; Dyke v. Elliott, L. R. 4 P. C. 184; U. S. v. Huggett, 40 Fed. 636.

[17] Shaw v. Clark, 49 Mich. 384, 13 N. W. 786.

[18] State v. Finch, 37 Minn. 433, 34 N. W. 905.

tioned by the older writers. "If the law," says Dwarris, "be that for a certain offense a man shall lose his right hand, and the offender hath before had his right hand cut off in the wars, he shall not lose his left hand, but the crime shall rather pass without the punishment which the law assigned than the letter of the law shall be extended." [19]

Construction not to Defeat Legislative Intent.

Although, as above stated, penal statutes are to be construed strictly, yet they are not to be construed so strictly as to defeat the obvious intention of the legislature, nor is the rule to be so applied as to exclude from the operation of the statute cases which the words in their ordinary acceptation, or in the sense in which the legislature manifestly used them, would comprehend. [20] "It is true," says the supreme court of Pennsylvania, "that a penal law must be construed strictly and according to its letter. But this strictness, which has run into an aphorism, means no more than that it is to be interpreted according to its language. Literal interpretation is but a figurative expression, meaning, perhaps, that we are to adhere so closely to the language that we are not to change the signification by dropping even a letter. The purpose of the rule is to prevent acts from being brought within the scope of punishment

---

[19] Potter's Dwarris on Stat. 247.

[20] U. S. v. Wiltberger, 5 Wheat. 76; U. S. v. Hartwell, 6 Wall. 385; Dyke v. Elliott, L. R. 4 P. C. 184; King v. Inhabitants of Hodnett, 1 Durn. & E. 96; In re Coy, 31 Fed. 794; Walton v. State, 62 Ala. 197; Crosby v. Hawthorn, 25 Ala. 221; Doe v. Avaline, 8 Ind. 6; Parkinson v. State, 14 Md. 184; Comm. v. Loring, 8 Pick. 370; Melody v. Reab, 4 Mass. 471; Butler v. Ricker, 6 Me. 268; Pike v. Jenkins, 12 N. H. 255; Wilson v. Wentworth, 25 N. H. 245; Mayor v. Davis, 6 Watts & S. 269; Bartolett v. Achey, 38 Pa. St. 273; People v. Bartow, 6 Cow. 290; Randolph v. State, 9 Tex. 521. In one of the text-books on this subject it is said: "The rule that statutes of this class are to be construed strictly is far from being a rigid or unbending one; or rather, it has in modern times been so modified and explained away as to mean little more than that penal provisions, like all others, are to be fairly construed according to the legislative intent as expressed in the enactment, the courts refusing, on the one hand, to extend the punishment to cases which are not clearly embraced in them, and, on the other, equally refusing by any mere verbal nicety, forced construction, or equitable interpretation, to exonerate parties plainly within their scope." Sedgwick, Stat. Constr. (2d edn.) 282.

because courts may suppose they fall within the spirit of the law, though not within its terms.   To create offenses by mere construction is not only to entrap the unwary, but to endanger the rights of the citizen." [21]   This subject received the careful consideration of Chief Justice Marshall in a leading case before the supreme court of the United States, and was explained and commented on by him as follows: "The rule that penal laws are to be construed strictly is perhaps not much less old than construction itself.   It is founded on the tenderness of the law for the rights of individuals, and on the plain principle that the power of punishment is vested in the legislative, not in the judicial, department.   It is the legislature, not the court, which is to define a crime and ordain its punishment. It is said that notwithstanding this rule the intention of the lawmaker must govern in the construction of penal as well as other statutes.   This is true.   But this not a new, independent rule which subverts the old.   It is a modification of the ancient maxim, and amounts to this, that though penal laws are to be construed strictly, they are not to be construed so strictly as to defeat the obvious intention of the legislature.   This maxim is not to be so applied as to narrow the words of the statute to the exclusion of cases which those words, in their ordinary acceptation, or in the sense in which the legislature has obviously used them, would comprehend.   The intention of the legislature is to be collected from the words they employ.   Where there is no ambiguity in the words, there is no room for construction.   The case must be a strong one indeed which would justify the court in departing from the plain meaning of words, especially in a penal act, in search of an intention which the words themselves did not suggest.   To determine that a case is within the intention of a statute, its language must authorize us to say so.   It would be dangerous indeed to carry the principle, that a case which is within the reason or mischief of a statute is within its provisions, so far as to punish a crime not enumerated in the statute, because it is of equal atrocity, or of kindred character, with those which are enumerated.   If this principle has ever been recognized in expounding criminal law, it has been in cases of considerable irritation, which it would be unsafe to consider as

[21] Comm. v. Cooke, 50 Pa. St. 201.

precedents forming a general rule for other cases." [22]   The true doctrine, thus set forth, is carried somewhat further by Story, J., in
the following expressions: "Penal statutes are not to be enlarged by
implication, or extended to cases not obviously within their words
and purport.   But where the words are general and include various
classes of persons, I know of no authority which would justify the
court in restricting them to one class, or in giving them the narrowest interpretation, where the mischief to be redressed by the
statute is equally applicable to all of them.   And where a word is
used in a statute which has various known significations, I know
of no rule that requires the court to adopt one in preference to another, simply because it is more restrained, if the objects of the statute equally apply to the largest and broadest sense of the word.
In short, it appears to me that the proper course in all these cases
is to search out and follow the true intent of the legislature, and
to adopt that sense of the words which harmonizes best with the context and promotes in the fullest manner the apparent policy and
objects of the legislature." [23]   To much the same effect are the following instructive remarks by a learned judge in North Carolina:
"It is an old but not very precisely defined rule of law that penal
statutes must be construed strictly.   By this is meant no more
than that the court, in ascertaining the meaning of such a statute,
cannot go beyond the plain meaning of the words and phraseology
employed in search of an intention not certainly implied by them.
If there is no ambiguity in the words or phraseology, nothing is
left to construction,—their plain meaning must not be extended by
inferences; and when there is reasonable doubt as to their true
meaning, the court will not give them such interpretation as to
impose a penalty.   Nor will the purpose of the statute be extended
by implication so as to embrace cases not clearly within its meaning.   If there be reasonable doubt arising as to whether the acts
charged to have been done are within its meaning, the party of
whom the penalty is demanded is entitled to the benefit of that
doubt.   The spirit of the rule is that of tenderness and care for
the rights of individuals, and it must always be taken that penal-

[22] U. S. v. Wiltberger, 5 Wheat. 76, 95.

[23] U. S. v. Winn, 3 Sumn. 209, Fed. Cas. No. 16,740. See, also, The Schooner
Enterprise, 1 Paine, 32, Fed. Cas. No. 4,499.

ties are imposed by the legislative authority only by clear and explicit enactments; that is, the purpose to impose the penalty must clearly appear. Such enactments, as to their words, clauses, several parts, and the whole, must be construed strictly together, but as well, and as certainly in all respects, in the light of reason. This rule, however, is never to be applied so strictly and unreasonably as to defeat the clear intention of the legislature. On the contrary, that intention must govern in construing penal as well as other statutes. This is a primary rule of construction, applicable in the interpretation of all statutes. The meaning of words or sentences should not be narrowed or strained so as to exclude the meaning intended; and while the purpose of the statute should not be extended by implication, it should not, on the other hand, be narrowed so as to abridge the intention that reasonably appears from its words, phraseology, and constituent parts. If words and sentences, and parts of sentences, having no very definite signification in their ordinary use, are employed and clearly intended to have a particular and definite meaning and application, and this appears from their particular use, connection, and application in the statute, that meaning and application must be accepted as proper and controlling. If the intention to impose the penalty certainly appears, that is sufficient and it must prevail. Otherwise the legislative intent would or might be defeated by mere interpretation, which can never be allowed." [24]

One or two illustrations will suffice to make plain the manner of the application of these principles. In Connecticut, a statute enacted penalties against any person who should keep "houses of bawdry." It was held to be applicable to a person who kept but one such house. It was urged that the act, being penal, should be taken according to its strict letter, and therefore would not apply to a case not explicitly provided for, viz., where one house only was so kept. But the court rejected this view, saying that while the statute was undoubtedly penal, the construction contended for would defeat its manifest purpose and object and frustrate the obvious intention of the legislature. [25] So again, a statute which contained simply mandatory provisions imposed a penalty for a failure

[24] Hines v. Wilmington & W. R. Co., 95 N. Car. 434.
[25] State v. Main, 31 Conn. 572.

to comply with the "conditions" of the section. It was held that the intent was plain to cast upon the delinquent the prescribed penalty for a failure to comply with the mandatory provisions. "It is insisted," said the court, "that the statute imposes the penalty for a failure to comply with the conditions of the section; that in fact there are no conditions, but simply mandatory provisions; that this, being a penal statute, is to be construed strictly; and hence, there being no conditions, no penalty is recoverable. Whatever criticism may be placed upon the use of the word 'conditions,' the intent of the legislature is plain, and although this be a penal statute, it is not to be so construed as to defeat the manifest intent of the law-making power." [26]

What are Penal Statutes.

The words "penal" and "penalty," in their strict and primary signification, denote a punishment, whether corporal or pecuniary, imposed and enforced by the state for a crime or offense against its laws; and "penal laws," strictly and primarily, are those imposing a punishment for an offense against the state, which the executive of the state has the power to pardon, and the expression does not include statutes which give a private action against the wrong-doer or provide for the numerous forfeitures or penalties growing out of breaches of duty that partake of the nature of a civil grievance or a merely local wrong, and which do not come within the category of criminal conduct. [27] This is the meaning to be attached to the term in applying the rule of international law that the courts of one state or country will not enforce the penal laws of another. But it is evident that, for the purposes of statutory construction, and with reference to the rule now under consideration, the term must be taken in a very much wider sense than this. "Among penal laws which must be strictly construed, those most obviously included are all such acts as in terms impose a fine or corporal punishment under sentence in state prosecutions, or forfeitures to the state as a punitory consequence of violating laws made for the preservation of the peace and good order of society. But these are

[26] State v. Kansas City, Ft. S. & G. R. Co., 32 Fed. 722.
[27] Huntington v. Attrill, 146 U. S. 657, 13 Sup. Ct. 224; Rumball v. Schmidt, L. R. 8 Q. B. Div. 603; Fennell v. Common Council of Bay City, 36 Mich. 186; Wayne County v. City of Detroit, 17 Mich. 390.

not the only penal laws which have to be so construed. There are to be included under that denomination also all acts which impose by way of punishment any pecuniary mulct or damages beyond compensation for the benefit of the injured party, or recoverable by an informer, or which, for like purposes, impose any special burden or take away or impair any privilege or right." [28] And to determine whether a liability to which a person is subjected is by way of penalty, it is not necessary that the statute, in the language imposing it, should so denominate it. When, for instance, the statute subjects an officer of a corporation, as such officer, to a liability to pay money, either for omitting to perform a duty enjoined or for doing an act prohibited, and does this in a case where, but for such omission of duty or wrongful act, he would be under no liability, he is thereby subjected to a forfeiture of the sum which he is made liable to pay, and so far as he is concerned, the imposition of liability is by way of punishment. [29] But if a statute in the nature of a police regulation gives a remedy for private injuries resulting from the violation thereof, and also imposes fines and penalties at the suit of the public for such violation, the former will not be regarded in the nature of a penalty, unless so declared. [30]

Examples of Penal Statutes and Their Construction.

Any statute which may involve, as a consequence of its violation, the depriving a citizen of his life or his liberty, is to be construed with strictness. [31] So also, if there is any doubt in the case, penal statutes are not to be so construed as to multiply felonies. [32] A statute declaring that "any person convicted of the offense of insurrection or an attempt at insurrection shall be punished with death," will not include the case of an attempt to incite insurrection. [33] A statute which prohibits, under penalties, the laying of a bet or wager on the result of "any election within this commonwealth," is penal and must be strictly construed, and therefore it does not apply to a primary election for the choice of party can-

---

[28] Sutherland, Stat. Constr. § 358.
[29] Merchants' Bank v. Bliss, 13 Abb. Pr. 225.
[30] Pittsburgh, Ft. W. & C. R. Co. v. Methven, 21 Ohio St. 586.
[31] Case of Pierce, 16 Me. 255; Ramsey v. Foy, 10 Ind. 493.
[32] Comm. v. Macomber, 3 Mass. 254; Comm. v. Barlow, 4 Mass. 439.
[33] Gibson v. State, 38 Ga. 571.

didates.[34] Again, an act providing for testing the accuracy of the weights and measures used in selling commodities, and affixing a penalty for "selling" by unmarked weights and measures, cannot be extended beyond its terms, although there may appear no other good reason for not applying it to buyers' weights and measures also.[35] An act which imposes a penalty on any telegraph company which shall fail to "transmit over its wires" a message delivered to it for transmission, will be strictly construed; and hence such a company will not be liable to a penalty for refusal to deliver a message after it has been transmitted.[36] The same is true of a statute which prohibits attorneys at law from buying "any bond, bill, promissory note, bill of exchange, book debt, or other thing in action, with the intent and for the purpose of bringing any suit thereon." Such an act will not apply to a purchase of corporate stock by an attorney, though it be for the purpose of enabling him to sue, as such stock does not come within the letter of the statute.[37] In Wisconsin, a law prohibited the county treasurer and clerk, or any of their deputies, or any other person for them, to purchase, directly or indirectly, property sold for taxes at any tax sale, or to purchase any tax certificate or tax deed held by the county, except for and in behalf of the county. It was held that this act, being subjected to a strict construction, would not prohibit the county treasurer or his deputy from buying a tax certificate from any other party than the county and having a deed issued to him thereon.[38] A penal statute which is local in its character, and refers to persons, places, or things, will be restricted, unless it be otherwise expressed, to such persons, places, or things as existed at the time of its passage, and not extended to those afterwards coming into being or coming under the policy or general purpose of the law. Hence a statute prohibiting the sale of intoxicating liquors within the vicinity of certain manufacturing establishments in three designated counties will be confined to such manufacturing establishments as existed in those counties at the time of its enactment.[39]

[34] Comm. v. Wells, 110 Pa. St. 463, 1 Atl. 310.
[35] Southwestern R. Co. v. Cohen, 49 Ga. 627.
[36] Brooks v. Western Union Tel. Co., 56 Ark. 224, 19 S. W. 572.
[37] Ramsey v. Gould, 57 Barb. 398.
[38] Coleman v. Hart, 37 Wis. 180.
[39] Hall v. State, 20 Ohio, 7.

And where one class of persons is designated as subject to the penalties of the statute, all persons not belonging to such class are to be deemed exonerated.[40] Again, a statute which confiscates the property of an individual will be understood as operating only upon the interest of that individual, and not as defeating the rights of those who held or might claim the property to the prejudice of the individual himself.[41] An act causing a forfeiture of a life-estate does not work a forfeiture of the estate in remainder.[42] A statute authorizing punishment for contempts of court is a penal law, and must be strictly construed in favor of those accused of violating its provisions.[43] The same is true of a statute imposing penalties on railroad companies for making unjust discriminations in the rates charged by them for the transportation of freight.[44] And a law making a mortgagee liable to an action for the recovery of a stated sum if he neglects or refuses to enter satisfaction of the mortgage or cancel the same of record, when it has been paid, is penal in its character, and will not be extended by construction to persons or cases not plainly within its terms.[45] So also it is with a statute which requires the payment of one per cent. a month on all taxes remaining unpaid and delinquent.[46] And the penalty prescribed for the violation of a statute cannot be applied for the violation of a later statute repealing the former one, if there is no express or implied legislative declaration to that effect.[47]

Statutes Giving Costs.

It is generally held that statutes allowing the recovery of costs are to be construed with reasonable strictness, as being in the nature of penal statutes.[48] But a law which provides that a plaintiff who becomes nonsuit shall pay the costs of the first action before he

---

[40] State v. Jaeger, 63 Mo. 403, citing Howell v. Stewart, 54 Mo. 400.

[41] Russel v. Transylvania University, 1 Wheat. 432.

[42] Archer v. Jones, 26 Miss. 583.

[43] Maxwell v. Rives, 11 Nev. 213.

[44] Hines v. Wilmington & W. R. Co., 95 N. Car. 434.

[45] Grooms v. Hannon, 59 Ala. 510; Marston v. Tryon, 108 Pa. St. 270.

[46] People v. Peacock, 98 Ill. 172; Comm. v. Standard Oil Co., 101 Pa. St. 119.

[47] State v. Gaunt, 13 Oreg. 115, 9 Pac. 55.

[48] Cone v. Bowles, 1 Salk. 205; Aechternacht v. Watmough, 8 Watts & S. 162; Dent v. State, 42 Ala. 514. Compare King v. Justices of York, 1 Ad. & El. 828.

shall be allowed to proceed in a subsequent action "should be interpreted liberally in behalf of defendants. It imposes no unreasonable burden on a plaintiff to require him to pay costs, which he has put upon a defendant without cause, before he can proceed again." [49]

Usury Laws.

It has been held that usury laws, when they prescribe the forfeiture of all interest upon contracts affected by unlawful charges of interest, are penal laws and to be strictly construed.[50] But on the other hand, it is said that a statutory provision that when a bank shall demand or receive more than the legal rate of interest, there shall be a forfeiture of the entire interest which the note or bill carries with it, or which has been agreed upon, is remedial as well as penal, and is to be liberally construed to effect the object which the legislature had in view in enacting it.[51]

Civil Damage Laws.

Civil damage laws are statutes which give a right of action against liquor dealers in favor of innocent parties who sustain injury by the intoxication of persons supplied with liquor by the defendants, or by the consequences of such intoxication, or by the acts of intoxicated persons, or by the furnishing of liquor to minors or habitual drunkards after warning given not to do so. These laws, being highly penal in their character, and introducing remedies unknown to the common law, and, as the statutes are framed in some jurisdictions, giving to the party prosecuting a decided advantage over the party defending, should receive a strict construction.[52] Hence, for example, no person can maintain an action under their provisions to whom a right of action is not given by their terms.[53] But on the other hand, while a statute of this character should not be enlarged, it should be interpreted, where the language is clear and explicit, according to its true intent and meaning, hav-

---

[49] Smith v. Allen, 79 Me. 536, 12 Atl. 542.

[50] Coble v. Shoffner, 75 N. Car. 42.

[51] Farmers' & Mechanics' Nat. Bank v. Dearing, 91 U. S. 29; Ordway v. Central Nat. Bank, 47 Md. 217.

[52] Meidel v. Anthis, 71 Ill. 241; Freese v. Tripp, 70 Ill. 496; Fentz v. Meadows, 72 Ill. 540.

[53] Schneider v. Hosier, 21 Ohio St. 98.

ing in view the evil to be remedied and the object to be attained. It would be a gross failure of justice to put so narrow a construction upon these acts as to impair the effects which they were intended to produce. Their beneficent purpose is not to be defeated by technical or verbal niceties.[54]

Statutes Giving Double and Treble Damages.

The rule that penal statutes are to be construed strictly does not apply to a case where the party has a remedy at common law and the statute merely gives an increase of damages.[55] But where the law, by way of punishing given acts or omissions, authorizes a judgment to be entered for double or treble the amount of damages found by the jury, it is in the nature of a penal statute and is to be construed accordingly.[56] Thus, a statute providing for the recovery of treble damages for the cutting of timber on the lands of another, in certain cases, is penal in its character, and must be held to apply, not to every case of a technical trespass or conversion, but only to cases in which some element of wilfulness, wantonness, or evil design enters into the acts complained of.[57] So, where a statute provided that any person who had lost money at gambling might recover the same in an action to be brought within three months, but that if he neglected to sue, any third person who might thereafter choose to sue should be entitled to recover three times the amount lost, it was held that the statute was penal and should be construed with strictness.[58]

Laws Imposing Liability on Stockholders.

Although there is considerable diversity of opinion as to the proper construction of statutes imposing on stockholders in private corporations an individual liability for the debts of the corporation, into the details of which we cannot now enter, the better opinion appears to be that if such liability is to be regarded as at all in the nature of a penalty, such laws should receive a strict construction.[59] But in a case in New York, it is said: "A personal liabil-

[54] Mead v. Stratton, 87 N. Y. 493.
[55] Ellis v. Whitlock, 10 Mo. 781; Phillips v. Smith, 1 Strange, 137.
[56] Bay City & E. S. R. Co. v. Austin, 21 Mich. 390.
[57] Cohn v. Neeves, 40 Wis. 393.
[58] Cole v. Groves, 134 Mass. 471.
[59] O'Reilly v. Bard, 105 Pa. St. 569.

ity of stockholders for the debts of a corporation, in virtue of the charter, is not in the nature of a penalty or forfeiture, and does not exist solely as a liability imposed by statute. It is not enforced simply as a statutory obligation, but is regarded as voluntarily assumed, by the act of becoming a stockholder." But at the same time, "the operation and effect of the statute, or the liability of the stockholder, which is measured by it, cannot be extended by implication. There is no implied undertaking of the defendant as a stockholder of the bank, and there is no obligation resulting from that relation other than such as is expressed, in terms or by necessary implication, in the act of incorporation." [60]

Statutes Both Remedial and Penal.

While penal statutes are to be construed strictly, and remedial statutes liberally, it does not follow that any given statute must belong irrevocably to one or the other of these two classes. The two terms are not in exact antithesis. Moreover, an act of the legislature may be penal in part and remedial in part, with a corresponding difference in the construction. That penal provisions are found in it does not necessarily make it penal in its whole extent or for all purposes.[61] A statute may well be penal in some of its parts, provisions, aspects, applications, or consequences, and remedial in others; or it may be penal as to some of the persons to be affected by it, and remedial as to others. For instance, a law making void assignments for the benefit of creditors, when made with the view of giving preferences, might contain penal provisions to be applied to the insolvent debtor, and yet be remedial in its relation to the creditors whom it enabled to share in the distribution of the estate. In general it is said that when a prohibitory act gives the right to enforce the penalty for its violation to the party aggrieved, it will be construed as remedial in its nature; but it is a penal act when such right is given to the public or the government.[62] In the interpretation of a statute of this character, a greater or less latitude of construction should be indulged according to whether the question is as to the party's being able to take advantage of the beneficial and remedial features of the act, or as

---

[60] Lowry v. Inman, 46 N. Y. 119. And see Gray v. Coffin, 9 Cush. 192.
[61] Hyde v. Cogan, 2 Dougl. 699; Short v. Hubbard, 2 Bing. 349.
[62] Ordway v. Central Nat. Bank, 47 Md. 217.

to the applicability of the penalty to the particular case before the court. But as a general rule (and especially where these two questions cannot be separated) the courts are disposed to lay the greater stress upon the penal features of the act and to construe it accordingly.[63] Thus, it is said that, so far as statutes for the regulation of trade impose fines or create forfeitures, they are to be construed strictly as penal laws, and not liberally as remedial laws.[64] So also, statutes authorizing arrest and imprisonment for debt, although remedial to the extent that they are designed to coerce payment, are also regarded as penal, and they are not to be extended by construction so as to embrace cases not clearly within them. Thus, when the statute authorizes an arrest "when the defendant has been guilty of a fraud in contracting the debt or incurring the obligation upon which the action is brought," it applies only to cases of actual personal fraud on the part of the defendant, and does not include merely legal or constructive fraud.[65] Again, an act conferring on creditors of an attachment defendant the right to intervene and defend in case of his failure to do so, and providing that if judgment be in favor of the intervenor, it shall be for any damage found by the jury, whether actual or exemplary, and shall abate the suit and writ, while remedial as to the intervenor, is penal as to the plaintiff, and is therefore not applicable to suits pending at the time of its passage, unless expressly made so.[66]

Statutes Abolishing the Rule.

In several of the states, the common-law rule requiring the strict construction of penal statutes has been displaced or abrogated by legislative authority. Thus, in California, the Penal Code provides that "the rule of the common law, that penal statutes are to be construed strictly, has no application to this code. All its provisions are to be construed according to the fair import of their terms, with a view to effect its objects and to promote justice."[67] So,

---

[63] Abbott v. Wood, 22 Me. 541. But on the other hand, in Sickles v. Sharp, 13 Johns. 497, it is said that a statute, penal as to some persons, if it is generally beneficial, may be equitably construed.

[64] Mayor v. Davis, 6 Watts & S. 269.

[65] Hathaway v. Johnson, 55 N. Y. 93.

[66] Powers v. Wright, 62 Miss. 35.

[67] Penal Code Cal. § 4; People v. Soto, 49 Cal. 67.

also, in Kentucky, the common-law rule has been abrogated by statute, and penal laws, like all others, are to be construed with a view to carry out the intention of the legislature.[68]

STATUTES AGAINST COMMON RIGHT.

115. Statutes which are in derogation of common right are to be construed strictly.

It is a well-settled rule that statutes which are in derogation of common right, and which confer special privileges, or impose special burdens or restrictions, upon individuals or upon one class of the community, not shared by others, should receive a strict construction; and the courts will require that cases coming before them shall be brought clearly within the terms of such statutes before they will be held applicable thereto.[69]   But a statute cannot be said to be in derogation of common right unless it is confined in its operation to a particular individual or set of men, separate and apart from the rest of the community.[70]   Moreover, the rights infringed upon by the statute must be such as would be enjoyed by the persons affected at common law, or as a part of the general liberty which belongs to them under our system of government.   Thus, laws for the protection of married women, infants, and persons of unsound mind are not regarded as being in derogation of their common rights.   But if a statute, for any cause, disables any persons of full age and sound mind (such as "spendthrifts") from making contracts and otherwise dealing freely with their own property, it is to be construed strictly; for although it may be founded in wise policy and a just regard for the public welfare, it is in derogation of private rights.[71]   So also, statutes requiring gratuitous services from any class of citizens are against common right and to be construed strictly.   For this reason, a law requiring attorneys at law to act as counsel for indigent persons in civil cases, without compensation, when assigned to that duty by the court, cannot be extended

[68] Comm. v. Davis, 12 Bush, 240.

[69] Rothgerber v. Dupuy, 64 Ill. 452.

[70] Flint River Steamboat Co. v. Foster, 5 Ga. 194.

[71] Smith v. Spooner, 3 Pick. 229; Jones v. Semple, 91 Ala. 182, 8 South. 557; Strong v. Birchard, 5 Conn. 357.

by construction so as to include criminal cases.[72]   Again, the exclusion of any citizen or class of citizens from the privilege of giving
evidence in the courts is opposed to natural right, and ought not to
be extended beyond the letter of the statute.[73]   And an act imposing upon suitors in the courts an "oath of expurgation," that is, an
oath of past loyalty to the government, and providing that if any
person shall refuse to take such oath his suit shall be dismissed,
must be subjected to a restrictive interpretation.[74]   For the same
reason, laws which impose restrictions upon trade or common occu-
pations, or upon the alienation of property, are to be strictly construed, and are never extended to cases not within the expressed
will of the legislature.[75]   It is also said that an act authorizing an
assessment for a street improvement is in derogation of individual
rights, and must be strictly construed and rigorously observed.
If there is a failure to comply with any material requirement of the
statute, a sale of property for nonpayment of the assessment, or a
lease based upon such a sale, will be invalid to convey either the
title or the right of possession.[76]   The same is true of estray laws.
These, it is said, "like all others prescribing modes by which a party
may be divested of his property without his consent, must be strictly construed, and a party claiming to have acquired a right and title
to property by virtue of their provisions as against the original
owner must affirmatively allege and prove that the mode prescribed by the statute for the acquisition of such title has, in every
particular, been strictly followed."[77]   Again, the policy of the law
favors an equal distribution of the effects of a failing debtor among
his creditors, and a statute which, by giving a lien to certain
creditors, gives them a preference, should be construed with reasonable strictness.[78]   In the opinion of some of the courts, bankruptcy
and insolvency laws are also in derogation of common right and

[72] Webb v. Baird, 6 Ind. 13.

[73] Pelham v. Steamboat Messenger, 16 La. Ann. 99.

[74] Harrison v. Leach, 4 W. Va. 383.

[75] Richardson v. Emswiler, 14 La. Ann. 658; Sewall v. Jones, 9 Pick. 412;
Mayor, etc., of Savannah v. Hartridge, 8 Ga. 23.

[76] Hopkins v. Mason, 61 Barb. 469.

[77] Trumpler v. Bemerly, 39 Cal. 490.

[78] Chapin v. Persse & Brooks Paper Works, 30 Conn. 461.   But see ante,
p. 245, as to construction of mechanics' lien laws.

should be strictly construed.   Such statutes, it is said, are intended
to deprive creditors of all remedy for the recovery of their debts,
and therefore cannot be extended by implication beyond the fair
and legitimate meaning of the terms used by the legislature.[79] But
this opinion has been disputed, and there are respectable authorities
holding that such statutes ought to be construed with liberality, as
being remedial in their nature and beneficial in their effects.[80]   It
is true that laws relating to bankruptcy and insolvency operate with
severity upon the debtor, since they deprive him of the control and
disposition of all his property and subject him to heavy penalties for
any fraud, concealment, or false dealing.   It is true also that they
restrict the creditors to one particular mode of obtaining payment
of their claims, and often compel them to accept less than the full
amount in discharge and satisfaction of their debts.   And in these
respects such statutes ought not to be enlarged by intendment or
implication beyond the clear expression of the legislative meaning.
But yet such laws are founded in a sound and wise public policy
and are designed to accomplish beneficent results, and it would be
an abuse of the power of interpretation if they were subjected to so
narrow and severe a construction as to defeat the very objects which
they are intended to promote.   The construction should be strict as
to the imposition of penalties, liberal as to the powers of the assignee
and as to the rights of the creditors, and liberal also as to the discharge of an honest debtor.   In Louisiana, it is held that laws in
derogation of the commercial law, as, for instance, statutes changing the rules of the law-merchant with respect to the negotiabil-
ity of notes or the validity of a verbal promise to accept a bill to be
thereafter drawn, must be strictly construed.[81]   It is also a corollary from the rule we are considering that where the intention of
the legislature is to confer a privilege upon persons whose rights
are to be affected by a statutory proceeding (such proceeding being
in derogation of their rights of property), and the language is doubtful as to the extent of the privilege, it is the duty of the courts to
give to it the largest construction, in favor of the privilege, which the
language employed will fairly permit.[82]

---

[79] Salters v. Tobias, 3 Paige, 338; Calladay v. Pilkington, 12 Mod. 513.
[80] Campbell v. Perkins, 8 N. Y. 430; Mines v. Lockett, 20 Ga. 474.
[81] Crowell v. Van Bibber, 18 La. Ann. 637.
[82] Walker v. City of Chicago, 56 Ill. 277.

Eminent Domain.

Since the exercise of the power of eminent domain is in derogation of common right, and is a high exertion of the paramount rights
of the sovereign, it must be hedged about with all needful precautions for the protection and security of the citizen. And for this
reason it is held that statutes authorizing the appropriation of
private property for public use must be strictly construed. An intention to authorize such taking will never be presumed, nor deduced from anything but clear and unambiguous terms. Especially
is this the case with regard to the delegation of this power to private corporations. Such a corporation will never be presumed to be
invested with the power. If it claims the right to condemn property for its uses, it must show a grant of such power.[83] Nor will a
grant of the power be enlarged by mere implication. Thus, if the
charter of a corporation gives it the right to appropriate private
property for certain enumerated purposes, it will possess no authority to take property for any other purposes, and no such extension of its powers can be deduced by mere inference from the
terms of the grant.[84] At the same time, laws delegating this power
to corporations are not to be construed so strictly or literally as to
defeat the evident purposes of the legislature. They are to receive
a reasonably strict and guarded interpretation, and the powers
granted will extend no further than expressly stated or than is necessary to accomplish the general scope and purpose of the grant.
If there remains a doubt as to the extent of the power, after all
reasonable intendments in its favor, the doubt should be solved
adversely to the claim of power.[85] It is held that a statute giving
to railroad companies the right of eminent domain will not be so
construed as to allow such a company to appropriate a portion of
the right of way of another railroad for the purposes of a parallel
line, if such a result can be avoided by any reasonable construc-

[83] Phillips v. Dunkirk R. Co., 78 Pa. St. 177; Allen v. Jones, 47 Ind. 438;
Matter of Water Comm'rs of Amsterdam, 96 N. Y. 351; Adams v. Washington & S. R. Co., 10 N. Y. 328; Fork Ridge Baptist Cemetery Ass'n v. Redd,
33 W. Va. 262, 10 S. E. 405; Gilmer v. Lime Point, 19 Cal. 47; In re Opening of Roffignac Street, 7 La. Ann. 76; Martin v. Rushton, 42 Ala. 289.

[84] Currier v. Marietta & C. R. Co., 11 Ohio St. 228.

[85] New York & H. R. Co. v. Kip, 46 N. Y. 546. See, also, Tide Water Canal
Co. v. Archer, 9 Gill & J. 479.

tion of the act.[86] On the same general principle, it is held that a
statute authorizing the impressment of private property, to serve
the military necessities of the government in time of war, or for
the use of health officers in times of dangerous epidemic sickness,
must be strictly construed, and exactly followed by those acting
under it.[87]

Police Regulations.

Statutes enacted by the legislature in the exercise of the police
power, for the· promotion or preservation of the public safety,
health, or morals, may sometimes impinge upon the liberty of individuals, by restricting their use of their property, or abridging
their freedom in the conduct of their business. When this is the
case, such statutes ought always to receive such a construction as
will carry out the purpose and intention of the legislature with the
least possible interference with the rights and liberties of private
persons.[88] For example, a law regulating the practice of medicine,
and imposing penalties upon persons who engage in the practice
of that profession without complying with its provisions, though
a valid and wholesome police regulation, is penal in its character
and should be strictly construed.[89] The same is true of statutes
or ordinances establishing fire-limits in populous cities, and prohibiting the erection of wooden buildings within such limits.[90]
And similar principles will be found to be applicable to laws regulating the operation of railways in the interests of the public
safety, to those which concern the purity of food products, to those
which restrict the right to engage in the sale of intoxicants and
other articles deemed noxious or dangerous, to those which place
restrictions upon the freedom of contract, and to many other classes
of enactments designed to further the general welfare by derogating from the liberty of a few.

[86] Illinois Cent. R. Co. v. Chicago, B. & N. R. Co., 122 Ill. 473, 13 N. E. 140.

[87] White v. Ivey, 34 Ga. 186; Pinkham v. Dorothy, 55 Me. 135.

[88] See In re Jacobs, 98 N. Y. 98; Stewart v. Comm., 10 Watts, 306; Carberry v. People, 39 Ill. App. 506; Shiel v. Mayor, etc., of Sunderland, 6 Hurl.
& N. 796; Brady v. Northwestern Ins. Co., 11 Mich. 425.

[89] Brooks v. State, 88 Ala. 122, 6 South. 902.

[90] Brown v. Hunn, 27 Conn. 332.

LAWS AUTHORIZING SUMMARY PROCEEDINGS.

116. Statutes authorizing summary proceedings must be construed with strictness, and must be exactly followed by those who act under or in pursuance of them.

When the object of a statute is remedial, it is to be construed liberally so that it may accomplish the purposes for which it was designed. But when a remedy is sought to be obtained by a summary proceeding, under a statute which is in derogation of the common law, the statute is to be strictly construed. Hence the courts, when looking at the remedy, will take care that it shall be made effectual, if possible, in the manner intended. But when scanning the proceedings to obtain that remedy, the courts will be strict and rigid in exacting a compliance with all the requirements of the statute.[91] "An act of parliament," says Best, C. J., "which takes away the right of trial by jury, and abridges the liberty of the subject, ought to receive the strictest construction; nothing should be holden to come within its operation that is not expressly within the letter and spirit of the act."[92] For example, statutes authorizing proceedings by attachment must be construed strictly, and hence cannot be held applicable to cases which are not plainly within their terms.[93] "The proceeding in attachment, as authorized by the statutes of the several states, is always viewed as a violent proceeding, a proceeding wherein the plaintiff, at the inception of his suit, seizes upon the property of the defendant without waiting to establish his claim before the judicial tribunals of the land, and the statute authorizing it has invariably received a strict construction."[94] But it must be remarked that this rule has been changed by statute in some of the states, the legislature directing

[91] Smith v. Moffat, 1 Barb. 65; Logwood v. Planters' & Merchants' Bank, Minor (Ala.) 23.

[92] Looker v. Halcomb, 4 Bing. 183.

[93] Van Norman v. Circuit Judge, 45 Mich. 204, 7 N. W. 796; Mathews v. Densmore, 43 Mich. 461, 5 N. W. 669; Whitney v. Brunette, 15 Wis. 61; Blake v. Sherman, 12 Minn. 420 (Gil. 305); Wilkie v. Jones, 1 Morr. (Iowa) 97; Musgrave v. Brady, Id. 456; Burch v. Watts, 37 Tex. 135.

[94] Wilkie v. Jones, 1 Morr. (Iowa) 97.

that the attachment laws shall be liberally construed. "The property of one person," says the court in Ohio, "cannot be subjected to the payment of the debt of another without invading the right of private property; and whatever may be the competency of the legislative power to create such a liability by way of forfeiture, penalty, or confiscation, upon the ground of public policy, it cannot be done by mere implication; and in the absence of any provision expressly declaring the public duty exacted and providing for such liability, a statute providing for the collection of claims by a summary proceeding against property by its seizure or attachment must be construed as simply providing a remedy for the enforcement of liabilities, and not as creating new liabilities upon the owners of the property, not arising at common law."[95] So also, any statute which authorizes an arrest without a direct charge of guilt should be construed with great strictness. Thus, where a statute authorizes the issuance of a warrant, in certain cases, upon the oath of the prosecutor that he "has good reason to believe" that an offense has been committed, it must be exactly followed; and if he merely swears that he "has been credibly informed," etc., this will not be enough to justify the issuing of a warrant.[96] So again, the terms and conditions prescribed by a statute, providing for constructive service of process, must be strictly complied with.[97] And a statute requiring a defendant in civil actions to file an affidavit of defense to the action, and authorizing the plaintiff, on failure of such affidavit, to have judgment entered up, is in derogation of the defendant's right to a trial by jury, and must be strictly construed.[98] A statute giving a remedy by motion against public officers on their official bonds, being summary and in derogation of common law, should be construed with strictness.[99] Thus, a statute which authorizes a summary proceeding against a sheriff, and his amercement in damages, for a failure to return a writ of execution at the proper time, is highly penal in its character, and any

[95] Steamboat Ohio v. Stunt, 10 Ohio St. 582.

[96] State v. Dale, 3 Wis. 795.

[97] Stewart v. Stringer, 41 Mo. 400.

[98] Wall v. Dovey, 60 Pa. St. 212.

[99] Hearn v. Ewin, 3 Coldw. 399; Rice v. Kirkman, 3 Humph. 415; Scogins v. Perry, 46 Tex. 111; Robinson v. Schmidt, 48 Tex. 13.

person who claims that this process should be put into effect against
the officer must bring his case within both the letter and the spirit
of the law.[100] So a statute authorizing the courts to render judgment, without a separate action, against sureties on bonds given in
the course of legal proceedings, must be construed strictly and
not extended by implication.[101] Again, a party who claims goods
under a constable's sale upon a distress for rent must prove affirmatively that all the statutory requirements of such a sale have been
complied with.[102] So if, by a private act, the property of a person
is directed to be sold by the surveyor-general without any warranty,
and the money to be paid to certain creditors, it does not take away
the rights of third persons, but amounts only to a quitclaim of any
right or interest of the state.[103]

REMEDIAL STATUTES.

**117. Remedial statutes are to be liberally construed with
a view to effectuate the purposes of the legislature;
and if there be any doubt or ambiguity, that construction should be adopted which will best advance the remedy provided and help to suppress
the mischief against which it was aimed.[104]**

It is "an old and unshaken rule in the construction of statutes that
the intention of a remedial statute will always prevail over the literal sense of its terms, and therefore when the expression is special
or particular, but the reason is general, the expression shall be
deemed general." [105] "The rule in construing remedial statutes,
though it may be in derogation of the common law, is that every-

100 Moore v. McClief, 16 Ohio St. 51.
101 Willard v. Fralick, 31 Mich. 431.
102 Murphy v. Chase, 103 Pa. St. 260.
103 Jackson v. Catlin, 2 Johns. 248.
104 Smith v. Moffat, 1 Barb. 65; Hudler v. Golden, 36 N. Y. 446; White v.
The Mary Ann, 6 Cal. 462; Cullerton v. Mead, 22 Cal. 95; Jackson v. Warren, 32 Ill. 331; Wilber v. Paine, 1 Ohio, 251; Litch v. Brotherson, 16 Abb.
Pr. 384; Hoguet v. Wallace, 28 N. J. Law, 523; State v. Blair, 32 Ind. 313;
Fox v. Sloo, 10 La. Ann. 11; Sprowl v. Lawrence, 33 Ala. 674; State v. Can-
ton, 43 Mo. 48; Mason v. Rogers, 4 Litt. 375.
105 Brown v. Pendergast, 7 Allen, 427.

thing is to be done in advancement of the remedy that can be done consistently with any fair construction that can be put upon it." [106] Especially in the construction of a remedial statute which has for its end the promotion of important and beneficial public objects, a large construction is to be given where it can be done without doing actual violence to its terms. [107]   But still it is to be remembered that the rule of construction whereby the operation of a statute may sometimes be judicially extended beyond its words does not apply, even in the case of a remedial statute, where the words are too explicit to admit of the belief that such an extension of its operation was intended by the legislature. [108]

What are Remedial Statutes.

"Remedial statutes are those which are made to supply such defects, and abridge such superfluities, in the common law, as arise either from the general imperfection of all human laws, from change of time and circumstances, from the mistakes and unadvised determinations of unlearned (or even learned) judges, or from any other cause whatsoever.   And this being done, either by enlarging the common law where it was too narrow and circumscribed, or by restraining it where it was too lax and luxuriant, hath occasioned another subordinate division of remedial acts of parliament into enlarging and restraining statutes." [109]   To this it should be added that a law is equally entitled to be considered a remedial statute whether it remedies a defect of the common law or of the pre-existing body of statute law.   "The object of this kind of statutes being to cure a weakness in the old law, to supply an omission, to enforce a right, or to redress a wrong, it is but reasonable to suppose that the legislature intended to do so as effectually, broadly, and completely as the language used, when understood in its most extensive signification would indicate." [110]

Examples of Remedial Statutes and their Construction.

It may be stated in general terms that any statute which gives a remedy or means of redress where none existed before, or which

[106] Chicago, B. & Q. R. Co. v. Dunn, 52 Ill. 260.
[107] Town of Wolcott v. Pond, 19 Conn. 597.
[108] Farrel Foundry v. Dart, 26 Conn. 376; Learned v. Corley, 43 Miss. 687.
[109] 1 Bl. Comm. 86.
[110] Endlich, Interp. § 107.

creates a right of action in an individual, or a particular class of individuals, is remedial, within the meaning of this rule.[111]　Thus, a statute giving to a person injured by reason of a defect in a highway a right of action in damages against the municipal corporation which was charged with the duty of keeping the highway in repair, is remedial, even though it authorizes the recovery of double damages.[112]　So also, a statute for the collection of claims against steamboats and other water-craft, which authorizes proceedings against the same by name, is remedial in its nature, being designed to afford a convenient and speedy remedy against the property of the persons liable, and to provide some means of safety in the collection of the claims by fixing the liability of the property.[113] Again, where an act authorized suits to be brought against insurance companies in the county where the "property insured" might be located, and a supplementary act provided that all the provisions of the former statute should be applicable to life insurance companies, it was held that, under said acts, suit might be brought against a life insurance company in the county where the person insured resided.[114]　On this principle, it is generally held (although there are some decisions to the contrary) that statutes giving a right of action in damages to the surviving relatives or next of kin of a person whose death is caused by the wrongful act, neglect, or default of another are remedial and should be liberally construed.[115]　The court in New Jersey, speaking of such a statute, says: "It is entirely and in the highest sense remedial in its nature.　Its object was to

[111] Neal v. Moultrie, 12 Ga. 104.

[112] Reed v. Inhabitants of Northfield, 13 Pick. 94.

[113] Steamboat Ohio v. Stunt, 10 Ohio St. 582.

[114] Quinn v. Fidelity Beneficial Ass'n, 100 Pa. St. 382.

[115] Haggerty v. Central R. Co., 31 N. J. Law. 349; Merkle v. Bennington Tp., 58 Mich. 156, 24 N. W. 776; Bolinger v. St. Paul & D. R. Co., 36 Minn. 418, 31 N. W. 349; Wabash, St. L. & P. Ry. Co. v. Shacklett, 10 Ill. App. 404; Hayes v. Williams, 17 Colo. 465, 30 Pac. 352; Beach v. Bay State Co., 16 How. Pr. 1. See, per contra, Pittsburgh, C. & St. L. Ry. Co. v. Hine, 25 Ohio St. 629; Hamilton v. Jones, 125 Ind. 176, 25 N. E. 192. The case last cited holds such a statute to be subject to the rule of strict construction, not, however, on the ground that it is not a remedial statute, but solely on the ground of its being in derogation of the common law, as to which, see ante, pp. 237–241. On the subject of the proper construction of these statutes, see Tiffany, Death by Wr. Act, § 32.

abolish the harsh and technical rule of the common law, actio personalis moritur cum persona.   The rule had nothing but prescriptive authority to support it; it was a defect in the law, and this statute was designed to remove that defect.   It is therefore entitled to receive the liberal construction which appertains to remedial statutes.   The mischief to be redressed was the non-existence of a remedy for an admitted wrong.   It is clearly therefore the duty of the court to advance the remedy." [116]   So again, statute provisions for indemnity for loss accruing to one citizen, by means of a privilege given to another by the legislature, ought to receive a liberal construction in favor of the citizen damnified. [117]   And a statute providing for the determination of claims to real estate and to quiet title to the same is remedial and should be liberally construed. [118]

In the next place, statutes made relative to the administration of justice in the courts, and designed to render the same more simple, speedy, or efficacious, are to be liberally construed, for the attainment of that important object. [119]   Thus an act which tends to simplify procedure in the courts, by abolishing all the forms of action ex contractu except that of assumpsit, should receive a liberal construction. [120]   The same is true of statutes providing for amendments in pleadings or legal process.   They are to be liberally construed in furtherance of the object of securing trials upon the merits. [121]   And a law altering the mode of procedure in point of form, in a suit pending when the act was passed, so as to prevent a delay and hasten the time of trial, is remedial in its nature and should be liberally construed. [122]   Again, statutes authorizing a change of venue in cases where it is alleged that a fair and impartial trial cannot be had in the court where suit is originally brought are very important to the due administration of justice, and ought to be so construed as to secure the right and make it effective. [123]   So also,

[116] Haggerty v. Central R. Co., 31 N. J. Law, 349.
[117] Boston & R. Mill Corp. v. Gardner, 2 Pick. 33.
[118] Holmes v. Chester, 26 N. J. Eq. 79.
[119] Mitchell v. Mitchell, 1 Gill, 66.
[120] Jones v. Gordon, 124 Pa. St. 263, 16 Atl. 862.
[121] Bolton v. King, 105 Pa. St. 78; Fidler v. Hershey, 90 Pa. St. 363; Bulkley v. Andrews, 39 Conn. 523.
[122] People v. Tibbetts, 4 Cow. 384.
[123] Griffin v. Leslie, 20 Md. 15.

statutory provisions in relation to the submission of controversies to arbitration are beneficial in their nature and founded in good public policy, and should be construed with liberality.[124]   On the same general principle, statutes giving or extending a right of appeal are always liberally construed in furtherance of justice, and the courts will endeavor to avoid putting upon them such a construction as would work a forfeiture of the right in the particular case.[125]

A statute intended to legitimate the issue of marriages otherwise void is remedial in its nature and to be liberally construed; and hence, in such an act, the words "inherit," "heir," and "joint heir" will be construed to give to legitimated children all the rights of inheritance and succession which would attach to them had they been born in lawful wedlock.[126]   Acts providing for the recording of conveyances, making such records constructive notice, and relieving subsequent purchasers and incumbrancers in good faith from the effect of unrecorded conveyances, are remedial and to be construed liberally.[127]   The same rule was applied, in a case in Illinois, to a statute designed to remedy the evils consequent upon the destruction of public records by a fire, which provided for the recording of certified copies of conveyances and extracts from court records, provided a form of action to establish a destroyed record, and gave the courts jurisdiction to inquire into and settle titles. It was said to be emphatically a remedial act and entitled to a liberal construction.[128]   Again, statutes exempting homesteads from forced sale on judicial process should receive such a construction as to carry out the liberal and beneficent policy of the legislature. But parties must bring themselves within their provisions, at least in spirit, before they can claim exemption under them; for without some special statute making the exemption, all the property of

[124] Tuskaloosa Bridge Co. v. Jemison, 33 Ala. 476; Bingham's Trustees v. Guthrie, 19 Pa. St. 418.

[125] Pearson v. Lovejoy, 53 Barb. 407; Houk v. Barthold, 73 Ind. 21; Womelsdorf v. Heifner, 104 Pa. St. 1; Arceneaux v. Benoit, 21 La. Ann. 673; Converse v. Burrows, 2 Minn. 229 (Gil. 191). See, also, Vigo's Case, 21 Wall. 648.

[126] Brower v. Bowers, 1 Abb. App. Dec. 214; Beall v. Beall, 8 Ga. 210; Swanson v. Swanson, 2 Swan, 446.

[127] Connecticut Mut. Life Ins. Co. v. Talbot, 113 Ind. 373, 14 N. E. 586.

[128] Smith v. Stevens, 82 Ill. 554.

a debtor will be subject to levy and sale.[129] A statute exempting from attachment and execution "the tools of any debtor necessary for his trade or occupation" is a beneficent and remedial statute and should not be narrowly construed; and hence it will be held to include not merely the tools used by the tradesman with his own hands, but also such, in character and amount, as are necessary to enable him to prosecute his appropriate business in a convenient and usual manner, including also, in a proper case, the tools used by journeymen or apprentices and constituting the necessary means of their employment.[130] A law validating irregularities in proceedings for the formation of school districts is to be liberally construed in furtherance of its object.[131] And a statute authorizing a court to open, re-examine, and correct the accounts of a public officer is highly remedial.[132] So also, an act relating to the official bonds of public officers concerns the public rights and interests, and should be liberally construed with a view to making it effective against the evil which it was intended to abate, where that can be done without depriving any individual of his just rights.[133] On the same principle, a statute authorizing and requiring an officer of a city to take proper steps to procure the opening and reversal of all judgments against the city which he may have reason to believe were founded in fraud or obtained by collusion, is for the benefit of the public and designed to prevent fraud, and should therefore be liberally construed.[134]

[129] Charles v. Lamberson, 1 Iowa, 435.
[130] Howard v. Williams, 3 Pick. 80. See, also, Alvord v. Lent, 23 Mich. 369.
[131] First School District v. Ufford, 52 Conn. 44.
[132] White County v. Key, 30 Ark. 603.
[133] Ex parte Plowman, 53 Ala. 440.
[134] Sharp v. Mayor, etc., of New York, 31 Barb. 572.

STATUTES AGAINST FRAUDS.

118. Statutes against frauds, in so far as they operate upon the fraud or offense, are to be liberally construed, in order that justice may be promoted by counteracting the fraud or annulling the fraudulent transaction.

"Statutes against frauds are to be liberally and beneficially expounded. This may seem a contradiction to the last rule (that penal statutes are to be construed strictly), most statutes against frauds being in their consequences penal. But this difference is to be here taken: where the statute acts upon the offender, and inflicts a penalty, as the pillory or a fine, it is then to be taken strictly; but when the statute acts upon the offense, by setting aside the fraudulent transaction, here it is to be construed liberally. Upon this footing, the statute of 13 Elizabeth, c. 5, which avoids all gifts of goods, etc., made to defraud creditors and others, was held to extend by the general words to a gift made to defraud the queen of a forfeiture."[135] So in this country also, statutes intended to prevent frauds upon creditors by secret and pretended transfers of property, as those which provide that the title to goods and chattels shall not pass by a sale without delivery, the vendor remaining in possession, unless the same is evidenced by a writing duly acknowledged, etc., are held to be salutary and beneficial and entitled to a liberal construction.[136] And a statute authorizing general assignments for the benefit of creditors, so framed as to prevent an insolvent debtor from giving preferences to some among his creditors at the expense of others, and thus tending to prevent fraud and injustice, should be liberally construed to the furtherance of that end.[137] The same rule and principle apply to the case of a statute which provides that "every sale, mortgage, or assignment which shall be made by debtors in contemplation of insolvency, and with

[135] 1 Bl. Comm. 88. See, also, Gorton v. Champneys, 1 Bing. 287; Cumming v. Fryer, Dudley (Ga.) 182; Carey v. Giles, 9 Ga. 253.

[136] Bank of United States v. Lee, 13 Pet. 107; Cadogan v. Kennett, 2 Cowp. 432.

[137] Hahn v. Salmon, 20 Fed. 801.

the design to prefer one or more creditors to the exclusion in whole
or in part of others, shall operate as an assignment and transfer
of all the property and effects of such debtor, and shall inure to the
benefit of all his creditors." An act of this character should be
liberally construed to effectuate the intention of the legislature.[138]
In New York, a statute provided that no member of the common
council of a city, or any other officer of the municipality, should be
directly or indirectly interested in any contract, work, or business,
the price or consideration of which was to be paid out of the city
treasury. It was held that this law should not be narrowed by
construction, but should be interpreted broadly and liberally to
promote the end which the legislature had in view.[139] Still, there
is a limit to the application of this rule. It is not permissible, in
the endeavor to hunt out and extirpate frauds, to subject the words
of the legislature to a fantastic or extravagant interpretation, nor
to put upon them a meaning which they could not reasonably be
made to bear. For example, a statute annulling any "wilfully false
claim" should not be construed as applying to a case of mere dis-
crepancy in the amount of a claim as filed, such as may not be inconsistent with good faith.[140] Again, a statute of New York was
designed to prevent persons from transacting business under ficti-
tious names. One W. brought an action against a railroad company
for damages for an injury to a carriage belonging to him, but which
was marked with the name of "W. Brothers." The railroad company attempted to defend on the ground that W. was amenable to
the statute, since he was carrying on the business alone, after his
brother's retirement, in the former firm name. But it was held that
the statute was not applicable to such a case as this, and the defense
should not prevail.[141]

[138] Terrill v. Jennings, 1 Met. (Ky.) 450.
[139] Mullaly v. Mayor of New York, 6 Thomp. & C. 165.
[140] Barber v. Reynolds, 44 Cal. 519, 533.
[141] Wood v. Erie Ry. Co., 72 N. Y. 196.

LEGISLATIVE GRANTS.

119. Statutory grants by the legislature, when they delegate sovereign power, derogate from sovereign authority, or confer special benefits or exemptions, in derogation of common and equal rights, are to be construed strictly against the grantee.

Statutory grants, made by congress or the legislature of a state, are not to be construed by the same rules which are applicable to grants or contracts between private persons. The words of a private grant are to be taken most strongly against the grantor. In the interpretation of a private contract, the courts are to adopt the construction which the parties mutually put upon it at the time of its making. But in the case of a legislative grant or contract, the fact that the instrument is a law, as well as a grant or contract, changes the aspect of the case and renders these rules inapplicable. Thus, in a case in Michigan, where the principles recognized as applicable to transactions between private parties were urged upon the court in connection with the interpretation of a legislative grant, it was said: "The fault of this reasoning is that it seeks to apply the principles which relate to common-law grants between private persons to an act of the legislature, which differs from a grant of a private person in that it is both a grant and a law, and, as such, the intent of the law is to be kept in view, and its purpose effectuated, whenever the subject-matter of the grant comes in controversy; and that construction must be placed upon it which will preserve and carry out the object of the legislature, however such construction may conflict with the principles of the common law, or prevent the attaching of equities which would spring from transactions between private parties." [142] Again, although a statute may contain the elements of a compact between the government and an individual, nevertheless it should be construed according to the rules for construing statutes, and not according to those which are applicable in the case of contracts. In cases of contract, the court is to give effect to the real intention of the parties, and therefore adopts their own interpretation, as shown by the contemporary construction which they have mu-

---

[142] Jackson, L. & S. R. Co. v. Davison, 65 Mich. 416, 32 N. W. 726.

tually put upon it. But in cases resting upon a statute, there is no mutuality of agreement to be sought out. The only will is that of the legislative power. Hence the contemporary construction of a statute given to it by an officer intrusted with its execution cannot be allowed to prevail against the true construction of the statute, on the ground of its embodying a contract.[143] This difference, however, between private and legislative grants, does not exclude the operation of all the subsidiary rules of interpretation. For instance, the familiar rule that a party cannot be allowed to claim under, and at the same time repudiate, any instrument, is applicable not only to contracts and conveyances but also to that class of statutes which grant new rights or privileges subject to certain conditions.[144] In general, however, the rule is well settled that statutory grants of property, franchises, or privileges in which the government has an interest are to be construed strictly in favor of the public and against the grantee, and nothing will pass except what is granted in clear and explicit terms.[145] And when there is any doubt as to the proper construction of a statute granting a privilege, that construction should be adopted which is most advantageous to the interests of the government.[146] But yet, where the grant admits of two interpretations, one of which is more extended and the other more restricted, so that a choice is fairly open, and either may be adopted without a violation of the apparent objects of the grant, if, in such a case, one interpretation would render the grant inoperative, and the other would give it force and effect, the latter should be adopted.[147] The rule that a grant by the United States is strictly construed against the grantee applies as well to grants to a state to aid in building railroads as to one granting special privileges to a private corporation.[148]

[143] Union Pac. R. Co. v. U. S., 10 Ct. Cl. 548.

[144] Burrows v. Bashford, 22 Wis. 103.

[145] Coosaw Min. Co. v. South Carolina, 144 U. S. 550, 12 Sup. Ct. 689; Water Comm'rs of Jersey City v. Mayor, etc., of Hudson, 13 N. J. Eq. 420; Bennett v. McWhorter, 2 W. Va. 441.

[146] Hannibal & St. J. R. Co. v. Missouri River Packet Co., 125 U. S. 260, 8 Sup. Ct. 874.

[147] Black, Const. Prohib. § 52; Mills v. St. Clair, 8 How. 569.

[148] Leavenworth, L. & G. R. Co. v. U. S., 92 U. S. 733.

Delegation of Powers to Municipal Corporations.

Municipal corporations "possess and may exercise those powers which are granted in express terms, also those necessarily implied or necessarily incident to the powers expressly granted, and lastly, those which are absolutely indispensable to the declared objects and purposes of the corporation. In this connection it may also be stated that it is regarded as a settled principle of law that where there is a fair and reasonable doubt as to the existence of a power in such corporation, the courts will not uphold or enforce its execution."[149] For example, statutes or charters delegating the power of taxation to municipal corporations will be strictly construed, and such delegation should be made in clear and unambiguous terms, and the grant will not be extended by implication or inference.[150] The reason is that the power of taxation, being a sovereign power, can be exercised by the legislature only when and as conferred by the constitution, and by municipal corporations only when unequivocally delegated to them by the legislative body. The charter of a municipality, in respect to the powers of taxation which it grants, will not therefore receive a liberal or expansive interpretation, and the municipality will not have authority to lay any other taxes, or to tax any other property, or to impose taxes for any other purpose, than as its charter or the general laws of the state relating to municipal corporations expressly or by necessary implication allow.[151] The grant to a municipal corporation of the power to provide for the levy and collection of special taxes for the improvement of streets

[149] Paine v. Spratley, 5 Kans. 525.   See, also, Ottawa v. Carey, 108 U. S. 110, 2 Sup. Ct. 361; Cooley, Const. Lim. 192–194; Black, Const. Law, 381.

[150] City of St. Louis v. Laughlin, 49 Mo. 559; Moseley v. Tift, 4 Fla. 402; City of Alton v. Aetna Ins. Co., 82 Ill. 45; Wisconsin Tel. Co. v. City of Oshkosh, 62 Wis. 32, 21 N. W. 828; Mason v. Police Jury, 9 La. Ann. 368, per Buchanan, J.

[151] Mays v. City of Cincinnati, 1 Ohio St. 268; Lima v. Cemetery Ass'n, 42 Ohio St. 128. "When the power (of municipal taxation) is found to have been conferred, if any question arises upon its extent or application, the rule is that the power must be strictly construed. It is a reasonable presumption that the state, which is the depositary and source of all authority on the subject, has granted in unmistakable terms all it has intended to grant at all. Municipal authorities, therefore, when they assume to tax, must be able to show warrant therefor in the words of the grant, which alone can justify their action." Cooley, Tax'n, 276.

and alleys upon real estate adjacent to such improvements, does not include the power to provide for the sale and conveyance of such real estate in case of nonpayment.[152]   So also, in the absence of an express grant of power, a municipal corporation can neither borrow money, nor issue negotiable paper, nor become a party to such paper, nor become a stockholder in a private corporation, nor incur debts in aid of such private corporation.[153]   To take another illustration, authority given to a municipal corporation by general statute to "cause the streets of the city to be lighted," and to make "reasonable regulations" with reference thereto, does not empower the city government to grant to one company the exclusive right to furnish gas for a long period of years.[154]   A board of commissioners of a county is a quasi-corporation, a local organization which, for purposes of civil administration, is invested with a few of the functions characteristic of a corporate existence.   A grant of powers to such a corporation must be strictly construed.   When acting under a special power, it must act strictly on the conditions under which it is given.[155]

Grants of Power to Officers.

Where statutes confer special ministerial authority, the exercise of which may affect rights of property, or incur a municipal liability, it must be strictly observed, and any material departure will vitiate the proceedings.[156]   And the principle that every grant of power carries with it the usual and necessary means for the exercise of that power, and that the power to convey is implied in the power to sell, cannot be admitted in the construction of statutes which are in derogation of common law and the effect of which is to divest a citizen of his real estate, as in the case of sales of land for the nonpayment of taxes.   Such statutes, although enacted for the public good, must be strictly construed.[157]

---

[152] Paine v. Spratley, 5 Kans. 525.

[153] Mayor, etc., of Wetumpka v. Wetumpka Wharf Co., 63 Ala. 611; City of Aurora v. West, 22 Ind. 88.

[154] Saginaw Gaslight Co. v. City of Saginaw, 28 Fed. 529.

[155] Treadwell v. Comm'rs of Hancock Co., 11 Ohio St. 183, 190.

[156] Board of Comm'rs of Shawnee Co. v. Carter, 2 Kans. 115.

[157] Sibley v. Smith, 2 Mich. 486.

Grants of Charters and Franchises to Corporations.

Acts of incorporation, and statutes granting other franchises or special benefits or privileges to corporations, are to be construed strictly against the corporators; and whatever is not given in un-equivocal terms is understood to be withheld.[158] As already ex-plained, the common-law rule that words are to be taken in the strongest sense against the party using them is not applicable to a statute of this character. Or if it be supposed that this rule should nevertheless be applied, the true view is that the organizers or "pro-moters" of the corporation are to be regarded as framing the in-strument of incorporation and so using the words in which it is expressed.[159] The principle which should govern the interpreta-tion in this class of cases was explained in an important and lead-ing case before the United States supreme court, as follows: "A great deal of the argument at the bar was devoted to the considera-tion of the proper rules of construction to be adopted in the inter-pretation of legislative contracts. In this there is no difficulty. All contracts are to be construed to accomplish the intention of the parties; and in determining their different provisions, a liberal and fair construction will be given to the words, either singly or in connection with the subject-matter. It is not the duty of a court, by legal subtlety, to overthrow a contract, but rather to uphold it and give it effect; and no strained or artificial rule of construction is to be applied to any part of it. If there is no ambiguity, and the meaning of the parties can be clearly ascertained, effect is to be given to the instrument used, whether it is a legislative grant or not. In the case of the Charles River Bridge [11 Pet. 544] the rules of construction known to the English common law were adopted and applied in the interpretation of legislative grants, and the prin-ciple was recognized that charters are to be construed most favor-ably to the state, and that in grants by the public nothing passes by implication. This court has repeatedly since re-asserted the same doctrine, and the decisions in the several states are nearly all the

---

[158] Moran v. Comm'rs of Miami Co., 2 Black (U. S.) 722; Parker v. Great Western Ry. Co., 7 Man. & G. 253; Proprietors of Stourbridge Canal v. Wheeley, 2 Barn. & Ad. 792; Young v. McKenzie, 3 Ga. 31; Coolidge v. Wil-liams, 4 Mass. 140.

[159] Raleigh & G. R. Co. v. Reid, 64 N. Car. 155.

same way. The principle is this: That all rights which are asserted against the state must be clearly defined, not raised by inference or presumption, and if the charter is silent about a power,
it does not exist. If, on a fair reading of the instrument, reasonable doubts arise as to the proper interpretation to be given to it,
those doubts are to be solved in favor of the state; and where it is
susceptible of two meanings, the one restricting and the other extending the powers of the corporation, that construction is to be
adopted which works the least harm to the state. But if there is
no ambiguity in the charter, and the powers conferred are plainly
marked, and their limits can be readily ascertained, then it is the
duty of the court to sustain and uphold it, and to carry out the
true meaning and intention of the parties to it. Any other rule of
construction would defeat all legislative grants and overthrow all
other contracts." [160] No strained or extravagant interpretation
should be resorted to, to defeat the grant or render it inoperative.
For instance, if a statute grants to a turnpike company a power to
erect a toll-gate "near" a particular spot, they may place it on the
spot where an old road intersects, provided only that the gate be
near the place designated, for in such a case, "near" is not to be
construed as meaning "nearest." [161] So again, where a statute gives
to a corporation power to mortgage its land for the erection of
buildings, this will be construed as extending to a mortgage for the
cost of painting the same. [162]

Grants of Bounties and Pensions.

Where the object of an act of congress, or of a state legislature,
is to confer a bounty or reward, in consideration of meritorious
services rendered to the state, or in aid of a deserving charity, or
for the compensation of public officers, it should not be subjected
to a restrictive interpretation. On the contrary, such a statute
ought to be liberally construed, in furtherance of its beneficent purpose and policy, and any doubts or ambiguities arising upon its
terms should be resolved in favor of the intended beneficiaries.
Thus, a statute which grants pensions or half pay to retired, dis-
abled, or superannuated military officers should be interpreted in

---

[160] The Binghamton Bridge, 3 Wall. 51, 74.
[161] People v. Denslow, 1 Caines, 177.
[162] Miller v. Chance, 3 Edw. Ch. 399.

the manner most beneficial to the officers, even though it may be susceptible of another construction.[163]　So also, in a grant of public lands by statute, by way of donation, any language which expresses the legislative intention to invest the party with the title is sufficient.[164]　So, where an act of congress made donations of land to the first settlers upon an exposed part of the frontier, it was considered that, as the statute was intended to confer a bounty upon a numerous class of individuals, but was expressed in somewhat ambiguous terms, it was the duty of the court to adopt the construction which would best effect the liberal intentions of the legislature.[165]　So again, where a statute fixes the compensation of a public officer in loose and obscure terms, admitting of two meanings, it should be given that construction which is most favorable to the officer.[166]

Grants of Monopolies.

The legislature of a state, if the public interests may seem to make it desirable, may grant to a person or corporation a monopoly or exclusive franchise or privilege (unless forbidden by the constitution), and the grant may assume the form of a contract, the obligation of which must not thereafter be impaired.　But monopolies are not favored in law, and grants of this kind are subject to the following limitations:

(1) The grant is to be construed strictly against the grantee and in favor of the public.　Nothing will pass by implication, and the extent of the privileges granted will not be enlarged by inference or construction.　Thus, the grant will not be understood to prevent the legislature from according rival or competing franchises to other persons, unless its plain terms convey that meaning.[167]

(2) The intention to grant a monopoly will never be presumed, but on the contrary it will be presumed that the legislature did not intend thus to limit its own power or that of its successors.　And

---

[163] Roane v. Innes, Wythe (Va.) 62; Walton v. Cotton, 19 How. 355.

[164] Trustees of Kentucky Seminary v. Payne, 3 T. B. Mon. 161.

[165] Ross v. Doe, 1 Pet. 655.

[166] Butler v. U. S., 23 Ct. Cl. 162; U. S. v. Morse, 3 Story, 87, Fed. Cas. No. 15,820.

[167] Charles River Bridge v. Warren Bridge, 11 Pet. 420; Turnpike Co. v. Maryland, 3 Wall. 210; The Binghamton Bridge, Id. 51.

this presumption can be overcome only by clear and satisfactory inferences from the terms of the grant. Thus, the privileges granted in an act of incorporation will not be deemed exclusive, unless it appears from the charter, in terms too clear and explicit to be mistaken, that it was the actual and deliberate intention of the legislature to preclude the state from granting similar franchises to any subsequent corporation.[168]

But here it should be mentioned that patents for inventions and copyrights upon literary property are not monopolies, in the sense of being in derogation of the rights of the community, nor are they granted as restrictions upon those rights, but to promote the progress of science and the useful arts; and hence they are entitled to be liberally construed.[169] "Patents for inventions are not to be treated as mere monopolies, and therefore odious in the eyes of the law, but they are to receive a liberal construction, and under the fair application of the rule 'ut res magis valeat quam pereat' are, if practicable, to be so interpreted as to uphold, and not destroy, the right of the inventor."[170]

Grants of Exemptions; Exemption from Taxation.

Statutes which strip a government of any portion of its prerogative, or give exemption from a general burden, should receive a

[168] Black, Const. Law, 528; Stein v. Bienville Water-Supply Co., 34 Fed. 145; Pennsylvania R. Co. v. Canal Comm'rs, 21 Pa. St. 9; Detroit v. Detroit & H. P. R. Co., 43 Mich. 140, 5 N. W. 275; Bridge Proprietors v. Hoboken Co., 1 Wall. 116; Parrott v. Lawrence, 2 Dill. 332, Fed. Cas. No. 10,772; Lehigh Water Co.'s Appeal, 102 Pa. St. 515; Ruggles v. Illinois, 108 U. S. 526, 2 Sup. Ct. 832; State v. Curry, 1 Nev. 251.

[169] Wilson v. Rousseau, 4 How. 646, 704; Hogg v. Emerson, 6 How. 437; Brooks v. Fiske, 15 How. 212; Blanchard v. Sprague, 3 Sumn. 535, Fed. Cas. No. 1,518; Davoll v. Brown, 1 Woodb. & M. 53, Fed. Cas. No. 3,662; Hamilton v. Ives, 6 Fish. Pat. Cas. 244, Fed. Cas. No. 5,982; 2 Rob. Pat. § 735. "The law has always regarded monopolies as hostile to the rights and interests of the public. One method of obtaining them in early times was by a grant from the sovereign to a particular individual of the sole right to exercise a particular trade. The mischief arising from these monopolies became so intolerable that the practice was suppressed by a clause in Magna Charta. This clause does not, however, apply to grants for the sole use of a new invention for a limited period. These grants, it is said, are indulged for the encouragement of ingenuity. Patent right and copyright laws rest on this ground." Taylor v. Blanchard, 13 Allen, 370.

[170] Turrill v. Railroad Co., 1 Wall. 491.

strict interpretation.[171] Hence, statutes exempting a particular class of men (as, officers of the militia) from general burdens borne by all other citizens of the state, such as jury duty or poll taxes, ought to be subjected to a strict construction.[172]

It is well settled that the legislature of a state may agree, by an explicit grant founded upon a consideration, to exempt specified property from taxation, either for a limited period or indefinitely, or that taxation of the property in question shall be had only on a certain basis, and not otherwise, or shall not exceed a certain rate; and this will constitute a contract with the grantee which succeeding legislatures may not impair by imposing taxes contrary to the grant.[173] But the exemption of property from the burden of taxation is against public policy and in derogation of the sovereign rights of the state. Hence the rule of construction is strictly against the person or corporation claiming such exemption and in favor of the public. The right of taxation, like any other power of sovereignty, will not be held to have been surrendered, unless such surrender has been expressed in terms too plain to be mistaken and admitting of no reasonable construction consistent with the reservation of the power. And it is never to be presumed that the legislature has in this respect fettered its power for the future, except upon clear and irresistible evidence that such, in the particular instance, was the actual and deliberate intention.[174] For example, where a statute granting exemption from taxation to educational institutions employs the term "academies," it means only those designed for purposes of education of a general character; and it is not properly applicable to an institution for the study and exhibition of works of art, although called an "academy of fine arts."[175] So also, it is a generally admitted rule that when the property of a railroad or business corporation, or of a church, school, hospital, or other

171 Academy of Fine Arts v. Philadelphia County, 22 Pa. St. 496.

172 State v. Mills, 34 N. J. Law, 177.

173 Black, Const. Law, 537; Pacific R. Co. v. Maguire, 20 Wall. 36.

174 Providence Bank v. Billings, 4 Pet. 514; Charles River Bridge v. Warren Bridge, 11 Pet. 420; Gilman v. City of Sheboygan, 2 Black (U. S.) 510; Delaware Railroad Tax, 18 Wall. 206; Vicksburg, S. & P. R. Co. v. Dennis, 116 U. S. 665, 6 Sup. Ct. 625; Yazoo & M. V. R. Co. v. Thomas, 132 U. S. 174, 10 Sup. Ct. 68; Cincinnati College v. State, 19 Ohio, 110.

175 Academy of Fine Arts v. Philadelphia County, 22 Pa. St. 496.

charitable corporation, is by constitution or statute exempted from "all taxation" or from "taxation of every kind," such property is nevertheless liable for its proportionate share of assessments levied for the cost of local improvements.[176] "Yet, while an exemption from taxation cannot be implied from the apparent spirit or general purpose of a statute, this rule does not call for a strained construction, adverse to the real intention of the legislature; and to ascertain that intention, the courts will look to the context, as well as to the particular words used, taking into consideration the contemporaneous surroundings and the purposes which the legislature had in view."[177] Moreover, a statute granting exemption from taxation to a corporation, which does not receive such exemption as a bonus, but is required to pay into the state treasury an equivalent for taxes in the shape of a license, should be construed fairly, and even liberally, in favor of the company.[178]

LAWS AUTHORIZING SUITS AGAINST THE STATE.

120. Statutes allowing private persons to maintain suits against the state are in derogation of sovereign rights and must be strictly construed.

No private individual has a right to institute and maintain an action against a state, unless the state has consented thereto. If such consent is given, whether for the particular case only or by a general law, the right of action accorded is a matter of favor, conferred by the state in derogation of that immunity which every sovereign enjoys. For this reason it is to be strictly construed.[179]

---

[176] Black, Tax Titles, § 81; Lima v. Cemetery Ass'n, 42 Ohio St. 128; Seamen's F. Soc. v. Boston, 116 Mass. 181; Roosevelt Hospital v. New York, 84 N. Y. 108; First Presb. Church v. Fort Wayne, 36 Ind. 338.

[177] Black, Tax Titles, § 57; Louisville & N. R. Co. v. Gaines, 3 Fed. 266.

[178] Milwaukee & St. P. R. Co. v. City of Milwaukee, 34 Wis. 271.

[179] Rose v. Governor, 24 Tex. 496; Raymond v. State, 54 Miss. 562; State v. Stout, 7 Neb. 89. It appears that only in the state of Arkansas does a contrary doctrine prevail. It is there held that laws authorizing actions against the state should be liberally construed, and hence that the state may be sued as well in chancery as at law. It is said that the right of a citizen to sue a state is not derogatory of common right or subversive of the true principles of the common law, but is in harmony with both. It cannot be

Hence such suits can be brought only upon such claims and demands as are mentioned in the statute, and only in those courts which the statute specifies for the purpose. Thus, if the act provides that suits against the state may be brought in the circuit court of the district where the plaintiff resides, it cannot be brought in the chancery court.[180] And again, if the law provides that claims must first be presented to the auditor of public accounts for audit, and that the jurisdiction of the courts shall attach only by way of appeal from a decision of such auditor rejecting the claim in whole or in part, these requirements are imperative and must be obeyed, or else the judicial tribunals can have no rightful authority to proceed with the case.[181]

REVENUE AND TAX LAWS.

121. Statutes imposing taxes and providing means for the collection of the same should be construed strictly in so far as they may operate to deprive the citizen of his property by summary proceedings or to impose penalties or forfeitures upon him; but otherwise tax laws ought to be construed with fairness, if not liberality, in order to carry out the intention of the legislature and further the important public interests which such statutes subserve.

In regard to the general rule to be applied in the construction of revenue and tax laws, at least three contrariant opinions have received support from the adjudications of the courts. In England it is well settled (and many authorities in this country have adopted the same view) that any law which imposes a tax or charge upon the subject must be strictly construed; that the intention to impose such

supposed that the people, as represented in the constitutional convention, in directing that the legislature should provide in what courts, and in what manner, suits might be commenced against the state, intended that these provisions should be any other than such as would advance this right in the citizen to apply to the courts of justice for the redress of grievances. State v. Curran, 12 Ark. 321.

[180] Ex parte Greene, 29 Ala. 52.

[181] State v. Stout, 7 Neb. 89.

a burden cannot be made out by inference or intendment, but must in all cases be shown by clear and unambiguous language; and that all doubts are to be resolved against the government and in favor of the tax-payer.[182]   In some few of our states, a diametrically opposite doctrine has been maintained.   Thus, the court in New Jersey says: "In laying the burden of taxation upon the citizens of the state, while it must be the object of every just system to equalize this charge by a fair apportionment and levy upon the property of all, it is equally the duty of the courts to see that no one, by mere technicalities which do not affect his substantial rights, shall escape his fair proportion of the public expenses, and thus impose them upon others.   A liberal construction must therefore be given to all tax laws for public purposes, not only that the offices of government may not be hindered, but also that the rights of all tax-payers may be equally preserved." [183]

Between these two extreme views lies the truth. "There must surely be a just and safe medium," says Judge Cooley, "between a view of the revenue laws which treats them as harsh enactments to be circumvented and defeated if possible, and a view under which they acquire an expansive quality in the hands of the court, and may be made to reach out and bring within their grasp, and under the discipline of their severe provisions, subjects and cases which it is only conjectured may have been within their intent. Revenue laws are not to be construed from the standpoint of the tax-payer alone, nor of the government alone. Construction is not to assume either that the tax-payer, who raises the question of his legal liability under the laws, is necessarily seeking to avoid a duty to the state which protects him, nor, on the other hand, that the government, in demanding its dues, is a tyrant which, while too powerful to be resisted, may justifiably be obstructed and defeated by any

182 Oriental Bank Corp. v. Wright, L. R. 5 App. Cas. 842; Warrington v. Furbor, 8 East, 242; Denn v. Diamond, 4 B. & C. 243; Gurr v. Scudds, 11 Exch. 190; Green v. Holway, 101 Mass. 243; Cahoon v. Coe, 57 N. H. 556; Sewall v. Jones, 9 Pick. 412; Moseley v. Tift, 4 Fla. 402; Barnes v. Doe, 4 Ind. 132; Mayor, etc., of Savannah v. Hartridge, 8 Ga. 23; Inhabitants of Williamsburg v. Lord, 51 Me. 599; Boyd v. Hood, 57 Pa. St. 98; City of Alton v. Aetna Ins. Co., 82 Ill. 45; Wisconsin Tel. Co. v. Oshkosh, 62 Wis. 32, 21 N. W. 828.

182 State v. Taylor, 35 N. J. Law, 184.

subtle device or ingenious sophism whatsoever. There is no legal presumption either that the citizen will, if possible, evade his duties, or, on the other hand, that the government will exact unjustly or beyond its needs. All construction, therefore, which assumes either the one or the other, is likely to be mischievous and to take one-sided views, not only of the laws, but of personal and official conduct."[184] To much the same effect is the following language from an opinion of the supreme court of Connecticut: "A law imposing a tax is not to be construed strictly because it takes money or property in invitum (although its provisions are for that reason to be strictly executed), for it is taken as a share of a necessary public burden; nor liberally, like laws intended to effect directly some great public object; but fairly for the government and justly for the citizen, and so as to carry out the intention of the legislature, gathered from the language used, read in connection with the general purposes of the law, and the nature of the property on which the tax is imposed and of the legal relation of the tax-payer to it."[185] "There may and doubtless should be a distinction taken in the construction of those provisions of revenue laws which point out the subjects to be taxed, and indicate the time, circumstances, and manner of assessment and collection, and those which impose penalties for obstructions and evasions. There is no reason for peculiar strictness in construing the former; neither is there reason for liberality."[186] But there may be some forms of tax laws which should, in all circumstances, receive a strict interpretation. Thus, it is said that a law imposing a privilege tax must be construed favorably to the citizen, and no occupation is to be taxed unless clearly within the provisions of the law.[187]

Statutes which provide that, if the taxes upon land are not duly paid, the land shall thereupon become forfeited to the state, and the title thereto shall vest in the state, are to be strictly construed. "It is certain that the legislature will not be understood as intending to declare a forfeiture of private lands to the state for nonpay-

---

[184] Cooley, Tax'n, 272.

[185] Hubbard v. Brainard, 35 Conn. 563. See, also, Cornwall v. Todd, 38 Conn. 443.

[186] Cooley, Tax'n, 271.

[187] Vicksburg & M. R. Co. v. State, 62 Miss. 105.

ment of taxes, if construction can put any less severe meaning on the language of the statute."[188] Again, those provisions of the revenue laws which authorize the officers of the revenue to make public sale of lands on which the taxes remain delinquent are to be construed with strictness, so far as to require an exact compliance with all those provisions which are designed for the security and protection of the tax-payer, though less stress may be laid upon such provisions as are merely directions to the officers. The reason is that laws of this character operate to deprive the citizen of his estate, not, indeed, without due process of law, but by the agency of ministerial officers and in a summary manner, which may result in injustice or even oppression if his rights are not carefully guarded.[189] "When the statute under which land is sold for taxes directs an act to be done, or prescribes the form, time, and manner of doing any act, such act must be done, and in the form, time, and manner prescribed, or the title is invalid, and in this respect the statute must be strictly, if not literally, complied with. But in determining what is required to be done, the statute must receive a reasonable construction, and when no particular form or manner of doing an act is prescribed, any mode which effects the object with reasonable certainty is sufficient. But special stress should always be laid upon those provisions which are designed for the protection of the tax-payer."[190]

---

[188] Black, Tax Titles, § 196; Bennett v. Hunter, 9 Wall. 326; Fairfax v. Hunter, 7 Cranch, 625; Schenck v. Peay, 1 Dill. 267, Fed. Cas. No. 12,451; Dickerson v. Acosta, 15 Fla. 614.

[189] Young v. Martin, 2 Yeates, 312; Wills v. Auch, 8 La. Ann. 19; Powell v. Tuttle, 3 N. Y. 396. "Strict construction is the rule in the case of statutes which may divest one of his freehold by proceedings not in the ordinary sense judicial, and to which he is only an enforced party. It is thought to be only reasonable to intend that the legislature, in making provision for such proceedings, would take unusual care to make use of terms which would plainly express its meaning, in order that ministerial officers might not be left in doubt in the exercise of unusual powers, and that the citizen might know exactly what were his duties and liabilities. A strict construction in such cases seems reasonable, because presumptively the legislature has given in plain terms all the power it has intended should be exercised. It has been very generally supposed that the like strict construction was reasonable in the case of tax laws." Cooley, Tax'n, 266.

[190] Black, Tax Titles, § 155; Chandler v. Spear, 22 Vt. 388.

On the other hand, but for a similar reason, it is held that statutes allowing the owner of land sold for taxes to redeem the same,
on prescribed conditions, are to be construed liberally and gener-
ously in favor of the redemptioner, and not to be applied with any
greater severity or narrowness than the terms of the law absolutely
require.[191] And again, statutes intended to cure defects and irregularities in tax proceedings should receive an effective construction at the hands of the courts, and should be so interpreted, if
possible, as to carry into operation all the designs which the legislature may reasonably be supposed to have had in mind at the time
of the enactment.[192]

United States Internal Revenue and Tariff Acts.

In some of the earlier cases involving the interpretation of the
internal revenue and customs laws of the United States, the courts
adopted and applied the English rule, that statutes levying duties
or taxes upon the citizen are to be construed most strongly against
the government and in favor of the citizen, and their provisions are
not to be extended by implication beyond the clear import of the
language used.[193] But afterwards, without going so far in the
opposite direction as to hold that these laws should be construed
with liberality, the federal tribunals reached the conclusion that

[191] Cooley, Tax'n, 532; Black, Tax Titles, § 350; Dubois v. Hepburn, 10
Pet. 1, 22; Corbett v. Nutt, 10 Wall. 464; Gault's Appeal, 33 Pa. St. 94;
Karr v. Washburn, 56 Wis. 303, 14 N. W. 189; Nelson v. Central Land Co.,
35 Minn. 408, 29 N. W. 121; Jones v. Collins, 16 Wis. 594; Alter v. Shepherd,
27 La. Ann. 207.

[192] Belcher v. Mhoon, 47 Miss. 613; Clementi v. Jackson, 92 N. Y. 591;
Clark v. Hall, 19 Mich. 357; McCallister v. Cottrille, 24 W. Va. 173; Paxton
v. Valley Land Co., 67 Miss. 96, 6 South. 628. But in Dean v. Charlton, 27
Wis. 522, it is said that acts of the legislature authorizing municipal corporations to re-assess and re-levy special taxes which were void for irregularities in the proceedings are in derogation of individual rights and likely to
work great injustice, and therefore should be strictly construed.

[193] U. S. v. Wigglesworth, 2 Story, 369, Fed. Cas. No. 16,690. Also in a late
case in the circuit court of appeals, it is said that revenue statutes, including
those fixing duties on imports, are neither remedial laws nor laws founded on
any permanent public policy, and should be construed most strongly against
the government; for burdens should not be imposed on the tax-payer beyond
what such statutes expressly and clearly import. Rice v. U. S., 4 C. C. A.
104, 53 Fed. 910.

there was no adequate reason for subjecting them to a restrictive interpretation, but that they should be construed with fairness and justice and in a manner such as to make them accomplish the purpose designed. In one of the important decisions of the supreme court it was said, in substance, that while there was one sense in which every law imposing a penalty or forfeiture might be deemed a penal law, yet in another sense such laws were often deemed, and truly deserved to be called, remedial; that it must not be understood that every law which imposes a penalty is legally speaking a "penal" law, in such sense that it must be construed with great strictness in favor of the citizen. Laws enacted for the prevention of fraud, for the suppression of a public wrong, or to effect a public good, are not, in the strict sense, penal acts, although they may inflict a penalty upon those persons who violate them. It was in this light, the court considered, that revenue laws should be viewed. They should be construed in such a manner as most effectually to accomplish the intention of the legislature in enacting them.[194] In another case it was said: "Penalties annexed to violations of general revenue laws do not make such laws penal in the sense which requires them to be construed strictly. Nor, on the other hand, are they to be construed with an excess of liberality. But it is the duty of the court to study the whole statute, its policy, its spirit, its purpose, its language, and, giving to the words used their obvious and natural import, to read the act with these aids in such a way as will best effectuate the intention of the legislature. Legislative intention is the guide to true judicial interpretation."[195] And in a late case, which involved the question of the infliction of penalties for illicit distilling and forfeiture of the liquors and apparatus, it was declared to be "the now settled doctrine" of the supreme court that "statutes to prevent frauds upon the revenue are considered

---

[194] Taylor v. U. S., 3 How. 197, 210. See, also, Cliquot's Champagne, 3 Wall. 114.

[195] U. S. v. One Hundred Barrels of Spirits, 2 Abb. U. S. 305, Fed. Cas. No. 15,948; U. S. v. Thirty-Six Barrels of High Wines, 7 Blatchf. 459, Fed. Cas. No. 16,468; Twenty-Eight Cases, 2 Bened. 63, Fed. Cas. No. 14,281; U. S. v. Olney, 1 Abb. U. S. 275, Fed. Cas. No. 15,918; U. S. v. Three Tons of Coal, 6 Biss. 379, Fed. Cas. No. 16,515; U. S. v. Twenty-Five Cases of Cloths, Crabbe, 356, Fed. Cas. No. 16,563; U. S. v. Willetts, 5 Bened. 220, Fed. Cas. No. 16,699.

as enacted for the public good, and to suppress a public wrong, and therefore, although they impose penalties or forfeitures, not to be construed, like penal laws generally, strictly in favor of the defendant; but they are to be fairly and reasonably construed, so as to carry out the intention of the legislature."[196] At the same time, the courts have no rightful authority to tax, by construction, subjects not taxed by the terms of the law, nor to create penalties or forfeitures by an expansive system of interpretation. "It is the duty of the courts of the Union, undoubtedly, so far as they are invested with any agency in carrying out the financial purposes of the government, fairly to enforce the revenue laws of the country, and see that they are not fraudulently evaded. But they are not at liberty, by construction or legal fiction, to enlarge their scope to include subjects of taxation not within the terms of the law."[197] Hence, in cases of serious ambiguity in the language of a tariff act, or in case of a doubtful classification of articles, where the real meaning of congress cannot be ascertained by a careful and rational study of the act, nor by comparison with provisions of prior statutes relating to the same subject, that construction must be adopted which is more favorable to the importer.[198]

STATUTES OF LIMITATION.

122. Statutes of limitation are statutes of repose and remedial in their nature. Their purposes should not be defeated by undue strictness of construction.[199]

"This class of statutes," says Sutherland, "has a harsh effect upon the creditor, which consideration leads to a strict construction; and a debtor who takes advantage of long forbearance to be utterly discharged on his own account has little right to favor. But all per-

---

[196] U. S. v. Stowell, 133 U. S. 1, 10 Sup. Ct. 244, citing Taylor v. U. S., 3 How. 197, 210; Cliquot's Champagne, 3 Wall. 114, 145; U. S. v. Hodson, 10 Wall. 395, 406; Smythe v. Fiske, 23 Wall. 374, 380.

[197] U. S. v. Watts, 1 Bond, 580, Fed. Cas. No. 16,653.

[198] Powers v. Barney, 5 Blatchf. 202, Fed. Cas. No. 11,361; McCoy v. Hedden, 38 Fed. 89; American Net & Twine Co. v. Worthington, 141 U. S. 468, 12 Sup. Ct. 55.

[199] Toll v. Wright, 37 Mich. 93; Coffin v. Cottle, 16 Pick. 383.

sons are not provident enough to have indestructible evidence of all their transactions, and it is for the general good that a period be fixed after which there is an arbitrary exemption from liability. In this sense these statutes are remedial, to afford protection against stale claims, after a period sufficient to the diligent, and when in a majority of instances a defending party would be placed at a disadvantage by reason of the delay." [200] "Of late years the courts in England and in this country have considered statutes of limitation more favorably than formerly. They rest upon sound policy and tend to the peace and welfare of society. The courts do not now, unless compelled by the force of former decisions, give a strained construction to evade the effect of these statutes. By requiring those who complain of injuries to seek redress by actions at law within a reasonable time, a salutary vigilance is imposed and an end is put to litigation." [201] But if the statute itself is to be construed liberally, necessarily it follows that the exceptions which it makes in favor of particular persons or classes are to be construed with strictness. Accordingly, the doctrine is now very fully established that implied and equitable exceptions are not to be ingrafted upon the statute of limitations where the legislature has not made the exception in express words in the statute; the courts cannot allow them on the ground that they are within the reason or equity of the statute. [202] "The general rule in regard to the application of statutes of limitation is that all persons, whether under disability or not, are barred by them, unless excepted from their operation by a saving clause. General words of a statute are to receive a general construction, and unless there is found in the statute itself some ground for restraining it, it cannot be restrained." [203] "Whenever the situation of the party was such as, in the opinion of the legislature, to furnish a motive for excepting him from the operation of the law, the legislature has made the exception. It would be going far for this court to add to those exceptions. * * * If the difficulty be produced by the legislative

[200] Sutherland, Stat. Constr. § 368.

[201] McCluny v. Silliman, 3 Pet. 270. And see Roddam v. Morley, 1 DeG. & J. 1; U. S. v. Wilder, 13 Wall. 254.

[202] Dozier v. Ellis, 28 Miss. 730; Bedell v. Janney, 9 Ill. 193; Sacia v. De-Graaf, 1 Cow. 356; Allen v. Mille, 17 Wend. 202.

[203] Favorite v. Booher's Adm'r, 17 Ohio St. 548.

power, the same power might provide a remedy; but courts cannot on that account insert in the statute of limitations an exception which the statute does not contain." [204] Thus, a statute of limitations, general in its nature, binds minors and married women, although they are not specially named, if they are not specially excepted. [205] And so, where it was urged that the case at bar ought to be excepted out of the statute of limitations, because the complainant had been prevented, for a time, from asserting his claims, by reason of an injunction against him, but the statute made no express exception in favor of persons so circumstanced, the court held that it could make no exception. [206]

[204] McIver v. Ragan, 2 Wheat. 25.

[205] Warfield v. Fox, 53 Pa. St. 382.

[206] Kilpatrick v. Byrne, 25 Miss. 571. A statute providing that where an action, commenced within the time limited by law, is defeated "for any matter of form," the plaintiff may commence a new action for the same cause of action within one year, is a beneficial statute and is to be construed very liberally. Johnston v. Sikes, 56 Conn. 589.

CHAPTER XII.

MANDATORY AND DIRECTORY PROVISIONS.

DEFINITIONS.

123. A provision in a statute is said to be mandatory when disobedience to it, or want of exact compliance with it, will make the act done under the statute absolutely void; but if the provision is such that disregard of it will constitute an irregularity, but one not necessarily fatal, it is said to be directory.

"To answer the purposes of definitions," says a learned writer on this subject, "it would seem to be more logical, as well as precise, to say that a statute or statutory provision is directory when the legislature intended that strict compliance with it should be left to the discretion of the party empowered to act under it and the convenience and necessities of the occasion upon which it was to be applied, and did not intend that a failure to exercise the power conferred, or a failure of exact conformity with all the prescribed details in the execution of it, should render the same void; while a mandatory statute or provision would be one which the legislature intended to be strictly complied with, contemplating an exercise of the power conferred in it at all events, and in exact conformity with the prescribed details in the execution of it as a condition of the legality and validity of the same."[1] The conditions of the problem, and the

---

[1] Endlich, Interp. § 431, note. "A provision in a statute is said to be directory when it is considered as a mere direction or instruction, of no obligatory force, and involving no invalidating consequence for its disregard, as

form in which it is usually presented to the courts, are thus lucidly stated by Judge Cooley: "All the provisions of a statute, not on their face merely permissory or discretionary, are intended to be obeyed, or they would not be enacted at all; and therefore they come to the several officers who are to act under them as commands. But the negligence of officers, their mistakes of fact or law, and many other causes, will sometimes prevent a strict obedience, and when the provisions which have been disregarded constitute parts of an important and perhaps complicated system, it becomes of the highest importance to ascertain the effect the failure to obey them shall have on the other proceedings with which they are associated in the law. The form the question most commonly assumes is this: Some official act which the law provides for, and which constitutes one step to be followed by others in reaching a specified result, having failed to be taken, does the authority to proceed toward the intended result terminate when that particular step has been neglected, or may the proceedings go on to a conclusion, treating the neglect as immaterial? If the proceeding fails at that point, the requirement of the official act which has been neglected is said to be mandatory; but if it may still proceed, the requirement is directory only; that is to say, the law directs that particular act to be performed, but does not imperatively command it as a condition precedent to anything further." [2] This explains the difference between directory and mandatory provisions so far as concerns their effect on the rights of private persons and on the conduct of public busi-

opposed to an imperative or mandatory provision, which must be followed." Maxwell, Interp. 330. "A statute is termed directory when a part or all of its provisions operate merely as advice or direction to the official or other person who is to do something pointed out, leaving the act or omission not destructive of the legality of what is done in disregard of the direction." Bishop, Wr. Laws, § 255. "Directions given by a sovereign in regard to a matter over which his power is conceded would, according to the ordinary use of language, be held to involve, as their correlative, obedience. But as, in the cases now under consideration, obedience is dispensed with by the judiciary, the statute might be better called advisory. The phrase is the more calculated to mislead as it is frequently used in the strict and proper sense of the word." Sedgwick, Stat. Constr. (2d edn.) 318, note.

[2] Cooley, Tax'n (2d edn.) 280. Under a directory statute, a duty should be performed at the time specified, but may be valid if performed afterwards. Under a mandatory statute, the act must be done at the time specified. Web-

ness. But with the officer, whose official action is regulated by the statute, the case is somewhat different. To say that the statute is directory does not mean that he is at liberty to disobey it at his mere pleasure or caprice. To him it is a command. His omission to discharge a duty prescribed by a directory statute may not vitiate the proceedings as to third persons, but it will certainly render him liable to any person injured by his failure to act.[3]

It does not necessarily follow that because a statute is directory in some of its parts or provisions, or in some of its aspects, or as to some of the persons who are to act under it, it must be held directory throughout its whole extent. It is most frequently the case that some particular clause or provision of the act is construed as directory only, while the remainder is held to be imperative. The two classes of provisions may even coexist in the same section or other division of the enactment. For example, where an act directs a certain officer to take certain action and within a certain time, it may be directory as to the time of performance, but mandatory as to the doing of the act itself.[4]

It may be that the statute itself will point out which of its provisions are to be considered as mandatory and which as directory. But this is not usually the case. And in the absence of such authoritative guidance, the courts must determine the question for themselves. Their proper object in construing any statutory provision as merely directory is not to defeat the legislative will, but to avoid the delay, confusion, and overturning of rights and titles which would result from ascribing an invalidating effect to every trifling irregularity in official action. But it must be admitted that this power to declare statutes directory, instead of imperative, is sometimes employed by the courts as a means of modifying the rigor of the law or escaping the harsh and severe consequences which would follow its strict enforcement, and sometimes as a convenient method of avoiding the necessity of putting into active operation laws which are obsolete and ill-adapted to contemporary conditions, but still unrepealed. This is well illustrated by a decision in Pennsyl-

ster v. French, 12 Ill. 302. "An absolute enactment must be obeyed or fulfilled exactly, but it is sufficient if a directory enactment be obeyed or fulfilled substantially." Woodward v. Sarsons, L. R. 10 C. P. 733.

[3] Brown v. Lester, 13 Sm. & Mar. 392.

[4] See Hardcastle, Stat. Constr. (2d edn.) 281.

vania, where the question arose upon a very ancient statute of that state which provided that "all marriages shall be solemnized by taking each other for husband and wife before twelve sufficient witnesses." The court said: "To escape from a conclusion imputative of guilt to the parties, and destructive of the civil rights of their offspring, it is necessary to hold, not only this clause, but those which require a certificate of the marriage under the hands of the parties and the twelve witnesses to be registered in the proper office, as well as publication of banns by posting on the church or courthouse doors, with other matters fallen into disuse, to be but directory." [5] Although the power of the courts in this regard can be vindicated, not only upon authority, but also by the necessities of the case, yet it is a power dangerously liable to abuse, and one which should be most carefully guarded in its exercise. "This mode of getting rid of a statutory provision by calling it directory is not only unsatisfactory on account of the vagueness of the rule itself, but it is the exercise of a dispensing power by the courts which approaches so near to legislative discretion that it ought to be resorted to with reluctance, only in extraordinary cases, where great public mischief would otherwise ensue, or important private interests demand the application of the rule. There is no more propriety in dispensing with one positive requirement than another; a whole statute may be thus dispensed with when in the way of the caprice or will of a judge. And besides, it vests a discretionary power in the ministerial officers of the law which is dangerous to private rights, and the public inconvenience occasioned by a want of uniformity in the mode of exercising a power is a strong reason for bridling this discretion. It is dangerous to attempt to be wiser than the law; and when its requirements are plain and positive, the courts are not called upon to give reasons why it was enacted. A judge should rarely take upon himself to say that what the legislature have required is unnecessary. He may not see the necessity of it; still it is not safe to assume that the legislature did not have a reason for it; perhaps it only aimed at certainty and uniformity. In that case, the judge cannot interfere to defeat that object, however puerile it may appear. It is admitted that there are cases where the requirements may be deemed directory. But it may safely be affirmed that it can never be where the act, or the omission of it, can by any possibility work advantage or injury, however slight, to any one affected by it. In such case, the requirement of the statute can never be dispensed with." [6]

MEANS OF DETERMINING CHARACTER OF PROVISION.

124. There is no absolute formal test for determining whether a statutory provision is to be considered mandatory or directory. The meaning and intention of the legislature must govern; and these are to be ascertained, not only from the phraseology of the provision, but also by considering its nature, its design, and the consequences which would follow from construing it in the one way or the other.

Many different tests have been proposed for determining whether a statutory provision is to be regarded as mandatory or merely directory. But none of them is entirely satisfactory as a fixed rule, or adequate to the solution of all possible cases. Of course the language of the act is first to be resorted to, as a clue to the intention of the legislature. But it is not always conclusive. For instance, the use of the word "may" does not always show that the act to which it relates is left to the discretion of the officer who is to perform it; and the use of the term "shall" does not necessarily make the provision imperative. As we have already seen,[7] these two words, as used in a statute, may be read interchangeably, as the one or the other reading will best express the legislative meaning. The word "may" will be construed to mean "shall" or "must" when the public interests and rights are concerned, and when the public or third persons have a claim de jure that the power shall be exercised. And conversely, the word "shall" may be understood as equivalent to "may" when no right or benefit to any one depends upon the imperative use of the term.[8] Again, it is often said that the use of negative terms will make a statute imperative.

[6] Koch v. Bridges, 45 Miss. 247.

[7] Ante, pp. 155–158.

[8] Fowler v. Pirkins, 77 Ill. 271; Seiple v. Mayor, etc., of Elizabeth, 27 N. J. Law, 407.

Thus, if the law directs that a particular proceeding shall be taken at a particular time or in a particular manner "and not otherwise," or if it makes the act void if not done as directed, or if it gives it effect only on condition that it be so done, or if it declares that if the proceeding is not taken subsequent proceedings shall not be had, or if it prohibits the doing of the act except at the time or in the manner prescribed, in these and similar cases, the wording of the statute is generally to be taken as indicating the intention of the legislature to exact a strict compliance with its terms.[9]   But this rule is not invariable.   There are cases which have been ruled in direct opposition to its purport.   And still less reliance can be placed upon the converse of this rule, namely, that the absence of negative words shows that the provision was designed to be only directory.[10]   Where the words of a statute are affirmative, and relate to the manner in which power or jurisdiction vested in a public officer or body is to be exercised, and not to the limits of the power or jurisdiction itself, they may be, and often are, construed to be directory.[11]   But affirmative words may make the statute imperative, if they are absolute, explicit, and peremptory, and show that no discretion is intended to be given.[12]

Another line of cases suggests, as the proper test of the imperative or directory character of a statute, the question whether the thing directed to be done is of the essence of the thing required or relates to matters of form.[13]   "When a particular provision of a statute relates to some immaterial matter, where compliance is a matter of convenience rather than substance, or where the directions of a statute are given with a view to the proper, orderly, and prompt conduct of public business merely, the provision may generally be regarded as directory."   But "when a fair interpretation

[9] Cooley, Tax'n (2d edn.) 283;   Hurford v. City of Omaha, 4 Neb. 336;   Hardcastle, Stat. Constr. (2d edn.) 277.

[10] Cooley, Const. Lim. 74.

[11] Bladen v. Philadelphia, 60 Pa. St. 464.

[12] Potter's Dwarris on Stat. 228.   If an affirmative statute, introductive of a new law, directs a thing to be done in a certain manner, that thing cannot, even although there are no negative words, be done in any other manner. Cook v. Kelley, 12 Abb. Pr. 35.   And see Comm'rs of the Poor v. Gains, 3 Brev. 396.

[13] Norwegian Street, 81 Pa. St. 349.

of the statute, which directs acts or proceedings to be done in a certain way, shows that the legislature intended a compliance with such provisions to be essential to the validity of the act or proceeding, or when some antecedent and prerequisite conditions must exist prior to the exercise of the power, or must be performed before certain other powers can be exercised, then the statute must be regarded as mandatory." [14] Again, it is said that the question should be in the main governed by considerations of convenience and justice; and when nullification would involve general inconvenience or great public mischief, or injustice to innocent persons, or advantage to those guilty of neglect, without promoting the real aim and object of the enactment, such an intention should not be attributed to the legislature. [15] Still a different aspect of the question is developed by the United States supreme court in a case where it was said: "There are undoubtedly many statutory requisitions intended for the guidance of officers in the conduct of business devolved upon them, which do not limit their power or render its exercise in disregard of the requisitions ineffectual. Such generally are regulations designed to secure order, system, and despatch in proceedings, and by a disregard of which the rights of parties interested cannot be injuriously affected. Provisions of this character are not usually regarded as mandatory, unless accompanied by negative words, importing that the acts required shall not be done in any other manner or time than that designated. But when the requisitions prescribed are intended for the protection of the citizen and to prevent a sacrifice of his property, and by a disregard of which his rights might be and generally would be injuriously affected, they are not directory but mandatory. They must be followed, or the act done will be invalid. The power of the officer in all such cases is limited by the manner and conditions prescribed

---

[14] Hurford v. City of Omaha, 4 Neb. 336. "Those directions which are not of the essence of the thing to be done, but which are given with a view merely to the proper, orderly, and prompt conduct of the business, and by the failure to obey which the rights of those interested will not be prejudiced, are not commonly to be regarded as mandatory; and if the act is performed, but not at the time or in the precise mode indicated, it will still be sufficient, if that which is done accomplishes the substantial purposes of the statute." Sutherland, Stat. Constr. § 447.

[15] Endlich, Interp. § 433.

for its exercise." [16]   Again, it has been said that if it is clear that the legislature did not intend to impose any penalty for a noncompliance with the directions of the statute, it is but carrying out the legislative will to declare the statute in that respect to be simply directory.[17]   But in regard to all these rules and criteria, it must be remarked that while each of them contains some valuable and helpful truth, no one of them should be set up as a fixed and invariable standard.   Much will depend upon the circumstances of the individual case.   Each of these rules may furnish a clue or indication of the meaning of the legislature, but none of them can take the place of that meaning when it is discoverable.   If the language of the enactment does not certainly disclose it, the legislative design is to be determined mainly from a consideration of the antecedent probability or improbability of a particular construction having been intended.

TERMS OF AUTHORIZATION CONSTRUED AS MANDATORY.

125. Where a statute provides for the doing of some act which is required by justice or public duty, or where it invests a public body, municipality, or officer with power and authority to take some action which concerns the public interests or the rights of individuals, though the language of the statute be merely permissive in form, yet it will be construed as mandatory, and the execution of the power may be insisted upon as a duty.[18]

The most frequent illustrations of the application of this rule are found in statutes authorizing the settlement of claims held by pri-

[16] French v. Edwards, 13 Wall. 506, 511.

[17] Corbett v. Bradley, 7 Nev. 106.

[18] Rex v. Barlow, 2 Salk. 609; King v. Inhabitants of Derby, Skinner, 370; Supervisors v. United States, 4 Wall. 435; City of Galena v. Amy, 5 Wall. 705; Ralston v. Crittenden, 13 Fed. 508; People v. Supervisors of Otsego Co., 51 N. Y. 401; Phelps v. Hawley, 52 N. Y. 23; Mayor of New York v. Furze, 3 Hill (N. Y.) 612; People v. Supervisors of New York, 11 Abb. Pr. 114; Inhabitants of Veazie v. Inhabitants of China, 50 Me. 518; Inhabitants of Milford v. Inhabitants of Orono, Id. 529; Wendel v. Durbin, 26 Wis. 390; Kellogg v. Page, 44 Vt. 356; Jones v. State, 17 Fla. 411.

vate persons against the state or its municipal corporations and those making provision for the levy and collection of municipal taxes. If, for instance, the act provides that the proper officers of a city or county "may" audit and pay a specified claim against the municipality, or that they are "authorized and empowered" so to do, its requirements are to be considered as mandatory, and not as merely investing them with a choice or discretion in the matter.[19] Thus, an act of the legislature of New York "authorized and empowered" a board of supervisors to cause taxes illegally assessed and paid in their county to be repaid. This was held to be imperative; and it became the duty of the supervisors to take the action indicated whenever valid claims for such taxes were duly presented to them.[20] Again, a law which authorizes a municipality to levy and collect taxes is to be construed as mandatory whenever the purposes to which such taxes are to be devoted are such as concern the necessary public duties of the corporation or the just rights of private persons.[21] Thus, where a statute declared that the common council of a city was "authorized" to audit and adjust the amount of damage done to certain private property by the opening of a street, and provided that, on the appraisal of such damage, the city should raise the same by taxation and pay it over to the owner of the property, this was held to be imperative.[22] Even where the act provides that certain public officers, "if deemed advisable," or "if they believe the public good and the best interests of the city require it," "may" levy a certain tax, though these words are purely permissive in form, yet the act will be held to be peremptory whenever the public interest or individual rights call for the exercise of the power granted.[23] And in general, where the statute enacts that a public officer "may" act in a certain way which is for the benefit of third persons, he must act in that way. For example, where it is enacted that the officers of a municipal corporation "may" proceed, in selling

---

[19] Bowen v. City of Minneapolis, 48 Minn. 115, 49 N. W. 683; People v. Supervisors of Erie, 1 Sheld. (Super. Ct. Buffalo) 517.

[20] People v. Supervisors of Otsego Co., 36 How. Pr. 1.

[21] Kennedy v. City of Sacramento, 19 Fed. 580; People v. Supervisors of Livingston Co., 68 N. Y. 114.

[22] People v. Common Council of Buffalo, 140 N. Y. 300, 35 N. E. 485.

[23] Supervisors v. United States, 4 Wall. 435; City of Galena v. Amy, 5 Wall. 705.

land for delinquent taxes, in cases where there are several lots assessed to the same person, to sell one or more of such lots for the taxes and expenses due on the whole, or that "it shall be lawful" for them so to do, these expressions are mandatory; that is, the officers must offer one lot at a time, and stop selling if one lot produces enough to pay the debt of all.[24]

STATUTES REGULATING TIME OF OFFICIAL ACTION.

126. **When a statute specifies the time at or within which an act is to be done by a public officer or body, it is generally held to be directory only as to the time, and not mandatory, unless time is of the essence of the thing to be done, or the language of the statute contains negative words, or shows that the designation of the time was intended as a limitation of power, authority, or right.[25]**

"Where there is no substantial reason why the thing to be done might not as well be done after the time prescribed as before, no presumption that by allowing it to be so done it may work an injury or wrong, nothing in the act itself, or in other acts relating to the same subject-matter, indicating that the legislature did not intend that it should rather be done after the time prescribed than not to be done at all, there the courts assume that the intent was that, if not done within the time prescribed, it might be done afterwards; but when any of these reasons intervene, there the limit is established."[26] "In general, where a statute imposes upon a public officer the duty of performing some act relating to the interests of the public, and fixes a time for the doing of such act, the requirement as

[24] Mason v. Fearson, 9 How. 248.

[25] Rex v. Loxdale, 1 Burr. 445; Caldow v. Pixell, L. R. 2 C. P. Div. 562; Juliand v. Rathbone, 39 N. Y. 369; United States Trust Co. v. United States Fire Ins. Co., 18 N. Y. 199; People v. Allen, 6 Wend. 486; St. Louis County Court v. Sparks, 10 Mo. 117; People v. Lake County, 33 Cal. 487; Hart v. Plum, 14 Cal. 148; Walker v. Chapman, 22 Ala. 116; Ryan v. Vanlandingham, 7 Ind. 416; Pond v. Negus, 3 Mass. 230; Wilson v. State Bank of Alabama, 3 La. Ann. 196; Bell v. Taylor, 37 La. Ann. 56; Swenson v. McLaren (Tex. Civ. App.) 21 S. W. 300.

[26] State v. Lean, 9 Wis. 279, 292.

to time is to be regarded as directory, and not a limitation of the exercise of the power, unless it contains some negative words, denying the exercise of the power after the time named, or from the character of the act to be performed, the manner of its performance, or its effect upon public interests or private rights, it must be presumed that the legislature had in contemplation that the act had better not be performed at all than be performed at any other time than that named." [27]

For example, where the statute requires a public officer to take an official oath within fifteen days after his appointment, this is directory as to the time, and it will be sufficient if he qualifies before any official act is done by him. [28]   So also, statutes fixing the time for public officers to file their official bonds are merely directory; they may file such bonds at any time before entering upon the duties of their office. [29]   Again, a statutory provision that grand jurors "shall be summoned at least five days before the first day of the court" at which their attendance is required, is merely directory to the sheriff and for the convenience of the jurors.   Probably a juror not so summoned might refuse to attend, but the requirement is not essential to be observed in order to constitute a legal grand jury. [30]   So where a statute under which a county issued bonds, a series of which fell due annually for a period of ten years, provided that "as soon as" certain prescribed conditions were complied with, "and annually thereafter for a period of ten years," the county commissioners should levy and assess a tax sufficient to pay the series falling due each year, it was held that the failure to assess and collect the tax within the time prescribed did not thereafter limit or destroy the power to levy and collect the tax, but that the power existed so long as the legal obligation to pay the debt subsisted. [31] Where an act provided that "the commissioners shall return the assessment-roll within forty days," but no public or private rights required that the word "shall" should be construed in an imperative

[27] State v. Smith, 67 Me. 328. See, also, Magee v. Comm., 46 Pa. St. 358.

[28] Howland v. Luce, 16 Johns. 135.

[29] McRoberts v. Winant, 15 Abb. Pr. N. S. 210.

[30] Johnson v. State, 33 Miss. 363; State v. Pitts, 58 Mo. 556; State v. Smith, 67 Me. 328.

[31] Commissioners' Court of Limestone Co. v. Rather, 48 Ala. 433. And see State v. Harris, 17 Ohio St. 608.

sense, it was held to be merely directory as to the time.[32]   Where
the charter of a municipal corporation enacts that the council, on
or before the first day of March in each and every year, shall direct
and authorize the city solicitor to proceed to sell lands for delinquent taxes, this is so far directory in fixing the time that valid sales
may be made afterwards.[33]   Again, where the statute makes provision for the issuing of a warrant against a defaulting tax collector and the sureties on his official bond, and specifies the time
within which such warrant shall issue, the sureties are not discharged from liability by the omission of the county treasurer to
issue the warrant within the designated time.   For since the provision as to time is for the benefit of the public, it is directory only, in
that respect, as regards the defaulter; and if directory as to him,
it is so also with respect to his sureties and others who may be incidentally affected by the warrant or the proceedings on it.[34]   On
the same principle, a statute requiring a judge of an inferior court
who tries a cause without a jury to give his decision on or before
the first day of the term succeeding that in which the cause was submitted, is only directory.[35]   And so, where the officers of a municipal corporation are directed to be elected annually, the words are
directory, and do not take away the power incident to the corporation to elect afterwards, when the annual day has, by some means,
free from design or fraud, been passed by.[36]   Again, where state
officers are required by statute to advertise for sealed proposals for
supplies or work to be done for the state, this direction is imperative.
But if the act also requires that the proposals shall be deposited
in a certain office on or before a designated day, this is not to be
construed as a limitation upon the power of the officers in receiving
and accepting such proposals.[37]   For similar reasons, it is held that

32 Wheeler v. Chicago, 24 Ill. 105.

33 Hugg v. City Council of Camden, 39 N. J. Law, 620.

34 Looney v. Hughes, 30 Barb. 605.

35 Rawson v. Parsons, 6 Mich. 401.   "It imposes a duty upon the judge, but
as the parties have no control over his action, it would be a harsh construction which should deprive them of the fruits of the litigation because the
judge fails to decide by a particular day."   Id.

36 People v. Trustees of Fairbury, 51 Ill. 149.

37 Free Press Ass'n v. Nichols, 45 Vt. 7.   But compare Webster v. French,
12 Ill. 302.

a provision in a statute, that the secretary of state shall cause it to be published "three months," etc., is only directory, and consequently his neglect to do so will not affect the operation of the statute.[38]

But the specification of time in a statute may be imperative, and may operate as a limitation upon the power of those who are to act under it. This will depend upon the intention of the legislature; and an intention to make time of the essence of the thing to be done may be disclosed either by the express language of the law or by necessary implications from its terms. Thus, where a statute directs the doing of a thing, but expressly prohibits its performance until another thing shall have been done, the prohibition cannot be disregarded or construed as merely directory.[39] Again, where a duty is required by statute to be performed on a certain day, and the object contemplated by the legislature cannot otherwise be carried into effect, the time prescribed must be considered as a mandatory and imperative requirement.[40] And so, a provision of a city charter which prohibits the passing or adoption of certain kinds of resolutions by the common council, until two days after the publication thereof in all the newspapers employed by the corporation, is not merely directory. It imposes a limitation upon the power of the council, and is therefore to be regarded as mandatory; and an ordinance or resolution not so published is void, and action taken under it is invalid.[41]

STATUTES REGULATING OFFICIAL ACTION IN MATTERS OF FORM.

127. Statutory provisions regulating official action in matters of form are to be regarded as merely directory, where they are designed only to promote order and convenience in the discharge of the public business, and where the public interests or private rights do not depend upon their strict observance.

Irregularities in official action, consisting in the neglect or lack of strict compliance with statutory directions, should not be allowed to vitiate the proceedings taken under a statute, when the

---

38 State v. Click, 2 Ala. 26.   40 Colt v. Eves, 12 Conn. 243.
39 Stayton v. Hulings, 7 Ind. 144.   41 In re Petition of Douglass, 46 N. Y. 42.

objects and ends of the statute have been substantially accomplished, and neither the public nor private persons are injured by the course of proceedings. For instance, a statute required that the official bonds of certain officers should be made to the people as obligee. But inasmuch as the obligee named in such a bond has no active duty to perform, and no voice in taking or approving the bond or in bringing suit upon it, and there is no importance in the people being named as obligee rather than the county, it being important only that some party shall be named as promisee in whose name suits may be brought, the provision for naming the people was considered as merely directory; so that a bond, otherwise good and sufficient, would not be void simply because it was made to the county instead of the people.[42] So also, it has been held that a statute which requires sales of land on execution, where the property consists of known lots or parcels, to be made separately and not in gross, is directory. A sale made in gross would be irregular, and might be set aside at the instance of the party aggrieved, but would not be void.[43] And a statute requiring a sheriff, after selling land on execution, to file a certificate of sale in the clerk's office is likewise directory only. His omission to comply will not invalidate the sale nor be regarded as taking away the right to issue a deed

[42] Bay County v. Brock, 44 Mich. 45, 6 N. W. 101.

[43] Cunningham v. Cassidy, 17 N. Y. 276. In this case, Denio, J., said: "A judgment is a general lien upon all the land owned by the debtor at the time it was docketed. It is the recovery of the judgment which affects the owner's title, by charging it with the burden of the debt, and the subsequent proceedings relate to the method in which the lien is enforced and executed. A departure from the prescriptions of the statute, in conducting these proceedings, may or may not prejudice the debtor or his other creditors. * * * It would be an inconvenient rule which should make the validity of the sale depend upon a difficult question of fact. It would be a safer rule to hold that the power exists to sell premises so divided together, and that the title passes by a conveyance made pursuant to such a sale. A party in interest, applying within a reasonable time, would have a right to set such a sale aside; but that he may waive by an express act of ratification or by a neglect to assert his rights by a seasonable application to the court. It was repeatedly held, before the adoption of the Revised Statutes, that sales of several lots or farms in a single parcel were oppressive and wrong; but it was considered that a title passed, and that the party aggrieved was obliged to apply to have the sale set aside."

in pursuance of the sale.[44] A statutory provision that, at the meeting of the board of supervisors of a county, the minutes of the
board shall be read over and signed by the president is merely
directory; it should be scrupulously observed, but yet the omission to do so will not affect the validity of the proceedings of the
board.[45] So also, a law requiring the minutes of a court to be
signed by the judge is merely directory; and the minutes are valid,
though not so signed, unless it is shown that the court rejected
them.[46] Again, an act authorizing a town to issue bonds declared
that they should be signed by the chairman of the town board of
supervisors and the town clerk, "and have annexed to them the official certificate of the clerk of the county board of supervisors, under
his official seal, that they are such officers and that their signatures
are genuine." The act did not provide who should obtain such
certificate, nor when it should be made, nor what should be its
effect, nor that it should be annexed to the bonds before they were
issued, nor that without it they should be invalid; nor did it contain any language raising a presumption that the legislature intended that the annexing of such certificate should precede the delivery of the bonds or be essential to their validity. It was accordingly held that the provision as to such certificate was designed
merely to facilitate the negotiation of the bonds, and it was not
essential to their valid execution and issue that such certificate
should be annexed.[47] On similar principles, it is held that a clause
in the charter of a corporation providing that its stock shall be
transferable only on its books is for the security of the corporation, and does not prevent the title to stock from passing, as between vendor and vendee, by any other mode of transfer.[48] Again,
a statute requiring the court to limit the time of sentence of a
convict, so that his imprisonment in the state prison shall expire
some time between March and November, is merely directory, and
a failure to comply with such requirement does not render the sentence void.[49] So the statute of Vermont, providing that all warn-

[44] Jackson v. Young, 5 Cow. 269.
[45] Arthur v. Adam, 49 Miss. 404.
[46] Justices v. House, 20 Ga. 328.
[47] Lackawana Iron, etc., Co. v. Town of Little Wolf, 38 Wis. 152.
[48] Duke v. Cahawba Nav. Co., 10 Ala. 82.
[49] Miller v. Finkle, 1 Park. C. R. 374.

ings for school-district meetings shall, before the same are posted, be recorded by the clerk, is regarded as directory only, so that a failure to record the warning will not render a meeting illegal.[50]

Even in the case of provisions found in the constitution of the state, instead of acts of the legislature, a similar rule obtains, and it is held that mere directions as to matters of form, not involving the public interests or private rights, may be considered as not imperative. Thus, where the constitution provides that the style of all laws of the state shall be "Be it enacted," etc., this requirement is not mandatory; an act regularly passed by the legislature may be valid though this clause is omitted.[51] And it is said that a clause in the state constitution requiring the supreme court to "decide every point fairly arising upon the record and give its reasons therefor in writing," is merely directory.[52] But, as we have pointed out in an earlier chapter, the courts should proceed with great hesitation and diffidence in assuming to dispense with the imperative force of any provision incorporated in so solemn and enduring an instrument as the constitution.[53]

The language, or the purport, of a statute may show that it was the legislative intention that its requirements, even in matters of form, should be exactly followed; and of course where this is the case, the rule under consideration has no application. For instance, where a statute provides that orders of a certain kind may be made by two of a board of three commissioners, provided it appears in the order that they all met and deliberated on the subject-matter or were duly notified to attend a meeting for the purpose of deliberating thereon, an order made by two of the commissioners, which does not show the above jurisdictional facts, will have no validity.[54] Especially in carrying out proceedings conducted under the power of taxation or that of eminent domain, which are in their nature summary and liable to abuse, to the prejudice of the citizen, the courts are not prone to dispense with any requirements which may possibly be for the benefit or protection of the individ-

[50] Adams v. Sleeper, 64 Vt. 544, 24 Atl. 990.

[51] City of Cape Girardeau v. Riley, 52 Mo. 424; McPherson v. Leonard, 29 Md. 377; Swann v. Buck, 40 Miss. 268.

[52] Henry v. Davis, 13 W. Va. 230.

[53] See ante, p. 21.

[54] Fitch v. Comm'rs of Kirkland, 22 Wend. 132.

ual. "In carrying out laws for condemning private property to public uses, it has always been held necessary to strictly observe every material requirement, and the courts have been equally constant in insisting that the proceedings should affirmatively show upon their face a substantial adherence to the course prescribed by the legislature." [55]

LAWS REGULATING TAX PROCEEDINGS.

128. In statutes regulating the assessment and collection of taxes, those provisions which are designed to secure equality of taxation and are intended for the benefit and protection of the tax payer are to be construed as mandatory; such as are meant only for the guidance of officers, and to secure uniformity, system, and dispatch in the conduct of the proceedings, may be considered as directory.

It would be beyond the scope of the present work to enter upon a detailed examination of the complicated system of laws and official proceedings by which the public revenues are levied and collected. It will be sufficient for the purposes of the discussion now in hand to explain the general rule which should govern the courts in determining whether any given provision of these laws is mandatory or merely directory, and to illustrate its practical workings by references to some of the more important steps in these proceedings. And first, as to the general rule: "One rule," says the supreme judicial court of Massachusetts, "is very plain and well settled: that all those measures which are intended for the security of the citizen, for insuring an equality of taxation, and to enable every one to know, with reasonable certainty, for what polls and for what real and personal estate he is taxed, and for what all those who are liable with him are taxed, are conditions precedent, and if they are not observed he is not legally taxed, and he may resist it in any of the modes authorized by law for contesting the validity of the tax. But many regulations are made by statute, designed for the information of assessors and officers, and intended to promote

[55] Kroop v. Forman, 31 Mich. 144.

method, system, and uniformity in the modes of proceeding, the compliance or noncompliance with which does in no respect affect the rights of tax-paying citizens. These may be considered directory; officers may be liable to legal animadversion, perhaps to punishment, for not observing them, but yet their observance is not a condition precedent to the validity of the tax." [56] Thus, specifically in regard to the assessment of the tax, "those legislative directions which have for their object the protection of the tax payer against spoliation or excessive assessment must be treated as mandatory. But if there be enough to show that the assessment is so made and evidenced as to be understood, then regulations designed for the information of the assessors or other officers, intended to promote dispatch, method, system, and uniformity in modes of proceeding, are merely directory. So, clerical and ministerial duties, the observance or nonobservance of which does not affect the tax payer injuriously, must be classed as directory." [57] For example, a statute enacting that "taxes on real estate shall be assessed to the owners, and separate tracts or parcels shall be separately described and valued as far as practicable," is mandatory, being for the benefit and protection of the tax payer.[58] But on the other hand, a statutory provision that "the taxable property of nonresidents shall be arranged in separate assessment lists" is merely directory to the assessors, and an assessment is not invalidated by their neglect to comply with this direction.[59] Where the statute makes provision for a board of equalization, to review tax assessments, and expressly provides the time and place of the meeting of such board and the number of days it may remain in session, these provisions are imperative, and the board will have no authority to meet at any other time or place, or to do any official act after the expiration of the time limited. For if it were otherwise, great injury and injustice might be done to tax payers.[60] On the same principle, a

---

[56] Torrey v. Millbury, 21 Pick. 64. And see People v. Auditor General, 41 Mich. 728, 1 N. W. 890; Stockle v. Silsbee, Id. 615; Cromwell v. MacLean, 123 N. Y. 474, 25 N. E. 932.

[57] State Auditor v. Jackson County, 65 Ala. 140.

[58] Young v. Joslin, 13 R. I. 675.

[59] Adams v. Town of Seymour, 30 Conn. 402.

[60] Wiley v. Flournoy, 30 Ark. 609; Sumner v. Colfax Co., 14 Neb. 524, 16 N. W. 756. But in the case of a board before which the statute contemplates

statutory provision that the collector of taxes shall "attend at his office at the county seat until the 20th day of April in each year, to receive taxes from persons wishing to pay the same," is mandatory. "This provision," said the court, "was evidently intended for the benefit of tax payers. All the authorities, everywhere, are uniform in holding that all such provisions are mandatory, and the observance of them is a condition precedent to any valid sale of land for taxes."[61] So, where the statute provides that the collector of taxes, before proceeding to sell land for taxes, shall give notice thereof by public advertisement, specifying the time and place of sale, the property to be sold, the amount due thereon, etc., this requirement is imperative, and its omission, or incomplete observance, will nullify all subsequent proceedings.[62] And with regard to all the provisions of the statute which relate to the time, place, and manner of conducting the sale of land for delinquent taxes, the courts are very strict in requiring an exact compliance on the part of those who are charged with the execution of the law. It is at this point that it is especially necessary to guard the rights of the tax payer against fraud, imposition, or unfair dealing. Thus, the sale must be held at the exact time and place specified by the law for that purpose, or designated in the advertisements. If not, it is a nullity. So strictly is this rule applied that there are cases holding that where the statute requires that the sale shall be made before the courthouse door of the county, and the sale is in fact made inside the courthouse, it is void and no title will pass.[63] So, where the law directs that tax sales shall be held "on the first Monday of November in each year, between the hours of nine o'clock A. M. and four o'clock P. M.," the sale must be kept open, for the

ex parte proceedings only, making no provision for contests by parties interested (as, a state board of equalization acting between counties), a statutory provision that it shall meet on a designated day in each year, for the purpose of transacting its official business, is merely directory as to the day. State Auditor v. Jackson Co., 65 Ala. 142; Perry Co. v. Selma, etc., R. Co., Id. 391.

[61] Hare v. Carnall, 39 Ark. 196.

[62] Milner v. Clarke, 61 Ala. 258; Black, Tax Titles, § 205, and many cases there cited.

[63] Rubey v. Huntsman, 32 Mo. 501; Koch v. Bridges, 45 Miss. 247; Richards v. Cole, 31 Kans. 205, 1 Pac. 647; Black, Tax Titles, § 227.

reception of bids, from nine to four; otherwise it is not valid.[64] And where the law contemplates that separate parcels of land shall be separately offered for sale, though they are all assessed to the same owner, and that only so much shall be sold as may be needed to pay the taxes and charges against all, this provision is mandatory, and must be strictly followed, even though the language of the statute, on this point, is only permissive in form.[65] And so, where, as is most commonly the case, statutes providing for the sale of land for the nonpayment of taxes provide that a period of time shall be allowed for the owner to redeem from the sale, and· that the purchaser at the tax sale, or the officer whose duty it is, shall give to such owner a notice of the expiration of the time for redemption, such a provision is to be construed as mandatory. It must be strictly complied with; and the omission to give the prescribed notice, or the service of a notice not conforming to the statute, will invalidate the subsequent tax deed.[66]

LAWS REGULATING ELECTIONS.

129. Statutory provisions regulating the conduct of public elections, if not made mandatory by the express terms of the law, will be construed as so far directory that the election will not be nullified by mere irregularities, not fraudulently brought about, when the departure from the prescribed method was not so great as to throw a substantial doubt on the result, and where it is not shown that there was any obstacle to a fair and free expression of the will of the electors.

"If the law itself declares a specified irregularity to be fatal, the courts will follow that command, irrespective of their views of the importance of the requirement. In the absence of such declaration, the judiciary endeavor, as best they may, to discern whether the

[64] State v. Farney, 36 Neb. 537, 54 N. W. 862.

[65] Mason v. Fearson, 9 How. 248.

[66] Doughty v. Hope, 3 Denio, 594; Hendrix v. Boggs, 15 Neb. 469, 20 N. W. 28; Black, Tax Titles, § 329.

deviation from the prescribed forms of law had or had not so vital an influence on the proceedings as probably prevented a free and full expression of the popular will. If it had, the irregularity is held to vitiate the entire return; otherwise, it is considered immaterial. It has been sometimes said, in this connection, that certain provisions of election laws are mandatory and others directory. These terms may perhaps be convenient to distinguish one class of irregularities from the other. But strictly speaking, all provisions of such laws are mandatory, in the sense that they impose the duty of obedience on those who come within their purview. But it does not therefore follow that every slight departure therefrom should taint the whole proceedings with a fatal blemish. Courts justly consider the chief purpose of such laws, namely, the obtaining of a fair election and an honest return, as paramount in importance to the minor requirements which prescribe the formal steps to reach that end; and in order not to defeat the main design, are frequently led to ignore such innocent irregularities of election officers as are free of fraud and have not interfered with a full and fair expression of the voters' choice."[67] Thus, for example, a statutory provision as to the place at which the polls shall be maintained for an election is directory, in so far as that the election will not be invalidated by being held at another place, if there were necessary and sufficient reasons for making the change, and all the voters knew of it, and there was no fraud or improper motive for making the change, and no voter complains that he was deprived thereby of an opportunity to vote.[68] So, where a statute regulating the law of elections provides that the polls shall be kept open, on the day of the election, between certain hours, it is presumably the intention of the legislature that there should be no closing of the polls between those hours, and, on the other hand, that they should not be open after the hour limited. But this provision is so far directory that an

[67] Bowers v. Smith, 111 Mo. 45, 20 S. W. 101. "It is a well recognized principle of statutory construction that election laws are to be liberally construed when necessary to reach a substantially correct result; and to that end their provisions will, to every reasonable extent, be treated as directory rather than mandatory." Duncan v. Shenk, 109 Ind. 26, 9 N. E. 690.

[68] Dale v. Irwin, 78 Ill. 170; Farrington v. Turner, 53 Mich. 27, 18 N. W. 544; Preston v. Culbertson, 58 Cal. 198; Wakefield v. Patterson, 25 Kans. 709.

election is not invalidated by the fact that the election officers opened the polls a short time before the hour fixed, or closed them a short time before the proper hour, or closed the polls for an hour in the middle of the day, if it is not shown that any fraud was practised or any substantial right violated, or that there was any obstruction or impediment to a full and fair expression of the will of the people.[69] But on the other hand, a statute which forbids the vote of any person to be received at any election within the state, unless his name be on the registry made on a previous day, or unless he shall furnish to the board of inspectors a certain affidavit and certain specified proof of his residence in the district, is imperative; and all votes received in violation of those provisions will be rejected by the court in an action to try title to an office.[70]

[69] Fry v. Booth, 19 Ohio St. 25; Holland v. Davies, 36 Ark. 446; Cleland v. Porter, 74 Ill. 76.

[70] State v. Hilmantel, 21 Wis. 574. And so, the statute requiring the governor to issue his proclamation of election to fill vacancies in certain offices is mandatory and an essential prerequisite to all such elections. People v. Weller, 11 Cal. 49.

CHAPTER XIII.

AMENDATORY AND AMENDED ACTS.

130. Construction of Amendments.
131. Construction of Statute as Amended.
132. Scope of Amendatory Act.
133. Amendment by Way of Revision.
134. Identification of Act to be Amended.

CONSTRUCTION OF AMENDMENTS.

130. An original act and an amendment to it should be read and construed as one act.

When an amendment to a statute is adopted, there are not two separate enactments, the old and the new, but by their union there is produced one law, namely, the statute as amended. From this it follows that the legislative intention, in making the amendment, is to be learned from a consideration of the original act and the amendment as one act. And consequently, on the principle that the interpretation is to be such, if possible, as to give effect to every clause and provision of every statute, no portion of either the original act or the amendment should be declared inoperative if it can be sustained by any rational construction and without putting upon the language employed a forced or unnatural meaning.[1] For the same reason, of two constructions, either of which is warranted by the words of an amendatory act, that is to be preferred which best harmonizes the amendment with the general tenor and spirit of the act amended.[2] So also, in construing an amendatory statute, the mischiefs or hardships produced by the old law must be considered, together with the remedy proposed by the new.[3] And it will be presumed that a word used in a certain sense in the original act is used in the same sense where it occurs in the amendatory act.[4]

---

[1] Harrell v. Harrell, 8 Fla. 46.

[2] Cæsar Griffin's Case, Chase, 364, Fed. Cas. No. 5,815.

[3] People v. Greer, 43 Ill. 213; Maus v. Logansport, etc., R. Co., 27 Ill. 77.

[4] Robbins v. Omnibus R. Co., 32 Cal. 472.

CONSTRUCTION OF STATUTE AS AMENDED.

131. An amended statute is to be construed as if it had read from the beginning as it does with the amendment added to it or incorporated in it.[5]

An amendment of a statute by a subsequent act operates precisely as if the subject-matter of the amendment had been incorporated in the prior act at the time of its adoption, so far as regards any action had after the amendment is made.[6] For it must be remembered that an amendment becomes a part of the original act, whether it be a change of a word, figure, line, or entire section, or a recasting of the whole language.[7] For example, the act of congress "to correct errors and supply omissions in the Revised Statutes" amends the Revised Statutes by adding to them certain provisions of existing statutes; but the amendments are not in the nature of new enactments; they are to be construed as though the Revised Statutes were originally adopted with these alterations incorporated therein.[8] And where an amendatory act uses the language "under the limitations herein provided," this must be taken to refer to the limitations in the original act as it stands after all the amendments made thereto are introduced into their proper places therein.[9] Nevertheless, the rule that an amended statute is to be understood as if it had read from the beginning as amended, must not be so applied as to defeat the plain intent of the legislature in amending it. This doctrine was applied in a case where an amendment, adopted more than twenty years after the statute was passed, provided that actions on judgments "heretofore rendered" should be brought within ten years after entry thereof. It would obviously be incorrect, in such a case, to confine the provision to judgments

[5] Goldman v. Kennedy, 49 Hun, 157, 1 N. Y. Supp. 599; Peters v. Vawter, 10 Mont. 201, 25 Pac. 438; Kamerick v. Castleman, 21 Mo. App. 587.

[6] Holbrook v. Nichol, 36 Ill. 161; Turney v. Wilton, Id. 385; Conrad v. Nall, 24 Mich. 275; Farrell v. State, 54 N. J. Law, 421, 24 Atl. 725; McKibben v. Lester, 9 Ohio St. 627.

[7] People v. Sweetser, 1 Dak. 308, 46 N. W. 452.

[8] Ludington's Case, 15 Ct. Cl. 453.

[9] McKibben v. Lester, 9 Ohio St. 627.

rendered before the passage of the original act. The true reading is that "heretofore" means before the passage of the amendment.[10]

SCOPE OF AMENDATORY ACT.

132. An amendatory statute is to be confined, in its scope and operation, to the limits of the act to which it is an amendment, unless the intention of the legislature to give it a wider field of operation is manifest.

For example, where a statute is limited, in its operation, to certain localities, an act amendatory thereof can have no wider scope than the original act, unless it is expressly so provided in the amendment.[11] And an amendment of a section of the statutes prescribing the practice in the circuit court does not, by implication, amend another section wherein a similar practice has been prescribed for justices' courts.[12] On similar principles, an act which declares that the provisions of a special act shall apply to another city than that for which it was passed has not the effect of making subsequent amendments to the original act applicable to the second city.[13]

[10] People v. Circuit Judge of Wayne County, 37 Mich. 287.
[11] U. S. v. Crawford, 6 Mackey, 319.
[12] Jones v. St. Onge, 67 Wis. 520, 30 N. W. 927.
[13] Knapp v. Brooklyn, 97 N. Y. 520.

AMENDMENT BY WAY OF REVISION.

133. Where an amendment is made by declaring that the original statute "shall be amended so as to read as follows," retaining part of the original statute and incorporating therein new provisions, the effect is not to repeal, and then re-enact, the part retained, but such part remains in force as from the time of the original enactment, while the new provisions become operative at the time the amendatory act goes into effect, and all such portions of the original statute as are omitted from the amendatory act are abrogated thereby and are thereafter no part of the statute.[14]

When an amendatory act provides that the original statute shall be amended "so as to read as follows," and thereupon repeats some of the clauses or provisions of the amended statute and omits others, and at the same time introduces certain new clauses or sections, there are three points which must be chiefly noticed in regard to its operation and effect. In the first place, as to those portions of the original statute which the amendatory act simply retains, it is not generally to be construed as a new enactment. It does not repeal those provisions and then re-enact them in the same terms, but they are to be considered as remaining in force from the time of the original enactment, and as being merely continued in operation by the amendatory statute.[15] In some of the states, this principle has been made into a statutory rule of construction. Thus, in Kansas, it is provided that "the provisions of any statute, so far as they are the same as those of any prior enactment, shall be construed as a continuation of such provisions, and not as an amend-

[14] Ely v. Holton, 15 N. Y. 595; Moore v. Mausert, 49 N. Y. 332; Matter of Peugnet, 67 N. Y. 441; Goillotel v. Mayor, etc., of New York, 87 N. Y. 440; The Louis Olsen, 6 C. C. A. 608, 57 Fed. 845; Central Pac. R. Co. v. Shackelford, 63 Cal. 261; Burwell v. Tullis, 12 Minn. 572 (Gil. 486); Kamerick v. Castleman, 21 Mo. App. 587; State v. Mines, 38 W. Va. 125, 18 S. E. 470.

[15] Moore v. Mausert, 5 Lans. 173, s. c. 49 N. Y. 332.

ment, unless such construction would be inconsistent with the manifest intent of the legislature." But under this rule it is held that where the legislature enacts a law which is the same in terms as a former statute, yet if such former statute has prior thereto wholly accomplished its purpose and exhausted its force, the latter law must be held to be a new enactment, and not merely a continuation of the former; for this case comes within the exception.[16] In the second place, those provisions which are newly added by the amendatory statute are not to be considered as having been in force from the beginning. They take effect from the time of the enactment of the amendatory act, and derive their whole efficacy and vitality from the amending law and not from that amended. In other words, such new provisions will not have any retrospective effect, unless it is explicitly so declared.[17] In the third place, all those provisions of the original statute which are not repeated in the amending statute are abrogated or repealed thereby, and are thereafter of no force or effect whatever.[18] In this particular, the amendatory act is to be considered as a new enactment, and it is not even to be construed as in pari materia with the provisions of the old law which it has superseded or displaced. That is to say, the intention of the legislature, in the new portions of the amendatory act, is to be ascertained from that act itself, and such intention cannot be limited or modified by anything contained in the abrogated portions of the old law, on the theory that they are acts in pari materia and should therefore be construed together.[19]

When a statute, purporting to be amendatory of a former law, and declaring that the earlier act shall be amended "so as to read as follows," covers the entire ground occupied by the provisions of the original act, and is repugnant to its further operation, and is plainly designed to furnish the sole and complete system of legislation on that subject-matter, it must be construed as a new and independent enactment, and as entirely abrogating and repealing the former statute.[20]

---

[16] City of Emporia v. Norton, 16 Kans. 236.

[17] Kelsey v. Kendall, 48 Vt. 24.

[18] State v. Andrews, 20 Tex. 230; Goodno v. City of Oshkosh, 31 Wis. 127; People v. Supervisors of Montgomery Co., 67 N. Y. 109.

[19] Cortesy v. Territory (New Mex.) 32 Pac. 504.

[20] Comm. v. Kenneson, 143 Mass. 418, 9 N. E. 761.

"A law purporting to be an amendment of another law may operate as a repeal of the original law, or it may not.   If an amendment does not change the original law, but simply adds something to it, the amendatory law would not operate as a repeal of the old law.   Where an amendment is made which changes the old law in its substantial provisions, it must, by a necessary implication, repeal the old law so far as they are in conflict.   And when a new law, whether it be in the form of an amendment or otherwise, covers the whole subject-matter of the former, and is inconsistent with it and evidently intended to supersede and take the place of it, it repeals the old law by implication." [21]

IDENTIFICATION OF ACT TO BE AMENDED.

134. Unless the constitution otherwise specifically directs, it is sufficient if an amendatory act refers to the act to be amended in such a manner as to identify it substantially.

Thus, for example, where an amendatory act refers to the act to be amended by its date, title, and subject-matter, a mistake in the two former is immaterial, provided the reference to the latter renders certain the identity of the amended act.[22]   And so, where the amendatory act first declares what the amendments shall be, and then makes a mistake in reciting the law as it will read when amended, such mistake will not vitiate the act.[23]   But in many of the states the constitutions now contain a provision substantially as follows: "No act shall ever be revised or amended by mere reference to its title, but the act revised or section amended shall be set forth and published at full length."   "As we understand this clause of the constitution," says the court in Ohio, "it requires, in the case of an amendment of a section or sections of a prior statute, that the new act shall contain, not the section or sections which it proposes to amend, but the section or sections in full as it purports to amend

---

[21] Longlois v. Longlois, 48 Ind. 60.

[22] Madison, W. & M. Plank Road Co. v. Reynolds, 3 Wis. 287. And see Dowda v. State, 74 Ga. 12.

[23] Custin v. City of Viroqua, 67 Wis. 314, 30 N. W. 515.

them.   That is, it requires, not a recital of the old section, but a full
statement, in terms, of the new one.   *   *   *   The constitutional
provision was intended, mainly, to prevent improvident legislation;
and with that view, as well as for the purpose of making all acts,
when amended, intelligible, without an examination of the statute as
it stood prior to the amendment, it requires every section which is intended to supersede a former one to be fully set out. No amendments
are to be made by directing specified words or clauses to be stricken
from, or inserted in, a section of a prior statute which may be referred to, but the new act must contain the section as amended." [24]
A constitutional provision of this character is generally regarded as
mandatory; and it is said that the intention of the legislature in
reference to an amendment of a statute is unimportant, unless manifested in the manner directed by the constitution.[25]

[24] Lehman v. McBride, 15 Ohio St. 573, 602, 603.
[25] Dodd v. State, 18 Ind. 56.

CHAPTER XIV.

CONSTRUCTION OF CODES AND REVISED STATUTES.

CODE CONSTRUED AS A WHOLE.

135. The various parts and sections of a code, or of a body of revised or compiled laws, though collected from independent laws of previous enactment, are to be construed as making up one entire and harmonious system. Conflicts between them are to be avoided by construction, if possible. But if there is an irreconcilable repugnancy between different parts or sections, that which was last adopted or enacted must prevail.

Although a code or revision may be made up of many provisions drawn from various sources, though it may include the whole or parts of many previous laws and reject many others in whole or in part, though it may change or modify the existing law, or though it may add to the body of law previously in force many new provisions, yet it is to be considered as one homogeneous whole, established "uno flatu." All its various parts or sections are to be considered and interpreted as if they were parts of a single statute. And hence, according to a well known rule, the various provisions, if apparently conflicting, must, if possible, be brought into harmony and agreement. In order to bring about this harmony and agreement, the court which is called upon to interpret the code will look through the entire work, and gather such assistance as may be afforded by a complete survey of it. In such a review, the order of time in which the various parts were originally enacted will be disregarded, if, by such a course, and looking at the work as a whole, harmony can be produced. But if there is still a conflict between different parts or provisions which cannot be reconciled by any allowable use of the processes of construction, then that part or provision which was last adopted must prevail, because it is the latest expression of the legislative will.[1] "In construing the revised statutes," says the court in Massachusetts, "we are to bear in mind that the whole was passed at one and the same time and constitutes one act, and then the rule applies that in construing one part of a statute we are to resort to every other part, to ascertain the true meaning of the legislature in each particular provision. This rule is peculiarly applicable to the revised statutes, in which, for the convenience of analysis and classification of subjects, provisions are sometimes widely separated from each other in the code which have so immediate a connection with each other that it is quite necessary to consider the one in order to arrive at the true exposition of the other."[2] But where two statutes, passed at different times, both relating to the same subject-matter, but inconsistent with each other, are both incorporated into a code or revision, the court will inquire as to the dates of their respective enactments, and will give effect to that which is last in point of time, rejecting the other.[3] And in case of a conflict between the two parts or provisions which is not so radical as to require that one or the other shall be absolutely disregarded, the court will endeavor to so modify the earlier provision as to bring it into harmony and consistency with the later. But any one who contends that an article or section of the code is void for repugnancy to some other must assume the burden of showing the repugnancy beyond all doubt, and also that the law so abrogated is older in date than the repealing statute.[4]

[1] Gibbons v. Brittenum, 56 Miss. 232; State v. Heidorn, 74 Mo. 410; Mobile, etc., R. Co. v. Malone, 46 Ala. 391; Ashley v. Harrington, 1 D. Chip. 348.

[2] Comm. v. Goding, 3 Metc. (Mass.) 130. See, also, Bryant v. Livermore, 20 Minn. 313 (Gil. 271); Ex parte Ray, 45 Ala. 15; Gallegos v. Pino, 1 New Mex. 410.

[3] Mobile Savings Bank v. Patty, 16 Fed. 751; Haritwen v. The Louis Olsen, 52 Fed. 652; Hamilton v. Buxton, 6 Ark. 24.

[4] Gee v. Thompson, 11 La. Ann. 657.

REFERENCE TO ORIGINAL STATUTES.

136. The provisions of a code or revision are primarily to be interpreted in and by themselves alone; reference to the originals of the statutes embodied in the code is justifiable only on special grounds, as where the provisions of the code are of doubtful import, or are susceptible of more than one construction, or where language is used which had previously acquired a technical meaning.

On this point, in a recent English case, Lord Bramwell is reported as having used the following language: "I think the proper course is in the first instance to examine the language of the statute, and to ask what is its natural meaning, uninfluenced by any considerations derived from the previous state of the law, and not to start with inquiring how the law previously stood, and then, assuming that it was probably intended to leave it unaltered, to see if the words of the enactment will bear an interpretation in conformity with this view.   If a statute, intended to embody in a code a particular branch of the law, is to be treated in this fashion, it appears to me that its utility will be almost entirely destroyed, and the very object with which it was enacted will be frustrated.   The purpose of such a statute surely was that on any point specifically dealt with by it the law should be ascertained by interpreting the language used, instead of, as before, roaming over a vast number of authorities in order to discover what the law was, extracting it by a minute critical examination of the prior decisions, dependent upon a knowledge of the exact effect even of an obsolete proceeding such as a demurrer to evidence. I am of course far from asserting that resort may never be had to the previous state of the law, for the purpose of aiding in the construction of the provisions of the code.   If, for example, a provision be of doubtful import, such resort would be perfectly legitimate.   Or again, if, in a code of the law of negotiable instruments, words be found which have previously acquired a technical meaning, or been used in a sense other than their ordinary one, the same interpretation might well be put upon them in the code. I give these as examples merely; they of course do not exhaust the category. What, however, I am venturing to insist upon is that the first step taken should be to interpret the language of the statute, and that an appeal to earlier decisions can only be justified on some special ground."[5] To the same effect is the following language of the supreme court of Massachusetts: "Where the language of the public statutes is distinct, clear, and admits of but one possible interpretation, it must be followed, although it assumes the law to have been as we should not have held it, and although we are not able to ascertain, from the reports of the legislature, its committees, or otherwise, that there was any intention to amend or change it. Where the law as expressed in the public statutes is ambiguous or doubtful, or susceptible of two constructions, it is then most proper to examine the statutes as they previously existed, in order that it may be construed in the light afforded by them."[6] So also, according to the court in Ohio: "Where the language used in a revised statute is of such doubtful import as to call for a construction, it is both reasonable and usual to refer to the statute or statutes from which the revision has been made. But where the language is plain, and leads to no absurd or improbable results, there is no room for construction, and it is the duty of the courts to give it the effect required by the plain and ordinary signification of the words used, whatever may have been the language of the prior statute or the construction placed upon it. If the plain language of a revised statute is to be departed from, whenever the language of the prior one may require it, then it may be asked, what is gained by a revision? The definition of crimes must, in such case, be sought, not in the statutes as they are found to exist, but in the language of those that have been repealed. The more rational rule must be, as we think, to resort to the prior statute for the purpose of removing doubts, not for the purpose of raising them."[7]

The same rule is applied to the construction of the Revised Statutes of the United States. The body of law thus named must be accepted as the law on the subjects which it embraces, as it existed

---

[5] Bank of England v. Vagliano, (1891) App. Cas. 107, 144. And see, also, Robinson v. Canadian Pac. Ry. Co., (1892) App. Cas. 481; Myer v. Car Co., 102 U. S. 1; Viterbo v. Friedlander, 120 U. S. 707, 7 Sup. Ct. 962.

[6] Pratt v. Street Comm'rs of Boston, 139 Mass. 559, 2 N. E. 675.

[7] Heck v. State, 44 Ohio St. 536, 9 N. E. 305.

at the date of the enactment, December 1, 1873. When the meaning of any part or section of the Revised Statutes is plain and clear, the courts cannot recur to the original acts of congress to see if errors were committed in revising them or to obtain light as to their proper interpretation; but such recourse to the original statutes may be had when it becomes necessary in order to put a construction upon obscure, doubtful, or ambiguous language used in the revision.[8]

Where, in the revision of statutes, by incorporating several former acts into one, the natural construction of the words would give a meaning clearly at variance with the law, the true construction may be arrived at by giving such words the meaning in which they were used in the old statute.[9] In Alabama, a statute authorizing the codification of the laws of the state into one revised code provided that there should be no change in "the substance or meaning of any statute to be included therein." It also directed that marginal references to the session acts should be inserted. The evident design of the latter provision was that the sections of the code should be compared with the original acts, when necessary, and that the marginal notes should promote facility of reference for such purposes. It was accordingly held that when any section of the code is found to differ, in meaning or substance, from the statute which purports to be incorporated therein, the original statute is the law and must govern.[10]

---

[8] U. S. v. Bowen, 100 U. S. 508; Arthur v. Dodge, 101 U. S. 34; Vietor v. Arthur, 104 U. S. 498; Deffeback v. Hawke, 115 U. S. 392, 6 Sup. Ct. 95; Cambria Iron Co. v. Ashburn, 118 U. S. 54, 6 Sup. Ct. 929; U. S. v. Lacher, 134 U. S. 624, 10 Sup. Ct. 625; Bate Refrigerating Co. v. Sulzberger, 157 U. S. 1, 15 Sup. Ct. 508; Wright v. U. S., 15 Ct. Cl. 80. Where it is found that an act of congress which is an independent statute, permanent in character, though special in its application, and not repealed by any act prior to the revision of the statutes, has been omitted from the Revised Statutes, it nevertheless continues in force. Peters v. U. S. (Okl.) 33 Pac. 1031.

[9] In re Murphy, 23 N. J. Law, 180.

[10] Nicholson v. Mobile & M. R. Co., 49 Ala. 205.

EFFECT OF CHANGE OF LANGUAGE.

137. When statutes are codified, compiled, or collected and revised, a mere change of phraseology should not be deemed to work a change in the law, unless there was an evident intention, on the part of the legislature, to effect such change.[11]

"It is a well settled rule," says the court in Ohio, "that in the revision of statutes, neither an alteration in phraseology nor the omission or addition of words, in the latter statute, shall be held, necessarily, to alter the construction of the former act. And the court is only warranted in holding the construction of a statute, when revised, to be changed, where the intent of the legislature to make such change is clear, or the language used in the new act plainly requires such change of construction."[12]   It should be remembered that condensation is a necessity in the work of compilation or codification. Very frequently words which do not materially affect the sense will be omitted from the statutes as incorporated in the code, or the same general idea will be expressed in briefer phrases. No design of altering the law itself could rightly be predicated upon such modifications of the language. And again, in the construction of such a body of laws, "the manifest purpose to express in general words the substance of former statutes must be borne in mind; and from the omission of special words found in former statutes, embraced by the general words, an intention to change the former statutes will not be implied."[13]   When the language of the code or revision, as it stands, would lead to absurd or highly improbable results, it may be compared with the language of the original statute, to ascertain if the phraseology has not been changed by mistake or inadvertence. Thus, in Louisiana, a section of the revised statutes provides that all crimes, offenses, and misdemeanors shall be construed according to the common law of England. This was intended to be a reproduction of an

[11] McDonald v. Hovey, 110 U. S. 619, 4 Sup. Ct. 142; The E. W. Gorgas, 10 Bened. 460, Fed. Cas. No. 4,585; Hughes v. Farrar, 45 Me. 72; Conger v. Barker, 11 Ohio St. 1; Burnham v. Stevens, 33 N. H. 247; Overfield v. Sutton, 1 Metc. (Ky.) 621; Douglass v. Howland, 24 Wend. 35, 47; Case of Yates, 4 Johns. 317, 359; Ennis v. Crump, 6 Tex. 34.

[12] Conger v. Barker, 11 Ohio St. 1.

[13] Posey v. Pressley, 60 Ala. 243.

act of 1805, which named and described certain crimes, and then provided that the offenses "hereinbefore named" should be construed according to the common law.   It was held that the omission, in the revised statutes, of the words "hereinbefore named" was not intended to extend or alter the meaning of the provision so as to embrace all crimes and misdemeanors, however obscure or obsolete, known to the common law of England, but that such omission was an oversight.[14] But while the presumption is against an intention to change the law, yet when the language used in the revision cannot possibly bear the same construction as the revised and repealed act, full effect must be given to the new enactment.[15]

ADOPTION OF PREVIOUS JUDICIAL CONSTRUCTION.

138. When the legislature revises the statutes of the state, after a particular statute has been judicially construed, without changing that statute, it is presumed that the legislature intended that the same construction should continue to be applied to that statute.[16]

This rule is strictly analogous to that already noticed, that when a statute or a constitutional provision is adopted from the legislation or the constitution of another state, which has there received a settled judicial construction, it is presumed to be adopted in view of that construction, which is thereby sanctioned and intended to be continued in force; and also to the rule which produces a like consequence when a statute of the same state is re-enacted.[17]   In either case, the interpretation of the law becomes a part of the law; and in the instance of a revision or codification of the statutes, it would require an unmistakable alteration of the language employed to indicate an intention, on the part of the legislature, that a different construction should thereafter be put upon it.

[14] State v. Gaster (La.) 12 South. 739.

[15] The Bark Brothers, 10 Bened. 400, Fed. Cas. No. 1,968.

[16] Gulf, C. & S. F. Ry. Co. v. Fort Worth & N. O. R. Co., 68 Tex. 98, 3 S. W. 564; Anthony v. State, 29 Ala. 27; Duramus v. Harrison, 26 Ala. 326. And see Smith v. Smith, 19 Wis. 522; Scheftels v. Tabert, 46 Wis. 439, 1 N. W. 156; Posey v. Pressley, 60 Ala. 243.

[17] See ante, pp. 159, 161.

CHAPTER XV.

DECLARATORY STATUTES.

139. Definition.
140. Declaratory Statutes not Retrospective.
141. Construction of Declaratory Acts.

DEFINITION.

139. A declaratory or expository statute is one passed with the purpose of removing a doubt or ambiguity as to the state of the law, or to correct a construction deemed by the legislature to be erroneous. It either declares what is, and has been, the rule of the common law on a given point, or expounds the true meaning and intention of a prior legislative act.

According to Blackstone, a statute is called declaratory "where the old custom of the kingdom is almost fallen into disuse, or become disputable; in which case the parliament has thought proper, in perpetuum rei testimonium, and for avoiding all doubts and difficulties, to declare what the common law is and ever hath been." [1] In modern usage, however, the term carries a much wider signification than this. "It is a matter of frequent occurrence that the common law, or previous statute law, on a particular subject, is found to be ambiguous and uncertain, and that the legislature passes an act declaring what the common law is and has been on that topic, or explaining the meaning of the language employed in the former act, and the inferences to be drawn from its terms. A declaratory statute in effect promulgates a rule of construction or interpretation. Such laws are usually enacted in consequence of the establishment, by the judicial department, of a settled doctrine in regard to an ambiguous law. But the legislative exposition is not always in affirmance of the view taken by the courts." [2] "Mr. Fox's libel act declared that, by the law of England, juries were

---

[1] 1 Bl. Comm. 86.   [2] Black, Const. Prohib. § 194.

judges of the law in prosecutions for libel; it did not purport to introduce a new rule, but to declare a rule already and always in force. Yet, previous to the passage of this act, the courts had repeatedly held that the jury in these cases were only to pass upon the fact of publication and the truth of the innuendoes, and whether the publication was libellous or not was a question of law which addressed itself exclusively to the court. It would appear, therefore, that the legislature declared the law to be what the courts had declared it was not." [3]

Declaratory statutes, to have the force of law and be binding on the courts, must of course be made by the proper legislative power of the jurisdiction where the law to be expounded is in force. Thus, for example, an English statute expository of the common law, enacted after the separation of America from the British kingdom, has not technically the force of law in the United States. Hence, considered as a declaratory law, it is not authoritative or binding on our courts, in such sense that they would not be at liberty to disregard it and put their own interpretation upon the common law. Yet such an act, as an aid in the elucidation of an obscure point of the common law, will be entitled to respectful consideration. [4]

DECLARATORY STATUTES NOT RETROSPECTIVE.

140. A declaratory statute, in so far as it is applicable to facts and transactions occurring after its enactment, is binding on the courts; but in so far as it is intended to have a retrospective effect upon vested rights, pending controversies, or past transactions, it is invalid, as an unlawful assumption of judicial power, and consequently not obligatory upon the courts. [5]

"In the very nature of things," says the supreme court of Pennsylvania, "interpretation follows legislation, and is not to be con-

[3] Cooley, Const. Lim. 93.

[4] Bull v. Loveland, 10 Pick. 9.

[5] Koshkonong v. Burton, 104 U. S. 668; Union Iron Co. v. Pierce, 4 Biss. 327, Fed. Cas. No. 14,367; Stebbins v. Pueblo Co., 4 Fed. 282; Gorman v. Sinking Fund Comm'rs, 25 Fed. 647; Singer Manuf. Co. v. McCollock, 24 Fed.

founded with it, either as an act or as an authority. The duties
are as distinct as possible, and the performance of them is given
to different offices, yet without preventing the legislature from embodying in a statute rules for its interpretation, or from making a
new law, by changing the interpretation or application of an old
one relative to future cases." [6] The rule is more fully explained
by the New York court of chancery in the following terms: "In
England, where there is no constitutional limit to the powers of
parliament, a declaratory law forms a new rule of decision, and is
valid and binding upon the courts, not only as to cases which may
subsequently occur, but also as to pre-existing and vested rights.
But even there the courts will not give a statute a retrospective
operation, so as to deprive a party of a vested right, unless the language of the law is so plain and explicit as to render it impossible
to put any other construction upon it. In this country, where the
legislative power is limited by written constitutions, declaratory
laws, so far as 'they operate upon vested rights, can have no legal
effect in depriving an individual of his rights, or to change the rule
of construction as to a pre-existing law. Courts will treat such
laws with all the respect which is due to them as an expression of
the opinion of the individual members of the legislature, as to what
the rule of law previously was. But beyond that they can have
no binding effect, and if the judge is satisfied the legislative construction is wrong, he is bound to disregard it." [7] Especially is this
principle applied with firmness when the effect of the declaratory
law, by reversing the construction previously put upon the common law or statutes by the judiciary, would unsettle titles or change
the legal effect of acts performed by parties in reliance upon the

667; Lambertson v. Hogan, 2 Pa. St. 22; Greenough v. Greenough, 11 Pa. St. 489;
Reiser v. William Tell Saving Fund Ass'n, 39 Pa. St. 137; Haley v. City of Philadelphia, 68 Pa. St. 45; Cambridge v. Boston, 130 Mass. 357; Todd v. Clapp,
118 Mass. 495; Shallow v. City of Salem, 136 Mass. 136; Dash v. Van Kleeck,
7 Johns. 477; People v. Board of Sup'rs of New York, 16 N. Y. 424; Lincoln
Building & S. Ass'n v. Graham, 7 Neb. 173; Kelsey v. Kendall, 48 Vt. 24;
McNichol v. United States Mercantile Reporting Agency, 74 Mo. 457; Mc-
Manning v. Farrar, 46 Mo. 376; Dequindre v. Williams, 31 Ind. 444; James
v. Rowland, 52 Md. 462.

[6] West Branch Boom Co. v. Dodge, 31 Pa. St. 285.

[7] Salters v. Tobias, 3 Paige, 338.

stability of the judicial interpretations.   So also in regard to pend-ing controversies; a party has a right to the decision of the court as to the meaning of a statute applicable to his case, independently of a declaratory act on the subject passed while the suit was pend-ing.[8]

But if no rights or titles will be affected, there is authority for holding that a declaratory statute may be accorded a retroactive operation.   It is said that while it is not within the competency of the legislative power to deprive a person of a vested right by means of a declaratory act, yet where no right has been secured under the former act or its judicial interpretation, the legislature may declare its meaning by a subsequent law, and this will have the effect of giving to the former act the same meaning and effect as if the declaratory statute had been embodied in the original act at the time of its enactment.[9]   In Georgia, it is said that a legislative exposition of a doubtful law is the exercise of a judicial power; yet if it interferes with no vested rights, impairs the obligation of no contract, and is not in conflict with the primary principles of the social compact, it is in itself harmless, and may be admitted to re-troactive efficiency; but if rights have grown up under a law of ambiguous meaning, then it cannot interfere with them.[10]   It should also be noticed that a subsequent act, which, considered as an ex-position of a previous one, may have no force, may still be of ef-fect as a new grant of power.   Thus, while the legislature has no authority to construe the charter of a corporation, yet a statute purporting to do so may, if the words will carry such a meaning, operate as a new grant of power to the corporation.[11]

---

[8] Ogden v. Blackledge, 2 Cranch, 272; Stephenson v. Doe, 8 Blackf. 508.

[9] Washington, A. & G. R. Co. v. Martin, 7 D. C. 120; State v. Trustees of Orphans' Home, 37 Ohio St. 275.

[10] McLeod v. Burroughs, 9 Ga. 213.

[11] Aikin v. Western R. Co., 20 N. Y. 370.

CONSTRUCTION OF DECLARATORY ACTS.

141. A declaratory statute will be so construed as to carry out the intention of the legislature in enacting it, so far as that is legally possible; but it will not be extended beyond its terms.

The judicial department of government must determine the construction of all laws involved in cases before them; but it is also their duty to give to a declaratory statute its intended practical operation so far as that is possible.[12] This is the generally admitted rule. But in some few states, the courts have been reluctant to concede even this much to the legislative body. Thus, in an early case in Minnesota, it is said that the opinion of a subsequent legislature upon the meaning of a prior statute is entitled to no more weight than that of the same men in a private capacity.[13] In Kentucky, a clause of the general statutes provides that "all words and phrases shall be construed and understood according to the common and approved usage of language." This, it is said, is only declaratory of a part of the common law on the subject; and there are other rules of construction which are of equal dignity and importance, which, although not incorporated in the statute, are as binding upon the courts as if embodied in it.[14] In general, a declaratory statute will be held down to its natural and intended scope, and will not be considered as modifying received or legitimate constructions beyond its terms. For instance, a section of a code provided that "signature, or subscription, includes mark, when the person cannot write, and when his mark is attested," etc. It was held that this did not define the word when found elsewhere than in the code. "If this clause," said the court, "avoids writings to the validity of which signature or subscription is by mark, and not attested as prescribed, it would not affect a mortgage of personal property, which is valid without writing, and to which the signature of the mortgagor is not required by the code or any provision thereof."[15]

[12] Bassett v. U. S., 2 Ct. Cl. 448. And see Townsend Savings Bank v. Epping, 3 Woods, 390, Fed. Cas. No. 14,120.

[13] Bingham v. Supervisors of Winona Co., 8 Minn. 441 (Gil. 390).

[14] Bailey v. Comm., 11 Bush. 688.

[15] Alabama Warehouse Co. v. Lewis, 56 Ala. 514.

CHAPTER XVI.

THE RULE OF STARE DECISIS AS APPLIED TO STATUTORY CON-
STRUCTION.

142. The General Principle.
143. Effect of Reversing Construction.
144. Federal Courts Following State Decisions.
145. Construction of Statutes of Other States.

THE GENERAL PRINCIPLE.

**142. A settled judicial construction put upon a statute has
almost the same authority as the statute itself; and
though the courts have the power to overrule their
decisions and change the construction, they will not
do so except for the most urgent reasons.**

The rule just stated is not a modern invention.   It has for a very
long period of time been respected by the courts, and is now supported by a multitude of authorities.[1]   It is an ancient maxim of the
law that "legis interpretatio legis vim obtinet;" that is to say, the
authoritative interpretation put upon the written law by the courts acquires the force of law, by becoming, as it were, a part of the statute
itself.[2]   The importance of adhering to this rule is seen in the fact
that the judicial explanation of an obscure or ambiguous statute is
at once accepted as correct by those whose rights or actions may be
affected by the statute, and innumerable transactions will thereafter
depend for their validity and effect upon the permanence of the judicial construction in view of which they were had.   "The court almost always, in deciding any question, creates a moral power above

[1] Hammond v. Anderson, 4 Bos. & P. 69; King v. Younger, 5 Durn. & E.
449; King v. Inhabitants of Eccleston, 2 East, 299; Queen v. Chantrell, L. R.
10 Q. B. 587; People v. Albertson, 55 N. Y. 50; Wolf v. Lowry, 10 La. Ann.
272; State v. Thompson, Id. 122; New Orleans v. Poutz, 14 La. Ann. 853;
Beck v. Brady, 7 La. Ann. 1; Seale v. Mitchell, 5 Cal. 401; Sheridan v. City
of Salem, 14 Or. 328, 12 Pac. 925; Despain v. Crow, 14 Or. 404, 12 Pac. 806;
Davidson v. Biggs, 61 Iowa, 309, 16 N. W. 135.

[2] Branch, Principia (1st Am. edn.) 76.

itself; and when the decision construes a statute, it is legally bound, for certain purposes, to follow it as a decree emanating from a paramount authority, according to its various applications in and out of the immediate case." [3]   So, Lord Chancellor Cairns, speaking of revenue acts, observes: "The object must be, above that of all other acts, to maintain them and to expound them in a manner which will be consistent, and which will enable the subjects of this country to know what exactly is the amount of the charge and burden which they are to sustain. I think that, with regard to statutes of that kind, above all others, it is desirable, not so much that the principle of the decision should be capable at all times of justification, as that the law should be settled, and should, when once settled, be maintained without any danger of vacillation or uncertainty." [4]   Even though the court, when the question of the construction of the statute comes up a second time, should be satisfied that the original construction was founded in error, yet, if it is seen that great mischief would ensue from a change in the interpretation, the court will yield the construction which it would otherwise regard as the true one, in favor of that interpretation which has been universally received and long acted on. [5]   More especially when the construction given to a statute has become what is called a "rule of property" (that is, a rule under which titles have become fixed and upon the continuance of which property rights depend), it should be adhered to, even though questionable, so long as the statute itself remains unchanged. [6]   And the same opinion has been expressed with regard to the interpretation of statutes which involve questions of practice; decisions under which a practice has grown up, though erroneous, will still be followed. [7]

Although, in general, this doctrine applies only to judicial interpre-

[3] Bates v. Relyea, 23 Wend. 336.

[4] Comm'rs of Inland Revenue v. Harrison, L. R. 7 H. L. 1.

[5] Van Loon v. Lyon, 4 Daly, 149.

[6] Day v. Munson, 14 Ohio St. 488; Aicard v. Daly, 7 La. Ann. 612; Farmer's Heirs v. Fletcher, 11 La. Ann. 142. In Windham v. Chetwynd, 1 Burr. 414, Lord Mansfield said that when solemn determinations, acquiesced under, had settled precise cases, and become a rule of property, they ought, for the sake of certainty, to be observed as if they had originally made a part of the text of the statute.

[7] Succession of Lauve, 6 La. Ann. 529.

tations of statutes settled by the deliberate judgments of the court of last resort in the state, yet the rule has sometimes been extended so as to include adjudications of minor authority. Thus, in Mississippi, it is said that when the true meaning of a statute is doubtful, a construction which has been adopted by the inferior courts for a long period of time, and under which important rights have accrued, will not be disturbed by the supreme court of the state.[8]   And in Kentucky, in a similar case of doubt, a legislative exposition of the statute, together with an extra-judicial dictum of the supreme court formerly made, were allowed to have a decisive influence.[9]   A contemporaneor practical construction of a statute, under which rights of property have been acquired, will be upheld, when this can properly be done.[10]

EFFECT OF REVERSING CONSTRUCTION.

143. Where rights of property have accrued, and contracts have been made, in reliance upon the judicial construction of a statute, and were valid at the time of their inception under such construction, a subsequent decision, overruling prior decisions and reversing the construction established thereby, will not be allowed to retroact, so as to destroy those rights or invalidate those contracts.

Judicial decisions are evidences of the law; but when they are not long established, and are palpably erroneous and plainly productive of injustice, they should be overruled, and it is the right and duty of the courts to do so.[11]   But the settled judicial construction of a statute, so far as contract rights were acquired thereunder, is as much a part of the statute as the text itself; and a change of decision is the same in its effect on pre-existing contracts as a repeal or an amendment by legislative enactment.[12]   "We hold the doctrine

[8] Plummer v. Plummer, 37 Miss. 185.

[9] Comm. v. Miller, 5 Dana, 320.

[10] Matter of Warfield's Will, 22 Cal. 51.

[11] Paul v. Davis, 100 Ind. 422.

[12] Douglass v. Pike County, 101 U. S. 677; Ohio Life Ins. Co. v. Debolt, 16 How. 432; Taylor v. Ypsilanti, 105 U. S. 72; Geddes v. Brown, 5 Phila. 180;

to be sound and firmly established," says the supreme court of Alabama, "that rights to property and the benefits of investments acquired by contract, in reliance upon a statute as construed by the supreme court of the state, and which were valid contracts under the statute as thus interpreted, when the contracts or investments were made, cannot be annulled or divested by subsequent decisions of the same court overruling the former decisions; that as to such contracts or investments, it will be held that the decisions which were in force when the contracts were made had established a rule of property, upon which the parties had a right to rely, and that subsequent decisions cannot retroact so as to impair rights acquired in good faith under a statute as construed by the former decisions." [13]

FEDERAL COURTS FOLLOWING STATE DECISIONS.

144. The settled construction put upon a public statute of a state by the courts of that state will be accepted as authentic by the courts of the United States, and will be adopted and applied by them, without inquiry as to its soundness, unless some question of federal law is involved, such as the conformity of the statute to the constitution or laws of the United States.

This rule was announced by the supreme court of the United States at an early day, and has ever since been consistently followed and adhered to.[14] But the rule "has grown up and been held with constant reference to the other rule, stare decisis; and it is

Farrior v. New England Mortgage Co., 92 Ala. 176, 9 South. 532; Levy v. Nitsche, 40 La. Ann. 500, 4 South. 472; Paulson v. City of Portland, 16 Or. 450, 19 Pac. 450.

[13] Farrior v. New England Mortgage Co., 92 Ala. 176, 9 South. 532.

[14] McKeen v. Delancy's Lessee, 5 Cranch, 22; Elmendorf v. Taylor, 10 Wheat. 152; McDowell v. Peyton, Id. 454; Shelby v. Guy, 11 Wheat. 361; Leffingwell v. Warren, 2 Black (U. S.) 599; Christy v. Pridgeon, 4 Wall. 196; Nichols v. Levy, 5 Wall. 433; Walker v. State Harbor Comm'rs, 17 Wall. 648; Tioga R. Co. v. Blossburg & C. R. Co., 20 Wall. 137; Lamborn v. County Comm'rs, 97 U. S. 181; Douglass v. Pike Co., 101 U. S. 677; Bucher v. Cheshire R. Co., 125 U. S. 555, 8 Sup. Ct. 974; Cornell University v. Fiske, 136 U. S. 152, 10 Sup. Ct. 775; Dundee Mortgage Co. v. Parrish, 24 Fed. 197.

only so far and in such cases as this latter rule can operate that the other has any effect.　If the construction put by the court of a state upon one of its statutes was not a matter in judgment, if it might have been decided either way without affecting any right brought into question, then, according to the principles of the common law, an opinion on such a question is not a decision.　To make it so, there must have been an application of the judicial mind to the precise question necessary to be determined to fix the rights of the parties and decide to whom the property in contestation belongs. And therefore this court and other courts organized under the common law has never held itself bound by any part of an opinion, in any case, which was not needful to the ascertainment of the right or title in question between the parties."[15]　If there is no decision by the courts of the state on the interpretation of a statute of the state, and nothing on which to found a practical construction, or if the decisions of the state courts are conflicting and the interpretation unsettled, then the federal courts will decide for themselves as to the true construction of the statute.[16]　And if the highest judicial tribunal of a state adopts new views as to the proper construction of a statute of the state, and reverses its former decisions, the federal courts will follow the latest settled adjudications.[17] But the rule that the courts of the United States must accept as binding the interpretation of a state statute by the courts of that state is subject to this exception, that in cases where the federal courts are called upon to interpret the contracts of states, they will not follow the construction adopted by the supreme court of the state in such a matter when they entertain a different opinion; and this, whether the contract alleged be claimed to be such under the form of state legislation, or has been made by a covenant or agreement by the agents of a state by its authority.[18]　"Since the ordi-

[15] Carroll v. Carroll's Lessee, 16 How. 275, 286.

[16] Gardner v. Collins, 2 Pet. 58; Sohn v. Waterson, 17 Wall. 596; Burgess v. Seligman, 107 U. S. 20, 2 Sup. Ct. 10; Myrick v. Heard, 31 Fed. 241; Southern Pac. R. Co. v. Orton, 32 Fed. 457.

[17] Leffingwell v. Warren, 2 Black (U. S.) 599; Green v. Neal, 6 Pet. 291; Suydam v. Williamson, 24 How. 427.

[18] Jefferson Branch Bank v. Skelley, 1 Black (U. S.) 436; Bridge Proprietors v. Hoboken Co., 1 Wall. 116.

nary administration of the law is carried on by the state courts, it necessarily happens that by the course of their decisions certain rules are established which become rules of property and action in the state, and have all the effect of law, and which it would be wrong to disturb. This is especially true with regard to the law of real estate and the construction of state constitutions and statutes. Such established rules are always regarded by the federal courts, no less than by the state courts themselves, as authoritative declarations of what the law is. But where the law has not been thus settled, it is the right and duty of the federal courts to exercise their own judgment, as they also always do in reference to the doctrines of commercial law and general jurisprudence. So, when contracts and transactions have been entered into, and rights have accrued thereon, under a particular state of the decisions, or when there has been no decision, of the state tribunals, the federal courts properly claim the right to adopt their own interpretation of the law applicable to the case, although a different interpretation may be adopted by the state courts after such rights have accrued. But even in such cases, for the sake of harmony and to avoid confusion, the federal courts will lean towards an agreement of views with the state courts, if the question seems to them balanced with doubt." [19] Where two or more states have adopted statutes in the same or substantially the same terms, but their courts differ in regard to the interpretation of the statute, the federal courts will administer the laws of each state, as therein construed, without regard to the apparent inconsistency which will result in their own decisions. In this event, such local statutes are treated as different laws, each embodying the particular construction of its own state, and enforced in accordance with it in all cases arising under it. [20] As a deduction from the general rule that the decisions of the supreme court of a state, interpreting a statute of such state, are binding on the federal courts, it has been held that where the supreme court of the United States, upon a mistaken view of the purport and effect of a decision of the supreme court of the state in

[19] Burgess v. Seligman, 107 U. S. 20, 2 Sup. Ct. 10.

[20] Shelby v. Guy, 11 Wheat. 361; Christy v. Pridgeon, 4 Wall. 196; Louisiana v. Pillsbury, 105 U. S. 278, 294; Randolph's Ex'r v. Quidnick Co., 135 U. S. 457, 10 Sup. Ct. 655; Bauserman v. Blunt, 147 U. S. 647, 13 Sup. Ct. 466.

such a case, renders a decision in conflict therewith, that decision is not binding on the state courts.[21]

CONSTRUCTION OF STATUTES OF OTHER STATES.

145. The construction put upon a state statute by the courts of that state will be accepted as correct, and followed, by the courts of another state, when called upon to interpret and apply the statute.[22]

If it does not appear that the particular statute has ever been judicially construed in the state of its origin, or if no proof is given of the interpretation given to it by the courts of that state, the courts of the state where the case is on trial will construe the statute as they would a like statute in their own state.[23] But in a case in Tennessee, where the court was called upon to interpret the Arkansas statute of frauds, as applicable to the contract in suit, which was made and to be performed in Arkansas, and no decisions of the Arkansas courts could be found construing the statute, but in New York, where that part of the statute was expressed in the same terms, it had received a judicial interpretation, the Tennessee court adopted the construction settled by the New York courts.[24] In Louisiana, it is said that while, in ordinary cases, the decisions of the courts of other states on their own statutes, not involving questions under the federal constitution, will be adopted as decisive, yet where they differ from the supreme court of the United States, the interpretation of the latter, if more in harmony with the Louisiana jurisprudence, will be adopted, and particularly when the matter is one which may be reviewed by the federal courts.[25]

[21] Goodnow v. Wells, 67 Iowa, 654, 25 N. W. 864.

[22] Blaine v. Curtis, 59 Vt. 120, 7 Atl. 708; Jessup v. Carnegie, 80 N. Y. 441; Savings Ass'n v. O'Brien, 51 Hun, 45, 3 N. Y. Supp. 764; Howe v. Welch, 17 Abb. New Cas. 397; Hoyt v. Thompson, 3 Sandf. 416; American Print Works v. Lawrence, 23 N. J. Law, 590; Lane v. Watson, 51 N. J. Law, 186, 17 Atl. 117; Van Matre v. Sankey, 148 Ill. 536, 36 N. E. 628; Johnston v. Southwestern R. R. Bank, 3 Strobh. Eq. 263; Carlton v. Felder, 6 Rich. Eq. 58; McMerty v. Morrison, 62 Mo. 140; Hamilton v. Hannibal & St. J. R. Co., 39 Kans. 56, 18 Pac. 57; Croocker v. Pearson, 41 Kans. 410, 21 Pac. 270.

[23] Smith v. Bartram, 11 Ohio St. 690; Bond v. Appleton, 8 Mass. 472.

[24] Anderson v. May, 10 Heisk. 84.

[25] Davis v. Robertson, 11 La. Ann. 752.

CHAPTER XVII.

INTERPRETATION OF JUDICIAL DECISIONS AND THE DOCTRINE OF PRECEDENTS.

THE NATURE OF PRECEDENTS.

146. In law, a precedent is an adjudged case or decision of a court of justice, considered as furnishing a rule or authority for the determination of an identical or similar case afterwards arising or a similar question of law.

Value and Importance of Precedents.

One of the best explanations of the value and importance of precedents to be found in the books is given by Chancellor Kent in the following terms: "A solemn decision upon a point of law arising in any given case becomes an authority in a like case, because it is the highest evidence which we can have of the law applicable to the subject; and the judges are bound to follow that decision so long as it stands unreversed, unless it can be shown that the law was misunderstood or misapplied in that particular case. If a decision has been made upon solemn argument and mature deliberation, the presumption is in favor of its correctness, and the community have a right to regard it as a just declaration or exposition of the law, and to regulate their actions and contracts by it. It would therefore be extremely inconvenient to the public if precedents were not duly regarded and implicitly followed. It is by the notoriety and stability of such rules that professional men can give safe advice to those who consult them, and people in general can venture to buy and trust and to deal with each other.   If judicial decisions were to be lightly disregarded, we should disturb and unsettle the great landmarks of property.   When a rule has once been deliberately adopted and declared, it ought not to be disturbed unless by a court of appeal or review, and never by the same court, except for very cogent reasons; and if the practice were otherwise, it would be leaving us in a state of perplexing uncertainty as to the law." [1]   In the same line of thought, Judge Cooley observes: "All judgments are supposed to apply the existing law to the facts of the case, and the reasons which are sufficient to influence the court to a particular conclusion in one case ought to be sufficient to bring it or any other court to the same conclusion in all other like cases where no modification of the law has intervened.   There would thus be uniform rules for the administration of justice, and the same measure that is meted out to one would be received by all others.   And even if the same or any other court, in a subsequent case, should be in doubt concerning the correctness of the decision which has been made, there are consequences of a very grave character to be contemplated and weighed before the experiment of disregarding it should be ventured on.   That state of things when judicial decisions conflict, so that a citizen is always at a loss in regard to his rights and his duties, is a very serious evil, and the alternative of accepting adjudged cases as precedents in future controversies resting upon analogous facts, and brought within the same reasons, is obviously preferable.   Precedents, therefore, become important, and counsel are allowed and expected to call the attention of the court to them, not as concluding controversies, but as guides to the judicial mind." [2]   A still stronger view of the binding nature of precedents is taken by Blackstone, where he says: "It is an established rule to abide by former precedents where the same points come again in litigation, as well to keep the scale of justice even and steady, and not liable to waver with every new judge's opinion, as also because the law in that case being solemnly declared and determined, what before was uncertain, and perhaps indifferent, is now become a permanent rule, which it is not in the breast of any subsequent judge to alter or vary from according to his private senti-

[1] 1 Kent, Comm. 475.   [2] Cooley, Const. Lim. 49.

ments, he being sworn to determine, not according to his own private judgment, but according to the known laws and customs of the land; not delegated to pronounce a new law, but to maintain and expound the old one." [3]

Opinion of the Court.

The reader should remember that it is the decision, that is, the judgment rendered in the case, and not the opinion of the court, which settles the point of law involved and makes the precedent. The decision is the conclusion of the court on the premises; the opinion sets forth the reasons of the determination, and usually states and explains them at greater or less length. The opinion, disclosing the reasons of the judge for his decision, is of course of great importance in the information it imparts as to the principles of law which influenced the court and were supposed to govern the case, and which should guide litigants. But even if there is no opinion written or filed, the decision is a precedent for the similar disposition of similar cases. In that event, its nature and exact scope are to be ascertained by examining the record, to find the precise point of law which it involved, and considering the judgment given thereon. [4]

Ratio Decidendi.

A case is to be cited as an authority for the particular proposition of law which was held to govern the rights of the parties and to determine the judgment which should be given. This proposition or doctrine of law is called the "ratio decidendi" of the particular case; that is, the legal reason which caused the case to be decided as it was decided. It may or may not be explicitly set forth in the opinion of the court. Sometimes it is assumed, and the reasoning of the court is directed to the application of the rule to the special state

---

[3] 1 Bl. Comm. 69. "The decisions of this court, while unreversed. always form the absolute law of the case, and enter with very decisive effect into the body of precedents. They must, from the nature of our legal system, be the same to the science of law as a convincing series of experiments is to any other branch of inductive philosophy. They are, on being promulgated, immediately relied on according to their character, either as confirming an old or forming a new principle of action, which, perhaps, is at once applied to thousands of cases. These are continually multiplying throughout the whole extent of our jurisdiction. Numerous and valuable rights, offensive and defensive, may be claimed under them." Bates v. Relyea, 23 Wend. 336.

[4] Houston v. Williams, 13 Cal. 24.

of facts before it. Sometimes the rule is categorically or broadly stated. But it is not the very words of the court, but the underlying principle of law, which fixes the position of the decision as an authority. Even if the opinion of the court should be concerned with unnecessary considerations, or should state the proposition of law imperfectly or incorrectly, yet there is a proposition necessarily involved in the decision and without which the judgment in the case could not have been given; and it is this proposition which is established by the decision (so far as it goes) and for which alone the case may be cited as an authority. The fact that a particular case was decided in a particular way is an argument to induce the courts to decide a similar case in a similar way, even though the judges, in the first case, imperfectly apprehended, or incorrectly stated, the legal reason which led them to their decision.[5] "Without minutely examining all the cases," says Lord Kenyon, "or saying whether I do or do not agree with them, it is sufficient for me to abide by the principle established by them; the principle is the thing which we are to extract from cases, and to apply it in the decision of other cases."[6]

Principles Assumed by the Court.

If the case could not have been decided as it was without the recognition and application of a given rule or principle of law, the decision is an authority for that rule or principle, although it may not have been expressly stated or mentioned by the court, but only tacitly assumed. This fact is referred to by the supreme court of Alabama in the following statement: "It was contended in the discussion of this case that the only point decided, or in the mind of the court, was that made in the argument. The result of that position would be to take from judicial decisions, where there is no opinion, the authority of an adjudication upon all propositions which were too plain or too well recognized by the bench and bar to be questioned; and thus the universal and undisputed sanction of a legal principle would become a barrier to proof by judicial decisions of its existence. It better accords with reason to regard a judicial tribunal as asserting, and intending to assert, every proposition which is indispensable to the conclusions expressed, and nec-

---

[5] See Austin, Jurisprudence (Campbell's edn.) § 908.
[6] Lord Walpole v. Earl of Cholmondeley, 7 Durn. & E. 138, 148.

essarily involved in it, at least when the contrary does not appear." [7] Perhaps this matter can be made more plain by a specific illustration. Let it be supposed that an appellate court reverses a judgment for plaintiff rendered in the court below, in an action for damages caused by the alleged negligent conduct of the defendant, the particular ground for the decision being that the evidence shows such contributory negligence on the part of the plaintiff as should have prevented a recovery. The fundamental principle of law involved in this decision is that, in actions of this character, the plaintiff cannot recover if it is shown that the accident would not have happened but for his own negligence. Unless this principle were recognized and applied, the appellate court could not render the decision it has rendered. Yet the principle may not be even mentioned in the decision. The opinion may be wholly taken up with a consideration of the facts in the case, as tending to prove or disprove contributory negligence. Nevertheless, the decision will be an authority supporting the general rule as to contributory negligence, because that rule was necessarily involved or implied in the judgment.

Questions not Raised or Decided.

Questions in a case which were not raised by the parties, not presented to the attention of the court, and not considered by the judges, are not concluded by the decision in the case, and the judgment is not an authority upon such questions, even though they are logically present in the case and might have been argued as affecting its decision, and even though such questions, if raised and deliberated upon, would have caused a different judgment to be given. [8]

---

[7] Bloodgood v. Grasey, 31 Ala. 575, 587.

[8] "It is not enough to afford a binding precedent for us that these questions may have been lurking in the record of a former case, and might have been raised and considered. If they were not considered, it is as if they were not in the case at all." State v. Pugh, 43 Ohio St. 98, 121, 1 N. E. 439. On the same principle, the question of the constitutionality of a statute is never concluded by any number of decisions construing the act and applying it to particular states of fact. "The fact that acts may in this way have been often before the court is never deemed a reason for not subsequently considering their validity, when that question is presented. Previous adjudications upon other points do not operate as an estoppel against the parties in new cases, nor conclude the court upon the constitutionality of the acts, because that

For example, if an appeal is taken from a judgment of conviction in a trial for murder, and numerous objections are urged and considered by the appellate court, including some objections to the form of the indictment, and the judgment is affirmed, this is to be considered as settling the law only as to those points which were so argued and considered.　If, afterwards, a question is raised as to the sufficiency of an indictment, which might have been raised in the former case, and which, if raised, would have caused the judgment below to be reversed instead of affirmed, but which in fact was not raised or thought of, the decision in the former case is not to be regarded as an authority to the effect that the indictment in that case was in all respects good and sufficient.　In other words, in the later case, the court is not precluded, by anything in the former case, from considering the question newly raised as still undetermined.[9]　The same principle applies to questions which the court expressly leaves open and undetermined, because it deems them unnecessary to the decision of the particular issue before it.

Hypothetical Cases.

It is the duty of appellate courts, as well as of those of first instance, to pass judgment only upon the cases actually before them. They have no jurisdiction to pronounce judgment on moot questions or hypothetical cases.　"If the judiciary were to assume to decide hypothetical questions of law not involved in a judicial proceeding before them, even though the decision would be 'of great value to the general assembly' in the discharge of its duties, it would, nevertheless, be an unwarranted interference with the functions of the legislative department that would be unauthorized and dangerous in its tendency.　Not only this, but it would be an attempt to settle questions of law involving the rights of persons, without parties before it or a case to be decided in due course of law, thus violating the provision of the Bill of Rights which declares that every person shall have a remedy for an injury done him by due course of law."[10]

point might have been raised and determined in the first instance." Boyd v. Alabama, 94 U. S. 645, 648.

[9] Fouts v. State, 8 Ohio St. 98, 123; State v. Pugh, 43 Ohio St. 98, 122, 1 N. E. 439.

[10] State v. Baughman, 38 Ohio St. 455, 459.

It follows from this that the court must consider the whole of the case actually before it, and only the case as it is presented by the record. It is true that appellate courts will sometimes rest their decision on a particular point emerging from the facts or pleadings in the case, where the determination of that special point is enough to show the disposition which must be made of the controversy. But in general, if the decision is based upon a state of facts which does not exist in the case, or upon a state of facts which is in part assumed or imagined by the court, or upon a mistaken conception of the issues in the cause, or upon certain elements of the case which are misleading unless considered in their relation to others not referred to, the decision made will not be entitled to the authority of a precedent, because it will be without jurisdiction, and therefore unofficial. Just as a trial court acts without jurisdiction if it assumes to go beyond the issues in the case and pass upon matters not submitted by the parties and not connected with the controversy raised by the pleadings, or to render a judgment or decree not invited or asked for by the litigants,[11] so it is with the decision of an appellate court where the opinion does not correlate with the questions actually raised by the record.

Immaterial Differences in Cases; Distinguishing Cases.

In order that the decision in one case should be available as a precedent for the decision of another case, it is not necessary that the circumstances of the two cases should be identical. Each case actually in the courts involves numerous facts or circumstances which may never be present in any other. But many of them may be immaterial to the rule of law announced in the case. If the point of difference between the two cases is such that its presence or absence could make no difference in the determination of the rule of law by which the case is to be governed, it is immaterial, and will not affect the authority of the former case as a precedent in the latter. But if there be a fact or circumstance in the former case which is not present in the latter case, and which is of such a nature that the former case could not have been ruled as it was had that fact or circumstance been absent, then the former case is not an authority for the decision of the latter. The ascertainment

---

[11] Munday v. Vail, 34 N. J. Law, 418; 1 Black, Judgm. § 242.

of such material points of difference, and the indication of their influence upon the decision to be rendered, is known as "distinguishing" cases.

Arguing from Analogy; Combining Cases.

One case which presents exactly the same state of facts with another is said to be "on all fours" with it. As already explained,
this absolute identity is not necessary to justify the application of
the one to the other as a precedent. One case is a direct precedent
for another if it involves the same question of law arising out of a
substantially similar state of facts. But it also frequently happens that a case may be decided strictly on precedent, although no
earlier case can be found which is on all fours with it or even a
direct precedent for it. For several cases, all dealing with the
same general topic, though with dissimilar aspects of it, may, by
their combination, establish a general rule which is broader than
the doctrine of any one of the cases taken by itself, and broad
enough to include the novel case to which it is to be applied. Let
it be supposed, for example, that it has been decided that an inscription painted on glass is admissible as documentary evidence in a
proper case, notwithstanding the nature of the substance and the
method of putting the writing upon it. Suppose further that a second case has made a similar decision with regard to an inscription
cut into wood, and that a third case has laid down the same rule
with reference to an inscription carved on stone. A case now arises
in which the question is as to the admissibility of an inscription
engraved on a gem or a ring. No one of the three previous cases is
identical with it. Yet those cases, taken together, may be considered as having settled the general rule that neither the substance
on which a document is inscribed nor the manner of the inscription
is material, so long as it is legible and sufficiently enduring in character. And this general rule is broad enough to include the case
on trial and to furnish a principle for its decision.[12]

Advisory Opinions by the Courts.

Under the general principle of the constitutional separation of the
three departments of government, the courts cannot be required to
render their opinions upon questions of law, except in cases actu-

[12] See 1 Whart. Ev. §§ 219, 220, 614.

ally before them. But in a few of the states, the constitutions empower the executive or legislative departments to demand the opinion of the supreme court, or of the justices thereof, upon important questions of law and upon solemn occasions. The effect of the opinions thus rendered, as precedents for the determination of similar questions, propounded in the same way or arising in the ordinary course of judicial administration, varies in the different states which have adopted this constitutional provision. In Massachusetts, it is said: "In giving such opinions, the justices do not act as a court, but as the constitutional advisers of the other departments of the government, and it has never been considered essential that the questions proposed should be such as might come before them in their judicial capacity." [13] Hence these advisory opinions are not regarded as precedents, in such sense that the court, as such, will feel obligated to adhere to them and follow them in controversies between private persons. "As we have no means, in such cases, of summoning the parties adversely interested before us, or of inquiring in a judicial course of proceeding into the facts upon which the controverted right depends, nor of hearing counsel to set forth and vindicate their respective views of the law, such an opinion, without notice to the parties, would be contrary to the plain dictates of justice, if such an opinion could be considered as having the force of a judgment binding on the rights of parties." [14] But in Colorado, on the other hand, where the constitution provides that "the supreme court shall give its opinion upon important questions upon solemn occasions, when required by the governor, the senate, or the house of representatives, and all such opinions shall be publis..ed in connection with the reported decisions of the court," it is held that the opinions have the force and effect of judicial precedents. The reasons are explained by the supreme court of that state, as follows: "By the express words of the corresponding provisions in each of the other states, the questions are limited to questions of law, and the justices, not the court, are to respond. These officers appear to be merely legal advisers, occupying much the same relation in this regard to their respective general assemblies as does the attorney gen-

---

[13] Opinion of the Justices, 126 Mass. 557.

[14] Opinion of the Justices, 5 Metc. (Mass.) 596. See, also, Green v. Comm., 12 Allen, 155; Answer of the Justices, 122 Mass. 600; Opinion of the Justices, 148 Mass. 623, 21 N. E. 439.

eral of Colorado to the state legislature. Their written responses, when questioned, are not always published in the reports. They are not pronounced by the court, and hence are not technically judicial decisions, nor do they necessarily constitute judicial precedents. In this state, on the other hand, the interrogatories are not expressly limited to questions of law, and it is the court, not the justices, that must answer. For obvious reasons, we hold that the intent could not have been to authorize questions of fact, but our responses must be reported, as are other opinions, and they have all the force and effect of judicial precedents." [15]

INTERPRETATION OF JUDICIAL DECISIONS.

147. The language of a judicial decision is always to be construed with reference to the circumstances of the particular case and the question actually under consideration; and the authority of the decision, as a precedent, is limited to those points of law which are raised by the record, considered by the court, and necessary to the determination of the case. [16]

"A law or rule of law made by judicial decisions," says Austin, "exists nowhere in a general or abstract form. It is implicated with the peculiarities of the specific case or cases, to the adjudication or decision of which it was applied by the tribunals; and in order that its import may be correctly ascertained, the circumstances of the cases to which it was applied, as well as the general propositions which occur in the decisions, must be observed and considered. The reasons given for each decision must be construed and interpreted according to the facts of the case by which those reasons were elicited, rejecting as of no authority any general propositions which may have been stated by the judge, but were not called for by the facts of the case, or necessary to the decision. The reasons, when so ascertained, must then be abstracted from the detail of circumstances with which in the particular case they have been implicated. Look-

[15] In re Senate Resolution, 12 Colo. 466, 21 Pac. 478. And see In re House Resolutions, 15 Colo. 598, 26 Pac. 323; In re Priority of Legislative Appropriations, 19 Colo. 58, 34 Pac. 277.

[16] Wright v. Nagle, 101 U. S. 791.

ing at the reasons so interpreted and abstracted, we arrive at a ground or principle of decision, which will apply universally to cases of a class, and which, like a statute law, may serve as a rule of conduct. Without this process of abstraction, no judicial decision can serve as a guide of conduct or can be applied to the solution of subsequent cases. For as every case has features of its own, and as every judicial decision is a decision on a specific case, a judicial decision as a whole, or as considered in concreto, can have no application to another and therefore a different case."[17]   To much the same effect is the following remark of Chief Justice Marshall: "It is a maxim not to be disregarded that general expressions in every opinion are to be taken in connection with the case in which those ex-

---

[17] Austin, Jurisprudence (Campbell's edn.) § 900. At the risk of some tediousness, we think it desirable to quote further on this point from this acute though eccentric writer. "The primary index to the intention with which a statute was made, or the primary guide for the interpretation of a statute, is the literal and grammatical sense of the words in which it is expressed. * * * But the primary index to a rule created by a judicial decision is not the grammatical sense of the very words or terms in which the judicial decision was pronounced by the legislating judge; still less is it the grammatical sense of the very words or terms in which the legislating judge uttered his general propositions. As taken apart or by themselves, and as taken with their literal meaning, the terms of his entire decision, and, a fortiori, the terms of his general propositions, are scarcely a clue to the rule which his decision implies. In order to an induction of the rule which his decision implies, their literal meaning should be modified by the other indices to the rule, from the very commencement of the process. From the very beginning of our endeavor to extricate the implicated rule, we should construe or interpret the terms of his entire decision and discourse by the nature of the case which he decided, and we should construe or interpret the terms of his general or abstract propositions by the various specific peculiarities which the decision of the case must comprise. For it is likely that the terms of his decision were not very scrupulously measured, or were far less carefully measured than those of a statute; insomuch that the reasons for his decision, which their literal meaning may indicate, probably tally imperfectly with the reasons upon which it was founded. And his general propositions are impertinent and ought to have no authority, unless they be imported necessarily, and therefore were provoked naturally, by his judicial decision of the very case before him. It is even unnecessary that the general grounds should be expressed by the judge. In which case, the only index is the specialties of the decision as construed by or receiving light from the nature of the case decided; an inference ex rei natura." Id. §§ 903-905.

pressions are used. If they go beyond the case they may be respected, but ought not to control the judgment in a subsequent suit when the very point is presented for decision. The reason of this maxim is obvious. The question actually before the court is investigated with care, and considered in its full extent. Other principles, which may serve to illustrate it, are considered in their relation to the case decided, but their possible bearing on all other cases is seldom completely investigated." [18]   A still more specific and detailed exposition of this principle is given by the court in Tennessee, in the following terms: "It may not be out of place here to remark, as the subject seems to be so often and by so many misunderstood, that the generality of the language used in an opinion is always to be restricted to the case before the court, and it is only authority to that extent. The reasoning, illustrations, or references, contained in the opinion of the court, are not authority, not precedent, but only the points in judgment arising in the particular case before the court. The reason of this is manifest. The members of a court may often agree in a decision—the final result in a case—but differ widely as to the reasons and principles conducting their minds to the same conclusion. It is then the conclusion only, and not the process by which it is reached, which is the opinion of the court and authority in other cases. The law is thus far settled, but no farther. The reasoning adopted, the analogies and illustrations presented, in real or supposed cases, in an opinion, may be used as argument in other cases, but not as authority. In these the whole court may concur or they may not. So of the principle concurred in and laid down as governing the point in judgment, so far as it goes, or seems to go, beyond the case under consideration. If this were not so, the writer of an opinion would be under the necessity in each case, though his mind is concentrated upon the case in hand and the principles announced directed to that, to protract and uselessly encumber his opinion with all the restrictions, exceptions, limitations, and qualifications which every variety of facts and change of phase in cases might render necessary." [19]   "When a proposition is laid down generally," says Ram, "and is meant to be a general proposition appli-

[18] Cohens v. Virginia, 6 Wheat. 264, 399. And see Holcomb v. Bonnell, 32 Mich. 6; Pass v. McRae, 36 Miss. 143, 148; Miller v. Marigny, 10 La. Ann. 338.

[19] Louisville & N. R. Co. v. Davidson County Court, 1 Sneed, 636, 695.

cable to a variety of cases, it is important nevertheless to bear in mind that though, as a general proposition, it may be right, yet there may be circumstances, which may constitute a case, in which the rule may not be capable of being applied." [20]

DICTA.

148. A dictum is an expression of opinion in regard to some point or rule of law, made by a judge in the course of a judicial opinion, but not necessary to the determination of the case before the court. It may be either put forth as the personal opinion of the judge who delivers the judgment of the court, or introduced by way of illustration, argument, or analogy, but not bearing directly upon the question at issue, or it may be a statement of legal principle over and above what is necessary to the decision of the controverted questions in the case.

149. Dicta may be entitled to respect, on account of the learning or general accuracy of the judge who pronounces them; but as they are not the judicial determinations of the court, they are never entitled to the force and effect of precedents.

In the common speech of lawyers, all such extra-judicial expressions of legal opinion are referred to as "dicta" or "obiter dicta," these two terms being used interchangeably. In strict propriety of language, however, there are several kinds of dicta, not differing in their lack of authoritative force, but differing in their nature or in respect to the manner of their introduction into judicial opinions.

An "obiter dictum" is a remark made or opinion expressed by a judge, in his decision upon a cause, "by the way," that is, incidentally or collaterally, and not directly upon the question before the court; or it is any statement of law enunciated by the judge or court merely by way of illustration, argument, analogy, or suggestion.[21] For example, if the case involves a question as to the law

[20] Ram, Legal Judgment, 99.
[21] See Lucas v. Comm'rs of Tippecanoe Co., 44 Ind. 524.

relating to married women, and the judge who delivers the opinion, arguing in support of the conclusion reached by the court, draws an analogy from the law of the contracts of infants, his statement on that point is obiter dictum, and the opinion cannot be regarded as an authority upon the point referred to.[22]

Dicta of another class are found in the books, which, though they have not hitherto borne a special name, might properly be called "dicta propria," that is, personal or individual dicta, the private opinions of the judge who delivers the opinion, not necessarily concurred in by the whole court, and not essential to the disposition of the case at bar. Dicta of this kind most commonly occur in the case of an opinion written by a judge who, though he concurs in the general decision as to the rules of law which must govern the case, is not willing to accede to all the reasoning which has led the court to the conclusion reached. But there are also numerous examples of such dicta delivered by a judge who speaks for the court on the general lines of the decision, but incidentally steps outside the record to express his individual views as to some point or question.

A third kind of dicta are those which embody statements of legal principle more broad or general than is necessary for the determination of the case before the court, or, after the specific questions involved have been decided, add superfluous expressions of opinion on points or questions not in the record, or lay down rules for similar or analogous cases. These are properly called "gratis dicta,"[23] because they make judicial assertions of law over and above what is needed for the particular case. It must be remembered that the

---

[22] "Dicta are opinions of a judge which do not embody the resolution or determination of the court, and, made without argument or full consideration of the point, are not the professed deliberate determinations of the judge himself; obiter dicta are opinions uttered by the way, not upon the point or question pending, as if turning aside for the time from the main topic of the case to collateral subjects." Rohrbach v. Germania Fire Ins. Co., 62 N. Y. 47, 58.

[23] "An extra-judicial opinion given in or out of court is no more than the prolatum or saying of him who gives it, nor can it be taken for his opinion, unless everything spoken at pleasure must pass as the speaker's opinion. An opinion given in court, if not necessary to the judgment given of record, but that it might have been as well given if no such or a contrary opinion had been broached, is not judicial opinion, nor more than a gratis dictum." Bole v. Horton, Vaughn, 360, 382.

question presented to an appellate court is always specific—whether a new trial should be granted or refused, whether the judgment of the court below should be affirmed or reversed, whether or not the writ of mandamus should issue, etc.   This question is the one to which the decision and opinion of the court should be directed, and, ordinarily, when this question has been decided, anything that follows is merely gratis dictum, because unnecessary to the decision of the case.[24]   A perfect example of a gratis dictum is found in the important case of Pennoyer v. Neff,[25] in the supreme court of the United States.   In this case, the question was as to the validity and effect of a judgment rendered in a state court, against a non-resident of the state, upon a constructive service of process and the attachment of certain property of his within the jurisdiction.   It was held that such a judgment, being otherwise regular, would bind the property attached, but not the person of the defendant nor any other property belonging to him, though found within the state. When this conclusion was reached, the case before the court was disposed of.   But Mr. Justice Field, who wrote the opinion, added: "To prevent any misapplication of the views expressed in this opinion, it is proper to observe that we do not mean to assert, by anything we have said, that a state may not authorize proceedings to determine the status of one of its citizens towards a nonresident, which would be binding within the state, though made without service of process or personal notice to the nonresident.   The jurisdiction which every state possesses to determine the civil status and capacities of all its inhabitants involves authority to prescribe the conditions on which proceedings affecting them may be commenced and carried on within its territory.   The state, for example, has absolute right to prescribe the conditions upon which the

---

[24] It should be noted, however, that after the court has decided that a judgment should be reversed and a new trial granted, it will often proceed to pass upon the various questions of law raised by the record, in order that the court below may be correctly guided in the further proceedings in the case. Although perhaps it was unnecessary to do more than point out some one radical error which would require the reversal of the judgment, yet such additional rulings on points of law are not, in the case we have supposed, to be regarded as dicta, for the reason that such points are within the case and are decided upon argument and the full consideration of the judges.

[25] 95 U. S. 714.

marriage relation between its own citizens shall be created, and the causes for which it may be dissolved." This, it will be seen, was purely gratis dictum; and it is none the less so because the statement thus made has been universally accepted as a valuable contribution to the case-law on the subject of the validity of decrees of divorce, and has come to be relied on as having practically the effect of a direct decision. Another form of gratis dictum lurks under the word "semble," so frequently found in the reports. This term is often used to preface a statement by the court upon a point of law which is not directly decided, when such statement is intended as an intimation of what the decision would be if the point were necessary to be passed upon. It is also used to introduce a suggestion by the reporter, or his understanding of the point decided when it is not free from obscurity.

The reason usually assigned for not conceding to dicta the weight and effect of precedents is that they are expressions of opinion upon some matter which may not have been argued at the bar, or duly brought to the attention of the court, or that they do not embody the mature and deliberate opinion of the judges.[26] But this is not the true ground. The test is whether the statement made was necessary or unnecessary to the determination of the issues raised by the record and considered by the court. If it was merely an illustration or argument, or a private view of the judge speaking, or superfluous and not needed for the full determination of the case, it was, so to speak, rendered without jurisdiction, or at least extrajudicial. Official character attaches only to those utterances of a court which bear directly upon the specific and limited questions which are presented to it for solution in the proper course of judicial proceedings. Over and above what is needed for the solution of these questions, its deliverances are unofficial. Now a statement of law makes a precedent, not because it emanates from a wise and learned man, but because it is laid down by a judge, in his office of judge, and speaking to a question brought before him as a judge. Hence it follows that dicta of all kinds, however maturely they may have been considered, or however correctly they may state the law, are not technically entitled to the weight of precedents, because not within the limits of official decision. In effect, the difference

26 State v. Clarke, 3 Nevad. 566.

between a dictum and a judicial precedent is the difference between an unofficial assertion of a principle of law and a decision of a controverted question.   To this effect speaks the supreme court of the United States in the following language: "If the construction put by the court of a state upon one of its statutes was not a matter in judgment, if it might have been decided either way without affecting any right brought into question, then, according to the principles of the common law, an opinion on such a question is not a decision.   To make it so, there must have been an application of the judicial mind to the precise question necessary to be determined to fix the rights of the parties and decide to whom the property in contestation belongs.   And therefore this court, as other courts organized under the common law, has never held itself bound by any part of an opinion, in any case, which was not needful to the ascertainment of the right or title in question between the parties." [27]   We must remark, however, that in some few jurisdictions, and particularly in Maryland, these views are not accepted.   It seems to be there considered that any ruling made by the courts upon due argument and consideration, whether necessary or unnecessary to the decision of the particular case, is entitled to be considered a precedent.[28]

It should also be remarked that a dictum, though not originally entitled to rank as a precedent, may eventually come to occupy a position hardly distinguishable from that of a direct adjudication. This happens when the dictum is regarded as embodying a particularly correct or forcible statement of legal doctrine, and is frequently referred to with approval.   This is illustrated in the dictum in Pennoyer v. Neff, above referred to.   Again, a dictum is sometimes made the starting-point for a line of direct decisions, which, notwithstanding the origin on which they rest, are too weighty, in their accumulated strength, to be overthrown.

[27] Carroll v. Carroll's Lessee, 16 How. 275.

[28] "In Maryland, it is usual to limit the judgment to the question of right involved in the issue. But where a question of general interest is supposed to be involved, and is fully discussed and submitted by counsel, the court frequently decides the question with a view to settle the law; and it has never been supposed that a decision made under such circumstances could be deprived of its authority by showing that it was not called for by the record." Alexander v. Worthington, 5 Md. 471. And see Michael v. Morey, 26 Md. 239.

Several Questions in the Case.

It is seldom that a case in an appellate court will be found to involve but a single question. More frequently, many distinct and separable propositions of law are argued by counsel and considered by the court. For instance, the same case may present a question as to the competency of a juror, a question as to the admissibility of certain evidence, and a question as to the correctness of certain instructions given to the jury. So, the constitutionality of a statute may be attacked on many different grounds. In many cases before the supreme court of the United States, a preliminary question as to jurisdiction is raised, as well as the main question on the merits. In such cases, it is generally considered that the decision is an authority on each and every point which, being really and substantially involved in the case, was considered by the court and passed upon, not by way of analogy or illustration, but as affecting the judgment to be given. On a narrower view, however, the exact weight of such rulings as precedents will depend upon the disposition which is made of the appeal or writ of error. If several points are urged against the judgment of the court below, but all of them are found in favor of the appellee, the decision is an authority on each of such points, because a finding on each of them was necessary to the disposition which was made of the case. If, on the other hand, all of the points are found in favor of the appellant, and the judgment is reversed, the decision cannot be regarded as an authority of the strongest kind on any of such points, unless the court specifies the ground for its judgment of reversal; because a finding against the judgment on any one of such points would be sufficient to require its reversal, and therefore the decision on the other points must be regarded as unnecessary to the determination of the case. If some of the points are ruled in favor of one party and some in favor of the other, the same principle applies. If the judgment is reversed, the decision on the points found in favor of the appellee is immaterial and not authority. If the judgment is affirmed, then the points found in favor of the appellant must be considered as of no importance, because if they were material, the judgment could not have been affirmed.

But by many of the courts this narrow and technical view is not regarded with favor. Thus, in a case in Wisconsin, a bill in equity was dismissed in the court below, and on an appeal, two points of law were raised and argued by counsel for the defendant: first, that the damages complained of by the plaintiff were incidental merely and not such as would entitle him to recover in any action; second, that, assuming that he could recover in a proper action, yet his bill in equity was properly dismissed, that not being an appropriate remedy. The appellate court ruled the first point in favor of the plaintiff; that is, it was held that he could recover damages in a proper form of action. It found the second point in favor of the defendant; that is, it was held that the bill in equity was properly dismissed. When the case came again before the appellate court, it was contended that so much of the former opinion as related to the plaintiff's right to recover in a proper action was merely obiter dictum, because the ruling on the second point, as to the dismissal of the bill in equity, was sufficient to dispose of the appeal, and rendered any other ruling in the case unnecessary. But it was said that the first point, as it had been fairly presented by the bill, urged and relied upon on the argument, and considered and deliberately passed upon by the court, was so far involved in the case that the opinion expressed with regard to it could not reasonably be called a mere dictum.[29]

If there were two or more points in a case, either of which was sufficient to determine the disposition which should be made of it, and the conclusion of the court is expressly based on one only of such points, the case is not an authority upon any other of the points involved, although the same may have been discussed and reasoned out by the court in the opinion. But the fact that a decision might have been put upon a different ground, existing in the case, does not place the actual decision upon a ground also arising, although less satisfactory, in the category of a dictum.[30] And when the record fairly presents two points upon the merits in a case, upon either of which the appellate court might rest its decision, and the court actually decides both, without indicating that it is intended to rest the judgment upon one rather than the other, it cannot be said that the decision upon either of those points is dictum.[31]

---

[29] Buchner v. Chicago, M. & N. W. R. Co., 60 Wis. 264, 19 N. W. 56.

[30] Clark v. Thomas, 4 Heisk. 419.

[31] Starr v. Stark, 2 Sawy. 603, Fed. Cas. No. 13,317.

STARE DECISIS.

150. The doctrine of adherence to judicial precedents is expressed in the maxim "stare decisis et non quieta movere."

151. This maxim means that when a point or principle of law has been once officially decided or settled, by the ruling of a competent court in a case in which it was directly and necessarily involved, it will no longer be considered as open to examination, or to a new ruling, by the same tribunal or those which are bound to follow its adjudications, unless it be for urgent reasons and in exceptional cases.

"The cases are extremely rare in which the judgment of the highest appellate court can be properly departed from, when the same legal question again arises before a court of the same government. If it shall be thought that an erroneous rule has been established by the adjudication relied on as a precedent, it is better that it should be changed by the legislature by an act which cannot retrospect, than that the courts should overturn what they have themselves established, and thus disappoint all who have acted upon the rule which had been considered settled. If this is so where an abstract rule of law, determined in a prior case, is sought to be applied to new facts, the reason is stronger where * * * a series of particular acts has been passed upon and held to produce a given legal result, and the same identical facts are again before the court between other parties." [32] "As it is a well-known maxim in politics and jurisprudence," says Lieber, "that the certainty of the law is next in importance to its justice,—and by certainty of the law we understand both that it be well defined, known, and unwavering, as also that its penalties fall with unerring certainty upon those who deserve them,—it becomes necessary that doubtful points, springing up from a new state of things, should, if once settled, be considered so, until a weighty reason induces us to deviate from the settled decision." [33]

[32] Towle v. Forney, 14 N. Y. 423.   [33] Lieber, Hermeneutics, 195.

Stare Decisis Distinguished from Principle of Res Judicata.

"A judgment, as to all matters decided thereby, and as to all mat-ters necessarily involved in the litigation leading thereto, binds and estops all parties thereto and their privies in all cases where the same matters are again brought in question.   Such is the doctrine of res judicata.   There is also the doctrine of stare decisis, which is of a different nature.   When a court has once laid down a prin-ciple of law as applicable to a certain state of facts, it will adhere to that principle and apply it to all future cases where the facts are substantially the same, and this it does for the stability and cer-tainty of the law." [34]   In effect the two principles differ in three main particulars.   First, as to the parties affected.   A judgment (unless it be in rem) is conclusive only upon the parties to the for-mer litigation and those who are in privity with them.   But a ju-dicial precedent will be applied by the courts without any regard to the parties, it being necessary only that their legal rights and relations should be substantially the same as those passed upon in the former case.   Second, they differ as to the nature of the ques-tions settled.   The doctrine of estoppel by judgment applies to controverted questions of fact, and prevents the re-examination of issues of fact once judicially settled in a court of competent juris-diction.   The rule of stare decisis has no relation to matters of fact, but is applicable when disputed questions of law have been officially settled and determined.   Third, while both these rules are directed to the same general end, namely, to put an end to liti-gation, they differ in the modes by which they seek to accomplish this purpose.   A judgment is held to be conclusive in order that the parties may not be at liberty to renew the same litigation at their pleasure.   The object is to put a definite end to each individ-ual controversy when a final judgment has been reached, so that it may not be indefinitely protracted in the courts.   The doctrine of stare decisis, on the other hand, seeks to prevent litigation in gen-eral, by rendering it unnecessary.   Its object is to impart such certainty and stability to the law that every man may be certified of the nature and extent of his various rights and legal relations, and may be enabled to govern his conduct in such a manner as to

---

[34] Moore v. City of Albany, 98 N. Y. 396, 410.

make it unnecessary for him to come before the courts either as plaintiff or defendant.

Limitations of Rule; Decision Manifestly Erroneous.

The rule of stare decisis is admitted to be subject to this limitation: If a prior decision is clearly erroneous, whether from a mistaken conception of the law or through a misapplication of the law to the facts, and especially if it is injurious or unjust in its operation, while no injurious results would be likely to flow from a reversal of it, it is not only an allowable departure from the rule of stare decisis, but it is the imperative duty of the court, to overrule it.[35] "The doctrine of stare decisis, like almost every other legal rule, is not without its exceptions. It does not apply to a case where it can be shown that the law has been misunderstood or misapplied, or where the former determination is evidently contrary to reason. The authorities are abundant to show that, in such cases, it is the duty of courts to re-examine the question."[36] The same idea was forcibly expressed by a learned judge in Pennsylvania, where, after laying down the general principle of adherence to judicial precedents, he observed: "Of course I am not saying that we must consecrate the mere blunders of those who went before us, and stumble every time we come to the place where they have stumbled. A palpable mistake, violating justice, reason, and law, must be corrected, no matter by whom it may have been made. There are cases in our books which bear such marks of haste and inattention that they demand reconsideration. There are some which must be disregarded because they cannot be reconciled with others. There are old decisions of which the authority has become obsolete, by a total alteration in the circumstances of the country and the progress of opinion."[37] But it is better, when prior decisions must be overruled, to hold that the reversal of the rules which they established shall not be allowed to retroact so as to overturn acts done and contracts made in good faith and in reliance on those decisions. Many of the courts are disposed to maintain this doctrine, and especially in the case where the earlier decision turned

[35] Paul v. Davis, 100 Ind. 422; Sydnor v. Gascoigne, 11 Tex. 449; Linn v. Minor, 4 Nevad. 462; Lieber, Hermeneutics, 208.
[36] Rumsey v. New York & N. E. R. Co., 133 N. Y. 79, 30 N. E. 654.
[37] McDowell v. Oyer, 21 Pa. St. 417, 423.

upon the construction of a statute or established a rule of property.[38]

Two Extremes to be Avoided.

The progress of the law and the just and accurate administration of its commands are not promoted either by a blind and unreasoning adherence to precedent or by a lax disregard of the settled principles. Between these two extremes, equally undesirable, the courts must find the path of safety and justice. The philosophy of moderation in this respect is very well explained by the supreme court of Pennsylvania, in an opinion from which we quote as follows: "That doctrine, though incapable of being expressed by any sharp and rigid definition, and therefore incapable of becoming an institute of positive law, is among the most important principles of good government. But like all such principles, in its ideal it presents its medial and its extreme aspects, and is approximately defined by the negation of its extremes. The conservatism which would make the instance of to-day the rule of to-morrow, and thus cast society in the rigid molds of positive law, in order to get rid of the embarrassing but wholesome diversities of thought and practice that belong to free, rational, and imperfect beings, and the radicalism that, in ignorance of the laws of human progress and disregard of the rights of others, would lightly esteem all official precedents and general customs that are not measured by its own idiosyncrasies, each of these extremes always tends to be converted into the other, and both stand rebuked in every volume of our jurisprudence. And the medial aspect of the doctrine stands everywhere revealed as the only practical one. Not as an arbitrary rule of positive law, attributing to the mere memory of cases higher honor and greater value than belong to the science and natural instinct and common feeling of right; not as withholding allowance for official fallibility and for the changing views, pursuits, and customs that are caused by, and that indicate, an advancing civilization; not as indurating, and thus deadening, the forms that give expression to the living spirit; not as enforcing 'the traditions of the elders' when they 'make void the law' in its true sense; nor as fixing all opinions that have ever been pronounced by official functionaries; but as yielding

---

[38] See Hardigree v. Mitchum, 51 Ala. 151. And see ante, p. 377.

to them the respect which their official character demands, and which all good education enjoins." [39]

Conflicting Decisions.

When two or more decisions upon the same point or question of law have been rendered by the same court in which the question again arises, or by a court whose decisions are binding upon the court which is called upon to solve the question, and such earlier decisions are found to be contradictory or conflicting with each other, the general rule is to follow the latest decision and disregard the other.   This is because the later case must be supposed to have overruled the earlier and to stand as the final expression of the court's opinion.   But the rule is not invariable.   There may be cases in which the earlier decision should be preferred.   If that case, in comparison with the later case, is seen to be more consonant to legal principle and right reason, or more correctly decided on the facts involved, or to have been more thoroughly argued at the bar and considered by the court, or, generally, to be the stronger and more satisfactory authority, the court may feel impelled to adopt and follow it, at the expense of overturning the later decision.[40]

DECISIONS ESTABLISHING RULES OF PROPERTY.

152. Where a decision or series of decisions has established or settled a rule of property, the rule will be adhered to by the same court, and by those which are bound to follow its adjudications, even though it may be erroneous, unless it is seen that the erroneous rule itself works more harm than could result from its reversal.

There are some questions in the law the final settlement of which is vastly more important than how they are settled;   and among these are rules of property, long recognized and acted upon, and under which rights have vested.   Accordingly, when a principle of law, doubtful in its character or uncertain in the subject-matter of

---

[39] Callender v. Keystone Mut. Life Ins. Co., 23 Pa. St. 474.
[40] See Ram. Legal Judgment, 242.

its application, has been settled by a series of judicial decisions and acquiesced in for a considerable time, and important rights and interests have become established under such decisions, the courts will hesitate long before attempting to overturn the result, notwithstanding they may think the previous authorities to be entirely erroneous.[41] "When a rule of property," says a court in New York, "has been once deliberately adopted and declared, it ought not to be disturbed by the same court, except for very cogent reasons; otherwise the community would never be able to deal with safety, and would be in a state of perplexing uncertainty as to the law."[42]

Among the various questions which may come before the courts, those relating to titles to real estate are probably the most important in this aspect; that is, it is especially in this department of the law that a wise and conservative adherence to precedents will benefit the best interests of the community. On this point we quote the following from an instructive opinion of the supreme court of Indiana: "The question at the threshold is whether a rule of property thus repeatedly declared by the court of last resort, after earnest contest, and, it must be supposed, upon the most careful deliberation, should be deemed open to further controversy. The repose of titles is important to the public. Upon the faith of these decisions, our people have for a considerable period of years invested their money in real estate, the titles to which they were thus again and again assured were not liable to be disturbed. There must be a just basis of confidence in the stability of judicial decisions somewhere in the history of a controverted legal question, when it may be confidently relied on that the question is settled. It is not always that the courts may freely inquire, in determining a case before them, what is the law. Sometimes investigation should stop when it is ascertained what has been decided on the subject. We think the doctrine of stare decisis should be applied to the question now presented. Such is its relation to the interests of our people, among whom real estate is so much an article of traffic, that it is not possible to estimate the extent of the evil which would follow a decision of this

---

[41] Yorks' Appeal, 110 Pa. St. 69, 2 Atl. 65; Dugan v. Campbell, 1 Ohio St. 115; Pyles v. Furniture Co., 30 W. Va. 123, 2 S. E. 909; Bennett v. Bennett, 34 Ala. 53; Reed v. Ownby, 44 Mo. 204; Cooley, Const. Lim. 52.

[42] Goodell v. Jackson, 20 Johns. 693, 722.

court now overruling Strong v. Clem [12 Ind. 37,] and the cases which followed it. If the doctrine of those cases be admitted to be wrong, it is yet quite obvious that it has already accomplished most of the harm that ever can result from it, while a change now would sow a wide crop of serious evils to the injury of those who are innocent, and who have purchased and sold real estate upon the faith of a doctrine declared by this court no less than half a dozen times within the last ten years." [43]   Such also is the case with regard to decisions settling the law upon the descent and distribution of estates. "Our law of descents," says the same court, "is not remarkable for precision and clearness, and vexatious questions are often occurring, requiring judicial interpretations of the statute. We cannot change a decision without producing confusion in titles, as the ruling made would necessarily relate back to the time the law came into force. But if the canon of descent, as determined by the court of last resort, is unjust, or even distasteful, the legislature can change the rule by a new statute without interfering with vested rights. As now constituted, however much we may differ from the opinions of our predecessors, we shall not introduce doubt and confusion in questions of property, by overruling the previous decisions of this court." [44]   Moreover, when judicial decisions may fairly be presumed to have become a settled rule of property, they should be upheld and maintained, not only as to the points necessarily involved and decided, but also as to the principles declared by subsequent cases to have been established by them. [45]   And thus a mere dictum, when it relates to such a matter as the validity of titles to real estate, may acquire the sanctity and inviolability of a rule of property, if it is accepted by subsequent decisions of the same court, not as a dictum but as an official precedent.

But even in regard to rules of property, the maxim of stare decisis is not an iron-clad rule. If it can be shown that the evil resulting from the principle established by a previous erroneous decision or series of decisions must be productive of greater mischief to the community than can possibly ensue from diregarding the

[43] Harrow v. Myers, 29 Ind. 470.
[44] Rockhill v. Nelson, 24 Ind. 422.
[45] Matheson's Heirs v. Hearin, 29 Ala. 210.

former rulings on the subject, it is the duty of the courts to over-rule the prior case or cases, and strike into the true path.[46]

Precedents not Settling Rules of Property.

It should be observed that while a judicious adherence to prece-dents is important in all cases, for the purpose of imparting stability and certainty to the law, the rule of stare decisis applies with special and peculiar force in the case of rules of property, and that this force is much moderated when the question is as to the continued enforcement of a judicial rule which cannot be made the basis of titles, contracts, or other vested rights. In the latter case, the for-mer adjudications should be followed unless plainly erroneous; in the former case, they should be followed even though they are plain-ly erroneous.[47] "The maxim stare decisis has greater or less force according to the nature of the question decided; there are many questions upon which there is no objection to a change of decision other than grows out of those general considerations which favor cer-tainty and stability in the law. These are questions where the de-cision did not constitute a business rule, and where a change would invalidate no business transactions conducted upon the faith of the first adjudication. As an illustration, take a case involving personal liberty. A party restrained of his liberty claims to be discharged under some constitutional provision. The court erroneously decides against him. The same question arises again. To change such a de-cision would destroy no rights acquired in the past. It would only give better protection in the future. The maxim in such a case would be entitled to but very little weight, and mere regard for stability ought not to be allowed to prevent a more perfect admin-istration of justice. But where a decision relates to the validity of certain modes of doing business, which business enters largely into the daily transactions of the people of a state, and a change of deci-sion must necessarily invalidate everything done in the mode pre-scribed by the first, there, when a decision has been once made and acted on for any considerable length of time, the maxim becomes im-perative, and no court is at liberty to change. Take a case involving the validity of certain modes of executing deeds or wills. A deci-sion is made and the people act upon it for years, executing all such

[46] Boon v. Bowers, 30 Miss. 246; Sutherland, Stat. Constr. § 316.
[47] See Sutherland, Stat. Constr. § 314.

instruments in the manner prescribed. After that, some one raises the question again, and contends that the first decision is erroneous. Admit it to have been so; would the court be justified in overruling it? Every man, whether lawyer or layman, would answer, no." [48] Another apt illustration of this difference is found in the work of Dr. Lieber, as follows: "If the courts decide a certain form of guaranty to be good, it is evident that men will hereafter use that form and rely upon it, and no court can subsequently declare it bad without the risk of great mischief, by making worthless existing contracts and obligations. But if the former decision had been that it was bad, the only practice that could be founded on such a decision would be a practice of abstaining entirely from the use of such a form; and a subsequent decision, reversing the former, and holding the form to be good, would do little if any harm." [49]

THE FORCE OF PRECEDENTS.

153. Not all decided cases possess the same value as authority or the same weight as precedents. There are various circumstances which may either strengthen or weaken the force of a decision in this aspect. Among the considerations which may thus affect the degree of respect to be paid to an adjudication (in instances where they are severally found to be applicable) the most important are the following:

(a) **The nature of the question decided.**

(b) **Whether the case is one of first impression or one of a series.**

(c) **Whether it is an isolated decision, or has been already followed, or is a leading case.**

(d) **Whether it is an ancient or a modern case.**

(e) **Whether the decision has been overruled, or criticised, or reversed by legislative action.**

(f) **Whether the judgment passed ex parte or was contested.**

---

[48] Kneeland v. City of Milwaukee, 15 Wis. 454, 692, per Paine, J., dissenting.
[49] Lieber, Hermeneutics, 315, Hammond's note.

(g) The degree of care and thoroughness with which the case was argued by counsel.

(h) The rank or reputation of the court or judge.

(i) The bias of the judge, if any.

(j) The opinion of the court, in respect to the character and cogency of its reasoning, its length and general character, and the character and applicability of the authorities cited.

(k) Whether the opinion is signed by a judge or is anonymous.

(l) Whether the decision was unanimous or proceeded from a divided court.

(m) The nature, accuracy, and fullness of the report of the decision.

Nature of Question Decided.

If the decision cited as a precedent involved the solution of a question with which the court that rendered it could not be supposed to be specially familiar, it will not be entitled to so great weight as in the converse case. Or if the case turned upon the construction of a local statute, or some peculiarity of local law, it will not be regarded as of much importance in a jurisdiction where similar conditions do not prevail. Moreover, "precedents in regard to questions of doubted jurisdiction, assumed and decided by the same court whose power is doubted, are of less value than those which occur in the decision of ordinary law cases. The court here forms a party, and the doctrine of stare decisis does not apply with equal force as in a proper law decision on a question of meum and tuum." [50] But it should be remarked that a decision of the court of last resort in the particular system, on the boundaries of its own jurisdiction, while it may be open to re-examination in the same court, is imperatively binding on all the inferior courts of the same system.

Cases of First Impression.

A case is said to be "of first impression" (or res nova or res integra) when it presents an entirely novel question of law for the decision of the court, and cannot be governed by any existing precedent. Such

[50] Lieber, Hermeneutics, 203.

a case may grow out of the necessity of construing a recently enacted statute, or may be based upon the alleged applicability of a familiar rule of law to a new state of facts, or may arise from the need
of adjusting the body of the unwritten law to the increasing com-
plexities of industrial and commercial development and the discov-
ery and application of new forces and agencies in the material world.
The opinion of the court in a case of first impression is not ranked
so high, in the scale of authority, as one which is supported by concurring decisions in the same or other jurisdictions. Its weight
must depend upon the soundness of the court's reasoning and upon
the correctness of the analogies which it brings to bear in support of
the conclusion, and which, in the absence of direct authorities, are
the chief arguments which can be adduced. Moreover, it is difficult,
if not impossible, to foresee the effect which the new decision may
have on the existing law and on the course of dealings under it.
But decisions in cases of first impression are entitled to respect, if
well reasoned, and may furnish the starting point of a long and im-
pregnable line of cases. And such a decision gains force and strength
with every succeeding decision which rests upon it and conforms to
its doctrine.[51]

Isolated Cases.

A single decision may constitute a precedent which the courts
will positively refuse to overturn. It may have settled a rule of law
so elementary, and so universally regarded as just, that the question has not again been brought into contention before the courts.
Or the single case, being generally acquiesced in and made the basis
of private dealings and the foundation of private rights, and never
doubted or overruled, may have established a rule of property which
the judicial tribunals will be reluctant to disturb.[52] But speaking
generally, isolation tends to weaken the force of a precedent. Every
decision increases in weight in proportion as it is relied upon and
followed in succeeding cases. On the other hand, the fact that a
given case has not been cited or followed tends to show (unless it is a
recent decision) that it has not been regarded as good authority.
Hence we may lay down the general rule that a single decision upon

[51] See 23 Amer. Law Rev. 170, article by Mr. Justice Miller on "The Use
and Value of Authorities."
[52] Davidson v. Biggs, 61 Iowa, 309. 16 N. W. 135.

any given point of law is not regarded as authoritative or conclusive as a precedent in the same degree that a series of decisions upon that point would be.[53] Especially where a prior decision rests upon an unsound basis or an erroneous application of principles, the courts will be much more willing to overrule it than to disturb a connected line of cases holding the same views.[54] "When a question arises involving important public or private rights, extending through all coming time, which has been passed upon on a single occasion, and that decision can in no just sense be said to have been acquiesced in, it is not only the right but the duty of the court, when properly called upon, to re-examine the questions involved and again subject them to judicial scrutiny."[55] A still more advanced view is taken by the supreme court of South Carolina in an opinion from which we quote as follows: "When the court is asked to follow the line marked out by a single precedent case, it is not at liberty to place its decision on the rule of stare decisis alone, without regard to the grounds on which the antecedent case was adjudicated. There are three elements that enter into the authority of a case claimed to stand as a leading case on the general principles of the law: first, the unanimity with which its judgment was pronounced; second, the fact that it has been followed; and third, the duration of time during which it has been openly followed or tacitly assented to. As, then, the authority of such a case is distinctly fortified by the next succeeding case, it is obvious that in the decision of the latter the solidity of the grounds of the former conclusion should be inquired into; for it is only where resort is had to the original sources, and a concurring result obtained, that the first decision can be said to be fortified by that which follows it. An original case could not possibly gain authority by a mere perfunctory following on the principle of stare decisis."[56]

[53] Duff v. Fisher, 15 Cal. 375.

[54] Garland v. Rowan, 2 Sm. & Mar. 617. In California, it is said that the doctrine of stare decisis should lead the court to conform its decisions to a principle of commercial law established all over the world, rather than to follow a decision of its own made a few years before, where such decision is a decided and probably injudicious innovation upon that principle. Aud v. Magruder, 10 Cal. 282.

[55] Pratt v. Brown, 3 Wis. 603.

[56] State v. Williams, 13 S. Car. 546.

Leading Cases.

A leading case is one which, being either the first to deal with a given rule or principle of law or the first to investigate and discuss the same with special care, thoroughness, and learning, has been generally accepted as definitely settling the law on that point, and has been subscribed to and followed in many subsequent decisions. Leading cases are regarded as possessing exceptional importance and authority in the law; and the overruling of such a case is a very rare and remarkable occurrence.

Ancient and Obsolete Cases.

That a case is of ancient date may either strengthen or weaken its authority. If it involved the same questions which are now raised, and the same grounds of decision are considered as applicable, the fact that the earlier decision has for so many years stood unchallenged, that it has been acquiesced in and accepted as good law, that it has become a rule of property,—these are considerations which add to its authority, and directly in proportion to its age. On the other hand, if no rule of property is involved, but the decision in the earlier case depended upon the existence of a state of society which is now obsolete, or upon views of public policy or the policy of the law which have now given place to entirely different opinions, its authority should be held to have evaporated, and it is not incumbent on the courts to submit to its doctrines.

Overruled and Criticised Cases.

If a decision has been expressly overruled, either by the same court which rendered it or by a court exercising appellate jurisdiction, it can of course no longer be cited as a precedent.[57] The latest utterance of the court, on any given point, constitutes the authority which is not to be departed from without cause; and the same is true of decisions overruled by necessary implication in a subsequent case. But here it is necessary to show, beyond reasonable question, that the two authorities were really and necessarily inconsistent rulings on a substantially similar state of facts. An exception, however, would probably be made in the case of a single decision, clearly erroneous, which should overrule a series of previous authorities or unsettle the established principles of commer-

[57] Bradshaw v. Duluth Imperial Mill Co., 52 Minn. 59, 53 N. W. 1066.

cial or statutory law.[58] If a decision has been subjected to adverse criticism, or to doubts as to its correctness, or if the court's disapproval of it has been manifested in a reluctance to extend its doctrine beyond the very narrowest limits consistent with its continued recognition, its authority will be seriously impaired though not entirely destroyed. Often the courts of one state will thus disapprove or doubt the decisions of another state. That fact will prevent their being used with effect in the state where such criticism has been expressed; but adverse comment upon a case, made in a foreign state, does not usually impair the authority of the decision in the state where it was rendered. Where a rule of law has been settled by the decisions of the courts, but afterwards the legislature changes it by direct enactment, the authorities which announced it are no longer of any force or authority as precedents, though they may be used, in other jurisdictions, as evidence of what the law was before the interference of the legislature.[59]

Ex Parte Decisions.

A decision made upon an ex parte application or an uncontested proceeding is not regarded as being entitled to the same weight and authority as one which follows upon a contested suit. The reason is that in the latter case the points involved in the case are thoroughly brought into prominence and before the mind of the court, the questions implicated in the case are argued and discussed, and the judgment of the court is enlightened and its decision influenced by the exhaustive examination of both sides of the case and by the reference to pertinent authorities; whereas, in the former case, only one side is examined and discussed, and that usually with less thoroughness and care than in adversary proceedings. If no one is interested in opposing the judgment asked for, the court hears none of the reasons which avail against it, and which, if duly considered, might bring about a different result.

Arguments of Counsel.

The opinion in a case gains in weight and authority, and hence in importance as a precedent, in proportion as the point was the more fully discussed, more completely considered and comprehend-

[58] 25 Amer. Law Reg. (N. S.) 748.
[59] Lemp v. Hastings, 4 Greene (Iowa) 448.

ed by the court, and more elaborately elucidated in its judgment. Since it is the office of the briefs and arguments of counsel to bring to the knowledge of the court the precise questions involved in the case and the authorities in accordance with which they are to be decided, and since the arguments at the bar tend to explain and develop such points and questions, it is generally considered that an opinion in a case which was well and fully argued is entitled to more respect and authority than one which received little or no such attention. For a similar reason, if the decision should turn on a point not raised or argued by counsel, it is considered less valuable as an authority, and more easily to be disregarded, than where the reasoning and conclusions of the court are addressed to the very questions raised by the arguments at the bar.[60]

Rank or Reputation of Court or Judge.

The value of an authority depends, to a very considerable degree, upon the rank of the court which rendered the decision. The judgments of the inferior courts, whether of the same or another state, are not generally regarded as possessing much weight. The reasons for this comparatively low estimate of their importance will be explained hereafter. On the other hand, the decisions of the supreme court of the United States, even in cases where they are not technically binding on the state courts, are received by the latter with the very greatest respect. And so, when English cases are cited in our courts, their authority is esteemed in proportion to the rank of the court from which they proceed, much greater deference being paid to the rulings of the court of last resort than to those of a nisi prius court. And aside from the relative rank of the court, much may depend upon its reputation for learning, consistency, and sound judgment. Thus, it is said by Mr. Justice Miller: "It is obvious that in the courts of states where, by reason of great cities, the commerce is extensive and the moneyed transactions of great value, the commercial law is of supreme importance, and the decisions are of commanding weight. So also there are states in which the purity of the separate jurisdiction in equity has been preserved far beyond that of others, and this adds to the authority of their decisions in such cases. There also may be, and there probably are, courts in which the land laws have attained a uniformity

---

[60] 23 Amer. Law Rev. 170, article by Justice Miller, ut sup.

of administration rendering the decisions in regard to land titles of superior value. Then there are courts of the states which have long preserved their character for ability, care, and labor, and in regard to which it is sufficient to say at once that this is a case decided by the supreme court of Massachusetts, of New York, of Pennsylvania, or of South Carolina in her best days, to demand for it at once the consideration of the court." [61] And again, by the same eminent writer it is said: "While the main value of the authority of adjudged cases is in the character of the court which decided them, it often occurs that this value is very much enhanced by the standing of the judge who delivered the opinion. If he be a man who has attained high reputation as a jurist, as a judge, as a law-writer; if he be one of those members of the legal profession who stands out prominently as a leading man of the times in the law, or in any particular branch of it, this character in the man from whom the opinion emanated is often of more value than the character of the particular court which may have made the decision." [62]

Bias of Judge.

Although the courts steadily refuse to adjudicate questions of a political nature, it will sometimes happen that the decision in a case may turn upon the political aspects of an act of legislation, or the balance may incline, in a doubtful case, according to the political prepossessions of the members of the court. So also, views of statecraft, opinions in political economy, specialized modes of legal thinking, or other personal bias, may indirectly and unconsciously warp the judgment of a just and impartial judge to such an extent as to make his decision no true exponent of the law but a merely personal opinion. Criticism of decided cases on this ground is always permissible, if honest, but should not be allowed to detract from the weight of the decision as an authority unless the facts showing the bias of the judge are notorious and their influence upon the judgment is unmistakable.

Opinion of the Court.

As between a higher and a lower court of the same system, the decision of the former is binding and conclusive on the latter, as a precedent, in all cases where it is applicable, without inquiry into

---

[61] 23 Amer. Law Rev. 172.   [62] Id. p. 167.

the soundness of the views expressed or the correctness of the decision rendered. But when a court is asked to reconsider a rule formerly established by its own decisions, or when a decision of one court is cited as an authority to another court of a different system, the degree of respect to be paid to the precedent will depend largely upon the care and thoroughness with which the case was considered, and the logical correctness and legal soundness of the reasoning which led the court to its conclusions. To test a decision in these respects, we are to look to the reported opinion of the court. There are numerous particulars in which criticisms may be passed upon such opinions, whereby the authority of the decision may be impugned in the respects above indicated.

Same; Defective and Illogical Reasoning.

If the opinion embraces no more than a mere statement of the conclusions reached by the court, or a direction as to the disposition to be made of the case, without anything to indicate the course of reasoning which induced the decision to be made, it is in general unsatisfactory and not entitled to much weight as a precedent. For in that case we are unable to judge whether the case received a thoughtful attention and thorough investigation, such as to make the decision the result of the deliberate and reasoned judgment of the court. But there are exceptions to this principle. For instance, in those cases where the decision turns upon the application of a well-known rule of law to a particular state of facts, the mere judgment of the court that such rule was or was not applicable, without argumentation, may be weighty as a precedent for the decision of a future case based upon the same or similar facts. If the reasoning of the court is given in the opinion, but is found to be faulty, the force of the conclusion reached, as a precedent, is weakened. Faults of this kind may include violations of the ordinary rules of logic, as where a conclusion is based upon unfounded assumptions or is drawn from insufficient premises, or may consist in the disregard of the principles of legal dialectics, as where a rule is attempted to be supported upon a false analogy or a misconception of the spirit and policy of the law.

Same; Length and Character of Opinion.

More respect is naturally paid to an opinion in which the questions of law involved are fully and amply discussed and in which the conclusions reached are supported by an exhaustive examination of the legal principles concerned, than to one in which the court is contented with a hasty review of the case and a brief statement of its views.   In the latter case, there is always ground to suspect that the question did not receive that careful and thorough investigation which alone can produce an entirely satisfactory precedent for the determination of other similar cases.   Yet mere diffuseness adds nothing to the strength of an argument in law.   A rambling discussion may show that the court failed to grasp the precise questions which it was called upon to solve; while a well-reasoned opinion, confined strictly to what is necessary to be decided, gains force from its terseness.   It should also be remarked that when an opinion merely recognizes and reaffirms an already accepted rule or principle of law, it is respected as a cumulative authority on that point, although there may be no review of the reasoning which led originally to the establishment of the doctrine.

Same; Citation of Authorities.

Since the great mass of cases now before the courts are not cases of wholly first impression, but call only for the application of the established rules of law to particular states of fact, the character and applicability of the authorities cited in an opinion is an important point to be considered in judging of its value as a precedent.   If the opinion makes no reference to decisions of the courts or other authorities, where such authorities could have been discovered and applied, it is not only open to the criticism that the court could not have given the question a careful examination, but it also loses the force which it might have acquired by the support of pertinent precedents, either concurring in the conclusions reached or conducing thereto.   A well-reasoned opinion is like a strong wall; but a well-reasoned opinion fortified by the citation of well-considered and applicable authorities is like a strong wall made more firm by the support of buttresses.   On the other hand, if the opinion shows that the court relied on the authority of decisions which are found to be themselves ill-considered, obsolete, discredited, or overruled, its decision loses force in proportion as it depended upon such unreliable sources.   And the same is true if the decisions relied on can be shown to have been misunderstood by the court citing them.   If the court bases its conclusions wholly or in part upon what it supposes to have been the doctrine of a former case, whereas such former case in reality decided no such thing, then, in so far as the judgment was influenced by the mistaken conception of the former case, it is without value.   Still, it may be that the reasoning of the judge is itself so sound, logical, and consistent, that the opinion may be entitled to great respect, notwithstanding the citation of inappropriate or untrustworthy cases.   And in particular, with reference to reliance placed upon overruled cases, it must be noticed that the effect is different according to whether the discredited case was ruled by the same court or proceeds from a different jurisdiction.   Cases decided in one state are not conclusive authorities in another state, but they are respected for their reasoning and correct views of the law.   If, now, such a case has been followed in a state other than that in which it was decided, and is afterwards overruled at home, it does not follow that the opinion which relied upon it must also be discredited as an authority.   The question will then be whether the original decision or that which overruled it is the more worthy of respect and adherence.   If the court which followed the original ruling should be of opinion that it was right, and that the overruling case was not correctly decided, it will be justified in adhering to its own decisions.

While no court is bound to notice or refer to all the decisions which may have been made on the general subject to which its decision relates, yet, as it gains force by referring to pertinent and well-reasoned concurring authorities, so also it loses force if it overlooks contrary decisions made at home or abroad.   If there are, in the same state or system, previous authorities which are inconsistent with the conclusion at which the court arrives, it is a safe inference that no exhaustive search was made for illumination upon the question at issue; and in this case the force of the authority is further diminished by the reflection that the authorities, if they had been discovered and referred to, would have put the court to the necessity either of overruling its previous decisions or else deciding the case at bar in a different manner.[63]   If a particular de-

[63] A decision is not of high authority when it is found that it was contrary to a prior decision of the same court, which earlier case was unknown to counsel by whom the later case was argued and not noticed by the court itself. Smith v. Doe, 2 Brod. & B. 473, 593.

cision is opposed to the preponderance of authority in other jurisdictions, but is consciously so, it may be respected for the vigor or
acumen of its reasoning, and may even be influential in bringing about
a change of opinion.   But if it is rendered without any reference
to the fact of such a body of opposing authorities, and without anything to show that the court was even aware of their existence, it
is entitled to no respect.   For it is possible that if the court had
been directed to the authorities contravening its own view, and had
carefully considered them, it might have been influenced to an entirely different conclusion.   But of course this remark does not apply to a case where the court merely follows a settled line of precedents in its own state, or decides a question of purely local law.

If it should be found that the court had taken its authorities at
second hand, by relying upon the statement of them made in text-
books or digests, and that they are really inapplicable or erroneous,
the opinion will lose force, not only by reason of the citation of
worthless cases, but also for the evidence of a lack of care and thoroughness which such a method of proceeding would disclose.   Reliance placed upon the opinions of text-writers or commentators,
where such opinions are private and personal and not founded upon
the authorities, will naturally add no force to the opinion, even if
it does not detract therefrom.

Anonymous and Per Curiam Decisions.

An anonymous opinion (that is, one not professing to have been
written by any particular judge, but to be promulgated by the whole
court, or "per curiam") is not entitled to the highest respect as a
precedent.   Such per curiam opinions are very seldom given forth
in any case which is considered by the court to possess inherent difficulty or great importance.   Hence they indicate that while the
court gave sufficient attention to the case to decide the rights of
the parties with justice and to its own satisfaction, it did not consider that the case demanded an exhaustive discussion of legal principles or a detailed examination of the authorities.   Moreover, the
natural inclination of a judge writing a per curiam opinion is to
devote to it less care and elaboration than would be demanded of
him by an opinion bearing his own name.   Still, such an opinion
is as much a judgment of the whole court as any other.   And it
may frequently be used with effect as showing that the principle of

law which it applied to the facts of the case, and in support of which it is cited, was deemed by the court to be so plain or so well settled as to require no discussion or elucidation.[64]

Unanimity and Dissent.

An opinion concurred in by the whole bench is naturally of higher rank and value than one from which one or more of the judges dissent.[65] As respects the lower courts of the same system, a decision accompanied by such dissent is as conclusive as any other, being a decision of a majority of the court. As respects the court which rendered it, it is more open to attack and more easily overruled than a unanimous opinion, both because the fact of dissent weakens the force of the precedent and because, if the dissenting judges remain on the bench, they will naturally retain their opinion and be ready to vote for a reversal of the decision. In other jurisdictions, the value of such an opinion depends very largely upon the number of judges who dissented, upon their personal reputation for learning and ability, and upon the force and character of the dissenting opinion as compared with that of the majority. It will often happen that a dissenting opinion is so well-reasoned, so well sustained by authorities, and so much more in harmony with the spirit and reason of the law, as to destroy, almost wholly, the value of the majority opinion as a precedent; and in extreme cases, it may even come to pass that the dissenting opinion will be cited and respected as an authority, while the majority opinion is discredited. If the dissent extends only to some particular point or points, it has no effect upon those other points, material to the issue, upon which the court is not divided. It may even tend to strengthen the opinion as to those points, by showing that full and careful deliberation was given to the entire case.

Judgment of Equally Divided Court.

When the judges of an appellate court are equally divided in opinion as to the disposition to be made of a case, the judgment of

---

[64] In Pennsylvania, it is judicially laid down that a per curiam opinion is the opinion of the court in a case in which the judges are all of one mind, and so clear that it is thought unnecessary to elaborate it by an extended discussion. Such an opinion is not entitled to less weight, as an authority upon the questions involved, than any other. Clarke v. Western Assurance Co., 146 Pa. St. 561, 23 Atl. 248.

[65] Bentley v. Goodwin, 38 Barb. 640.

the court below will be affirmed.   This is because the party who prosecutes an appeal or writ of error must assume the burden of satisfying the appellate tribunal that the inferior court rendered an erroneous judgment; and unless he induces a majority of the judges to hold this view, he has not made out his case.   Such a judgment of affirmance is as binding on the parties to the particular litigation as one rendered by the entire court.   But it is not regarded as settling the questions of law involved for the purposes of any other or subsequent suit.   It is not to be cited or relied on as a precedent.[66]

Judges Absent or not Participating in Opinion.

It sometimes happens that one or more of the judges of an appellate court will refrain from joining in the decision of a case or in the opinion, either because they were not present at the argument, or because they considered themselves disqualified from passing judgment on the case, by reason of having been formerly of counsel in the litigation or as being personally interested in the result.   This circumstance should not ordinarily weaken the force of the decision as an authority.   Even though the judgment should thus be rendered by a bare majority of the court, it still stands as the decision of the court, not of the individual judges.   The case is different from that of a dissent.   For it cannot be known whether the judges who abstained from participating in the decision would have entertained a different opinion from that of the rest, or would have concurred in the conclusions reached by them.   But there are some rare instances in which there are both dissenting opinions given and an abstention on the part of others of the judges from any participation in the decision.   When this combination occurs, the judgment may actually be cast by a minority of the court; and although such a judgment is as binding on the parties concerned, and on the inferior courts of the same system, as a unanimous opinion would have been, yet it is generally regarded as of less weight and value as a precedent.[67]   For example, the celebrated "Chicago Lake Front

[66] Etting v. Bank of United States, 11 Wheat. 59; Bridge v. Johnson, 5 Wend. 342; Morse v. Goold, 11 N. Y. 281.

[67] In a recent case in Virginia, it is said that where, in the absence of two justices of a bench of five, a case is decided on the written opinion of two justices, and the concurrence of the third in the result only, and it is probable

Case" was decided on the opinion of four out of the nine judges who compose the supreme court of the United States, less than a majority. The reason was that two of the judges, on account of interest, took no part in the decision of the cause, and three dissented.[68]

Judges Concurring in Result Only.

If all or a majority of the judges concur in the result (as that a new trial should be granted, that the judgment of the court below should be affirmed, that the writ prayed should issue) but differ as to the reasons which lead them to this conclusion, the case is not an authority, except upon the general result.[69] For if one judge announces certain rules, principles, or doctrines of law as the reasons which incline him to the decision to be made, and another is induced to the same end by a different view of the rules, principles, or doctrines, it cannot be said that any one of the rules considered, or any one of the steps in the reasoning, has received the assent of the court, but only that it is supported by the opinion of the particular judge.

It sometimes happens that the opinion of the court (that is, of the majority) is written by a judge who dissents from it or who concurs only in the general result. In this case, the authority of the case

---

that the latter assents on other grounds, the principle on which such written opinion is based is not a precedent under the rule of stare decisis. Whiting v. Town of West Point (Va.) 14 S. E. 698. And see Ram, Legal Judgment, 48.

[68] Illinois Cent. R. Co. v. Illinois, 146 U. S. 387, 13 Sup. Ct. 110.

[69] City of Dubuque v. Illinois Cent. R. Co., 39 Iowa, 56. In Oakley v. Aspinwall, 13 N. Y. 500, it is said: "It is urged in favor of a reversal that the judges of this court were not unanimous in pronouncing the former decision, and that those who concurred in the result were inharmonious in the reasoning which brought them to the same conclusion. However this may be, the precise question then passed upon was the very one now before us. There was but one point then before the court, and there is but one now. * * * The modes of reasoning among the judges may have been different, but their conclusion was united and single." The supreme court of Nebraska declares that it is an unwritten rule of that court that the members thereof are bound only by the points stated in the syllabus of each case. Each judge, in the body of an opinion, necessarily must be permitted to state his reasons in his own way, without binding the members of the court to assent to all such reasoning, although they may concur in the conclusions reached. Holliday v. Brown, 34 Neb. 232, 51 N. W. 839.

is diminished by the consideration that the personal opinion of the author of the opinion will almost invariably interfere with his full and forcible statement of the opinions of the rest of the judges.

Reports of Cases.

The precedent in any given case is made by the decision of the court in that case. The evidence of the decision is the report of the case. It is true that in a strict sense the written opinion of the court, if any was filed, is the best evidence of the decision made. But the original opinions, or authenticated transcripts of them, are now very seldom cited in our courts. Hence in a general sense we may say that it is by the reports that precedents are brought to the knowledge of the profession and made available for the purposes of litigation. Still it is important to remember that it is the ruling of the court—the disposition which was made of the case—which establishes the precedent, and not the report. Hence, even though a given case should never be reported at all, and even though there should be no written opinion of the court, still the fact that such a case was decided in such a manner is a precedent for a similar disposition of a similar case. It may be difficult, in that event, to prove the fact of the former ruling. But it is not unusual for counsel to refer the court to its own rulings made in cases alleged to be similar to the case on trial, where such rulings rest only in the recollection of the court and counsel. Courts have also been known to decide cases before them on the authority of an unreported but remembered prior decision. In some of the states, it is the rule or custom that only those decisions of the appellate court shall be included in the official series of reports as are specially designated for that purpose by the judges. None the less, all the decisions are precedents, and may be cited and relied upon, unless some rule of court restricts the sources of information which may be referred to in briefs and on arguments.

Those volumes of reports which are prepared by the reporters appointed by the courts, and published under authority, are commonly styled "official." There are many other reports of the decisions of most of the courts of last resort, some found in regular though unofficial series, others in legal journals and professional periodicals of various sorts. Bearing in mind that the decision establishes the precedent, and the report only evidences it, it will be perceived that nothing is added to the weight of a precedent by the fact that the account of the case is found in an official report.   The question is always as to the accuracy, completeness, and reliability of the report, and the skill, judgment, and learning of the reporter. When written opinions were not filed, and the report of the decision had to be made from hearing the argument and the deliverances of the judges, much depended upon the opportunities which the particular reporter enjoyed to gain a full knowledge of the case and of the judgment.   But at present, when practically all the reports are founded on printed records and arguments and the written opinions of the courts, this question is of little importance; and the value of the particular report will principally depend upon its completeness and the judgment of the reporter in stating the facts and pleadings and in making the syllabi or head-notes.

Since the exact value of a given precedent, and its exact scope, can be ascertained only by a complete understanding of the precise question or questions presented to the court, and of the rulings made thereon and the reasons by which they were supported, it is evident that the worth of a report, as evidence of the precedent, will greatly depend upon its completeness.   Scanty, incomplete, or partial reports of cases are therefore discredited in the courts, not because the precedents which they established may not be entitled to respect and authority, but because, from the nature of the evidence, it is not possible adequately to determine what the precedent precisely was.   These remarks are not generally applicable to modern reports of cases, at least when found in the books of authority or in professional journals; but many of the cases in the older volumes of the English reports are open to this objection, and are an unsafe reliance, for the reason that the arguments of counsel and the oral decisions of the courts are so imperfectly narrated that it is difficult to ascertain the precise nature of the problem before the court for adjudication.   The same observation applies to that form of report which attempts merely to give a synopsis of the decision, without the full opinion of the court, or a bare statement of the rule of law supposed to be established or applied.   Since the language of the judges, and indeed the decision itself, is always to be restricted to the very needs of the case before them, and cannot be relied on as a precedent except in so far as the decision was necessary to the determination of that case, it is very evident that such epitomes may embrace too broad a generalization or lay down a rule of law in terms much wider than the facts of the case would warrant.[70]

It is principally for this reason that reports of cases in the newspaper press are not regarded as of high authority or worthy of much reliance. They cannot be expected to recount all the features of the case with the accuracy and detail of a professional report, and moreover they are seldom, if ever, made by trained and skilled reporters. Newspaper reports of cases cannot be cited at all in the English courts; and in this country, while a court would not refuse to listen to such a report if no other could be discovered, yet it would not be admitted to possess authority or to furnish fully satisfactory evidence of the precedent established by the case reported.[71]

If the same case is reported by several reporters, or in several series of reports, and if the reports differ, in respect either to the statement of the case or the rulings made by the court, the authority of that case as a precedent is diminished, by reason of the conflicting evidence as to the points decided. In such circumstances, it is sometimes possible to discriminate between the different reporters, conceding a higher degree of authority to one than to another, and sometimes the intrinsic evidence will show that one of the reports is more complete or more credible than the others. But unless such a distinction can reasonably be made, the authority of the case suffers.

[70] Much valuable learning on the character and reliability of the older reporters is collected in the work of John William Wallace on "The Reporters."

[71] Townsend, in his edition of Ram on Legal Judgment (page 173), says: "The writer once cited a decision of Judge Nelson from a newspaper report, and the court [New York court of appeals] not only listened to it, but referred to it in the opinion, and stated a concurrence with 'the views ascribed to Mr. Justice Nelson.'" Stevens v. Hauser, 39 N. Y. 305.

AS BETWEEN FEDERAL AND STATE COURTS.

154. The courts of the United States are ordinarily bound to follow the precedents established by the decisions of the courts of a state in respect to the construction of its constitution and laws, and where such decisions have become a settled rule of property, and also upon questions of local law or custom, no federal question being involved. In other cases, they will accord to such precedents a due measure of weight and influence, but will not be bound by them.

155. Where the question in a case arises under the constitution, laws, or treaties of the United States, the state courts will be imperatively bound to follow the decisions of the supreme court of the United States, if any are found to be applicable to the case on trial. In other cases, they will yield great respect to the determinations of that court, but will not be absolutely concluded by its decisions.

The extent to which the federal courts will feel themselves bound to follow the precedents established by the decisions of the state courts has already been pointed out, with special reference to questions concerning the interpretation of state constitutions and statutes.[72] It may now be further stated that substantially the same rules apply in the case of decisions which have settled a rule of property (more particularly concerning the law of real estate) and in regard to those which have been occupied with the solution of questions arising out of peculiarities of local law or usage, where no question arises under the federal constitution or laws.[73] The cases in which the federal courts consider themselves as entirely independent of the judicial decisions of the states may be summarized as follows: First, where such decisions are inconsistent with the decisions of the supreme court of the United States on ques-

---

[72] See ante, pp. 378–380.
[73] Burgess v. Seligman, 107 U. S. 20, 2 Sup. Ct. 10.

tions of constitutional law, or involve a construction of the federal constitution, or a treaty or act of congress, or the determination of a federal question.[74] Second, where the question is one of general commercial law, not depending on state statutes or usages.[75] Third, where the question is one depending on general public policy.[76] Fourth, where the question is one of general equity jurisprudence.[77]

In the courts of the states, where the question arises under the constitution or laws of the United States, or treaties made by the authority of the national government, any decision of the United States supreme court on the point at issue is to be regarded by the state courts as not only a precedent entitled to consideration, but as absolutely binding and authoritative. And even though the supreme court of a state should entertain a radically different view, yet it will decide in accordance with the rulings of the supreme federal court, because, if its decision should be adverse to any right or claim made under the constitution or laws of the Union, that decision could be reviewed on error by the supreme court of the United States, and its judgment reversed.[78] As to similar decisions by the inferior courts of the federal system, the state courts are not bound by them, if the question has not been adjudicated by the supreme court, but they will receive a respectful consideration and be admitted to exercise a persuasive influence on the determination of the state court. The decisions of the supreme federal court, other than such as concern the construction of the constitution or laws of the Union, are not binding as authority on the courts of a state, although they are entitled to great respect.[79] This distinction is explained by the court in New York, as follows: "As between the judgments of our own courts and those of the general government,

---

[74] Piqua Branch of State Bank of Ohio v. Knoop, 16 How. 369; Branch Bank v. Skelley, 1 Black (U. S.) 436; Louisville & N. R. Co. v. Palmes, 109 U. S. 244, 3 Sup. Ct. 193.

[75] Swift v. Tyson, 16 Pet. 1; Chicago v. Robbins, 2 Black (U. S.) 418; Boyce v. Tabb, 18 Wall. 546; Town of Venice v. Murdock, 92 U. S. 494; Roberts v. Bolles, 101 U. S. 119; Thompson v. Perrine, 103 U. S. 806.

[76] Railroad Co. v. Lockwood, 17 Wall. 357.

[77] Neves v. Scott, 13 How. 268.

[78] Black v. Lusk, 69 Ill. 70.

[79] Lebanon Bank v. Mangan, 28 Pa. St. 452; Merchants' & Miners' Transp. Co. v. Borland (N. J. Ch.) 31 Atl. 272.

where there is a conflict between them, we ought to follow our own decisions, except in cases arising under the constitution and laws of the Union, where the judgments of the supreme court of the United States are of controlling authority.   In cases in which the federal courts acquire jurisdiction of controversies on account of the character or residence of the parties, such courts assume to administer the law of the state in which the matter arose, and, where the action relates to titles to real estate, the law of the state within which the real estate is situated.   Thus the legal rules of property existing in New York are those prescribed by the laws of New York, and such laws are the same whether they are administered by the courts of the state or by the courts of the nation.   There is no national code or system of laws respecting private property. The dispensing of private justice between individuals is in general a matter of state concern.   It is only in a few exceptional cases that the courts of the United States can be called upon to act.   Where the United States, as a political corporation, is a plaintiff, where an alien is a party, and where the action is between a citizen of the state within which the action is brought and a citizen of another state, concurrent jurisdiction is, from motives of policy and convenience, conferred upon the federal courts.   In these exceptional cases, of comparatively infrequent occurrence, the general government undertakes, through its courts, to administer the state laws. As evidence of these laws, it of course receives the state constitutions and statutes, and the adjudications of the state courts.   If a question is found to have been settled by the highest appellate court of a state, that decision is binding upon the courts of the United States to the same extent as upon the courts of the state in which it was made.   *   *   *   Upon such a question as this, the highest court of the Union has no legal pre-eminence over any of the courts of this state.   We listen to the views of its judges with the respect to which their eminent character and high position entitle them, but in inquiring what the law of this state upon a particular question is, we must look primarily to the judgments of our own tribunals, and when we find the point well settled by the decision of the highest state court, we cannot do otherwise than follow that decision, notwithstanding the supreme court of the United States has taken a different view of the matter." [80]

[80] Towle v. Forney, 14 N. Y. 423.

AS BETWEEN SUPERIOR AND INFERIOR COURTS.

156. The decisions of the court of last resort in a state furnish imperative and binding precedents for the guidance of all the courts over which it exercises an appellate jurisdiction. In like manner, the decisions of the supreme court of the United States are binding upon all the inferior courts of the federal system.

157. The decisions of an inferior court should be followed as precedents by the court which made them, unless reversed or overruled, and by any other courts of the same state or system which are of a still lower rank. But in the higher courts of the state or system, and in foreign jurisdictions, decisions of inferior courts have not the weight of precedents, and, in general, are not highly esteemed.

In each state, the decisions rendered by the court of last resort, upon the points in judgment duly presented and passed on, become a part of the law of the state until overruled or otherwise annulled or modified, and the inferior courts of the state are bound thereby; that is, the lower courts are imperatively required to take the law as laid down by the appellate court, and to follow its adjudications, wherever applicable, without inquiry into the legal correctness of its views.[81] There is but one possible exception to this rule. It is said that an inferior state court is not bound by the decisions of the supreme court of the state on a question arising under the constitution or laws of the United States, but only by those of the federal judiciary. Yet even in this case, the inferior court ought to follow the decisions of its own supreme court, because otherwise the case would merely be reversed and sent back for a new trial, and there is no appeal to the supreme federal court except from the court of last resort of a state.[82]

In the same manner and for the same reasons, the adjudications

[81] Attorney General v. Lum, 2 Wis. 507.
[82] Comm. v. Monongahela Nav. Co., 2 Pears. (Pa.) 372.

of the supreme court of the United States furnish a binding rule for the decision of like causes in the inferior federal courts. Where such lower courts are concerned with the solution of questions arising under the state constitution or laws or local customs, they are bound, in the absence of rulings of the supreme federal court, to follow the decisions of the supreme court of the state. But while they must adopt the settled construction put upon the statutes of a state by the supreme court of that state, yet it is held that when the supreme court of the United States has maturely adopted such construction, and the state court afterwards gives a different construction to the same statute, it is proper for the lower federal courts to hold the decision of the supreme court of the Union as binding upon them, and not that of the state court, until the question shall be reviewed by the highest tribunal of the federal system.[83]

A decision made by an inferior court, or one which is subject to the appellate or supervisory jurisdiction of a higher court, will be regarded by the court which made it as a precedent for its own future action, so long as it remains unreversed by the upper tribunal and so long as that court has not rendered any decision contrary to or conflicting with it; and, in the same circumstances, it may be cited and relied on as a precedent in other courts of the same system which are of the same rank or of an inferior rank. But in the higher courts, and in foreign jurisdictions, the decisions of the inferior courts are not so highly esteemed as those which proceed from the appellate tribunals. Aside from the supposition (not always well founded) that these courts are presided over by judges who do not possess the learning of the superior courts, and that there may be a lack of thorough and exhaustive consideration in their judgments, there are special reasons which account for the comparatively low regard placed upon those judgments. In the state where such a court sits, its determinations are not binding upon the appellate court, because the same case or a similar case might be brought before it, and it would then of course be at liberty and under an obligation to consider the questions involved unhampered by any but its own previous decisions. Still, a court of last resort will sometimes yield its own judgment to the decisions of the

[83] Neal's Lessee v. Green, 1 McLean, 18, Fed. Cas. No. 10,065.

inferior courts of the same system. This may happen when such decisions have been so frequently made, in the same way, and by different courts, as to have become a rule of property relied on by the people of the state generally.[84] In the courts of another system or jurisdiction, decisions of inferior courts are but little esteemed, for the reason that they may be reversed or modified by their own court of last resort. But considerable weight is sometimes allowed to a judgment of a lower court of another system, when its reasoning is such as to commend its conclusions to the mind of the court before which it is cited. And it should be observed that the pre-eminence of certain of the great judges gives a weight to all their rulings, even when made in the inferior courts. Thus, in England, great respect is paid to any decision of Coke or Mansfield, even though made at nisi prius, and in this country a similar authority is conceded to the decisions of Marshall and Story on circuit. Also, the decisions of the inferior federal courts are generally more respected than those of the lower courts of another state.

AS BETWEEN CO-ORDINATE COURTS.

158. Decisions of inferior courts are not imperatively binding upon courts of equal rank and co-ordinate jurisdiction, but may be respected for their reasoning and may be followed for the sake of uniformity.

When the point has not been decided by the court of last resort of the state or system, but there are decisions upon it, made by inferior courts of equal authority, such as the district courts of a state, or the circuit courts of the United States, or by co-ordinate branches of the same court in different districts, and especially when

---

[84] Thus, in Mississippi, it is said that when the true meaning of a statute is doubtful, a construction which has been adopted by the inferior courts for a long period of time, and under which important rights have accrued, will not be disturbed by the supreme court of the state. Plummer v. Plummer, 37 Miss. 185. Decisions of a circuit court of the United States, from which no appeals were taken, cannot be regarded as establishing a rule of property to which it is the duty of the circuit court of appeals to adhere under the doctrine of stare decisis. American Mortgage Co. v. Hopper, 12 C. C. A. 293, 64 Fed. 553.

two or more of these decisions concur upon the point in question, it is proper, for the sake of securing uniformity of decision, that they should be recognized as precedents and respected as such by the other courts of equal rank, until reversed by a higher authority.[85] At the same time, one court of such a character has no control over the decisions of another. The mere fact that a decision has been heretofore rendered by a court of equal rank with that which is trying the case does not preclude the latter from deciding the issue upon its own views of the law, if satisfied that the former ruling was erroneous.[86] For instance, in a case in the court of queen's bench, Lord Chief Justice Campbell is reported to have said: "We have been pressed with the authority of Drew v. Collins, 6 Exch. 670. To that authority we have paid the most sincere respect; but after a very careful examination, we are not able to assent to the reasoning on which it rests. As it is only the decision of a court of co-ordinate jurisdiction, we do not consider ourselves bound by it; and we have the less reluctance to decide according to our own opinion, as, the question being upon the record, it may be carried to the exchequer chamber and the house of lords." [87] And the opinion has also been advanced, by an inferior court of the state of New York, that where a question has been fully considered. and deliberately determined by one of the lower courts, and other co-ordinate courts of the same system have made decisions in conflict therewith, it is better that the decision should be adhered to in the court which made it, until the court of last resort shall have passed upon the same question.[88] And indeed it may be conceded that a court should not be expected to overrule its own decisions merely in view of the fact of contrary decisions having been made by another court which has no appellate jurisdiction over the first.

[85] Andrews v. Wallace, 29 Barb. 350; Bentley v. Goodwin, 38 Barb. 633; Reed v. Atlantic & P. R. Co., 21 Fed. 283.

[86] Northern Pac. R. Co. v. Sanders, 47 Fed. 604.

[87] Tetley v. Taylor, 1 El. & Bl. 521.

[88] Greenbaum v. Stein, 2 Daly, 223.

AS BETWEEN COURTS OF DIFFERENT STATES.

159. If the question at issue is to be governed by the common or statutory law of a foreign state, the judicial decisions of the court of last resort of that state must be accepted as authoritative expositions of such law, and must be followed by the court in which the case is on trial.

160. If the question is to be determined according to the lex fori, decisions made under a similar legal system prevailing in another state may be cited and respected for their reasoning, but are not binding as precedents.

We have already seen, in another connection, that the construction put upon a state statute by the courts of that state will be accepted as correct, and followed as conclusive, by the courts of another state, when called upon to interpret and apply the statute to causes pending before them.[89] It remains to be here stated that this rule has been extended beyond the mere question of statutory construction, and made to apply to all cases where the pending issue is to be governed by some law other than the lex fori, and where authoritative expositions of such foreign law can be found proceeding from the courts. The supreme court of Pennsylvania has recently ruled that, where it becomes necessary to determine what is the law of another state, in order to decide upon the rights of parties to contracts or other transactions which are to be governed by such foreign law, the judicial decisions of such other state, declaring the law in force there, are binding and conclusive, and in this respect there is no difference between judicial constructions of statute law and judicial decisions upon the common or commercial law. "It is argued," said the court, "that the validity of this contract is a question of commercial law, and therefore the mere decisions of the New York courts are not binding; and, in the absence of any statute in New York expressly authorizing such a contract, the courts of this state must follow their own views of the commer-

[89] See ante, p. 381.

cial as part of the general common law, though different views may be held as to such law by the courts of New York.   This is the main argument of the plaintiff, and, as it is one which is frequently advanced, and affects a number of important questions, it is time to say plainly that it rests upon an utterly inadmissible and untenable basis.   There is no such thing as a general commercial or general common law, separate from, and irrespective of, a particular state or government whose authority makes it law.   *   *   *   The point is the force of judicial decisions on the common law, and the assumption that there is any tenable basis for holding them less binding upon such law than upon statutes.   The so-called commercial law derives all its force from its adoption as part of the common law, and a decision on the commercial law of a state stands upon precisely the same basis as a decision upon any other branch of the common law.   The only ground upon which any foreign tribunal can question either is that it does not agree with the premises or the reasoning of the court.   But the same ground would enable it to question a decision upon a statute because a different construction seemed to it nearer the true intent of the legislative language, and this, it is universally conceded, no foreign court can do.   There is no difference in principle.   The decisions of a state court, upon its common law and on its statutes, must stand unquestioned, because it is the only authority competent to decide; or they must be alike questionable by any tribunal which may choose to differ with its reasons or its conclusions." [90]

A like authority is conceded to the rulings of foreign courts in the case of adopted statutes or constitutional provisions.   "Where a particular statute or clause of the constitution has been adopted in one state from the statutes or constitution of another, after a judicial construction has been given to it in such last-mentioned state, it is but just to regard the construction as having been adopted, as well as the words; and all the mischiefs of disregarding precedents would follow as legitimately here as in any other case." [91]

But aside from these special and exceptional cases, and generally where the determination of the issue is not complicated with any

[90] Forepaugh v. Delaware, L. & W. R. Co., 128 Pa. St. 217, 18 Atl. 503. But compare Franklin v. Twogood, 25 Iowa, 520.

[91] Cooley, Const. Lim. 52. And see ante, pp. 32, 159.

questions of the applicability of foreign law, decisions rendered in another state may be entitled to respectful consideration, in proportion to the learning and sound judgment which they display, but are not technically of force as precedents. "The doctrine of stare decisis is only applicable in its full force within the territorial jurisdiction of the courts making the decisions, since there alone can such decisions be regarded as having established any rules. Rulings made under a similar legal system elsewhere may be cited and respected for their reasons, but are not necessarily to be accepted as guides, except in so far as those reasons commend themselves to the judicial mind." [92] It should also be noted that a decision which is good authority at home may be of no value in another jurisdiction, on account of differences in the legal systems of the two states. For instance, if the judgment in the case turns entirely upon the provisions of a statute, it will not be available in another state, unless the statute law of the latter jurisdiction is substantially the same in this respect. So also, if the decision is made in accordance with some local custom or some settled peculiarity of the law of the state in which it was given.

English Decisions.

A decision by the superior courts of Great Britain, while it would not be conclusive upon the courts of this country, as a direct authority, will be entitled to high consideration, as an evidence of the law, where it does not turn upon a local statute or custom, but is explanatory of the common law or of the doctrines of equity.[93] "Great Britain and the thirteen original states had each substantially the same system of common law originally, and a decision now by one of the higher courts of Great Britain as to what the common law is upon any point is certainly entitled to great respect in any of the states, though not necessarily to be accepted as binding authority any more than the decisions in any one of the other states upon the same point. It gives us the opinions of able judges as to what the law is, but its force as an authoritative declaration must be confined to the country for which the court sits and judges.

[92] Cooley, Const. Lim. 51; Caldwell v. Gale, 11 Mich. 77; Boyce v. St. Louis, 29 Barb. 650; Koontz v. Nabb, 16 Md. 549; Nelson v. Goree, 34 Ala. 565; Jamison v. Burton, 43 Iowa, 282.

[93] Hilliard v. Richardson, 3 Gray, 349.

But an English decision before the Revolution is in the direct line of authority." [94]　Thus, the English decisions construing the common or statutory law, made before the separation of the two countries, are entitled to much higher authority than those which may have been rendered since that event.　In particular, with reference to statutes of the parent country which were adopted in the American states, or constituted a part of the original law which they assumed to live under after the War of Independence, English decisions upon their construction, made after the separation, are not to be received as absolute or imperative authority by our courts, except in so far as they show what was the course of judicial decisions prior to that event.[95]

THE LAW OF THE CASE.

161. When a case has been decided in an appellate court, and afterwards comes there again by appeal or writ of error, only such questions will be noticed as were not determined in the previous decision; the points of law already adjudicated become the law of the case, and are not to be reversed or departed from in any of its subsequent stages.[96]

The reasons of this rule are well explained in a decision of the supreme court of Vermont, from which we quote as follows: "The question is, will this court revise a former decision made by the same court in the same cause and on substantially the same state of facts?　Such a decision presses itself upon the consideration of the court with a twofold force: first, as an authority, as though it were a decision made in any other case; second, as an adjudication between the parties, not as one that is conclusive as a matter of law, for the court may revise and reverse it, but as an adjudication that practically is to be regarded as having much the same effect. The rule has been long established in this state, often declared from the bench, and we believe uniformly adhered to, that in the same

[94] Cooley, Const. Lim. 52.

[95] Mayor, etc., of Baltimore v. Williams, 6 Md. 235.

[96] Overall v. Ellis, 38 Mo. 209; Phelan v. San Francisco, 20 Cal. 39; Davidson v. Dallas, 15 Cal. 75, 82; Heinlen v. Martin, 59 Cal. 181.

cause this court will not revise or reverse their former decisions. It is urged, and there is force in the argument, that if there is error in the decision and it is ever to be reversed, it should be done in the same court. Although this position may be sound in theory as applicable to a single case, yet as a rule to be acted on in all cases it would lead to incalculable mischief. If all questions that have ever been determined by this court are to be regarded as still open for discussion and revision in the same cause, there would be no end of their litigation until the ability of the parties or the ingenuity of their counsel were exhausted. A rule that has been so long established and acted upon and that is so important to the practical administration of justice in our courts, we think, should not be departed from. And whatever views the different members of this court may entertain as to the soundness of the former decision, we all agree that the doctrine there enunciated is to be regarded as the law of this case." [97]   But when the supreme court has based its judgment in a case upon the concessions of counsel, it is not precluded, on another trial, from questioning the legal soundness of those concessions; but it seems that the parties themselves are not at liberty to dispute the ground of the judgment, but must be governed throughout by the rule first laid down. [98]

[97] Stacy v. Vermont Cent. R. Co., 32 Vt. 552
[98] Henry v. Quackenbush, 48 Mich. 415, 12 N. W. 634.

TABLE OF CASES CITED.

[The figures refer to pages.]

[The figures refer to pages.]

[The figures refer to pages.]

Bruce v. Schuyler, 251.
Brudenell v. Vaux, 164.
Bryan v. Sundberg, 148.
Bryant v. Livermore, 364.
   v. Merrill, 264.
Buchanan v. Smith, 246.
Bucher v. Cheshire R. Co., 378.
Buchner v. Chicago, M. & N. W. R.
   Co., 400.
Buckingham v. Moss, 262.
Buckley, Ex parte, 262.
Buckner v. Real Estate Bank, 131.
Bulkley v. Andrews, 310.
Bull v. Loveland, 371.
Bullard v. Bell, 63.
Bulwinkle v. Grube, 136.
Burch v. Watts, 305.
Burden v. Stein, 68.
Burgess v. Seligman, 379, 380, 427.
Burgett v. Burgett, 172.
Burke v. Jeffries, 117.
   v. Monroe Co., 168, 199.
Burnam v. Banks, 199.
Burnham v. Stevens, 368.
Burrows v. Bashford, 316.
Burt v. Rattle, 74.
Burwell v. Tullis, 249, 359.
Butler v. Ricker, 288.
   v. U. S., 321.
Byrne v. Byrne, 9.
Bywater v. Brandling, 168, 179.

C

Cadogan v. Kennett, 313.
Caesar Griffin's Case, 62, 356.
Cahoon v. Coe, 326.
Cail v. Papayanni, 90.
Calder v. Bull, 249.
Caldow v. Pixell, 343.
Caldwell v. Gale, 436.
   v. State, 249.
Calking v. Baldwin, 148.
Calladay v. Pilkington, 302.
Callaway v. Harding, 273.
Callender v. Keystone Mut. Life Ins.
   Co., 405.
Calvin's Case, 43.
Cambria Iron Co. v. Ashburn, 367.
Cambridge v. Boston, 372.
Camp v. Rogers, 94.
Campau v. Detroit, 96.

Campbell v. Hotl, 267.
   v. Perkins, 302.
   v. Quinlin, 159.
   v. Thompson, 132.
Cantwell v. Owens, 18.
Carberry v. People, 304.
Carey v. Giles, 313.
Carlton v. Felder, 381.
Carolina Sav. Bank v. Evans, 103.
Caroline, The, 106.
Carroll v. Carroll's Lessee, 379, 398.
   v. State, 271, 273.
Cary v. Marston, 138.
Casey v. Harned, 112.
Casher v. Holmes, 145.
Castner v. Walrod, 49.
Caston v. Brock, 188.
Cates v. Knight, 123.
Cathcart v. Robinson, 161.
Catlin v. Hull, 35.
Cearfoss v. State, 36, 41, 53.
Central Pac. R. Co. v. Shackelford,
   359.
Central R. Co. v. Hamilton, 208.
Chaffee's Appeal, 59.
Chamberlain v. Western Transp. Co.,
   243.
Chance v. Adams, 171.
Chancellor of Oxford's Case, 82.
Chandler v. Lee, 207.
   v. Spear, 328.
Chapin v. Persse & Brooks Paper
   Works, 245, 301.
Chapman v. State, 78.
   v. Woodruff, 146.
Charles v. Lamberson, 312.
Charles River Bridge v. Warren
   Bridge, 319, 321, 323.
Chartered Mercantile Bank v. Wilson,
   129.
Chase v. American Steamboat Co.,
   138.
   v. Dwinal, 49.
   v. Lord, 209.
Chegaray v. Mayor, etc., of New
   York, 141.
Chesnut v. Shane, 216.
Chew Heong v. U. S., 256.
Chicago v. Robbins, 428.
Chicago, B. & Q. R. Co. v. Dunn, 308.
Chicago, St. L. & N. O. R. Co. v.
   Pounds, 259.
Childers v. Johnson, 110.

[The figures refer to pages.]

[The figures refer to pages.]

[The figures refer to pages.]

Cummings v. Akron Cement & Plaster Co., 188.
   v. Coleman, 133.
   · v. Howard, 260.
   v. Missouri, 249.
Cunningham v. Cassidy, 347.
Currier v. Marietta & C. R. Co., 303.
Cushing v. Worrick, 150, 186, 273.
Custin v. City of Viroqua, 361.
Cutler v. Howard, 156.

D

Daily v. Burke, 136.
   v. Swope, 33.
Dale v. Irwin, 354.
Dale County v. Gunter, 134.
D'Allex v. Jones, 65.
Daniels v. Clegg, 159.
   v. Com., 208.
D'Aquin, Succession of, 174.
Darby v. Heagerty, 241.
Dash v. Van Kleeck, 372.
Davidson v. Biggs, 375, 411.
   v. Dallas, 437.
   v. Wheeler, 265.
Davis v. Robertson, 381.
Davoll v. Brown, 322.
Day v. Munson, 376.
   v. Savadge, 107.
Deake, Appeal of, 251.
Dean v. Charlton, 329.
   v. Metropolitan El. Ry. Co., 237.
Dean of Ely v. Bliss, 114, 194.
Deddrick v. Wood, 172.
Deffeback v. Hawke, 367.
Deitz v. Beard, 129.
Delafield v. Coldén, 56.
Delaplane v. Crenshaw, 219, 236.
Delaware Railroad Tax, 110, 323.
Denn v. Diamond, 326.
   v. Reid, 35.
Dent v. State, 295.
Depas v. Riez, 195.
Dequasie v. Harris, 244.
Dequindre v. Williams, 372.
Despain v. Crow, 375.
Detroit v. Detroit & H. P. R. Co., 110, 322.
De Veaux v. De Veaux, 128.
De Vries v. Conklin, 244.

Dewart v. Purdy, 251, 252.
Dewey v. Goodenough, 238.
De Witt v. San Francisco, 137.
Dickerson v. Acosta, 328.
Dillon v. Dougherty, 256.
Di Sora v. Phillips, 12.
District Court, In re, 280.
District of Columbia v. Washington Market Co., 227.
Division of Howard County, In re, 225.
Doane v. Phillips, 38.
Dobbins v. First Nat. Bank, 261, 272.
   v. Township Committee of Northampton, 176.
Dodd v. State, 362.
Dodge v. County Comm'rs of Essex, 235.
Dodsworth v. Anderson, 9.
Doe v. Avaline, 288.
   v. Considine, 36.
   v. Martin, 186.
Dole v. New England Mut. Ins. Co., 199.
Dollar Savings Bank v. United States, 281.
Donegall v. Layard, 226.
Donohue v. Ladd, 86.
Dorsey, In re, 19.
Doughty v. Hope, 353.
Douglass v. Chosen Freeholders of Essex Co., 38.
   v. Howland, 368.
   v. Pacific Mail Steamship Co., 138.
   v. Pike County, 377, 378.
Dousman v. O'Malley, 162.
Dowda v. State, 361.
Dozier v. Ellis, 332.
Drake v. Drake, 75.
Draper v. Emerson, 159.
Drayton's Appeal, 93.
Drennan v. People, 159.
Drew v. Collins, 433.
Dubois v. Hepburn, 329.
Duff v. Fisher, 412.
Dugan v. Bridge Co., 280.
   v. Campbell, 406.
Duke v. Cahawba Nav. Co., 348.
Duncan v. Shenk, 354.
Duncombe v. Prindle, 94.
Dundee Mortgage Co. v. Parrish, 378.

[The figures refer to pages.]

[The figures refer to pages.]

[The figures refer to pages.]

[The figures refer to pages.]

Hartley v. Hooker, 124.
Hartnett v. State, 125.
Hartson v. Elden, 258.
Harvey v. Travelers' Ins. Co., 162.
Haseltine v. Hewitt, 52.
Haskel v. City of Burlington, 263.
Hastings v. Lane, 251.
Hathaway v. Johnson, 299.
Hayes v. Williams, 309.
Heard v. Pierce, 68.
Hearn v. Ewin, 239, 306.
Hearne v. Garton, 54.
Heck v. State, 366.
Heilig v. City Council of Puyallup, 115.
Heinlen v. Martin, 437.
Hendrickson v. Fries, 91.
Hendrix v. Boggs, 353.
　　v. Rieman, 204.
Henry v. Davis, 349.
　　v. Quackenbush, 438.
　　v. Thomas, 56.
　　v. Tilson, 104.
　　v. Trustees of Perry Tp., 190.
Henschall v. Schmidtz, 263.
Hermance, In re, 142.
Herold v. State, 192.
Hershizer v. Florence, 257.
Hewey v. Nourse, 234.
Heydon's Case, 213.
Hicks v. Jamison, 80.
Higler v. People, 144.
Hill v. Boyland, 22.
　　v. Williams, 155.
Hilliard v. Richardson, 436.
Hillman, Ex parte, 133.
Hills v. City of Chicago, 16.
Hill's Adm'rs v. Mitchell, 224.
Hines v. Wilmington & W. R. Co., 39, 172, 291, 295.
Hing v. Crowley, 230.
Hoa v. Lefranc, 266.
Hogg v. Emerson, 322.
Hoguet v. Wallace, 307.
Holbrook v. Holbrook, 179.
　　v. Nichol, 357.
Holcomb v. Bonnell, 393.
Holland, Ex parte, 69.
　　v. Davies, 355.
Holliday v. Brown, 423.
Hollman v. Bennett, 231, 237.
Holman v. Johnson, 65.

Holman v. King, 12.
Holme v. Guy, 229.
Holmes v. Chester. 310.
　　v. Hunt, 266.
Hooker v. Hooker, 251.
Hopkins v. Jones, 251.
　　v. Mason, 301.
Horner v. State, 286.
Horton v. Mobile School Comm'rs, 38.
Hotaling v. Cronise, 239.
Houk v. Barthold, 311.
Houseman v. Com., 14, 27.
House Resolutions, In re, 391.
Houston v. Williams, 384.
Houston & T. C. Ry. Co. v. Travis County, 122.
Howard v. Moot, 266.
　　v. Williams, 312.
Howe v. Peckham, 233.
　　v. Welch, 381.
Howell v. Stewart, 147, 295.
Howes v. Newcomb, 237.
Howland v. Luce, 344.
Hoyt v. Thompson, 381.
Hubbard v. Brainard, 327.
　　v. Wood, 125.
Hudler v. Golden, 307.
Hudson v. Grieve, 170.
Huff v. Alsup, 183.
Huffman v. State, 286.
Hugg v. City Council of Camden, 345.
Huggins v. Ball, 94.
Hughes v. Farrar, 368.
Hull v. Hull, 58.
Hunt v. State, 21.
Hunter v. Nockolds, 171.
Huntington v. Attrill, 292.
Huntress, The, 27.
Hurford v. City of Omaha, 339, 340.
Hutchison v. Bowker, 10.
Hyatt v. Taylor, 38.
Hyde v. Cogan, 298.

I

Ihmsen v. Monongahela Nav. Co., 281.
Illinois Cent. R. Co. v. Chicago, B. & N. R. Co., 304.
　　v. Illinois, 423.
Illinois Land & Loan Co. v. Bonner, 260.

[The figures refer to pages.]

[The figures refer to pages.]

[The figures refer to pages.]

[The figures refer to pages.]

[The figures refer to pages.]

[The figures refer to pages.]

[The figures refer to pages.]

[The figures refer to pages.]

[The figures refer to pages.]

Stephenson v. Doe, 373.
   v. Taylor, 186.
Stevens v. Gourley, 64.
   v. Hauser, 426.
   v. Ross, 127.
Stewart v. Atlanta Beef Co., 227.
   v. Com., 304.
   v. Stringer, 306.
   v. Sup'rs of Polk Co., 93.
Stief v. Hart, 66.
Stockle v. Silsbee, 351.
Stone v. Mayor, etc., of Yeovil, 83.
   v. Stone, 141.
Stoneman v. Whaley, 81.
Stoughter's Case, 61.
Stowell v. Lord Zouch, 177.
Strong v. Birchard, 164, 300.
   v. Clem, 407.
Strother v. Hutchinson, 203.
Stuart v. Laird, 29, 32, 215, 222.
Stump v. Hornback, 61.
Sturges v. Crowninshield, 38.
Sturgis v. Hall, 261.
   v. Hull, 268.
Stutsman County v. Wallace, 159, 160.
Succession of D'Aquin, 174.
Succession of Lauve, 376.
Sullivan v. La Crosse & M. Steam Packet Co., 242.
Sumner v. Colfax Co., 351.
Supervisors v. U. S., 156, 341, 342.
Supervisors of Niagara v. People, 38.
Sussex Peerage Case, 177.
Sutton v. Sutton, 184.
Suydam v. Williamson, 379.
Swann v. Buck, 349.
Swanson v. Swanson, 311.
Swenson v. McLaren, 343.
Swift v. Luce, 58.
   v. Tyson, 428.
Swigert, In re, 141.
Swinney v. Ft. Wayne, M. & C. R. Co., 114.
Sydnor v. Gascoigne, 403.

T

Talbot's Lessee v. Simpson, 47.
Tarver v. Commissioners' Court, 156.
Taylor v. Blanchard, 322.
   v. Goodwin, 57.

Taylor v. Mitchell, 251.
   v. Newman, 171.
   v. Palmer, 169.
   v. Taylor, 16, 30, 227.
   v. U. S., 330, 331.
   v. Ypsilanti, 377.
Terrill v. Jennings, 314.
Territory v. Ashenfelter, 74.
   v. Clark, 71.
Tetley v. Taylor, 433.
Thames Manuf. Co. v. Lathrop, 254.
Thistleton v. Frewer, 260.
Thomas v. Huesman, 246.
   v. Mahan, 211.
   v. Owens, 23.
Thompson v. Bulson, 167.
   v. Mylne, 110.
   v. Perrine, 428.
   v. State, 106.
   v. Weller, 244.
Thorne v. San Francisco, 256.
Thorp v. Craig, 9.
Thurston v. State, 137.
Ticknor, Estate of, 56.
Tide Water Canal Co. v. Archer, 303.
Tierney v. Dodge, 115.
Tilton v. Swift, 262.
Tindall v. Childress, 123.
Tioga R. Co. v. Blossburg & C. R. Co., 378.
Toll v. Wright, 331.
Tollett v. Thomas, 78.
Tompkins v. First Nat. Bank, 48.
   v. Forrestal, 266.
Tonnage Tax Cases, 93.
Tonnele v. Hall, 212.
Tood v. Clapp, 372.
Torrance v. McDougald, 137, 168.
Torrey v. Corliss, 251.
   v. Millbury, 351.
Torreyson v. Board of Examiners, 172.
Towle v. Forney, 401, 429.
Town of Bethlehem v. Town of Watertown, 149.
Town of La Salle v. Blanchard, 250.
Town of Venice v. Murdock, 428.
Town of Wolcott v. Pond, 308.
Townsend v. Brown, 278.
Townsend Savings Bank v. Epping, 374.
Traders' Nat. Bank v. Lawrence Manuf. Co., 271.

[The figures refer to pages.]

[The figures refer to pages.]

INDEX.

[The figures refer to pages.]

BI-LINGUAL TEXTS,
comparison of, for purpose of construction, 170.
in case of conflict, English prevails, 170.

BILL OF RIGHTS,
construction of, with reference to constitution, 18.

BOUNTIES,
grants of, to be liberally construed, 320.

BRITISH STATUTES,
adopted here, how construed, 160.
see, also, "English Statutes."

BURNT RECORD ACTS,
to be liberally construed, 311.

C

CAPTIONS,
to articles of constitution, effect of, on construction, 27.
of chapters and sections of statute, as aids to interpretation, 181.

CASUS OMISSUS,
in statutes, not supplied by construction, 57.

CHANGE OF VENUE,
laws authorizing, liberally construed, 310.

CHAPTER HEADINGS,
in statute, effect of, on construction, 181.

CHARTERS,
of corporations, construed strictly, 319, 320.

CIVIL DAMAGE LAWS,
have no exterritorial effect, 92.
not construed retrospectively, 259.
to be construed strictly, 296.

CLERICAL ERRORS,
in statute, corrected by courts, 77-80.
in code, corrected by reference to original statute, 368.

CODES,
general rules for construction of, 363-369.
code construed as a whole, 363.
harmonizing conflicting sections, 363.
where parts are irreconcilable, 364.
reference to original statutes, when permissible, 365-367.
effect of change of language, 368.

[The figures refer to pages.]

[The figures refer to pages.]

[The figures refer to pages.]

F

[The figures refer to pages.]

        CONSTRUC.LAWS—31

482   INDEX.

N

O

[The figures refer to pages.]

[The figures refer to pages.]

[The figures refer to pages.]

[The figures refer to pages.]

[The figures refer to pages.]

[The figures refer to pages.]

WEST PUBLISHING CO., PRINTERS AND STEREOTYPERS, ST. PAUL, MINN.

Breinigsville, PA USA
30 March 2011
258732BV00003B/1/P